Popular Piety in Late Medieval England

The Diocese of Salisbury
1250–1550

ANDREW D. BROWN

CLARENDON PRESS · OXFORD

1995

Oxford University Press, Walton Street, Oxford OX2 6DP
Oxford New York
Athens Auckland Bangkok Bombay
Calcutta Cape Town Dar es Salaam Delhi
Florence Hong Kong Istanbul Karachi
Kuala Lumpur Madras Madrid Melbourne
Mexico City Nairobi Paris Singapore
Taipei Tokyo Toronto
and associated companies in
Berlin Ibadan

Oxford is a trade mark of Oxford University Press

Published in the United States
by Oxford University Press Inc., New York

British Library Cataloguing in Publication Data
Data available

Library of Congress Cataloging in Publication Data
Brown, Andrew (Andrew D.)
Popular piety in late medieval England : the Diocese of Salisbury,
1250–1550 / Andrew Brown.
p. cm. — (Oxford historical monographs)
Includes bibliographical references.
1. Catholics—England—Salisbury Region—Religious life.
2. Catholic Church. Diocese of Salisbury (England)—History.
3. Salisbury Region (England)—Religious life and customs.
I. Title. II. Series.
BR765.S25B76 1995
282′.42319′0902—dc20 94-31782
ISBN 0-19-820521-X

1 3 5 7 9 10 8 6 4 2

Typeset by Best-set Typesetter Ltd., Hong Kong
Printed in Great Britain
on acid-free paper by
Bookcraft Ltd., Midsomer-Norton, Avon

For my mother and father
with love

Acknowledgements

I have many people to thank, and I only wish that justice could be done here to all those who have helped me, in ways large and small, to complete this book. To John Maddicott, I owe a particular debt of gratitude for his wise comments and invaluable advice in supervising my original thesis; and also to Clive Burgess for starting me off on the subject. Among others who have so kindly, and stoically, read parts of this book, I single out John Blair, Thomas Charles-Edwards, Christine Peters, and Gervase Rosser. Their help and criticisms have improved the final product considerably. Before the book went to press, I also benefited greatly from the suggestions of Maurice Keen and Jeremy Catto; and from the eagle eyes of Matthew Williams and Tom Richardson. Over a longer period, I thank my siblings Phillip and Clare for consistently failing to take their older brother's work too seriously. (And in this context it would be unwise not to thank Neil Hayward—and therefore Steven Finch, Ian Hill, and the honorary historians Ben Mandry and Robert Walker.) I must particularly thank Rebecca Reader for her encouragement, inspiration, and perception throughout the writing of this book.

To the Warden and Fellows of Keble College, and to John and Sandy Feneley of the Centre for Medieval and Renaissance Studies, I owe the privilege of three enjoyable years as a Junior Research Fellow which gave me the time to write. At Keble, I have been especially helped by the critical insights of Ian Archer and the scholarly advice of Michael Hawcroft, both of whom made Keble an even more pleasant environment—and allowed me to get away with so little.

A.D.B.

November 1993

Contents

List of Maps		viii
List of Tables		viii
Abbreviations		ix
Introduction		1
1	Monks, Nuns, and Friars	26
2	Salisbury Cathedral and the Laity	49
3	The Parish and the Living	67
4	The Parish and the Dead	92
5	Parish Church-Building	111
6	Parish Fraternities and Craft Guilds	132
7	Guilds of Mayors and Burgesses	159
8	Hospitals, Almshouses, and Charity	181
9	Private Devotion and Lollardy	202
10	The Reformation	223
Conclusion		250
Bibliography		263
Index		285

Maps

1	Agricultural and economic regions	10
2	Parishes, chapels, and oratories	72
3	Perpetual chantries founded in parishes	98
4	Church-building	122
5	Procession of the tailors' guild in Salisbury	150
6	Lollardy	220
7	Visitations 1551, 1553, and 1556	232

Tables

1	Bequests to religious orders	29
2	Churchwardens' accounts: how money was raised	89
3	Perpetual chantry foundations in Wiltshire, Berkshire, and Dorset	95
4	Changes in church buildings, 1100–1540	113
5	Fraternities in Bridport	136
6	Bequests to Salisbury parish altars	138
7	Bequests to particular parish altars in Salisbury	139
8	Amount raised annually by the Jesus guild of St Edmund's, Salisbury	141
9	Salisbury civic processions	147
10	Benefactors of the mayor and commonalty of Salisbury	163
11	Obits celebrated by the mayor and commonalty of Salisbury before 1480	167
12	Hospital and almshouse foundations	182
13	Bequests to hospitals	188
14	Bequests to roads and bridges	198
15	The poor at funerals	199
16	Bequests for masses 1500–1547	226
17	Bequests for temporary chantries 1270–1545	235
18	Choice of burial places by gentry and others 1350–1538	253

Abbreviations

BAJ	*Berkshire Archaeological Journal*
BRO	Berkshire Record Office, Reading
BRUO	*A Biographical Register of the University of Oxford to A.D. 1500*, ed. A. B. Emden (Oxford, 1957–9)
Cal. Papal Reg.	*Calendar of Entries in the Papal Registers relating to Great Britain and Ireland: Papal Letters, 1198–1492* (15 vols.; London, 1893–1978)
CCR	*Calendar of the Close Rolls Preserved in the Public Record Office 1227–1550* (62 vols.; London, 1902–55)
CPR	*Calendar of the Patent Rolls Preserved in the Public Record Office 1216–1509* (54 vols.; London, 1891–1916)
D & C	Dean and Chapter Muniments of Salisbury Cathedral
DRO	Dorset Record Office, Dorchester
EHR	*English Historical Review*
Hutchins, *Dorset*	J. Hutchins, *The History and Antiquities of the County of Dorset* third edn. (4 vols.; Trowbridge, 1973)
JEH	*Journal of Ecclesiastical History*
LP	*Letters and Papers, Foreign and Domestic, of the Reign of Henry VIII*, ed. J. S. Brewer, J. Gairdner, and R. H. Brodie (21 vols. and addenda; London, 1862–1932)
NQSD	*Notes and Queries for Somerset and Dorset*
PCC	Prerogative Court of Canterbury, Public Record Office
Pevsner, *Berks.*	N. Pevsner, *The Buildings of England: Berkshire* (London, 1966)
Pevsner, *Dorset*	N. Pevsner and J. Newman, *The Buildings of England: Dorset* (London, 1972)
Pevsner, *Wilts.*	N. Pevsner and B. Cherry, *The Buildings of England: Wiltshire*, second edn. (London, 1975)

PRO	Public Record Office
Reg. Bp.	Bishops of Salisbury Registers 1298–1530 (four are in print: see Bibliography)
Reg. Dean Chandler	*The Register of John Chandler Dean of Salisbury 1404–17*, ed. T. C. B. Timmins (WRS 39; Devizes, 1984)
S. Edmund Accounts	*Churchwardens' Accounts of S. Edmund and S. Thomas, Sarum 1443–1702*, ed. H. J. F. Swayne (WRS; Salisbury, 1896)
TRHS	*Transactions of the Royal Historical Society*
VCH: Berks., ii–iv	*The Victoria County History of the Counties of England: A History of Berkshire*, ed. W. Page and P. H. Ditchfield (4 vols.; London, 1906–24)
VCH: Dorset, ii	*The Victoria County History of the Counties of England: A History of Dorset*, ii, ed. W. Page (London, 1908)
VCH: Wilts., iii–xiv	*The Victoria County History of the Counties of England: A History of Wiltshire*, ed. E. Critall, R. B. Pugh, and D. A. Crowley (13 vols.; Oxford, 1956–91)
WAM	*Wiltshire Archaeological and Natural History Magazine*
WRO	Wiltshire Record Office, Trowbridge
WRS	Wiltshire Record Society

Introduction

IN 1465, during the month of May, Sir Edmund Leversedge of Frome, a 'wretched and sinful creature', was struck down with 'the plage of pestylence'. His face turned black as coal, his swollen tongue black as pitch, and in his fevered state he had a horrible vision. His soul was led into a great valley where, suddenly, from the north side a terrible company of devils roared down, arrayed as 'galantes', those proud people who dressed themselves, as Edmund had himself, in short gowns and doublets, close-fitting hoses, shoes with pointed 'pykes', and high bonnets on their long-haired heads, puffed up with the sin of pride 'that rayneth most commonly in this realme of England'. Fortunately, Edmund's devotion to the Blessed Sacrament and his invocations to the name of Jesus and to the Virgin Mary spared him from eternal torment. He was led up a ladder and blessed with a vision of the Virgin herself. But he was warned that his beliefs had to be accompanied by good works. He was to dress more modestly, receive instruction from the vicar of Westbury in Wiltshire (not the three 'unlearned' chantry priests in Frome), and he was to offer candles to a certain image of Our Lady. Taking the name William Wreche, he was also to spend eight years, presumably grim ones, at the University of Oxford.[1]

Immediate light ought to be thrown on 'popular piety' in a late medieval diocese. Unfortunately, with Edmund's vision I have launched one stone at two birds and failed to kill either. Edmund originally came from Frome, in Somerset, outside the counties of Wiltshire, Berkshire, and Dorset, which constitute the region under study. Secondly, his vision exhibits a kind of personal, introverted, almost morbid piety, that was not strictly typical. This study will concentrate much more on collective forms of religion, the local activities, loyalties, and cults of lay people mostly below the rank of gentleman. This is not to assume that the religion of the gentry was essentially different. 'Popular piety' may indeed imply a distinction between it and an élite form of religion that was socially superior, more learned, clerical, or even 'unpopular'.[2] But 'popu-

---

[1] BL Add. MS 34193, fos. 126–130ᵛ; E. M. Thompson, 'The Vision of Edmund Leversedge', *NQSD* 9 (1904–5), 19–25.

[2] For problems with the label 'popular piety' see E. Duffy, *The Stripping of the Altars: Traditional Religion in England 1400–1580* (New Haven, Conn., 1992), 3; K. van Greyerz

lar' can mean, more neutrally, 'of the people' (gentry included), and 'piety' need not include only those religious practices that conformed to standards set by the Church hierarchy.

Edmund's personal vision does at least strike at the heart of devotional assumptions that were collectively shared. The sin of pride, the descent into purgatory, the torments of devils, even escape by ladder, had become topoi in the writings of theologians and the mouths of preachers.[3] The penitential works to be carried out by Edmund were central to the workings of late medieval religion. The idea of purgatory between heaven and hell had begun to assume an important place in Catholic theology after the eleventh century. The Gregorian effort to free the Church from excessive dependence on the lay lord had led the Church hierarchy to exploit sources of income (tithes especially) that could be collected from a wider section of the population. The willingness of the laity to contribute was stimulated by the elaboration of a doctrine of penance which made the effective remission of sin less arduous and more within the grasp of ordinary people. By the thirteenth century the laity was being made fully aware, through synodal decree and the teaching of friar and priest, that it was no longer necessary to undergo protracted penitential effort or to make huge benefactions during life (possible only for the monk and lord) to gain both forgiveness of sin and remission of punishment. Lighter penances (possible for all) could be executed, and punishment not completed would now be expiated in purgatory. Although usually an unpleasant region, as Edmund Leversedge testified, purgatory did not therefore loom, like hell, as an inevitable place for harrowing punishment: it lay instead as a half-way house for the truly penitent on the road to salvation.[4]

The doctrines of penance and purgatory bore prodigious fruit, from small offerings to shrines and altars, through to large endowments to

(ed.), *Religion and Society in Early Modern Europe 1500–1800* (London, 1983), esp. 3; N. Z. Davis, 'Some Tasks and Themes in the Study of Popular Religion', in C. Trinkaus and H. Oberman (eds.), *The Pursuit of Holiness in Late Medieval and Renaissance Religion* (Leiden, 1974), 307–36. See also C. Geertz, *The Interpretation of Cultures* (London, 1973), 87–125.

[3] D & C, MS 103, *c*.1450: *Jacob's Well: An English Treatise on the Cleansing of Man's Conscience* (Early English Text Society, 75; 1900–1), esp. 68–80, 171; G. Owst, *Literature and the Pulpit in Medieval England* (Oxford, 1961), 312–14, 407–14; G. R. Keiser, 'The Progress of Purgatory: Visions of the Afterlife in Late Medieval English Literature', *Analecta Cartusiana*, 117 (1987), 72–100.

[4] J. Le Goff, *La Naissance du Purgatoire* (Paris, 1981); R. W. Southern, 'Between Heaven and Hell: Review of J. Le Goff La Naissance du Purgatoire', *Times Literary Supplement* (18 June 1982), 651–2; C. R. Burgess, ' "A Fond Thing Vainly Invented": An Essay on Purgatory and Pious Motive in Late Medieval England', in S. J. Wright (ed.), *Parish, Church and People: Local Studies in Lay Religion, 1350–1750* (London, 1988), 56–84.

monasteries, chantries, guilds, for the perpetual celebration of mass, the most efficacious of all good works of penance. The benefits of these gifts and services for the donor's soul and for those still living could extend beyond the grave if remembered or kept going. Much could be done by the living for the soul that languished in purgatory, so much so that late medieval Catholicism is not unfairly called 'a cult of the living in the service of the dead', or 'the cult of living friends in the service of dead ones'.[5] Part of the aim of this study is to examine change and continuity in pious giving, the impact of the services required by the dead on the religious life of the living, and how these services came to be swept away when purgatory was abolished under Edward VI.

Yet pious giving and practice did not spring from a single source. Its many manifestations cannot be explained merely by clerical initiative, or by a conscious awareness of the soul's need for intercession. Not all of them were officially sanctioned by the Church: the mass might have been the most efficacious of all good works of penance, but promotion of the Eucharist could lead it, at one extreme, to be superstitiously abused or, at the other, to be heretically rejected. Over the last ten years or so, most recently in Eammon Duffy's emotively titled book, revisionist work has stripped late medieval religion of the 'rich Protestant varnish' that coloured earlier depictions.[6] It has revealed a religious landscape, still only partially uncovered, of remarkable depth and vitality.

Some areas of this landscape, however, have perhaps been touched up with a more Catholic gloss. The more panoramic of studies may overlook the variety in pious practice or ignore those corners of the landscape that do not support a particular vision.[7] A regional study affords an opportunity to look more closely at religion in its local setting and the uses to which it was put. The extent of pious giving might be significantly affected by economic wealth, social conditions, perhaps even by gender and class; its direction affected by the topography of local cults, shrines, monastic houses, and parish churches. The region in this study had certain characteristics that make it interesting: not because it was uniform (though it did form a kind of unit) but because of the points of contrast within it. The distinctive features of the region may be sought in three

[5] A. N. Galpern, 'The Legacy of Late Medieval Religion in Sixteenth-Century Champagne', in Trinkaus and Oberman (eds.), *Pursuit of Holiness*, 149; J. Bossy, 'The Mass as a Social Institution 1200–1700', *Past and Present*, 100 (1983), 42.

[6] Duffy, *Stripping of the Altars*, 1–6; K. B. McFarlane, *John Wycliffe and the Beginnings of English Nonconformity* (London, 1952), 10.

[7] Duffy's book deliberately excludes Lollardy and the possibility that certain areas harboured 'traditions' of Lollard dissent by the 1530s (see Ch. 9).

areas: ecclesiastical lordship, patterns of settlement, and socio-economic conditions.

The most important ecclesiastical lord of the region was the bishop and it is tempting to treat the whole region as his diocese. Just before the Conquest, the counties of Dorset, Wiltshire, and Berkshire had been gathered together to form the diocese of Salisbury. Old Sarum was sited as the bishop's seat in 1075, New Salisbury in 1220.[8] Bishops, some more than others, attempted to impose their stamp throughout the diocese not least in matters of pastoral care. In common with other diocesans after the reforming Lateran Council of 1215, which proclaimed the government of souls as the 'art of arts', the Salisbury bishops began to show an unprecedented interest in laying down the responsibilities of lay people to their local churches.[9] Visitations of parishes were undertaken with renewed vigour and widened scope from the mid-thirteenth century onwards (see Chapter 3). The cathedral chapter, too, exercised a pastoral role in its prebends and, later, in the city itself.[10] Bishops also appointed penitentiaries from the cathedral to hear confessions in the diocese. Some of the cathedral clergy made important contributions to the management of pastoral care: William Pagula with his manual for parish priests, the *Oculus Sacerdotis*, in the early fourteenth century, and William Lyndewoode, compiler of *Provinciale*, in the early fifteenth.[11]

The concerns of the Church hierarchy may have encouraged a kind of uniformity within the diocese, across all three counties. Bishop Richard Poore (1217–28), founder of New Salisbury, had also begun a scheme for the codification of cathedral customs and liturgy, containing much of what was to become the Use of Sarum.[12] About the same time, a campaign was under way to win the canonization of Bishop Osmund (1078–99), perhaps to encourage the spread of the Use, since it was Osmund who was believed to have been its founder. The attempt failed, but a second campaign, launched in the late fourteenth century and particularly during the episcopacy of Bishop Robert Hallum (1409–17), was eventually successful. When the wider problems of the Church were not exercising his mind—as leader of the English delegation at the Council of Constance

[8] *VCH: Dorset*, ii. 5; *Berks.* ii. 3; *Wilts.* iii. 1–7.
[9] *Councils and Synods with Other Documents relating to the English Church II (1205–1313)*, ed. F. M. Powicke and C. R. Cheney (2 vols.; Oxford, 1964), i. 57–95, 364–87, 510–15, 549–67.
[10] *Reg. Dean Chandler*, p. xiv; R. M. Haines, *Ecclesia Anglicana: Studies in the English Church of the Later Middle Ages* (Toronto, 1989), 39–46.
[11] *Reg. Bp. Hallum*, pp. ix–xvi. [12] *VCH: Wilts.* iii. 162–4.

in 1414—Bishop Hallum was concerned to promote uniform worship within his diocese. Both he and Archbishop Chichele sought to dissemi-nate the Sarum Use, to establish a sense of common worship within the diocese and the English Church as a whole.[13] Hallum was also believed to have attached indulgences to the mass of the Holy Name of Jesus, thereby helping to incorporate what was an increasingly popular form of private devotion into public worship.[14] As we shall see, the laity of the diocese could respond to clerical efforts at uniform worship.

Yet the diocesan boundaries impose a misleading kind of unity on the region. The three counties had not been united as a diocese since time immemorial and neither did they remain so: in 1542 Dorset was hived off to the newly created see of Bristol. The presence of bishop and dean was not ubiquitous and was perhaps felt more keenly in some places than in others. The fine, elaborate chancels of the parishes of Potterne or Bishops Cannings testify to the clerical concerns of thirteenth-century bishops rather more strongly than other churches that did not lie, as these two did, on episcopal manors or cathedral prebends.[15] Episcopal presence was strongest in the new city of Salisbury, which lay on episcopal land and had been established when the foundations of the new cathedral were being laid.[16] Bishop Richard Poore (1217–28) founded the city's first hospital and Bishop Giles de Bridport established Vaux college for poor scholars.[17] The parish structure was carefully regulated: only two more parishes were created, St Thomas's and St Edmund's, carved out of the older one of St Martin's which lay on the episcopal manor.[18] City government was kept firmly in episcopal hands. At the beginning of the fourteenth century the citizens had their own guild merchant, and later a council with their own officers. But they had no court of their own, and the fortnightly court that exercised civil and leet jurisdiction, including the supervision of city tenements, was presided over by the bishops' steward or bailiff. A newly elected mayor had to be presented to the same episcopal official.[19] As we

---

[13] *The Canonization of St. Osmund*, ed. A. E. Malden (WRS; Salisbury, 1901), 236–42; E. F. Jacob, *Essays in the Conciliar Epoch* (Manchester, 1943), 76–8; J. I. Catto, 'Religious Change under Henry V', in G. L. Harriss (ed.), *Henry V: The Practice of Kingship* (Oxford, 1985), 97–115; see Ch. 2.

[14] R. W. Pfaff, *New Liturgical Feasts in Late Medieval England* (Oxford, 1970), 62–83.

[15] *VCH: Wilts*. vii. 192, 211; Pevsner, *Wilts*. 111–14, 371.

[16] Bishop Poore's charter of 1225 demanded a quit rent of all services to be paid on city tenements; F. Street, 'The Relations of the Bishops and Citizens of Salisbury between 1225 and 1612', *WAM* 39 (1916), 187–92; K. H. Rogers, 'Salisbury', in M. D. Lobel (ed.), *Historic Towns* (London, 1969), i. 3.

[17] *VCH: Wilts*. iii. 369–70; BL Add. MS 28870.

[18] *VCH: Wilts*. vi. 144–51.   [19] Ibid. 95.

shall see, the bishops' hold over the city could cause conflict and affect the nature of religious celebrations in the city (see Chapter 7).

Elsewhere, it is doubtful whether the bishops could impose their concerns across the whole of the region. However active a bishop was in visiting his diocese, or however well oiled the machinery of his government, he was none the less a shepherd rather distant from his flock. All the Salisbury bishops of the period were university-educated, usually in both canon and civil law; almost all were 'Caesarian prelates', as John Wyclif would have called them, owing their appointments to the king whom they served as ministers in varying capacities. Bishop Richard Beauchamp (1450–81) admitted himself that he 'grew up almost from the cradle' under the patronage of Henry VI.[20] During Jack Cade's rebellion of 1450, Bishop William Aiscough (1438–50) was horribly hacked to death while saying mass in Edington church, mainly because of his role as the king's confessor, but perhaps too, as Thomas Gascoigne later claimed, because he was usually absent from his diocese.[21]

In any case, episcopal concerns did not limit the activities of lay people. If some bishops made attempts to propagate orthodox cults and liturgies uniformly, others found themselves suppressing cults that sprang up unbidden. In 1385 it was reported to Bishop Ralph Erghum that a newly discovered well at Bisham had become the object of idolatry by a credulous local people. The bishop was not greatly impressed by the two alleged miracles: a bird, resting in a tree overhanging the spring, which allowed itself to be freely handled, and the cure of a man with an inflamed eye ('a natural result of the wholesome application of cold water', one hears the bishop scoff).[22] Moreover, lay people were no respecters of diocesan boundaries. The multitudes who flocked to the Bisham well came from Wycombe and Great Marlow over the river Thames in the diocese of Lincoln. Some pilgrims travelled further afield where the spiritual wells of grace were perhaps deeper. Many a Salisbury citizen brought back badges and souvenirs from other shrines in England, Germany, France, Spain, Italy, and the Low Countries;[23] some belonged to guilds outside the

---

[20] Only Bishop Chandler (1418–26) seems to have risen up the ranks within the diocese (*VCH: Wilts.* iii. 13–15; R. G. Davies, 'The Episcopate', in C. H. Clough (ed.), *Profession, Vocation and Culture in Later Medieval England* (Liverpool, 1982), 51–89).

[21] *Thomas Gascoigne: Loci e Libro Veritatum*, ed. J. E. T. Rogers (Oxford, 1881), 158–9.

[22] Reg. Bp. Erghum, iii, fo. 76. See also the cult of John Schorne, whose bones were moved from North Marston to Windsor, and who was believed to have conjured the devil into a boot (*VCH: Berks.* ii. 168–9; Oxford Bodley Ashmole MS 1125, fo. 107).

[23] B. Spencer, *Salisbury Museum Medieval Catalogue, ii. Pilgrim Souvenirs and Secular Badges* (Salisbury, 1990), 12 and *passim*.

diocese.[24] Ships sailed from Weymouth full to the gunwales with seasick pilgrims bound for St James of Compostela;[25] very occasionally testators sent proxies to go on pilgrimage for their souls, to Compostela, Rome, and even Jerusalem.[26] One should not seek in a diocese a naturally self-contained unit of spiritual grace.

But the region may have had other focuses of unity, and other, narrower, devotional loyalties. The counties of Dorset, Wiltshire, and Berkshire once formed the heartland of the old Wessex kingdom, and even in the later Middle Ages memories reached back to an Anglo-Saxon past. In 1429 the parishioners of Littleton Drew had replaced the whole roof of their church and of one of its chapels which was said to commemorate the victory of King Athelstan and the death of his men in battle against the Danes in 936.[27] The parishioners of South Newton once enjoyed a ceremony that again celebrated King Athelstan's victory over the Danes. The burgesses of Malmesbury claimed, somewhat hopefully, that their ancestors around 930 had built a chapel in honour of the same king (and his alleged wife Maud) who had granted them land for their help against the Danes. In 1392 the burgesses of Devizes acquired letters patent for the founding of a chantry priest who was later said to pray for the soul of Queen Maud.[28]

Such traditions were not uniform throughout the region, and they were most prevalent in areas where old monasteries were dominant. The three places that remembered King Athelstan were close to the abbey of Malmesbury which, as a recipient of Athelstan's patronage, was probably responsible for keeping his memory alive.[29] The parishioners of South Newton also remembered an Abbot Loring of Malmesbury in their cer-

---

[24] See Ch. 6 nn. 7, 8.

[25] Hutchins, *Dorset*, ii. 420–1. For pilgrim seasickness see 'The Pilgrim's Sea-Voyage and Sea-Sickness', in *The Stacions of Rome*, ed. F. J. Furnivall (Early English Text Society, 13; 1867), 37–40.

[26] The only examples I have found from about 1,600 wills are: John de Homington of Salisbury (to Guildford and Canterbury in 1346), WRO G23/150/103; Geoffrey Barbour of Abingdon (to Rome in 1416), Holy Cross Almshouse muniments, Abingdon; Richard Pyton of Sherborne (to Compostela in 1436), PCC 21 Luffenham. A few testators mention their own impending expeditions to Compostela (William Boulard of Salisbury 1331, D & C, Press IV, Box 'W'; and Nicholas Soper of Sherborne 1507, PCC 32 Adeane), and to Jerusalem (Sir Thomas Trenchard 1493, PCC 27 Vox).

[27] D & C, Reg. Harding, fo. 96ᵛ. The battle was probably Brunanburh in 937 against the Scots (*The Anglo-Saxon Chronicle*, iv, ed. S. Taylor (Cambridge, 1983), 51).

[28] South Newton: BL Lansdowne MS 231, fos. 187–8; *John Aubrey: Remaines of Gentilisme and Judaisme 1667–87*, ed. J. Britten (London, 1881), 136–8. Devizes: *CPR* (1391–6), 115; PRO E133/2/347. Athelstan's wife was a late medieval invention.

[29] *VCH: Wilts*. iii. 213; *Willelmi Malmesbiriensis Monachi: De Gestis Pontificum Anglorum*, ed. N. E. S. A. Hamilton (Rolls Series; London, 1870), 396. See also the 15th-cent. panel

emony as another of their benefactors. Several monastic houses, two in
Berkshire, three in Wiltshire, and as many as nine in Dorset, had been
founded before the Conquest. Many of them remembered the names of
Anglo-Saxon kings, thegns, and abbots in their anniversary services.
Some were also repositories of local saints' relics which continued to be
venerated. Malmesbury abbey maintained the cult of St Aldhelm who
had once missionized by sitting on a bridge and singing ballads to the
passing heathen.[30] Other institutions also housed relics. Whitchurch
Canonicorum and Wimborne Minster (once a house of Benedictine nuns
before becoming a college of secular canons) retained, respectively, the
relics of St Whyte and St Cuthberga, which were still the objects of
popular veneration on the eve of the Reformation. Like the bishop in
Salisbury, some of these old monastic houses also dominated the areas
around them, affecting the structure of government and religious activity
within their towns, even breeding contempt as much as piety. Older
monasteries and churches that had once been minster churches could
exert an influence over their erstwhile daughter churches long after the
minster system of parishes had broken up (see Chapter 3). One theme
worth pursuing is how far older traditions influenced lay pious practice.

It was not only ecclesiastical lordship that gave the religious life of the
region some of its characteristics. In many ways, for instance, the parochial structure had little to do with clerical concerns and far more to do
with the pattern of settlement. Here again there are features about the
region that are distinctive, even if not unique.[31] There was more than a
proverbial contrast within it between chalk and cheese. The chalk soils
that ran through the middle of Berkshire, through eastern Wiltshire, and
down to their final escarpment in south-east Dorset supported sheep and
corn husbandry (see Map 1). By the fourteenth century, these regions

depicting Athelstan and his queen at Milton Abbey, founded by the same king (Pevsner, *Dorset*, 288).

[30] For monasteries see Ch. 1; *Reg. Malmesburiense*, ed. J. S. Brewer and C. T. Martin (2 vols.; Rolls Series; London, 1879–80); *Gestis Pontificum*, 336.

[31] For the following see J. Thirsk (ed.), *The Agrarian History of England and Wales*, iv (Cambridge, 1987), 1–15, 109–12, 462–5. For Wilts.: A. E. Nash, 'Population Change in Late Medieval Wiltshire', Ph.D. thesis (Cambridge, 1984), 3–20; J. N. Hare, 'Lords and Tenants in Wiltshire c.1380–c.1520', Ph.D. thesis (London, 1975), 9–25; *VCH: Wilts*. iii. 2–3. For Dorset: *VCH: Dorset*, ii. 123, 175, 275, 281; B. Reynolds, 'Late Medieval Dorset', MA thesis (London, 1958); C. C. Taylor, *Dorset: The Making of the Landscape* (London, 1970). For Berks.: *VCH: Berks*. i. 387–91; ii. 167–71; R. Faith, 'Berkshire: Fourteenth and Fifteenth Centuries', in P. D. A. Harvey (ed.), *The Peasant Land Market in Medieval England* (Oxford, 1984), 106–77.

were famous for their wool. Here settlements tended to be compact, nucleated, and strung out along the river valleys with their richer alluvial soils. Here, too, parishes followed this early pattern of settlement, their boundaries often climbing up the river valley to give them a distinctive elongated shape.

By contrast, the clay vales in the north-west section of Wiltshire supported dairy farming, and parts of these areas, like Braydon, Chippenham, and Melksham, were forested. Settlements tended to be more scattered and manorial customs perhaps less strong. Parishes in these areas tended to have more chapels within them, catering for the pastoral needs of the outlying hamlets. But other clay vales did not always have the same patterns of settlement. At the south-west end of the Vale of the White Horse in Berkshire, towards the rising scarp of chalkland, dairy farming predominated and parishes did contain scattered settlements and often more than one manor. In the north-east, however, one manor usually occupied the whole of one parish and arable farming held sway. Settlements of both the nucleated and scattered type can be found in the Vale of Blackmoor in Dorset. There were other soil types too: the extreme north-west of Wiltshire, in Cotswold country, had fewer scattered settlements; the south-east parts of Dorset lay on poor heathland.

The pattern of settlement was affected by demographic change during the later Middle Ages. Declining population in the early fourteenth century and the catastrophic visitations of the Black Death, which first struck the Dorset port of Melcombe Regis in 1349, severely depleted numbers all over the diocese. Two-thirds of the tenants on the bishop of Winchester's manor of Downton died in 1349; the Salisbury cathedral dean and chapter complained bitterly of a 'great shortage of artisans on account of the great pestilence' in 1362.[32] Population decline affected pastoral provision. Late-fourteenth-century bishops were faced with an acute shortage of priests, having to make a large number of institutions to benefices.[33] Some areas became deserted, wiped out by plague or emptied through migration. Beresford includes 189 places in the diocese among the lost medieval villages of England.[34] The value of landed rents declined and chapels fell out of use: in 1425 there was still a chapel, served by a stipendiary priest, at Witherington in Downton parish, but it disappeared shortly afterwards

[32] Nash, 'Population Change', 342 n. 120; D & C, Box 3, Press III, Box 'Chancellor'; *VCH: Dorset*, ii. 20.
[33] *VCH: Wilts.* iii. 22–3; *VCH: Dorset*, ii. 21; *VCH: Berks.* ii. 13, 18–19.
[34] M. Beresford, *The Lost Villages of Medieval England*, 4th edn. (London, 1963), 183, 186, 206–7.

MAP 1. Agricultural and economic regions

as the hamlet declined.[35] Even parish churches fell out of use: between
1361 and 1503 at least sixteen parishes were united in the diocese. Most of
the lost villages and the united parish churches were situated in the
chalklands where benefices were poorer and settlements, however nucleated, tended to be more precariously placed along the narrow river
valleys (see Map 2).

Differing parochial structures may have supported different religious
cultures.[36] To John Aubrey in the seventeenth century, the slow, dull,
contemplative, even malicious, inhabitants of the dairying parts were to be
unfavourably compared with the bucolic shepherds of the chalklands who
were hard-working, and without the leisure to read, or to contemplate
religion. The chalklands harboured pockets of traditional piety, where
shepherds still prayed to St Oswald, St Stephen, and St Osyth for protection, where parish priests might cry out to St Catherine when shooing
away cattle. It was perhaps in the nucleated villages of the chalklands that
communities shared a stronger sense of collective tradition, where, in
Aubrey's words, fiddlers and drummers with 'good cheer and strong beer'
enlivened sheep-shearing and harvest homes.[37] Even in the nineteenth
century the poet William Barnes could wax lyrical about 'the zwollen
downs w't chalky tracks':

> An hearty vo'k to laugh an' zing
> An parish churches in a string
> W' tow'rs o'merry bells to ring.[38]

Might the clay vales, where settlements were more scattered, parishes less
cohesive, where forests provided solitude for hermits,[39] have bred nonconformity? It is a compelling picture of contrast and one worth pursuing,
but at the same time we cannot be too ecologically deterministic, or be
beguiled by Aubreyesque nostalgia. As we have already seen, we cannot
divide up the region so easily. And there were other contrasts within the
region that partly reinforced the chalk–cheese division, but also partly cut
across it. These too potentially affected pious practices.

[35] Winchester college deeds, 4934, 5363, 4951, 4952, 5407; *VCH: Wilts.* xi. 77; Hare,
'Lords and Tenants', 165–87; R. K. Morris, 'The Church in the Countryside: Two Lines of
Inquiry', in D. Hooke (ed.), *Medieval Villages* (Oxford Univ. Committee for Archaeology,
Monograph 5; Oxford, 1985), 55–9.
[36] For an extravagant claim made of the same landscape affecting religious and secular
loyalties see D. Underdown, *Revel, Riot and Rebellion: Popular Politics and Culture in England
1603–1660* (Oxford, 1987), esp. 75–105. But see J. Morrill, 'The Ecology of Allegiance',
Journal of British Studies, 26 (1987), 457–62.
[37] Aubrey, *Remaines*, 9, 16, 27, 28–9, 136–8, 143.
[38] Quoted in Taylor, *Dorset*, 22.   [39] See Ch. 9 n. 26.

By the fifteenth century another regional division had developed: between cloth-producing areas and elsewhere (see Map 1). If the downlands had once been renowned for their sheep-shearing and production of wool, many of the region's towns, encouraged by Edward III's drastic increase in the wool custom, became famous for their cloth. The rate at which the alnage of Wiltshire was let to farm rose by a third between 1362 and 1390: Salisbury, the largest town in the diocese, rose in the national ranking of provincial towns from ninth to fifth between 1337 and 1525.[40] Abingdon, Reading, Newbury, and Windsor all came to rank in the top fifty of England's wealthiest provincial towns. Smaller towns could benefit in northern Dorset, like Sherborne, but particularly in the western parts of Wiltshire: Castle Combe gave its name to a fine woollen cloth.[41] The cloth industry had a profound effect on the distribution of population, perhaps keeping it to its pre-plague pattern.[42] Migration to cloth towns kept population levels buoyant within them: Salisbury was able to maintain a population of about 5,000 or 6,000 throughout the later Middle Ages. Not all towns outside these areas declined: Bridport supported a population of about 1,000 particularly from its monopoly of hemp-growing and rope-making. But others were more gravely affected: the inhabitants of Melcombe Regis and Lyme Regis complained about the inroads of the sea, the depredation of French pirates, and the desertion of their tenants in the late fourteenth and early fifteenth centuries.[43]

The wealth generated by the cloth trade also tended to set apart the religious life in cloth towns from that in other areas. Investment in penitential good works was determined by priorities rather than amounts of wealth, but wealth did allow a greater capacity to invest. Some very large investments were made. William Heynes of Castle Combe was reckoned to have amassed a huge fortune worth 3,000 marks. He was one of the first known users of the gig-mill, which speeded up the process of cloth manufacture—a protocapitalist, almost, investing in the means of production. We find him in 1435 giving £2 for a new grindstone within his corn

[40] *VCH: Wilts.* iv. 1–2, 115–47; Hare, 'Landlords and Tenants', 84–90; *VCH: Wilts.* vi. 124–5, 138; D. H. Carr, 'The Problem of Urban Patriciates: Office Holders in Fifteenth-Century Salisbury', *WAM* 83 (1990), 118–35.

[41] A. Dyer, *Decline and Growth: English Towns 1400–1640* (London, 1991), 64–5, 70–4; Hare, 'Landlords and Tenants', 86; Nash, 'Population Change', 31; J. L. Bolton, *The Medieval English Economy 1150–1500* (London, 1980), 268–9; E. M. Carus-Wilson, 'Evidence of Industrial Growth on Some Fifteenth-Century Manors', *Economic History Review*, second series, 12 (1959–60), 151–67.

[42] Nash, 'Population Change', 257, 301, 339–55.

[43] *VCH: Dorset*, ii. 246, 344–6; K. J. Penn, *Historic Towns in Dorset* (Dorset Natural History and Archaeological Society, Monograph series, 1; Dorchester, 1980), 23–7, 73.

mill and £30 for the construction of a new house in stone, but also contributing £20 to the building of the parish church tower.[44] Or take John Winchecombe of Newbury in the early sixteenth century, immortalized by the poet Thomas Deloney, who had 200 looms, 100 women carding wool, 200 boys making quills, 40 men in his dye house, 20 in his fulling mill; and who probably built the church of Newbury west of the pulpit to the tower.[45] It is difficult to class these men as merchants; some, like Thomas Horton of Bradford-on-Avon, styled themselves gentleman. And there cannot have been many who would have refused the offer of knighthood, as John Winchecombe was supposed to have done, bashfully preferring to remain a humble clothier till his dying day.[46] In any case, some gentlemen, with purer pedigrees, could benefit from cloth: Sir John Fastolf skilfully exploited cloth production on his manor of Castle Combe.[47] Even people lower down the social scale profited, since the production of cloth involved twice as much labour as that of wool. Artisans and labourers were in any case profiting from wage increases in the wake of labour shortages following the Black Death.[48] In a few towns, like Salisbury, Reading, and Castle Combe, craft guilds associated with the cloth trade sprang up. As we shall see, they were also accompanied by the advent of other kinds of guilds, hospital foundation, extensive church-building activity, investment in funerals, and other post-obit services.

Along with wealth, the cloth industry generated problems. Social and religious conformity was less easy to achieve. It was axiomatic under the Tudors for cloth workers to be linked with sedition,[49] and previous periods of unrest had lent some weight to that axiom. In the so-called

[44] Carus-Wilson, 'Industrial Growth', 161–3; BL Add. Ch. 18479; Hare, 'Landlords and Tenants', 249. See C. C. Dyer, 'Were There Any Capitalists in Fifteenth-Century England?', in J. Kermode (ed.), *Enterprise and Individuals in Fifteenth-Century England* (Stroud, 1991), 1–24.

[45] *VCH: Berks.* ii. 148; T. Deloney, 'The Pleasant History of John Winchecombe...' (1626), in *The Works of Thomas Deloney*, ed. F. O. Man (Oxford, 1912), esp. 20–1.

[46] Hare, 'Landlords and Tenants', 220. Cf. the Frenchman in the Heralds Debate in the 16th cent.: 'In England you clothiers dwel in gret farmes abrode in the country, havyng horses with commodities like unto gentlemen, where as wel they make cloth and kepe husbandry' (*Tudor Economic Documents*, ed. R. H. Tawney and E. Power, iii (London, 1924), 5).

[47] Carus-Wilson, 'Industrial Growth', 151–67; Hare, 'Landlords and Tenants', 89–90; G. D. Ramsay, *The Wiltshire Woollen Industry in the Sixteenth and Seventeenth Centuries* (London, 1965), 6–49.

[48] A. R. Bridbury, *Economic Growth: England in the Later Middle Ages* (London, 1962), 31, 35–6.

[49] J. F. Davis, *Heresy and Reformation in the South-east of England 1520–1559* (London, 1983), 2, 27.

Lollard uprising of 1431, a weaver from Westbury and a fuller from Abingdon had put up seditious posters in Salisbury with the help of a few citizens.[50] Support in 1450 for Jack Cade's rebellion, although essentially a political reaction to the mismanagement of the Duke of Suffolk's regime, had been fuelled in Wiltshire by a temporary slump in the cloth trade. Risings occurred in Devizes, Wilton, Biddeston, and Tilshead.[51] At Salisbury in the previous year the Hungerford Lord Moleyns, a notorious member of the Suffolk clique, had been set upon in a tavern; and on 30 May 1450 300 men were said to have converged on the city.[52] The civic authorities obviously responded with a visual display of their authority: the civic chamberlains' accounts of 1449/50 mention the payment of 2s. 6d. 'for the mending of the mace at the time of the insurrection'. Once the rebellion had been put down and Jack Cade disposed of, the mayor and burgesses paid two men a total of 23s. 4d. for the unsavoury task of riding to London to collect a quarter of Cade's body, presumably so that it might be displayed on the city gates.[53]

The preservation of a social order was inseparable from the articulation of a moral one. An undercurrent of moral concerns, a desire to enforce moral standards independently of any theological doctrine, surfaced in many forms throughout the later Middle Ages. The civic élite of Salisbury sought to control moral as well as social life. In 1387 the city council saw fit to protest to the dean and chapter about the behaviour of a certain vicar-choral who had been consorting with women of ill repute; in the mid-fifteenth century it sought to regulate prostitution in the city, by ordering prostitutes to wear striped gowns; around the same period it was restricting access to almshouses to inhabitants of the city rather than vagrants.[54] Authorities in other cloth towns were worried by 'proletarian' excesses. The manorial court of Castle Combe in the late fifteenth century sought to curb gambling, dicing, and drinking by closing the taverns at eight during winter and at nine during summer.[55] Immigration into cloth towns promoted disorder, and the problem of vagrancy was only to get

---

[50] See Ch. 9 n. 59.

[51] J. N. Hare, 'The Wiltshire Risings of 1450: Politics and Economic Discontent in Mid-Fifteenth-Century England', *Southern History*, 4 (1982), 13–31. I. M. W. Harvey, *Jack Cade's Rebellion of 1450* (Oxford, 1991), 121–30, distrusts the evidence (from indictments) showing large numbers of rebels from this region involved in the cloth trade.

[52] D & C, Reg. Burgh, fo. 1; see Ch. 2 nn. 3, 79.

[53] WRO G23/1/44, no. 2 (1449/50).

[54] D & C, Reg. Corffe, fos. 33ᵛ–34; R. Benson and H. Hatcher, *Old and New Sarum or Salisbury* (London, 1834), 133; see Ch. 8 n. 11.

[55] PRO CP 40/270; Carus-Wilson, 'Industrial Growth', 165.

worse in the early sixteenth century, as rising population and the beginnings of land enclosure served to increase unemployment.[56]

Disorder also had its effect on the character of religious life. Sedition
and heresy were linked. Taverns in cloth towns were indeed places of
sedition, secular but also religious. Richard Lillyngston of Castle Combe
openly preached heresy in the taverns of Devizes and Marlborough in
1481, just as William Ramsbury, one of the first Lollard preachers in the
diocese, had done a century before.[57] It may be too simplistic, however, to
see cloth towns as natural breeding grounds of heresy because of an
assumed susceptibility of cloth workers to dissidence. There were plenty
of heretics who had no connection with the cloth industry at all. But
authorities in cloth towns were acutely aware of the problems of disorder.
Through legislation they sought to contain social misfits, like tavern-
goers, prostitutes, and the migrant poor. At town councils like Salisbury
great store was set by the displays of civic ritual, processions that brought
together the craft guilds and emphasized the unity of the town (see
Chapters 6 and 7).

Disorder outside a town's élite, however, was matched by dissension
from within. The pride and fine living about which Sir Edmund
Leversedge felt so guilty were to be found in ample measure within late
medieval Salisbury. Quarrels about precedence and status bred dissension
amongst the city burgesses. In 1447 the city council banned the use of
certain phrases at its assemblies, 'fine examples of urban rhetoric'[58] according to the early historians of Salisbury, Benson and Hatcher:

I defy thee / what art thou / I am as rich as thou, churl, knave, harlot / I am as
rich as though and greater beloved than though / and thou sittest here in sembley
in contrary thee and never agree to thee / and am better of birth than thou, and
have born the worship and estate of this city and kept it as well as thou.[59]

Unfortunately, urban rhetoric was not always quite so fine. 'Torde, fart,'
quoth William Boket to Mayor William Tavener on the Friday before the
feast of the Annunciation in 1481, 'for I am worthe vi of the[e] / thou art
a fole.' For this and other 'ungoodly words' William Boket was in the next

---

[56] *VCH: Berks.* ii. 206, 216.
[57] *Reg. Bp. Langton*, 499; *Reg. Bp. Waltham*, fos. 222–223ᵛ. Bishop Chandler complained
in 1426 that too many people made for taverns on the sabbath rather than for church. Idle
talk in taverns could also prove treasonable, as the vicar of Tilehurst discovered in the Bear
Inn in 1539 when he speculated whether Bishop Longland was sufficiently anti-papal (*LP*,
xiv (1), 840).
[58] Benson and Hatcher, *Old and New Sarum*, 136.
[59] WRO G23/1/2, fo. 31b.

year to pay 13*s*. 4*d*. to the city treasurers.[60] As we shall see, fraternal feeling was encouraged not only by punishment but also by civic processions, membership of religious guilds, and involvement in parish life.

These religious practices and characteristics were not restricted to cloth towns like Salisbury. Regional distinctions cannot be pushed too far. There were many things that cut across a neat division between cloth and other regions, and indeed between chalk and cheese. Salisbury lay firmly in chalklands, and, like other cloth towns, the city was not an island of wealth within a sea of rural poverty. Its demand for grain, meat, and wool stimulated the economy of surrounding areas.[61] Moreover, the traffic was not all one way. We find cloth merchants extending their interests into rural areas, buying up leases on demesne land. The loosening of the land market benefited a new group of tenants who, by building up composite holdings from former demesne land, sprang from villeinage to yeoman status in the fifteenth century.[62] A significant number of these tenants were men who had been made wealthy by the cloth trade, acting as middlemen between the peasant farmer and export firms in distant ports. Many of these merchants—William Heynes of Castle Combe, James Terumber of Trowbridge, the Hortons at Bradford-on-Avon, the Stokes at Seend— also invested heavily in 'mills, sheep, pastures, farms and houses'.[63] As we shall see, they also invested substantially, as merchants within cloth towns did, in penitential good works.

Nevertheless, regional variations will be explored. If there is one impression to be gained about the differences in religious life between cloth towns and other areas in the region, it is one of intensity: greater wealth and investment in religious life but also greater fragmentation, more sedition and heresy. It will also be asked whether these differences help to explain the eventual progress of the Reformation.

Pious practices in the region, then, will be shown to be affected by geography, wealth, social and ecclesiastical concerns. But there are, first of all, problems of evidence to overcome. It is very difficult to fathom the

[60] WRO G23/1/2, fo. 141.

[61] Hare, 'Landlords and Tenants', 321–5; J. N. Hare, 'Durrington: A Chalkland Village in the Late Middle Ages', *WAM* 74–5 (1981), 141. In 1509 Robert Martyn of Durrington marked his family's ascent from villeinage to a higher stratum in peasant society by the bequest of a cow to the sacrament light in his parish church (PCC 26 Bennett). For the manumission of a Robert Martyn at Durrington in 1461 see D & C, Reg. Machon, fo. 65.

[62] Many did, however, recoil back into obscurity in the 16th cent. (Faith, 'Berkshire', 157; Hare, 'Landlords and Tenants', 93–137, 27–40).

[63] E. Power, *The Wool Trade in English Medieval History* (London, 1941), 35–40; 47–51; Bolton, *English Economy*, 272; Hare, 'Landlords and Tenants', esp. 220–9.

depth of belief in late medieval society. The occasional case crops up of sorcery or pre-Christian practice.[64] There are hints that some lay people were ignorant of the most basic prayers that the Church hierarchy expected them to know. The statutes of Heytesbury hospital (1472) hint that not everyone knew the basic prayers of Lady Psalter, Pater Noster, Ave, and Credo: if an inmate did not know them he was to 'do his besy labour to cunne say hit perfitely'.[65] The ubiquity of pious practice is sometimes suggested, ironically, by the protests of heretics against it (see Chapter 9). But then the problem of belief behind practices asserts itself: Edmund Leversedge's vision is an almost unique statement of religiosity. Only very occasionally did benefactors record the beliefs behind their pious gifts, and even then in a rather stylized form. In a gift to the Trinity hospital in Salisbury in 1396, John Chandler wrote: 'In expectation of heaven, but knowing that this is not attained except through good works', he sought to 'redeem by some office of piety the punishment of guilt incurred while imprisoned in the flesh'.[66] There were, in any case, plenty of reasons other than piety behind benefactions; it is easier to examine pious practices rather than to attempt to reveal underlying beliefs based on the assumption that 'by their works we shall know them'.

Particular problems of evidence used in this study place further barriers in the way of understanding pious practice. It is difficult to compare the thirteenth century, for which evidence is scarcer, with later periods, for which it is more abundant. Most of the early evidence comes from clerical sources, like the monastic cartularies of Reading, Malmesbury, Bradenstoke, and Lacock, made in the thirteenth or early fourteenth centuries (Chapter 1). They are hardly ideal indicators of attachment to monasteries. They record the gifts of land made by lay people, but do not make it clear if some were acquired by hidden purchase.[67] They also reflect the concerns of the religious who used them primarily for reference and information.[68] Many pressures went into their making: advances in literacy and land law, the growing practice of direct exploitation of the demesne by bailiff-farming, the administrative drive of a particular abbot like William Colerne of Malmesbury, perhaps even the apparent threat posed to the landed wealth of monastic houses by the Statute of Mortmain

[64] *Reg. Bp. Martival*, ii. 106–7 (1316).
[65] J. E. Jackson, 'Ancient Statutes of Heytesbury Almshouse', *WAM* 11 (1868), 301.
[66] WRO 1446/43.
[67] J. Wardrop, *Fountains Abbey and its Benefactors 1132–1300* (Cistercian Studies Series, 91; Kalamazoo, Mich., 1987), 85.
[68] G. R. C. Davis, *Medieval Cartularies of Great Britain* (London, 1958), p. xi.

in 1279.[69] Cartularies tend to peter out in the early fourteenth century (except for the unusual case of the fifteenth-century cartulary of Edington), which may indicate a decline in giving. It is as well, however, not to underestimate attachment to monasteries later on, just as it is unwise to exaggerate that attachment in the twelfth and thirteenth centuries. As to another branch of the religious, the friars, evidence is far sparser (not least because they did not make cartularies), and much of the work they did in the diocese remains hidden.

For Salisbury cathedral, evidence is more plentiful and mostly unpublished (Chapter 2). Early deeds are recorded in the register of St Osmund, and a large collection of them is still extant in the archives. Chapter act books survive from 1329 onwards, recording something of the cathedral's involvement with the laity, particularly in the prebendal parishes. The communars' account rolls (1363–1542) show cathedral lands and benefices and most of the obit and chantry services performed in the cathedral. Accounts of receipts of its appropriated church of St Thomas's from 1486 show its incomes from tithes and oblations from that parish. The fabric accounts (1464–1540) reveal some of the lay people's gifts and connections with guilds in the city. There are also the miracles of St Osmund, around the 1220s and the 1420s; others in the chapter act books, and a single account roll for St Osmund's shrine in 1493/4, show continuing support for the cult.

Whatever the evidence for lingering attachments to clerical institutions, it is much less abundant than sources for lay activity in their parishes. Not all of it is edifying: visitations of the cathedral prebends (1220–2, 1405, 1408/9, 1412, 1463, 1480, 1485/6), Bishop John Waltham's visitations of parishes in 1394, and miscellaneous cases in bishops' registers 1298–1530 reveal some of the failings of parishioners and of the parochial system (Chapter 3). Were all cases reported, one might ask, or were the pressures to report cases very strong? If they were, the few cases recorded suggest a lack of failings. Churchwardens' accounts allow us to make comparisons between different kinds of parishes, in larger, more urbanized, cloth towns like Salisbury through to villages like Winterslow on Wiltshire chalkland. Contrasts in endowments and services left by the dead, methods of collec-

[69] M. Chibnall, *Charters and Custumals of the Abbey of Holy Trinity of Caen* (London, 1982), p. xxxii. The list of Abbot Colerne's acquisitions is placed at the beginning of one of Malmesbury abbey's cartularies (*Reg. Malmesburiense*, i. 358–64). For an earlier link between collections of charters being amassed and fear of losing land see R. W. Southern, 'Aspects of the European Tradition of Historical Writing. IV: The Sense of the Past', *TRHS*, fifth series, 23 (1973), 247–51.

tion, numbers of services, plays, processions provided, cults catered for, are significant (Chapters 3 and 4). But accounts are frustrating, rarely revealing, for instance, how many contributed and how obligatory collections were. Finally, there is a great deal of visual evidence for activity in church-building: over 450 churches in the diocese are used in the survey. But it is difficult to be accurate about the chronology of building: efforts could take place over a number of decades; later rebuildings could be so extensive as to destroy evidence for rebuilding in earlier periods; use of Early English, Decorated, and Perpendicular styles does not date a building very accurately (Chapter 5).

Guild records are also abundant, particularly for Salisbury. The town books from *c*.1410 and chamberlains' account rolls from 1409 (though not complete) reveal a good deal about the activities of the guild of St George and the civic élite. Surviving too are the account books of the tailors' guild (from *c*.1444) and the Jesus guild in St Edmund's (from 1476, but incomplete). Some material comes from Abingdon, Reading, Windsor, Wallingford, and Marlborough; and unusual evidence comes from Bridport. Six account books of small guilds from the early fifteenth century show lists of members; the town books, the earliest dating from the early fourteenth century, show the activities of the town's élite in parishes and guilds. Indeed the links between parishes and guilds deserve to be explored more thoroughly (Chapters 6 and 7).

Evidence for hospitals and almshouses, their statutes and accounts, is also plentiful (Chapter 8). To some extent they can reveal something about the kind of poor admitted into almshouses, and even the attitudes to charity and the poor. Yet the evidence is extremely equivocal. Does the incidence of hospital foundation reveal more about the level of poverty and the wealth of the founder than about attitudes to the poor? There may have been a decline in gifts to hospitals during the later Middle Ages, but does this merely reflect a decline in charitable giving? The history of hospitals needs to be linked with the other institutions and services already mentioned because they performed functions that were similar to religious houses, parish churches, and guilds, which sometimes managed almshouses.

The problems of evidence for heresy have been well rehearsed (Chapter 9). There are records for heresy trials in the diocese from 1389 onwards: do they under- or overestimate levels of heresy? Do they mangle any sophisticated beliefs held by heretics or impose an order on their utterances that was not originally there? A regional study is less able to use the evidence of Lollard books (which are more revealing of Lollard belief), especially when their provenance is unknown. But careful attention can be given to the incidence of Lollardy and to the status of Lollards in local society (provided that it is remembered that trials reveal detection rates rather than true incidence of heresy, and that powerful heretics could have escaped punishment).

Wills provide one source of evidence for pious practice that is used throughout this study, yet they are deceptive in what they reveal. They tend to cover a limited period and restricted range of the population. About 1,600 wills (from the laity) survive for all three counties (360 of which come from Salisbury, fifty from Reading) between 1270 and 1547.[70] But only three survive for the thirteenth century, and only twenty-eight from before 1350. Moreover, wills tended to be made by wealthier people. Outside Salisbury, of the 263 testators whose status or profession is stated, 157 were members of the gentry; there were also twenty-six clothmen, thirteen yeomen, and seventeen husbandmen; the rest were a collection of merchants, weavers, tailors, fullers, dyers, bakers, barber-surgeons, and tanners. In Dorset there appears to be a more restricted range of professions represented, probably reflecting the county's lack of larger, busier towns, compared with Wiltshire or Berkshire. In Salisbury the range of professions was more varied, including artisans, like carpenters and dubbers, whose crafts were lowest placed in city processions. But there are still more merchants and wealthy burgesses represented than any other group in society (twenty-three out of eighty-nine). So the search for popular piety in wills tends to focus on the piety of wealthier members of society.

Moreover, wills do not allow us to measure piety very accurately.[71] They are less windows on to the soul than mirrors of social convention. The preambles of wills have sometimes been taken as expressions of personal piety, yet were more often than not frequently repeated formulas, even if drawn from the pages of primers.[72] Are we to read a private morbidity into

---

[70] Most of Salisbury's wills come from the WRO in the four Domesday Books (G23/1/212–215), among collections of deeds (G23), the Trinity hospital accounts (WRO 1446), the subdean's register act book 1476–8 (D4/3), in *Reg. Dean Chandler* and *The Tropenell Cartulary*, ed. J. S. Davies (2 vols.; WRS, 1908); most of the other wills for Salisbury and elsewhere come from the PCC, a few from archbishops' and bishops' registers, from D & C muniments, Winchester college deeds, PRO C146; DRO, Bridport muniments (DC/BTB), 'Weld of Lulworth'; BRO D/A1.

[71] Duffy, *Stripping of the Altars*, 504–23 and references cited there; C. R. Burgess, 'Late Medieval Wills and Pious Convention: Testamentary Evidence Reconsidered', in M. A. Hicks (ed.), *Profit, Piety and the Professions in Late Medieval England* (Gloucester, 1990), 14–33.

[72] Compare the elaborate, apparently individualistic, but identical preambles of Thomas

the will of one William Kellow, citizen of Salisbury, who in 1523 spoke of the 'uncertainty of life' and the 'wretchedness of the world', but considered his 'wretched body' worthy enough to be placed in the church of St Thomas 'under a stone of marbill'?[73] Historians of the sixteenth century, some less tentatively than others, have used preambles without the traditional invocation to God, the Virgin Mary, and all the saints to suggest a hidden attachment to Protestantism. Yet it was not unknown in the fifteenth century for testators (or was it merely a fashion of their clerical scribes?) to commend themselves to God alone.[74]

The depth of piety in a will is also very difficult to quantify. Take the will of William Swayne, a merchant of Salisbury, made in 1484.[75] He specified burial and funeral arrangements in St Thomas's church, doles to the poor, gifts to the high altar and to the shrine of St Osmund. He left 40s. to the friars of Salisbury to keep a dirige and a mass, and stipulated that part of the residue of his goods was to go to his chantry in St Thomas's church. Finally he gave his executors 10 marks and warned them sternly that if they did anything contrary to the provisions, they would answer for it before the celestial judge at the day of doom. Concern for the afterlife may be expressed, but the will may tell us little about William's priorities during life. He was not an entirely selfless individual. According to a rental of the city in 1455, he owned more property (some twenty-three tenements) than any other citizen in Salisbury but he was apparently greedy for more. In 1457 one Agnes Winchester accused him before the city council of pretending a title to a corner tenement 'before the Poultry cross' which had been bequeathed, or so she claimed, by her late husband to the almshouse of St Trinity: 'the said William Swayne had the said Agnes atte his hous in the Newstret of the said cite to mete w[i]t[h] hym atte which tyme he laboured and caused the seid Agnes to enseall a deede'. Other clashes with the city council hint that Swayne was proud as well as acquisitive. In 1447 he quarrelled with John Hall over a matter of personal honour; in 1465 he was expelled from the twenty-four (the inner ring of city aldermen) for defying the council's claim to a plot of land on which he wished to build a house for his chantry priest.[76]

Sextayn of Salisbury in 1401 and John Barbour in 1403 (WRO G23/1/213, fo. 43; PCC 6 Marche).

[73] PCC 12 Bodefeld.
[74] S. Brigden, *London and the Reformation* (Oxford, 1989), 380 and n. 7; *Reg. Dean Chandler*, p. xxiv and n. 4, nos. 402, 499, 505.
[75] PCC 20 Logge.
[76] E. R. Neville, 'Salisbury in 1455', *WAM* 37 (1911), 68; WRO G23/1/2, fo. 29ᵛ; see Ch. 7.

Whilst wills may exaggerate an individual's piety, they may also reveal too little about other good works performed during life. One might hope the wealthy to be more expansive and revelatory about pious concerns than the less wealthy, but this was not always the case. In William's will there is no reference to a gift of certain tenements to the mayor and commonalty of Salisbury for which he had been placed on the city's bede roll (list of benefactors). There is nothing about his part in the efforts to rebuild St Thomas's church after 1448. There is no mention of a substantial gift made in 1479 to the tailors' guild for the celebration of an anniversary. There is only the briefest allusion to a chantry that he had already endowed with at least four tenements by 1455.[77] Wills fail to tell us about a testator's good works made during his lifetime, many of which were probably more important than the provisions finally made in the will, especially if property was involved. To take one more example: the wills of twenty-one benefactors of the mayor and commonalty of Salisbury are extant; sixteen make no mention of these benefactions, and the five that do may only have reiterated what had already been decided orally. In 1412 William Walter declared his intention before the city council to bequeath a tenement to the mayor and commonalty five years before he made the bequest.[78] So statistics showing patterns of pious giving based on wills by no means give a fair indication of what services and institutions were preferred as objects of penitential works.

It is also very difficult to know whether the provisions of a will were always carried out. Some provisions may well have been left to the discretion of the executor, and some executors altered the proportion of money allocated in the will. In a will proved in 1538 Joanne Peerse asked her executors to give 20s. to the Trinity almshouse and a series of bequests to St Thomas's church in Salisbury that included £10 for gilding an image of St Anne. The accounts of the almshouse in 1539 show that the executors had indeed handed over the 20s. to the almshouse, but had decided to allocate the residue of the money assigned for gilding the image (£4. 10s.) to the almshouse and another £4. 10s. (said to have been bequeathed for the buying of an antiphoner for St Thomas's but not mentioned in the will) to the almshouse as well.[79] Executors were perhaps expected to alter a will's stipulations and divert funds to other institutions: if so, statistics based on wills may not fully indicate the preferences of testators or the final allocation of the bequest.

[77] WRO G23/1/1, fo. 77; G23/1/2, fos. 2, 188^{r-v}.
[78] WRO G23/1/214, fos. 32^v–33; G23/1/2, fo. 46^v; see Table 10.
[79] PCC 15 Dyngeley; WRO 1446, Trinity hospital accounts, 1539.

The provisions of some wills were clearly not performed at all. William Swayne had warned his executors of the terrible Day of Judgement, and some executors clearly needed reminding. In 1406 Alice Meriot of Salisbury made her will which was to be proved and read out, as was the custom, in the bishop's court before the bailiff and the mayor.[80] It begins in Latin with a typical list of provisions, but half-way through breaks into English. A few years earlier, Alice tells us, her former husband William Teynterer had made William Warmwell his executor to distribute 'gold and money', from the sale of a tenement, to the poor and for bridges and roads. Alice was adamant that William had failed to fulfil his brief:

I Aleise Meriot charge the William Warmwell this foreseid, upon the, utterly to be perfourmyd, as the [*sic*], savyng the mercy of God, wold be dampned to the fury of Helle. Myn holy father, Bishop of Salisbury, y forseid Aleise require you, in the name of Jesu Christ, and in wey of charitye, that ye sehe treu ordinance make, for the forseid matte[r], touchyng William Warmwell, of the summe foreseid, so that the soules of William Teynterer and me, foreseid Aleise, be dischargyd to fore God.

Nevertheless, despite the problems posed by wills, they remain among the best sources for pious practice. The rarity of protestations like Alice Meriot's may suggest that the stipulations of wills were generally performed. The execution of a will was in itself a good work; executors no doubt performed their duties as they would expect their successors to execute their own wills. And there may be some hope that the apparently conventional ('shallow and tranquil'[81]) statements of bequests hide a more personal sense of piety. The visionary Edmund Leversedge was finally laid to rest in 1496 in the parish church of Westbury (comfortably within the borders of Wiltshire) and he left posterity a will.[82] Conventionally, he bequeathed 20s. to the cathedral, 40s. to the church of Frome, 20s. to the vicar of Westbury; not unusually, he left 20s. each to the Carthusian charterhouses of Witham and Hinton; rather more untypically, he ordered £100 to be levied from his goods and chattels to found a fraternity in honour of Corpus Christi. Conventional he may have been, but he was surely not unaffected by the intense vision recorded thirty years before. He had been instructed to visit the vicar of Westbury, and his assumption of sober dress fits well with a bequest to the austere Carthusians (he also refers briefly to a 'friend in Witham' at the end of his testimony). He had

[80] WRO G23/1/213, fos. 73ᵛ–74.
[81] P. Heath, 'Urban Piety in the Late Middle Ages: The Evidence of Hull Wills', in R. B. Dobson (ed.), *Church, Politics and Patronage in the Fifteenth Century* (Gloucester, 1984), 229.
[82] PCC 6 Horne.

been afforded a vision of the Virgin Mary and instructed to make offerings to a Marian shrine. His devotion to the Blessed Sacrament had spared his soul from damnation and it was on the vigil of the feast of Corpus Christi itself that he had finished his record of the vision. Conventional gifts and bequests can reveal something of the piety and pious practices of the later Middle Ages.

I

Monks, Nuns, and Friars

WHEN, some time in the mid-twelfth century, Mauger of Malcuvenant, sheriff of Surrey, fell mortally ill in Reading, he chose a course of repentance different from that of Edmund Leversedge. He renounced the world and assumed the habit of a monk. The Reading monks were anxious, however, that the latest addition to their brethren should not die on them, since royal officials might transfer the debts owing from his shrievalty on to the abbey. Fortunately, the monks were able to produce an ampulla containing water in which their precious relic, the hand of St James, had been dipped. Mauger swallowed and was cured. He gave thanks for his recovery by attending mass, entering the confraternity of the monastery, and promising to offer 20s. a year at the high altar.[1]

In the twelfth century the power of laymen had been deliberately harnessed to the monastic ideal. Great families still relied heavily for their hope of salvation on large benefactions to monastic communities engaged in permanent prayer and penitential exercise. Yet by the time religious houses were suppressed in England in the 1530s, they no longer led society spiritually and intellectually.[2] It would indeed be possible to chart a decline in the value attached to the religious by the laity from the thirteenth century onwards. Declining gifts of land to the religious after 1300 might suggest that 'the springs of lay generosity had run dry', even that the relationship with lay society had become 'drained of spiritual content'.[3] Criticism of monastic wealth and virtue sharpened: the abbot of Abingdon was singled out for special satirical attention in Langland's *Vision of Piers Plowman*. Even the mendicant orders, who in theory owned no land, became the butt of late medieval satire.[4] Nevertheless, certain

---

[1] B. Kemp, 'The Miracles of the Hand of St. James', *BAJ* 65 (1970), 6. Mauger of Malcuvenant appears on the pipe rolls of 1155–6 as sheriff of Sussex.

[2] C. H. Lawrence, *Medieval Monasticism: Forms of Religious Life in Western Europe in the Middle Ages* (London, 1984), 61–2; D. Knowles, *The Monastic Orders in England*, second edn. (Cambridge, 1963), 668–77.

[3] C. Platt, *Abbeys and Priories of Medieval England* (London, 1984), 123; N. Saul, 'The Religious Sympathies of the Gentry in Gloucestershire 1200–1500', *Transactions of the Bristol and Gloucester Archaeological Society*, 98 (1980), 109.

[4] *William Langland: The Vision of Piers Plowman*, ed. A. V. C. Schmidt (London, 1982),

connections with lay society should be observed more closely: the incidence and purpose of benefaction to different religious orders; the relationship between different social groups and local religious houses.
Religious houses should not be shunted into some obscure sideline of
devotional interest.

By the mid-thirteenth century there were ten large Benedictine houses in
the region (five of which were in Dorset) and six smaller Benedictine
priories, two Cluniac houses, two Cistercian, four Augustinian, three
Gilbertine, and one Trinitarian. Five of these were nunneries. By then the
foundation of religious houses within the region, as elsewhere, had virtually ended. But even the older houses, which had acquired the bulk of
their temporal and spiritual possessions long before, were still attracting
gifts. Malmesbury was endowed with tithes, virgates, hides, acres, tenements, messuages, crofts, pasture, rents, food, and wax.[5] More grants of
land, albeit smaller ones, came to Reading abbey in the first half of the
thirteenth century than in the twelfth, after its refoundation in 1121.[6] The
houses of newer orders could do better still. The most important endowments of the Augustinian houses of Bradenstoke (founded in 1139)
and Lacock (1229) came with their foundation. But the cartulary of
Bradenstoke shows a peak in the number of gifts between *c.*1200 and
1250;[7] Lacock nunnery received more gifts of land in the second half of the
thirteenth century.[8] The picture of monastic endowment in the fourteenth
century is bleaker,[9] but one brightened by the foundation of two new

112 (*Passus* 10. 323); J. Mann, *Chaucer and Medieval Estates Satire* (Cambridge, 1973),
38–54.

[5] *Reg. Malmesburiense, passim*. For gifts to Stanley see W. de G. Birch, 'Collections
towards the History of the Cistercian Abbey of Stanley', *WAM* 15 (1875), 239–307, and PRO
E40/4619, 6552, 8529, 9360, 9371, 9375, 9377, 9382, 9390, 9535, 11972, 12097, and WRO
1213/1–17; for Wilton: WRO 1422/11, 28, 33, 34, 44, and WRO G25/1/205; for Maiden
Bradley: PRO E210/126, 1932, 2061, 2159, 2160, 2168, 2798, 2985, 3067, 3206, 3226, 3516,
3519, 5396, 5676, 6494, 7187, 7202, 7220, 7540, 8817.

[6] *Reading Abbey Cartularies*, ed. B. R. Kemp (2 vols.; Camden Society, fourth series, 31,
32; 1986–7): there were forty-five gifts in the 12th cent., sixty-four in 1200–49, forty in
1250–99, and eighteen in 1300–49. The largest gifts were made in the 12th cent., after the
refoundation of the abbey. Dates of gifts are not always precise; for other problems in
interpreting gifts see Intro.

[7] *The Cartulary of Bradenstoke Priory*, ed. V. C. M. London (WRS 35; Devizes, 1979),
passim: there were about six gifts in the 12th cent., about sixty-four in the early to mid-13th
cent., sixteen in the late 13th cent., and eight in the 14th cent.

[8] *Lacock Charters*, ed. K. Rogers (WRS 34; Devizes, 1977), *passim*: there were five gifts
from the founders, five gifts in 1230–49, eight in 1250–99, fifteen more from the 13th cent.
but undated, and six from the 14th cent.

[9] But see gifts to Wilton: WRO 1422/13, 34, 36, 38, 48; to Maiden Bradley: *CPR* (1307–

houses (even if both of them had been intended as chantries within parish churches). Poulton priory was founded by Sir Thomas Seymour for the Gilbertine order in 1348, and Edington priory by the bishop of Winchester in the 1350s for the Bonhommes.[10] Most of Edington's lands were painstakingly bought rather than liberally given, but as a newer foundation it could still attract generous gifts: Sir John Rous yielded up the manor of Baynton to the priory in 1444.[11]

Landed gifts, however, should not be the only criteria used to judge lay interest in religious orders. It had, of course, become harder to endow monastic houses after the Statute of Mortmain in 1279, even though the statute's provisions could be avoided by the payment of fines.[12] The evidence of wills suggests that, if the proportion of bequests was slowing down, religious houses could still attract money and goods even in the sixteenth century. In Salisbury more testators, about 10 per cent, gave to the closed orders between 1500 and 1536 than before (see Table 1(a)).[13] Moreover, testators did not particularly favour newer orders over older ones. More people, perhaps (like Edmund Leversedge), were prepared to leave money to the austere Carthusian houses of Hinton and Witham in Somerset, on the border of Wiltshire. Yet the Benedictines and Cistercians did not suffer much of a decline in the proportion of bequests that went to the religious as a whole (see Table 1(b)).[14] Despite the abundance of late medieval satire directed at the older and more wealthy orders—take Chaucer's Benedictine monk who 'a fat swan loved he best of any roost'—lay people did not apparently consider them any less worthy of bequest.

A closer look at the benefactors themselves shows that even the decline in proportion of bequests to the religious is more apparent than

13), 176; (1313–17), 630; (1334–8), 113, 227; PRO, Catalogue of Ancient Deeds, i. B 1703, ii, B 268 (1340); BL Harl. Ch. 57, E41 (349); *CPR* (1361–4), 394; (1367–70), 258; (1377–81), 598; to Ivychurch: *CPR* (1327–30), 267; (1334–8), 48; PRO C143/215/20 (1331); *Tropenell Cart.* ii. 165 (1340); *CPR*(1330–4), 434; *CCR*(1360–4), 445; *CPR*(1391–6), 184.

[10] *VCH: Wilts.* iii. 319–21.

[11] *CPR* (1361–4), 265; (1422–9), 398; *The Edington Cartulary*, ed. J. H. Stevenson (WRS 42; Devizes, 1987), 316; *CPR* (1441–6), 266; *Tropenell Cart.* i. 271. For other grants see *CPR* (1361–4), 113; (1377–81), 491, 508–9; *Edington Cart.* 330, 334 (1373). The appropriation of Keevil church cost over £527 (ibid., pp. xviii–xxvi).

[12] S. Raban, *Mortmain Legislation and the English Church 1279–1500* (Cambridge, 1982), 131–2.

[13] Cf. C. Cross, 'Monasticism and Society in the Diocese of York 1520–40', *TRHS*, fifth series, 38 (1988), 132: an eighth of testators gave to monastic houses, a quarter to the friaries; J. A. F. Thomson, 'Piety and Charity in Late Medieval London', *JEH* 16 (1965), 159: more than a third gave to the poor and friars, less than a sixth to the religious orders.

[14] Thomson, 'Piety and Charity', 159; Raban, *Mortmain Legislation*, 134, speaks of a 'preference for new orders'.

TABLE 1. Bequests to religious orders

(a) Bequests to monastic houses

	Salisbury			Rest of diocese		
	No. of testators	No. of bequests	%	No. of testators	No. of bequests	%
1270–1349	15	1	7			
1350–1399	65	6	9	114	23	20
1400–1449	129	8	6	292	44	15
1450–1499	53	2	4	277	43	16
1500–1536	60	6	10	648	100	15

(b) Distribution of bequests between monastic orders

	No. of bequests	Benedictines	Cistercians	Augustinians	Carthusians	Bonhommes
1300–1399	29	17 (59%)	3 (10%)	7 (24%)	1 (3%)	
1400–1449	48	26 (54%)	2 (4%)	10 (21%)	2 (4%)	5 (10%)
1450–1499	58	31 (53%)	8 (14%)	9 (16%)	7 (12%)	3 (5%)
1500–1536	132	56 (42%)	17 (13%)	26 (20%)	18 (14%)	9 (7%)

(c) Bequests to the mendicant orders

	Salisbury			Rest of diocese		
	No. of testators	No. of bequests	%	No. of testators	No. of bequests	%
1270–1349	15	6	40			
1350–1399	65	46	71	114	61	54
1400–1449	129	59	46	292	109	37
1450–1499	53	26	49	277	67	24
1500–1536	60	23	38	648	115	18

real. The most prominent group of benefactors mentioned in cartularies, and later in wills, were the knights and gentry. Almost as many gentry left bequests to the religious in the early sixteenth century as before. In particular, the gentry of Dorset, where the old Benedictine houses were thickest on the diocesan ground, seem the most attached to their religious.[15] Benefactions certainly came from lower down the social hierarchy, in the thirteenth century and later on. Kington St Michael celebrated the obit of one John Kynsman, husbandman, on 8 December; Robert Martyn, whose family had been villeins as late as 1450, gave 3s. 4d. to the prioress of Amesbury in 1509.[16] Wealthy clothiers with pretensions to gentry status left bequests to the religious.[17] But it was the gentry themselves who were the most consistent benefactors.

More precisely, it tended to be gentry families, rather than individual gentlemen, that maintained ties with particular houses. The Benedictines, Austin canons, and most nunneries often had close and well-defined links with their patrons.[18] The heraldic arms of knightly or gentry families often daubed monastic walls and cloisters: those of the Hungerfords at Lacock, those of the Beauchamps, Mortimers, Berkeleys, and Despensers at Malmesbury.[19] Family tradition did not always dictate benefaction. Some, like the Hungerfords, appear to have been highly individualistic in their testamentary choices[20] (though it may have been a somewhat atavistic individualism, born of a sense that ancestors' gifts to a religious house made further benefaction to the same house unnecessary). Traditions of benefaction, however, were kept alive particularly among families whose ancestors had founded a monastic house. The Longspees were attached to their houses of Lacock and Bradenstoke throughout the thirteenth century (see below). Even Cistercian houses could enjoy traditions of family patronage. Robert de Newburgh founded the Cistercian monastery of Bindon in 1172; his descendants maintained an abiding connection with the house such that in 1484 John Newburgh could ask for burial at his

[15] 63% of the Dorset gentry, 60% of the Wilts. gentry, but only 35% of the Berks. ones left bequests to the regular orders (from a total of 144 gentry).

[16] J. E. Jackson, 'Kington St. Michael', *WAM* 4 (1858), 67; PCC 26 Bennett; see Intro. n. 61.

[17] See below for clothiers. For other merchants see William Lightfoot 1459 (PCC 17 Stockton); Nicholas Martyn 1512 (PCC 16 Fetiplace); Thomas Martyn 1536 (PCC 1 Dyngeley); Reginald 'baker' of Calne (*Bradenstoke Cart.* 89); Henry Chubbe 'pistor' 1441 (WRO G23/1/214 fo. 3). For townsmen of Bristol see *Lacock Charters*, 441, 443, 444; Nicholas Russell, 'butcher' of Salisbury 1388 (D & C, Press IV, Box 'W'). For 'clothmen' see Henry Osborne 1496, John Horton 1496, John Lynde 1504, Richard Limbar 1510 (PCC 12 Horne, 17 Horne, 34 Holgrave, 8 Fetiplace).

[18] S. Wood, *English Monasteries and their Patrons in the Thirteenth Century* (Oxford, 1955), 3.

[19] H. Brakespear, 'Lacock Abbey', *WAM* 31 (1900–1), 216; H. Brakespear, 'Malmesbury Abbey', *WAM* 38 (1914), 489. For a Dauntsey family genealogy see *Reg. Malmesburiense*, i. 3. For the Berkeley family and Bradenstoke see *Bradenstoke Cart.* 423, 424, 426.

[20] M. A. Hicks, 'Chantries, Obits and Almshouses: The Hungerford Foundations 1325–1478', in C. M. Barron and C. Harper-Bill (eds.), *The Church in Pre-Reformation Society* (London, 1985), 123–42.

father's feet in the chapel of Holy Trinity built by him in the monastic church.[21]

Family tradition was not the only stimulant of benefaction. An appealing social exclusiveness tended to surround the enclosed orders. At the top end of the social scale was a nunnery like Amesbury, its close connections with the Crown making it the refuge of daughters of royalty. Other nunneries could also be useful 'dumping grounds' for the excess offspring of local families.[22] Nicholas Sambourne, a local gentleman, spent over £10 on the veiling of his daughter Joan at Lacock in 1395/6, a sum that included 12s. for coverlet and tester and 20s. for the furring of a pisch (undergarment).[23] The placement of daughters in nunneries may well have been restricted principally to gentry families, but it also appealed as an attractive investment to other aspirants of social status. Four Salisbury citizens left money for their daughters who were nuns;[24] in 1514 the clothier Walter Lucas, who was one of the main contributors to the rebuilding of his parish church of Steeple Ashton, left a plate of silver weighing six ounces to his daughter Jane, a nun at Wherwell abbey, and another to his daughter Elizabeth, a nun at Amesbury.[25] Some of the Lacock nuns in the fourteenth century were probably drawn from the prosperous burgess families at Bristol, Gloucester, and Cirencester.[26] Social ties were no doubt enhanced by educational ones: at Reading, Abbot Thorne apparently transferred the endowments of the old hospital of St John for a school famed, on the eve

---

[21] *VCH: Dorset*, ii. 82; PCC 20 Logge.

[22] E. Power, *Medieval English Nunneries* (Cambridge, 1922), 29–30.

[23] W. G. Clark-Maxwell, 'The Outfit for the Profession of an Austin Canoness at Lacock Wiltshire in the Year 1395', *Archaeological Journal*, 69 (1912), 117.

[24] John Cammel 1399 (Shaftesbury), Nicholas Hardyng 1419 (Shaftesbury), John Deng's daughters in William Warwick's will 1445 (Amesbury), John Chafyne 1498 (Amesbury) (WRO G23/1/214, fo. 87; D & C, Press IV, Box 'W'; Reg. Abp. Stafford, fo. 137; PCC 28 Horne). See also daughter of John Bromale at Amesbury in 1424 (*Canonization of St. Osmund*, 62).

[25] PCC 31 Fetiplace.

[26] *VCH: Wilts*. iii. 310. For others see Nicholas de Bonham 1386 (Wilton and Shaftesbury), BL Add. Ch. 15174; Matilda Delawey 1396 (Wilton), Reg. Bp. Mitford; Sir John Savage 1410 (unspecified nunnery), *Reg. Bp. Hallum*, 698; John Stone of Wilton 1412 (Wilton), WRO G23/1/213, fos. 113ᵛ–114ᵛ; Ivo Fitz Waryn 'miles' 1424 (sister at Wilton), *The Register of Henry Chichele*, ed. E. F. Jacob (Canterbury and York Society, 42; Oxford, 1937), ii. 118–22; Robert Gilpurne bequeathed £100 to his son in 1431 if he became a monk at Glastonbury (Winchester college deeds, 20294); John Mundy 1484 (Shaftesbury), PCC 14 Dogget; Henry Kelsall, clothier, 1493 (brother's daughter a nun of Romsey); Marion Baunfeld 1511 (Buckland), 11 Bennett; William Chubbe 1515 (daughter to be in custody of prior of Witham), 20 Holder; Thomas Goddard 1536 (daughters were nuns), 15 Dyngeley.

of the Reformation, for the humanistic education of noble or gentry children.[27]

Lay support for religious houses continued, if on a more modest scale, throughout the later Middle Ages. But was it a support based on spiritual links? The close ties, religious and social, that might exist between the religious and gentry families did not always breed an edifying spirituality. Abbots like Walter de Stokes of Abbotsbury in the mid-fourteenth century seemed to ape gentry habits, keeping hunting dogs, excessive retainers and servants, giving away lavish presents.[28] Ties with the outside world could even be dangerous to the welfare of a religious house. In 1330 the abbot of Bindon, John de Montacute, was deposed, much to the apparent displeasure of Sir Richard de Newburgh whose ancestor Robert had founded the abbey. The apostate monk was able to gather a large following who entered the abbey by night, drove away oxen and sheep, and carried away charters, vestments, and ornaments.[29]

Nevertheless, there were certain religious tasks that monastic houses could perform that also ensured continued benefaction. Social ties aside, religious motivations behind gifts should not be underestimated. Now a grant of land to a religious house need not have indicated a free gift, and some lay people, particularly in the early thirteenth century, sold land to religious houses because of 'urgent need'.[30] Whether these sales constituted any 'crisis of the knightly class' is doubtful, not least because there were comparatively few of them.[31] A few sellers were in debt to the Jews, but some sales did not preclude a religious motive. Two people 'in urgent need', who sold land to Reading abbey, required money to embark on pilgrimages, one to the Holy Land and the other to St James of Compostela.[32] Far more gifts were made with an explicit spiritual intent, as a work of penance for the soul in purgatory. The need for intercession

[27] *VCH: Berks.* ii. 69–70; C. Coates, *The History and Antiquities of Reading* (London, 1820), 322. For schools at Milton, Sherborne, and the Oxford connections of Abingdon and Wallingford see Hutchins, *Dorset*, iv. 396, 273; *Valor Ecclesiasticus temp. Henrici VIII Auctoritate Regia Institutio*, i, ed. J. Caley and J. Hunter (Record Commission; London, 1814), 68; *VCH: Berks.* ii. 58; *Accounts of the Obedientiars of Abingdon Abbey*, ed. R. E. G. Kirk (Camden Society, 1892), 25; BL Cott. MS Claud. Eiv, fo. 34ᵛ.

[28] Reg. Bp. Wyvill, fos. 166–167.   [29] PRO SC8/37/1829–31, 93/4613, 239/11943.

[30] *Bradenstoke Cart.* 74, 94, 128, 131, 183, 310, 314, 417; *Lacock Charters*, 58, 75, 76, 78, 88, 96, 224; *Reading Cart.*, 311–13, 403, 431–3, 590–1, 593, 642, 646, 708, 710, 717, 733–5, 892, 904, 1271, 1275 (before 1250); 316 (after 1250).

[31] D. A. Carpenter, 'Was There a Crisis of the Knightly Class in the Thirteenth Century? The Oxfordshire Evidence', *EHR* 95 (1980), 736.

[32] *Reading Cart.*, 733–5, 1052.

was one that monastic houses were equipped to satisfy: there may well be a link between the increasing number of benefactions, recorded in many cartularies in the early thirteenth century, and the growing dissemination of the doctrines concerning penance and purgatory.

The spiritual services required of the religious were also becoming more precisely defined. Some benefactors sought admission into 'all the prayers and benefits' of a monastic community, or into its more privileged 'fraternity', which could also imply the performance of specific masses and prayers. Originally this meant the obsequies and enrolment in the martyrology, but the content of spiritual benefits was becoming enlarged and more precisely defined in the thirteenth century.[33] As late as 1498, the obit roll of the Benedictine abbey of Kington St Michael recorded the admission of John Baker of Bridgewater and his wife, probably in return for gifts that included a bone of St Christopher, clothed in a cloth of gold, a book of saints in English, and a matins book.[34]

Larger endowments also began to be given in the thirteenth century for the perpetual celebration of mass, the chantry, for the soul of the benefactor. A quarter of all perpetual chantry foundations in the diocese before 1350 were set up in monastic churches (see Table 3). In 1311 Sir John Bluet chose to commission a side chapel at Lacock abbey to house his tomb and chantry.[35] There was certainly a drop in the number of such chantries after the mid-fourteenth century, but reasons are not to be found solely in a supposed decline of lay interest in the religious. The number of chantries founded in parish churches also seems to have fallen. Alienations to monastic houses for chantries may have been additionally discouraged by mortmain fines, and their avoidance became possible with the 'service' type of chantry, which entrusted endowments to feoffees rather than religious institutions.[36] After 1330 and especially after the Black Death, landlords were faced with high production costs, low prices,

[33] The foundress Ela was admitted to the 'fraternity' of Lacock by becoming a nun (*VCH: Wilts.* iii. 304). When Hugh de Burgoyne (1242) and Constance de Lega (1233) were admitted to the 'benefits and prayers' of the house, the term 'fraternity' was not used (*Lacock Charters*, 258, 353; see also *Reading Cart.*, 623, 803, 1079, 1193). On the changing definition of the term see B. Harvey, *Westminster Abbey and its Estates in the Middle Ages* (Oxford, 1977), 39, 370.
[34] Jackson, 'Kington St. Michael', 62–3 and n. 3. John Baker's will is not extant. Also on the obit roll were John Buttelar, gentleman of Badminton Magna, admitted to the fraternity; and at Stanley in the 12th cent. Hugh and Alice of Adena, and Henry and Milicent Bogent (Birch, 'Stanley Abbey', 287, 289). See also PRO E210/308; *Reg. Malmesburiense*, i. 171; BL Camb. Chart. xiii. Grants of fraternity had occasionally been accompanied by the granting of a corrody (annuity of hospitality) (ibid. ii. 348).
[35] *Lacock Charters*, 33–43.
[36] K. L. Wood-Legh, *Perpetual Chantries in Britain* (Cambridge, 1965), 8–16; see Table 3.

and shortages of tenants prepared to accept traditional terms: the costs of amortization when acquiring more land may have become too burdensome. Some monastic houses were less willing to accept landed endowments (especially if they entailed chantry obligations) which would lose their value; and potential chantry founders may have become less willing to involve the religious for fear that their endowments would be assimilated too readily into the general life of the house.[37] At Milton abbey, despite a scheme of retrenchment already under way in 1344, the monks needed to be warned against the withdrawal of chaplains serving the chantries in the abbey church.[38] Even so, economic difficulties did not deter everyone. Sir John Mautravers observed the debt-ridden state of Abbotsbury monastery when he was appointed one of its custodians in 1353 to promote financial reform; yet he later founded a chantry within the same house.[39] The Dorset gentry in particular continued to found perpetual chantries in local religious houses.[40]

There were, besides, less costly means of post-obit intercession. From the early thirteenth century, cartularies begin to record specific endowments for altar lights. Some time between 1230 and 1250, William son of Elis lord of Corton, left one acre to Bradenstoke for lights to be lit in the priory at the daily mass of the Virgin Mary; five similar grants were made soon after.[41] As cartularies peter out, so wills record a continuing desire to fund altar lights: in 1506 Thomas Audley left 40s. to Maiden Bradley priory, part of which was to fund two torches on the high altar and two on the altar of the Virgin Mary, to be lit at the raising of the host during mass.[42] A more elaborate form of commemoration was the anniversary service. Long celebrated by the religious, for monks, nuns, or for founders themselves, anniversaries, obits, or trental masses seem increasingly to have been demanded by other lay people in the thirteenth century.[43] The obit roll of Kington St Michael includes the names of possibly 150 lay

[37] Raban, *Mortmain Legislation*, 137, 174–82; Hare, 'Lords and Tenants', 93–110; Wood-Legh, *Perpetual Chantries*, 130 ff.

[38] Reg. Bp. Wyvill, fos. 130–131. Ivychurch and Marlborough also complained of poverty after the Black Death (*VCH: Wilts.* iii. 292, 317).

[39] PRO SC8/10470–10475; Reg. Bp. Wyvill, fos. 166ᵛ–167; *CPR*(1391–6), 116.

[40] All but one of the six perpetual chantries set up in monastic houses in the region after 1350 were founded in Dorset (see Table 3). The last was the Strangeway family's in Abbotsbury in 1505 (Reg. Bp. Audeley, fos. 172–73).

[41] *Bradenstoke Cart.* 69, 196, 234, 268, 416, 511; *Lacock Charters*, 122, 366; *Reg. Malmesburiense*, i. 100, 279, 480; ii. 158, 181, 199, p. lxxi.

[42] PCC 25 Adeane. Other testators asking for altar lights 1348 to 1535: six from Wilts., two from Dorset, one from Berks.

[43] Wood-Legh, *Perpetual Chantries*, 3; *Reg. Malmesburiense*, i. 176, 300; *Bradenstoke Cart.* 267.

people, belonging mainly, perhaps, to the thirteenth century.[44] Obits continued to be founded, if not with landed endowments, then with money. In 1510 Walter Cervington, esquire, asked for an anniversary 'by note' to be celebrated by Ivychurch priory: among the expenses was 20*d*. 'for the setting up of the hearse' over his grave.[45] Daily masses, even if on a temporary rather than perpetual basis, could also be demanded[46] and some benefactors gave neither money nor land, but liturgical goods. Sir John Mompesson the elder, for instance, chose to be remembered in 1500 by a gift of 20*s*. or a pair of vestments with 'the scochyn of my armes and my wyfe in the crosse on the back', to the houses at Shaftesbury, Wilton, Amesbury, Maiden Bradley, and Edington.[47] Gifts of vestments also suggest a willingness on the part of the laity to ensure the continuance in religious houses of the daily round of liturgical service.

Finally, a few lay people chose monastic houses for their place of burial. Most testators in the fourteenth and fifteenth centuries preferred burial in their own parish churches[48] but some burials in religious houses are still recorded: as late as 1536 Anne Stone, a widow from Salisbury, asked to be buried at Shaftesbury (if she died there) next to her father's grave.[49] Burial in a parish church, moreover, did not preclude intercession of the religious at the time of the funeral. John Wykes, buried in Trowbridge parish church, left money in 1460 to the houses at Bath, Kington St Michael, Edington, Monkton Farleigh, and Amesbury for them to say placebo and dirige for his soul and to have a potation on the day of his funeral.[50] After the funeral, intercession might continue. Endowments for chantries to be celebrated in parish churches could yet be entrusted to the

[44] Jackson, 'Kington St. Michael', 60–7: Ralph Bluet, early 13th cent.; Sir Hugh Mortimer, *c*.1227; Sir John Delamere, later 13th cent.; Sir Alexander Studley, *c*.1280; Nicholas Sambourne, 14th cent.? See also Sir John Rous at Edington after 1444 (*Tropenell Cart.* i. 271). For the obit of John Goodhyne 1352 (unrecorded in any cartulary) see *Lacock Charters*, 174.

[45] PCC 34 Bennett. Between 1456 and 1528 six testators from Dorset, four from Berks., and ten from Wilts. left gifts for obits.

[46] Between 1414 and 1528 eight testators from Wilts., five from Dorset, and one from Berks. asked for temporary masses from the religious. Almost all were of gentry stock.

[47] PCC 15 Blamyr. Between 1427 and 1533 ten testators from Wilts., one from Dorset, and two from Berks. (again mainly gentry) left bequests of vestments to the religious.

[48] Fewer than 5% of testators in the region chose burial in monastic houses. For earlier burials in monasteries see Bradenstoke (*Bradenstoke Cart.* 222, 284, 468, 510, 511, 518); Maiden Bradley (*VCH: Wilts.* iii. 296); Monkton Farleigh (*VCH: Wilts.* iii. 262); Birch, 'Stanley Abbey', 299; PRO E40/8529.

[49] PCC 38 Hogen. Between 1500 and 1535 nineteen (mainly gentry) testators asked for burial in monastic houses out of 708. Ten were from Dorset.

[50] PCC 40 Marche; 21 Stockton. See also Sir Thomas Tropenell (PCC 7 Milles) and his son Christopher (6 Holgrave); Alice Budde 1391 (DRO DC/BTB D2).

religious: even the 'service' type of chantry, like Thomas Horton's at Bradford-on-Avon around 1530, could involve the supervision of the religious (in Thomas's case, that of Hinton Charterhouse).[51]

Certain families chose religious houses as places of burial in preference to their local parish church. Bradenstoke and Lacock were the spiritual repositories of the Longspee family and the Salisbury earls during the thirteenth century: Stephen Longspee gave his heart to the priory and his body to the nunnery. The Seymours may have regarded Poulton priory as a family mausoleum: in 1389 Alice Seymour presented a petition to the bishop to allow her to move the bones of her progenitors from Poulton parish church to the priory which her ancestor had founded.[52] Easton priory retained enduring connections with two families who were descended from the nieces of the founder, Stephen of Tisbury. One of the families was still endowing the priory in the fourteenth century. In 1326 Robert Druweys, instead of founding a chantry in the parish church (to which he gave 12s. a year for altar lights and 200 sheep in compensation), was given licence to alienate land and rents to the priory to provide a chaplain to celebrate for his soul in the new chapel of St John the Baptist, near the north end of the parish church.[53] The other family, the Esturmeys, also maintained a tradition of family patronage. In 1389 Sir William confirmed the lands granted by his uncle Henry and minutely described the conditions under which they were to be held. Intercession for the souls of ancestors was required: the bodies of Sir Adam of Easton, Master Stephen, Geoffrey Esturmey the nephew of Stephen and his wife Matilda, Henry and his wife Matilda, Henry and his wife Mary, Henry and his wife Matilda had all been buried in the priory. On the evening before family anniversary days, candles were to be lit at placebo and dirige until vespers and compline were over; candles were also to burn during the commendation at the requiem on the morrow. Esturmey investment in the divine offices of Easton priory continued: in 1427 a later Sir William also requested burial in the priory church and bequeathed the canons, among other things, two volumes of Higden's Polychronicon.[54]

So some gentry families continued to enjoy amicable ties, religious and social, with monastic houses. But friendliness did not always characterize

[51] N. Orme, *Education in the West of England 1066–1548* (Exeter, 1976), 114–17.

[52] W. L. Bowles and J. G. Nichols, *Annals and Antiquities of Lacock Abbey* (London, 1835), app. 1, p. iii; Reg. Bp. Waltham, fo. 10.

[53] WRO Ailesbury MS 1300, 'Rough Lists', sect. 15, nos. 16–20, 24, 26. *Reg. Bp. Martival*, v. 519–23; *VCH: Wilts*. iii. 324–6.

[54] WRO Ailesbury MS 1300/1, 2; 'Rough Lists', sect. 15, no. 35; 1300/24, 30; PCC 7 Luffenham.

the relationship between monastic houses and certain townsmen. Old Benedictine abbeys that were overlords of borough towns, could be particularly fierce in holding on to long-established rights, in opposition to the aspirations of burgesses. Reading had grown up on the royal demesne but in 1121 had been granted to the new abbey: although a developing guild merchant gave the burgesses some measure of independence, an agreement reached in 1254 stamped monastic authority on town officers. Conflicts arose in 1302 and 1359 when the townsmen resisted the abbot's attempt to raise tallage; in the late fifteenth century when they flouted the abbot's right to select guild officers; and in 1450 and 1509 when they attempted to increase their hold over land given to the guild by claiming its status as a body corporate.[55] Frayed secular relations did not encourage spiritual links. Some people living in Reading did give land to the abbey in the thirteenth century, yet between 1311 and 1536, out of the forty-five testators who requested burial in Reading only one made a bequest to the monastery.[56]

At Abingdon disputes between townsmen and abbey could be more acrimonious still. Here, too, the town had grown up on monastic land, and there could be no harking back, as the Reading burgesses sometimes did, to a time before the monastery's foundation when townsmen were free of monastic overlordship. The abbot's authority was repeatedly questioned, his bailiffs attacked in 1296 and 1314, and in 1328 the abbot was forced to allow the townsmen their own bailiffs.[57] The abbey also prevented an attempt by the parishioners of St Helen's church or chapel, within the town, to found their own cemetery. In 1396 an appeal to Pope Boniface IX secured the abbey compensation for financial loss and the right to exhume the sixty-seven bodies in the new cemetery and to rebury them in the conventual one.[58]

A dispute of a different nature arose between parishioners and the monks at Sherborne. Here the monastic church was shared by monks and laity, and in the fourteenth century three aisles had been added to the west end of the nave for the exclusive use of the parish. In 1436 certain parishioners, with a multitude of others numbering about 100, were said to have moved the font from its old position in the nave of the monastic church to their own section of the church and to have narrowed the entrance between the two parts of the church. The monks complained that their divine service had been disturbed by the noisy baptismal procession conducted by the parishioners and the ringing of the parish bells at matins. But Bishop Aiscough's order to have the font returned to its

[55] *VCH: Berks.* ii. 62–8.
[56] William Knight 1535 (PCC 1 Crumwell).
[57] *VCH: Berks.* ii. 54–6.
[58] *Cal. Papal Reg.* v. 5, 6, 371.

traditional spot sparked a riot, led by Walter Gallor, a 'stoute butcher', who shot a burning shaft into the top of the monastic part of the church. The whole church was burned and its lead bells melted in the flames. The church had to be rebuilt by the parishioners and a new font was consecrated in 1450, presumably in the place they had so disliked.[59]

Yet the well-documented cases of disputes need not entirely colour our picture of relations between townspeople and their monasteries. Links between Reading abbey and the town were not always ones of secular enmity. By 1479 it was reported that the hospital run by the abbey's almoner admitted only the wives of burgesses who had fallen on hard times. The parishioners of St Laurence rang their great bell at the time of the abbot's death in 1520/1, and in 1521/2 allowed a seat for the abbot's mother in the church.[60] Abingdon abbey did not always clash with the aspirations of townsmen. When a new bridge was built across the Thames in 1416, a lengthy poem was written to commemorate the efforts of the townspeople and wealthy benefactors: among them, albeit referred to only briefly, was the abbot. The few surviving accounts of the abbey's warden of Trinity mention the repair of certain tenements on the new bridge in 1448/9.[61] Moreover, the sharing of a church by parishioners and religious did not always produce friction as it had done in Sherborne. The Edington Bonhommes shared their conventual church with the parishioners; proximity may explain why parishioners could leave bequests to the priory and require the canons to attend their funeral exequies.[62]

The closeness of such ties with the lay society, even in the later Middle Ages, did not always spell a decline in monastic virtue. The case for a sordid secularism creeping into late medieval monastic life[63] (and therefore a decline in respect and support for it) can be pressed too far. The religious could sometimes attempt to retain a certain holy isolation. Even in shared churches, monks wished to maintain the spiritual integrity of their services. Part of the abbot of Sherborne's displeasure with the parishioners centred on their ringing of bells at unreasonable hours. Part of the 1436 settlement was to ensure that a partition was put in the nave of the monastic church so that there would be a distinct separation between

[59] C. L. Kingsford (ed.), *English Historical Literature in the Fifteenth Century* (Oxford, 1913), 348–9.
[60] BRO D/P 97/5/2, pp. 128, 136; BL Add. MS 6214, fo. 7/16.
[61] *VCH: Berks.* iv. 439; F. Little, *A Monument to Christian Munificence; or An Account of the Holy Cross and the Hospital of Christ Church in Abingdon* (Oxford, 1871), 3–13; *Accounts of Obedientiars*, 124.
[62] Edward Lambert 1493 (PCC 3 Vox); John Newman 1501 (13 Blamyr).
[63] G. R. Elton, *Reform and Reformation, England, 1509–1558* (London, 1977), 240.

the monks and parishioners. At Abingdon the monks had also been disturbed by the tumult made by those who followed funeral processions into the conventual cemetery and who had even prevented the celebration of the office of the dead in church.

If worldly ties were not always fostered by the religious, some monastic houses, nevertheless, deliberately drew lay people towards their gates for spiritual reasons. The grant of papal indulgences, with remissions of days in purgatory, could encourage the penitent to make offerings, such as those who visited Amesbury at the Annunciation and Invention of the Holy Cross (after Lady Hungerford's lodgings in the nunnery had been burnt down in 1474).[64] In the early sixteenth century Tarrant Kaines abbey seems to have been undergoing repairs to which some testators left bequests; an indulgence granted for the rebuilding of a nearby bridge in 1505 may have been connected with the monastery's needs. In 1505 Lord Morgan Kyndeway left twenty marks or twenty sheep for the making of the abbey steeple.[65] Some abbots or priors also acquired licences to hear the confessions of those who visited their monastic houses.[66]

Other religious communities could attract the penitent to their chapels. The 1474 papal indulgence to Amesbury referred to the nunnery's chapel of Virgin Mary which contained an image of the crucified Saviour to which Sir Thomas de la Mare and many others were said to resort. Houses that kept relics of saints could reap further dividends. In the twelfth century Reading abbey benefited from the miraculous powers of the hand of St James given to the monastery by Henry I.[67] Wilton nunnery had its own cult of St Edith, the daughter of King Edgar, born in Kemsing in Kent, who spent most of her life in Wilton. It too attracted gifts, from royalty in the thirteenth century and from lay people in the lower ranks of society in the fourteenth: in 1398 Emma atte Mulle from Wilton left her wedding ring to the feretory of St Edith.[68] In the fifteenth century, moreover, there may also have been an attempt to encourage devotion to the cult. A poem about St Edith and her connection with Wilton was written around 1420, possibly by one of the chaplains of the nun-

[64] *Cal. Papal Reg.* (1362–1404), 342; (1471–80), 219.
[65] Reg. Bp. Audley, fo. 133; PCC 30 Holgrave; Thoms Audely 1506 (25 Adeane); Margaret Clement wished to be a 'sister' at Tarrant Kaines in 1505 (36 Holgrave); Margaret Twynhoo was already one in 1501 (15 Blamyr).
[66] *Cal. Papal Reg.* (1396–1404), 495; Reg, Bp. Mitford, i, fo. 113ᵛ.
[67] Kemp, 'Miracles', 1–19; see also gifts to the shrine or feretory of St Aldhelm at Malmesbury (*Reg. Malmesburiense*, ii. 158; 1478 Thomas Tanner or Pynnyng, PCC 35 Wattys).
[68] *VCH: Wilts.* iii. 231–2, 234; *CCR* (1237–42), 424; Winchester college deeds, 19466/3.

nery.[69] It tells of the former glories of Wilton, how kings 'dwelled there much', and of the generosity of royalty to Wilton and St Edith from King Egbert to Henry I. It describes how the blind, the crooked, the maimed, the sick, and lepers were healed by her intervention, how pilgrims from as far as Picardy visited the shrine. It encourages others to believe with the Duke of Cornwall, who told King Ethelred of his dream that the body of St Edith 'shuld be here in great honour and virtue'; it reminds the reader the 'contre of Wyltone' was 'full gladde' for relics 'the whyche ben there set in—to this day'. The poem may only have been for the benefit of the nunnery's inmates; whether it helped to put the cult of St Edith back on the religious map is not clear. But the cult may have enjoyed a local popularity: in 1426 an indulgence was granted to Wilton abbey for those who made offerings on the holiday of St Edith (16 September) and of the sixteen extant wills of Wilton testators between 1348 and 1529, twelve of them remembered the church of St Edith.[70]

Certain monastic houses had connections with chapels outside their walls that were also the focus of devotional cults. A Reading abbey cartulary records the gift of a stall in the town, in the mid-thirteenth century, to a chapel of the Holy Ghost on Caversham bridge for the support of a lamp in perpetuity. The same chapel was the focus of a Marian cult to which pilgrims resorted as late as 1536: the chapel was then a cell of Notley priory, but Reading abbey may have held some responsibility for its upkeep as the town burgesses claimed in 1479.[71] At Abingdon miracles were reported in a chapel which Edmund earl of Cornwall had built in the late thirteenth century. The wardens of the chapel accounted to the abbey, and in 1404/5 oblations from the altar yielded £6. 13s. 4d. (though by 1478/9 takings had dropped to 12s.).[72]

Monastic influence might also extend into the divine service of the parish. The appropriation of churches to monasteries did not always have desirable consequences for the pastoral care of the parish.[73] The responsi-

---

[69] *Chronicon Vilodunense*, ed. W. H. Black and R. Colt-Hoare (London, 1830); *S. Editha sive Chronicon Vilodunense im Wiltshire Dialekt*, ed. C. Horstmann (Heilbronn, 1883). The following extracts are from *Chronicon Vilodunense*, 64, 66, 68, 84, 92–5. Cf. the life of St Cuthbert in English verse (R. B. Dobson, *Durham Priory 1400–1500* (Cambridge, 1973), 30).

[70] Reg. Bp. Chandler, fo. 44. There also appears to have been a cult of St Edith at her birthplace in Kemsing which was popular and, according to Thomas Lamberd in 1570, worthy only of scorn (*A Perambulation of Kent by William Lambard 1570*, new edn. (London, 1827), 457–9).

[71] *Reading Carts.* 913; BL Add. MS 6214 fo. 14.

[72] *Annales Prioratus de Wigornia*, in *Annales Monastici*, ed. H. R. Luard (Rolls Series; London, 1869), 499; *Accounts of Obedientiars*, pp. xxxix, 67, 70, 95, 131, 137, 140.

[73] R. A. R. Hartridge, *A History of Vicarages in Middle Ages* (Cambridge, 1930), 157–88.

bility of a monastic house, as rector for the upkeep of the chancel in an appropriated church, was not always met. In 1437 the inhabitants of the chapelry of Charlton were complaining that it was the duty of the abbot of Malmesbury to maintain their chancel. To emphasize their bond with the abbey they mustered a group of 50- and 60-year-olds who touchingly recalled a time when the abbot had sent his officials and workmen to make repairs on the chancel roof, corner walls, and east window. The issue here was more complex than a mere shirking of monastic responsibility, for the chapelry was not directly linked with the abbey but was dependent on the parish of Westport which had been appropriated to the abbey.[74] Elsewhere, not a few parish churches bore the marks of abbots and abbesses, priors and prioresses, on their chancel walls, roofs, and windows, indicating monastic commitment to rectorial duties.[75]

Occasionally, religious houses met certain parochial needs. The monks of Abingdon had to be forbidden by the bishop to lend liturgical goods to parishioners in 1425. Malmesbury abbey may have given land to support the church of South Newton: John Aubrey was to record a traditional ceremony in which the parishioners remembered their benefactor Abbot Loring (abbot 1205–23).[76] In the late thirteenth century Bradenstoke priory 'generously conceded' a chapel at Draycot at the request of Ellis Cotel and other parishioners of Wilcot: the chaplain, charged with celebrating mass and regular hours, was to be appointed by the canons.[77] In 1368 the parishioners of Easton gained the bishop's permission to demolish their dilapidated church and take over a chapel, sixty paces away from the church, which belonged to the local priory (probably the one built by Sir Robert Druweys).[78] Chapelries dependent on monastic houses did not always experience the same difficulty as St Helen's in Abingdon in acquiring more parochial rights: in 1431 the inhabitants of Compton Hawy secured burial rights from the abbot of Sherborne.[79]

One final link between religious houses and society outside was through charitable works. Alms-giving was a task to which the monastic houses might have considered themselves well suited, for as the Stanley chronicle

[74] Reg. Bp. Neville, second series, fos. 52ᵛ–54.
[75] See chancels at St Nicholas Abbotsbury, Cranborne, Bradford Abbas, Oborne (Hutchins, *Dorset*, ii. 728; iii. 390; iv. 122, 201).
[76] Reg. Bp. Chandler, fos. 50–1; Aubrey, *Remaines*, 136–8; BL Lansdowne MS 231, fos. 187–188.
[77] *Bradenstoke Cart.* 69; see also 192.
[78] WRO Ailesbury MS 1300, 'Rough Lists', sect. 15 (Easton, Bradenstoke, Warren, and Priory), no. 41.
[79] Reg. Bp. Mitford, second series, fo. 13ᵛ, and *Cal. Papal Reg.* vii. 280 (1423).

put it, the religious were 'the stewards and dispensers of alms given by the faithful for their soul, for the use of monasteries, the poor, the sick, widows and orphans'.[80] Reading abbey was founded not merely for the sustenance of monks, but also for the reception of poor guests and way-farers. A hospital was founded outside the monastic gates to support thirteen resident poor and other needy travellers. In the thirteenth century the abbey attracted sixteen gifts (out of 104) specifically earmarked for the office of almoner who looked after the hospital.[81] Some grants refer to daily distributions of food to pilgrims and the poor.

How far casual doles were given out is not clear. Some monasteries apparently ceased to hand out casual alms to beggars as early as the thirteenth century, perhaps preferring to give, as the Reading monks did, to the poor resident in the almonry.[82] Monastic hospitals may have become discriminating as to whom they admitted. Monastic alms-giving seems generally to have been distributed in an organized, even ritualized form, particularly on Maundy Thursday and on anniversary days of benefac-tors. At Easton priory Sir William Esturmey's deed of 1389 stipulated that every year the prior was to render to twenty poor men 20*d*. and twenty good white loaves for Maundy Thursday 'such as the Prior and Brethren used to distribute in alms'. The feet of the poor were to be washed by the granter and subsequently by his heirs or by the prior 'as other religious do'.[83] Such forms of charity must have favoured the local poor, rather than the migrant or casual beggar, who were more likely to be apprised of the dates. Ela countess of Salisbury had made elaborate provision for her husband's and her own anniversary: late in the thirteenth century 100 poor were being given a wheaten loaf and two herrings for her own obit and thirteen poor were being fed for her husband's.[84] At the time of the *Valor Ecclesiasticus* in 1535, on average a modest 3 per cent of mon-astic income in 1535 was being spent on alms funded by endowments of benefactors.[85]

[80] *The Chronicles of Stephen, Henry II and Richard*, ed. R. Howlett (Rolls Series; London, 1885), 510–11.

[81] *VCH: Berks.* ii. 62; *Reading Carts.* 205, 208; for gifts see 492, 499, 710, 716, 721, 723, 724, 737, 739, 747, 904, 909, 933, 980, 991, 1097.

[82] Ibid. 737, 739, 909; and see B. Harvey, *Living and Dying in England, 1100–1540: The Monastic Experience* (Oxford, 1993), 17–23.

[83] WRO Ailesbury MS 1300/30.

[84] Clark-Maxwell, 'Austin Canoness', 120–1. In 1311 John Bluet asked for 1,000 poor to be given half a penny each on the day of his anniversary (*Lacock Charters*, 33; *Valor Ecclesiasticus*, ii. 117).

[85] A. Savine, *English Monasteries on the Eve of the Reformation* (Oxford Studies in Social

Measured in absolute terms, rather than in percentages of monastic incomes, the level of alms-giving could be substantial. Complaints that doles were not being distributed suggest that they were considered significant. Bishop Chandler had to warn the monks of Abingdon not to take for themselves the alms left for the poor. An inquiry in 1440 reported that the abbot of Cerne was distributing neither a halfpenny's worth of bread every Wednesday, nor a silver penny every Friday during the season of Lent, to all those who came for alms. At the manor court of Cookham around 1468 it was found that the abbot of Cirencester had withdrawn the three bushels of fine wheat that he and his predecessors had been accustomed to give to the poor every week between the first Sunday in Lent and the 'Yule of August'.[86] Moreover, the *Valor* does not generally record other expenditure on works of charity performed by the religious besides that for benefactors' alms. It also shows that the total amounts distributed to the poor by monasteries could be quite substantial, particularly by the old Benedictine abbeys in Dorset. At Milton £51. 16s. was being spent on alms, £30 of which was being spent on the daily necessities of thirteen poor men of the town chosen by the abbot. At Cerne £34. 6s. 8d. was spent, including weekly distributions of bread and ale for thirteen poor men.[87] The apparently greater attachment of the gentry in Dorset to their monastic houses, compared with their counterparts elsewhere in the diocese, may be explained by their approval of the level of alms-giving dispensed by the religious in the county.

The links between the closed orders and lay society were manifold, but ultimately they were restricted by the nature of the monastic calling. The friars, however, had a much clearer pastoral role to play. Nine places in the diocese are known to have housed friaries, though the role they played in the small towns of Dorchester, Gillingham, Bridport, and Lyme Regis is obscure. The friars, grey and black, were naturally attracted to the most populous towns of the region like Reading, Marlborough, and Sherborne. Salisbury had a Franciscan friary, and in 1281 the Dominicans moved

and Legal History, 1; Oxford, 1909, 228). Edington did not dispense any alms, according to the *Valor*, 238–9, but the priory celebrated obits which involved distributions.

[86] Reg. Bp. Chandler, fo. 50; PRO C270/309/72; BRO D/E SK M8. See also the substantial alms Abingdon distributed in the parishes of Culham and Cuddleston in 1383/4 (£11. 16s. and 66s. 8d.) (*Accounts of Obedientiars*, pp. li, 44, 50). The accounts of most of the monastic offices (excluding those of the almoner which do not survive) show distributions to the poor (ibid., pp. xxiii, li, 25, 44, 63, 113).

[87] *Valor Ecclesiasticus*, i. 51, 68.

from declining Wilton to Fisherton-Anger, a site much closer to the thriving city.[88]

In some ways the friars enjoyed links with the laity comparable to those of monastic houses. They had royal or aristocratic founders and patrons. Their churches could provide fashionable burial places for knightly or gentry patrons, though traditional connections with particular families were usually less important than for monastic houses. But, more often than with the closed orders, they received bequests to perform trentals, masses, and obits for donors, some of whom requested admission into the confraternity of the friary (see Table 1(c)).[89] Sir John Byconvil made a particularly elaborate gift to the friars of Dorchester in 1485. In return for the gift of certain water mills, he was recognized as chief founder of the house. The friars were to take turns week by week to pray for his soul; those who were lecturers, 'being diligently employed about their scholars', were exempted as long as they found substitutes. Sir John's obit was to be celebrated on the day after the feast of St Francis; young boys, called 'Byconvil's friars', were to be brought to the order and educated in good manners and learning, always respecting the memory of the benefactor.[90]

For all their connections with high society, the friars were not as exclusive as some monastic houses. Testators from Reading hardly ever made bequests to their abbey, but 28 per cent of them left money to the friary. At Salisbury almost 70 per cent of testators left money for the two friaries, and although this figure had dropped to 40 per cent in the fifteenth century, it was a larger percentage than bequests to monasteries. Many asked for the same intercessory services as knights or gentlemen, and a few asked for burial in the friary churches.[91]

Part of the relative popularity of the friars as intercessors for the dead must have sprung from the links forged with the living. Unfortunately, only a handful of references testify to the role friars actually played within local society. Their role as educators is alluded to in Sir John Byconvil's gift to the friars of Dorchester. Their role as confessors is confirmed by occasional licences granted by the bishop.[92] Friars were employed in the cathedral to give sermons during Lent and the large conventual church of the preaching friars in Salisbury suggests the need for space so that large

[88] *VCH: Wilts.* iii. 329–34; *VCH: Dorset*, 92–6; *VCH: Berks.* ii. 89–92; iv. 96.

[89] For an example of bequest for entrance into a friary fraternity see William Filliol, knight, in 1527 (PCC 23 Porche).

[90] Hutchins, *Dorset*, ii. 364–5; *VCH: Dorset*, ii. 93–6.

[91] Seven citizens out of seventy-nine asked for burial in their friaries during the 14th cent. and seven out of 178 in the 15th cent.

[92] Reg. Bp. Wyvill, ii. fo. 85 (1352).

congregations could attend sermons. Some lay fraternities in Salisbury, possibly craft guilds, may even have conducted their celebrations in mendicant churches.[93] The tailors' guild held its meetings in the church of the grey friars in 1444. In 1478 John Schotte, a goldsmith, left 3s. 4d. to the 'fraternity of St. Barbara' in the church of the friars minor; John Viresden made a bequest to the fraternity of St Peter in the same church in 1503.[94] Hints as to the friars' involvement in parishes are suggested by the 'Kaymes' play' (possibly involving friars) held at St Laurence's in Reading; in 1531/2 the church sold its old organ to the grey friars in Oxford for £10.[95] We also hear of layman Thomas Restwoode actually dwelling in the convent of the friars minor at Reading from his will of 1495.[96]

The friars may also have won regard from certain lay people because they were not always popular with the clergy, particularly with those clerics who feared that the friars would encroach on their pastoral—and financial—territory. Reading abbey, anxious to protect its right to tithes, legacies, and offerings, had originally made it difficult for the grey friars to establish themselves in the town. The abbey allowed the friars to settle on a stretch of wasteland leading to Caversham bridge in 1233, but the site proved to be one subject to flooding. Only the intervention of Archbishop Pecham in 1285, apparently at the request of 'many persons of conse-quence', forced the monks to allow the friars a more favourable site.[97] Perhaps the monks' protectionist stance helped to endear the friars to the townspeople, themselves at odds with monastic overlordship.

At Radipole the friars also found themselves in opposition to the exist-ing ecclesiastical structure and in harmony with lay concerns. Certain inhabitants of Melcombe Regis felt themselves to be ill served by the mother church of Radipole which lay a mile and a half away. In 1426 two knights, Hugh Deverill and John Rogers, and others complained to the bishop that there had been no place dedicated to God in the vill, which was difficult to reach even by merchants who visited by land and from the sea. Hence the inhabitants had remained notoriously ignorant. So a house

---

[93] D & C, Press II, Accounts of the Procurator of St Thomas's.

[94] WRO G23/1/251, fo. 5; WRO D4/3, fo. 16ᵛ; PCC 8 Holgrave. See also D. M. Palliser, 'The Trade Guilds of Tudor York', in P. Clark and P. Slack (eds.), *Crisis and Order in English Towns 1500–1700: Essays in Urban History* (London, 1972), 110–11.

[95] C. Kerry, *A History of the Municipal Church of St. Laurence Reading* (Reading, 1893), 237; BRO D/P 97/5/2, p. 130.

[96] PCC 28 Horne.

[97] BL Cott. MS Vesp. Exxv fo. 214; *Registrum Epistolarum Fratris Johannis Peckham Archiepiscopi Cantuarensis*, ed. C. T. Martin (3 vols.; Rolls Series, 77; London, 1882–5), i. 414–16; iii. 211–12.

for three Dominican friars had been established, about eight years earlier, who had already done much for the service of God and the salvation of men. But in the bishop's eyes the friars had established themselves without licence and had extracted oblations from the faithful who had flocked to the site. The friars had been subverting the rights of the mother church. Yet they had clearly fulfilled a popular role, satisfying a pastoral need that the parish framework did not meet. And when their presence was finally accepted by the bishop, we also find them active in other schemes, building a jetty against the ebb and flow of the tide, and attempting to add a tower to fortify the small town.[98] The friars could be closer to the concerns of lay people than the religious of enclosed orders.

The history of late medieval piety can be presented as a continuing search for novel expressions of spirituality.[99] The Cistercians overtook the Benedictines in the twelfth century, the mendicants rose to popularity in the thirteenth, and for laymen the parish, chantry, and private chapel became the focus of spiritual attention by the fourteenth. The flow of landed gifts to monastic houses slowed down after 1250 and the very accumulation of wealth became a source of friction and the object of satire. But to some extent the decline in landed gifts had little to do with changes in spiritual expression. The Statute of Mortmain in 1279 may have only accentuated the slowing down of landed accessions to the religious; yet in particular cases it may have acted as a more serious brake to lay generosity. The later fourteenth century saw many a religious house fall foul of debts and decay. Potential benefactors may have felt less favourably inclined to monasteries that sought to clutch their endowments, offerings, and oblations more tightly in the face of adverse conditions. Potential chantry founders may have become more fearful that any endowment would be swallowed up by the general needs of the house.

Moreover, the extent of giving to monastic orders was affected by changes not just in spirituality but also in patronage. Certain religious houses had benefited greatly from a close association with founding families: the interest of later families, once patronage had changed hands, could not be as great. The Esturmeys at Easton were succeeded by the Seymours and Ringbournes following the death of Sir William Esturmey in 1427. The Longspees were great patrons of Lacock and Bradenstoke; patronage passed, on the death of William Longspee (III), to his daughter

---

[98] Reg. Bp. Chandler, fos. 54–55; Reg. Bp. Neville, fo. 34.
[99] Raban, *Mortmain Legislation*, 131; see also N. Saul, *Scenes from Provincial Life: Knightly Families in Sussex 1280–1400* (Oxford, 1986), 140–60.

Margaret de Lacy, married to the earl of Lincoln. Her death in 1309 was cited as one of the reasons for the complete surrender of the advowson of Lacock parish church to the nunnery: Margaret de Lacy and other powerful people were gone, it was said, and the burdens daily increased. Patronage of Lacock and Bradenstoke passed on to the house of Lancaster and thence to the Crown, whose principal landed interests lay outside the county. Religious houses might also have had cause to regret the demise of local landlord families with whom close ties had been maintained. The Baynards took over the lordship of Lackham from the Bluet family in 1349 and never displayed the same interest in the convent as their predecessors: for five generations following, they chose to be buried not in the abbey, as Sir John Bluet had done, but in the local parish church.[100]

The decrease in landed accession does not necessarily indicate a waning interest in the religious. Bequests in money and liturgical goods continued to flow into monastic houses right up until the Dissolution, particularly from knights and gentry who had been the main group of benefactors. Nevertheless, the religious orders were indeed becoming less important in society. As we shall see, the parish, especially from the thirteenth century, was becoming the focus of pastoral and spiritual attention; the dissemination of the doctrines of purgatory, particularly in the thirteenth century, encouraged penitential gifts from a wider group of people who had not traditionally supported the monastic orders. But even these changes in piety and religious expression were not entirely detrimental to the religious. The general concern for a speedy passage through purgatory could still encourage gifts to religious houses. From the thirteenth century onwards, laymen had begun to stipulate specific services in return for their gifts to religious houses—altar lights, obits, pittances, doles to the poor, chantry services—in more detail than before. Many of these services were still being required in the sixteenth century, particularly from the upper echelons of local society. The growing importance of the parish did not mean isolation for monastic houses since they could become involved in parish chantry foundations, funeral services, and sometimes the wider pastoral and charitable needs of parishioners. The friars, of course, were far more involved in the religious life of townspeople than the closed orders.

In particular, certain conditions prompted more favourable links between lay people and the religious, even the closed orders. Distance, perhaps, lent a certain enchantment. Testators from Salisbury, without a

---

[100] *VCH: Wilts.* iii. 297, 265, 326, 276; *Lacock Charters*, 32; E. Kite, 'Baynard Monuments in Lacock Church', *WAM* 4 (1858), 1–7.

closed religious house in the city, were more likely to leave bequests to monasteries than those from Reading, who could be troubled by the immediate overlordship of their own abbey. Monks who shared their church with parishioners, as at Sherborne, did not always find that proximity made for a harmonious relationship. In some areas, however, religious houses could attract penitential bequests more readily. The Dorset gentry remembered local monastic houses more frequently in their wills than testators in Berkshire, perhaps because of the charitable distributions that monasteries like Cerne and Milton were making. Other monastic houses with saints' relics were the focuses of local cults. Even in the seventeenth century John Aubrey was able to recall that at Malmesbury St Aldhelm's bell was rung to drive away thunder and lightning.[101] On the eve of the Dissolution the religious still occupied a place in the devotional life of the laity, and memories of that place lingered long after.

[101]   Aubrey, *Remaines*, 22 (BL Lansdowne MS 231, fo. 110).

2

Salisbury Cathedral and the Laity

CATHEDRALS of secular clergy were potentially as detached from the laity as monastic houses. The daily round of liturgical service conducted by the Salisbury canons and vicars-choral—the seven canonical hours, daily mass, chantry masses, and anniversary services—tended to cut off the clerical members from lay people.[1] The cathedral's wealth and exclusiveness meant that the institution sometimes became a focus of discontent. The rebels of the Lollard uprising in 1431 drew up plans to disendow the cathedral and raze it to the ground.[2] Jack Cade's uprising of 1450 took on a local flavour in Salisbury, where one rebel indictment singled out the cathedral as the particular object of attack. Indeed some rebels were accused of assaulting two canons, Nicholas Upton and John Passelowe, on 28 June; the houses of these two and another canon, Richard Treve, were attacked and robbed on 1 July. In the minds of the mayor and city councillors, moreover, the cathedral was too often associated with episcopal overlordship that constrained their independent aspirations. When a group of insurgents, 'sons of perdition', burst into the cathedral during divine service in February 1474, the dean and chapter complained that the mayor and his brethren had done little to stop them.[3]

Unsavoury incidents like these do not suggest that the cathedral clergy were held in high esteem. They do not even imply that the laity regarded the cathedral at best with a mixture of 'respect and indifference'.[4] The primary aim of this chapter, however, is to stress that lay people were neither indifferent nor hostile to the cathedral. Particular incidents, like the 1450 uprising, may have been born of peculiar circumstances. They should also be offset by the influence that the cathedral could exercise over the diocese and over its collection of thirty-nine prebends. And links with the laity were perhaps strengthened, especially in the fifteenth century, by the promotion of the cult of Bishop Osmund, whose relics were housed

[1] K. L. Edwards, *The English Secular Cathedrals in the Middle Ages*, second edn. (Manchester, 1967), 56–7.
[2] See Ch. 9 n. 59.   [3] D & C, Reg. Machon, fo. 129; see Ch. 6.
[4] Cf. R. B. Dobson on the relations between the citizens of York and York minster, 'The Foundation of Perpetual Chantries by the Citizens of Medieval York', in G. J. Cuming (ed.), *The Province of York* (Studies in Church History; Leiden, 1967), 25.

within the cathedral fabric. In fact, an initially brighter picture of co-operation between cathedral clergy and lay people can be painted, by turning the clock back to the foundation of the cathedral itself.

In 1217 the bishop and canons decided to move from Old Sarum to a newer site down in the valley, exchanging the wind-swept, barren, treeless 'mountains of Gilboa', on which the old cathedral was built, for the bountiful, lush, corn-filled plain which 'Adam would have preferred to Paradise'.[5] On 28 April 1220 the first stones of the new cathedral were laid. Unlike a monastery, which could rely on the munificence of a high-born founder, a cathedral usually had to pool resources from a wider group of people. To the foundation service came not only 'counts and barons' but also 'a great multitude of people'. Canons were dispatched throughout the country to gather alms.[6] Although much of the money needed to rebuild the cathedral must have come from the dean and chapter's own resources and taxes on the prebends, the involvement of the laity is evident. Apart from the generosity of Henry III, the register of St Osmund records that magnates 'coming back from Wales' pledged themselves to seven years of contributions. Pyxes of silver gilt, or stone from quarries, came from other aristocrats.[7] From people lower down the social scale came smaller gifts of property, in Salisbury, Melksham, and Devizes.[8] There were no doubt many more gifts made (now no longer traceable), especially as remissions of days in purgatory were granted for the souls of benefactors: five separate indulgences were given, between 1225 and 1258, to those who contributed to the fabric or visited the cathedral.[9]

The building was consecrated in 1258, the roof was completed in 1266, and in the late thirteenth century the tower was heightened and the spire added.[10] The initial enthusiasm that may have accompanied the rebuilding

[5] According to Henry III's court poet, Hugh d'Avranches (A. R. Malden, 'A Contemporary Poem on the Translation of the Cathedral from Old to New Sarum', *WAM* 30 (1899), 210).

[6] *VCH: Wilts.* iii. 165; see also R. Graham, 'An Appeal about 1175 for the Building Fund of St. Paul's Cathedral', *Journal of the British Archaeological Association*, third series, 10 (1945–7), 73–6. *The Register of S. Osmund*, ed. W. H. Rich-Jones (2 vols.; Rolls Series; London, 1883), ii. 11–12.

[7] *CCR* (1231–4), 370; (1234–7), 279–80, 409; *Reg. S. Osmund*, ii. 13, 20; *Ceremonies and Processions of the Cathedral of Salisbury*, ed. C. Wordsworth (Cambridge, 1901), 30; Bowles and Nichols, *Lacock Abbey*, 145.

[8] D & C, Press IV, C6/5; Press I, Boxes 11–12, Salisbury 2/1a; Press I, Box 7, M–N/4; Press IV, E1, Cannings/3.

[9] C. Wordsworth, 'Wiltshire Pardons or Indulgences', *WAM* 38 (1913), 22–4.

[10] *VCH: Wilts.* iii. 165.

of the cathedral in the early years had probably slackened by the beginning of the fourteenth century when most of the work on the fabric had been finished. Bishop Martival spoke in 1320 of devotion to the cathedral growing cold.[11] Certainly, whereas thirteen gifts of land to the fabric from lay people can be traced between 1220 and *c.*1260, only five are known for the rest of the thirteenth century and only two for the whole of the fourteenth century.[12] But if the fabric fund found it increasingly difficult to attract outright gifts of land, the laity were still prepared to donate sums of money. A fifteenth- and early-sixteenth-century list of benefactors includes some fifty-four names of lay people.[13]

A closer look at these benefactors reveals a certain exclusivity in relations between cathedral and secular world. A large number on the list were aristocratic. Indeed the dean and chapter actively sought out the support of the most exalted people in society. In the late fourteenth century they began to admit lay people into a fraternity of the cathedral: in return for (presumably) liberal donations to the fabric, the benefactor could participate in all the prayers, fastings, vigils, and other meritorious works that were performed by the cathedral canons, vicars, and other ministers.[14] The first to be admitted was John of Gaunt, duke of Lancaster, in 1389, with his son, the future Henry IV, and seventeen of their attendants, both men and women. A succession of aristocratic brothers and sisters were admitted thereafter: Edward earl of Rutland in 1395, John earl of Somerset in 1406, the future Henry V and his brother Humphrey with their followers in 1408, Joanne wife of Henry IV with thirteen other women, five knights, and one cleric in her household, Walter Hungerford, in 1413, Joanna countess of Westmorland and Richard Neville with his wife Alice Montagu in 1417, Lady Matilda Lovell in 1417, Thomas duke of Exeter in 1419, Eleanor of St Amand in 1424, Thomas Montagu earl of Salisbury in 1427, and in 1430 Sir John Stourton. There was a gap of forty-one years before the next admissions to the fraternity were made: the duke of Clarence in 1471, Edward IV and Katherine Cheney, widow of

[11] *Statuta et Consuetudines Ecclesiae Cathedralis Sarisburiense*, ed. C. Wordsworth and D. Macleane (Salisbury, 1915), 194–201.
[12] 13th cent.: D & C, Press IV, C6/6; C6/7; E2, Knighton/5; 'Mixed'/22; Press I, Boxes 11–12, Salisbury 2/5; and WRO D1/1/2, Liber Evidentiarum B, p. 191, no. 469; *CCR* (1296–1302), 20; *Abstracts of Feet of Fines relating to Wiltshire for the Reigns of Edward I and Edward II*, ed. R. B. Pugh (WRS 1; Devizes, 1939), 2, 3, 13, 14. 14th cent.: Press IV, E3, Melksham/13, Boxes 13–15, 3/26; Press I, Boxes 9–10, Salisbury 1/466; Press I, Boxes 13–15, Salisbury 3/71.
[13] *Ceremonies and Processions*, 30–1.   [14] Ibid. 145–50.

Sir John, in 1474.[15] Admission to the brotherhood of the dean and chapter
was not granted to the low-born.

Admission into the prayers of the cathedral was not the only suffrage
sought by the well-connected benefactor. More specific post-obit commemoration was also required from the late thirteenth century onwards:
commemorative lights, anniversaries, and chantries. The coldness of devotion to the cathedral fabric was offset, as Bishop Martival also noted,
by a warm affection for masses to be said at cathedral altars. William
Longspee, earl of Salisbury, and Sir John Dacy were the earliest lay
founders of chantries in the cathedral, and each had anniversary services
celebrated for their souls on 19 May and 17 June respectively.[16] Edmund,
earl of Cornwall, some time between 1272 and 1300 gave a garden and a
small croft with a windmill for his obit: the communar account rolls
record that £1 was spent on his obit day between 1347 and 1536.[17] Most
of the other known founders of obits were members of the gentry. The
Hungerfords were the most consistent founders of divine service in the
cathedral, Walter founding an obit by 1449 and his wife, Margaret, founding a chantry for them both by 1472.[18]

Yet the suffrages of the cathedral had also been sought by those with
less distinguished pedigrees. Before the new cathedral had been finished
Elias Nichol, son of Master Nichol, mason, set aside the rent owed from
a tenement in the city in 1242 for the provision of a candle, one pound in
weight, to burn before the light of the Virgin Mary on the vigil of the feast
of the Assumption.[19] Five citizens of Salisbury were deemed worthy
enough to be included on the later list of benefactors: one of them,
William White, had asked in his will of 1440 that two windows be made in
the cathedral, one in the chapel of St Margaret and the other near the high
altar.[20] Some of them asked for altar lights. In 1406 John Chaundler the

---

[15] D & C, Reg. Dunham, fo. 59; Reg. Holmes, fo. 53; Reg. Draper, fo. 48; Reg. Viring,
fos. 17, 24ᵛ–25; Reg. Pountney, fos. 1, 24; Reg. Harding, fos. 45, 46, 99; Reg. Machon, fos. 56,
82, 83.

[16] *Charters and Documents Illustrating the History of the Cathedral City and Diocese of
Salisbury in the Twelfth and Thirteenth Centuries*, ed. W. Rich-Jones and W. D. Macray (Rolls
Series; London, 1891), 188; *Ceremonies and Processions*, 235–6.

[17] D & C, Press I, El, Mere/1; see also William Maudit lord of Warminster *c.*1257
(*Charters and Documents*, 277; D & C, Liber Evidentiarum C, fos. 130ᵛ–131).

[18] *Ceremonies and Processions*, 231; *CPR* (1340–3), 194; (1330–4), 434; (1334–8), 344;
D & C, Reg. Burgh, fo. 59ᵛ; *CPR* (1422–9), 390; (1467–77), 311.

[19] D & C, Press I, Box 7, M–N/4. Also Roger Brinkworth left a messuage (*c.*1220–5) to
find a taper to burn before the relics on festival days (D & C, Press I, Box 7, M–N/2; *Reg.
S. Osmund*, i. 234).

[20] PCC 20 Luffenham. The others are Nicholas Harding, Walter Shirley, and William
Swayne who made their wills in 1419, 1424, and 1484 respectively (D & C, Press IV, Box

elder provided rents enough for two torches to be carried in the canons' dawn procession on every Easter day for the next century.[21] He was also among the three Salisbury citizens who founded chantries in the cathedral. One of the others, William Teynterer, had founded his chantry and obit in 1362. The surviving rolls of fabric accounts after 1464 show that rents could yield over £20, half of which was spent on obit and chantry mass celebrated at the altar of St Margaret: the remainder swelled cathedral coffers.[22] Some layman valued the security that a perpetual institution such as the cathedral could provide for the celebration of services founded for their souls.

Even so, the cathedral supported more chantries and obits founded by clerics: lay people were responsible for only seven of the thirty-four perpetual chantries known to have been founded within the cathedral. Only seventeen out of seventy-six obit founders are known to have been lay people.[23] Yet if the cathedral tended to serve a clerical caste, it nevertheless had links with lay society outside the boundaries of the close. Laymen who set up chantries in parish churches could require the involvement of the dean and chapter. Robert Wodeford (1343), Robert Godmanstone (1380), William Warwick (1424), and William Swayne (by 1470) founded chantries in the parish churches of the city.[24] They were all of the benefice type, the bishop being required to present chaplains to the

'W'; PCC 3 Luffenham; PCC 20 Logge). Alice Charlyng, widow, gave £20 to the fabric in 1469 (D & C, Reg. Machon, fo. 18ᵛ). In 1270 William Pynnok left a tenement to the cathedral to celebrate an obit in his will (WRO G23/150/80), but his name does not appear in the cathedral list of benefactors.

[21] D & C, Press IV, Box 'Literae'. William Huntingdon gave two candles for the Morrow Mass altar in 1479 (D & C, Fabric accounts, no. 4).
[22] William Teynterer: *CPR* (1361–5), 237; WRO G23/1/212, fo. 37; D & C, Press IV, E1, 'New Salisbury', 1/12; Press II, Fabric accounts. John Chandler: *CPR* (1391–6), 300; D & C, Box O/a5 and Press I, Boxes 11–12, Salisbury 2/48. Walter atte Berghe: *CPR* (1358–61), 125. Endowments were also made for a chantry service of another Salisbury citizen, Thomas Chapleyn, and his wife in 1417 (WRO G23/1/214, fo. 23), but no record of it is to be found in the cathedral muniments.
[23] *VCH: Wilts.* iii. 168–9, 175, 181, modestly estimates that thirty-three chantries were being celebrated and between forty and fifty obits, but more can be found in the cathedral muniments. Chantries: 1219–99: 9; 1300–49: 5; 1350–99: 11; 1400–49: 4; 1450–99: 4; 1500–45: 1. Obits: 1219–99: 33; 1300–49: 12; 1350–99: 18; 1400–49: 8; 1450–99: 5; 1500–45: 0. Some of the early obits may have disappeared with time: the communar account rolls record expenditure on fifty-one obits between 1343 and 1540 and on a further twenty-five weekly masses; ten obits being celebrated in the 1340s were not celebrated after about 1360, perhaps because rents from endowments fell. These account rolls do not record all the obits that were being celebrated; others, especially if they were part of chantry endowments, were included in the fabric accounts.
[24] Reg. Bp. Wyvill, i, fos. 50, 189ᵛ; *CPR* (1343–5), 122; (1377–81), 561, 596; (1446–52), 48; D & C, Reg. Burgh, fo. 4.

chantries; but the dean and chapter are also to be found instituting priests to the same chantries during the fifteenth and sixteenth centuries.[25] Occasionally, the involvement of canons and vicars-choral was required for other services. Some testators demanded their presence at funeral exequies in parish churches. In 1403 Edmund Enfeld bequeathed 8s. 4d. so that vicars-choral should attend his funeral service in St Martin's church, Salisbury. John White, who asked to be buried in the cathedral, required that his exequies should begin in St Thomas's church: four vicars were to be paid 3d. each to carry his body from the church to the cathedral. A testator outside Salisbury, Christopher Twynyng in 1508, asked to be buried in 'sacred ground' and set aside 10s. for canons and vicars to attend his exequies.[26]

So the cathedral, like other religious houses, still retained a role, in the fourteenth and fifteenth centuries, as a performer of post-obit services for the dead. Unlike other religious houses, as mother church of the diocese, the cathedral could also expect small bequests in wills as a mark of its status. Most testators left modest donations to the fabric: in 1464/5, for instance, £3. 2s. 10d. was given to the fabric funds from forty-one bequests.[27] Gifts to the cathedral fabric were works of penance that attracted the laity throughout the later Middle Ages. But death was not the only means by which the cathedral and laity were brought into closer contact. As the mother church, the cathedral could expect Pentecostal obligations from parishes: the town of Wilton was paying banner-bearers to go to Salisbury at Pentecost in the fifteenth century.[28] As the mother church, too, the cathedral was sometimes the place in which penance had to be performed. In 1408 John Macy of Charminster, as punishment for fornication, was required to go on pilgrimage to the cathedral and distribute 6s. 8d. in alms on the way.[29]

Parishes that were also prebends were in more direct contact with the cathedral. The canons and vicars-choral expected their concerns to be relayed to the laity by the incumbent priest: in 1405 the vicar of Great

[25] Robert Wodeford's chantry foundation (1349) required the dean and chapter to present to his chantry in St Edmund's church if the provost of the college failed to (Reg. Corfe, fo. 24ʳ⁻ᵛ). Robert Godmanstone's chantry: Reg. Harding. fo. 87 (1427); Reg. Burgh, fos. 4, 35ᵛ (1447, 1451); Reg. Machon, fo. 61 (1473). William Warwick's chantry: Reg. Burgh, fo. 13ᵛ (1451); Reg. Newton, fo. 21 (1461). William Swayne's chantry: WRO G23/1/215, fo. 1; PCC 20 Logge.
[26] WRO G23/1/213, fos, 66ᵛ–67; PCC 20 Luffenham; 24 Bennett.
[27] D & C, Press II, Fabric accounts, no. 1.
[28] Accounts of the guild merchant, Wilton, WRO G25, *passim.*
[29] *Reg. Dean Chandler,* 197.

Faringdon was reported in the dean's visitational court for failing to publicize the business of the cathedral fabric.[30] Aside from conducting regular visitations in their prebends, the cathedral could also contribute to the divine service of those parishes. When the vicar of Stourpayne complained in 1342 that his benefice was too poor to pay for a priest to celebrate three times a week in the dependent chapel of Ashley, the dean and chapter gave him two marks a year for the purpose. In 1406 the dean and chapter gave a pair of vestments to the chapel of Knighton; in 1463 they donated a set of vestments and a chalice to the parish of Bramshaw. In 1429, when the parishioners of Littleton Drew were replacing the whole roof of their church and a chapel, the dean and chapter made their contribution as rectors, rebuilding the chancel with a large east window.[31]

In 1399 the church of St Thomas, Salisbury, was appropriated to the cathedral.[32] From then on, the oblations made on Easter day and at baptisms, marriages, funerals, anniversaries, and churchings of women by the parishioners were accounted for by two procurators from the cathedral. This money was used to fund the chantry service of Bishop Richard Mitford, who had permitted the appropriation to be made, and for certain festivities held in the parish on 'Frickfriday', probably in Whitsuntide. In 1507/8, for instance, 31s. 4d. was spent on 'lagenas' and 'potells' of red wine, claret, Malmsey, and cakes, and on wives, daughters, young women, and 'scholars' apparently for their dancing.[33] Moreover, when extensive rebuilding was being undertaken at St Thomas's in the early fifteenth century, the dean and chapter lent twelve marks to the parishioners; they also contributed, although with some reservation, to the rebuilding of the chancel after the structure had collapsed in 1448.[34]

The cathedral could also find itself entangled in the activities of guilds within the city. In the late fifteenth century a Jesus fraternity in St Edmund's church could use singers from the cathedral; within St Thomas's church many craft guilds made annual oblations to the high altar which were accounted by the procurators. Moreover, just as the canons could be drawn into the religious life of the parish, so guilds might involve themselves in the divine services celebrated in the cathedral.

[30] Ibid. 81.

[31] *Hemingsby's Register*, ed. H. M. Chew (WRS 18; Devizes, 1962), 143, 297, 299; D & C, Reg. Draper, fo. 26; Reg. Newton, fo. 29; Reg. Harding, fo. 96ᵛ.

[32] *CPR* (1399–1401), 392; *VCH: Wilts.* vi. 147.

[33] D & C, Press II, Procurator's accounts, with Accounts of the masters of the fabric (1487–1538).

[34] C. Haskins, 'The Church of St. Thomas of Canterbury, Salisbury', *WAM* 36 (1909), 3; see Ch. 5 n. 2.

Small oblations were given to the cathedral high altar by guilds who appear to have had altars in the cathedral: the barber-surgeons, the carpenters, the roofers or plasterers, and the tanners.[35] The guild of St George, the fraternity of the mayor and burgesses, also gave similar annual oblations. The tailors made their oblations both in St Thomas's church and in the cathedral on 24 June, the feast of the nativity of St John the Baptist, their patron saint (see Chapters 6 and 7).

There are hints, too, that lay involvement in the liturgical life of the cathedral was not restricted to fraternities alone. Other cathedral altars could attract oblations. Offerings were being made in the fourteenth century to the altars of St Nicholas and the 'Gysine' altar (for women in pregnancy), and (later) to the high altar on the feast days of the Virgin Mary.[36] One altar may have served as the parish altar for the inhabitants of the cathedral close; and arrangements were made to ensure that there should always be a mass which workmen, travellers, or other passers-by could attend from dawn till ten or eleven in the morning.[37] Lay people certainly attended some of the cathedral processions. There was, for instance, the annual ceremony of the boy bishop when, in Salisbury's case, a chorister was elected 'bishop' to perform the daily offices, bless the people, and even conduct visitations in the cathedral and outside. At vespers on the eve of Holy Innocents' day a procession headed by the boy bishop would go from the choir to the altars of Holy Innocents or Holy Trinity and All Saints: in 1319 such was the apparent eagerness of crowds of people who were wont to press upon the boys in the procession that Bishop Martival had to regulate against the dissolute behaviour.[38]

The cathedral must also have made distributions to the poor. There was a fund called 'Our Lady Chamber' for making distributions in the late thirteenth and early fourteenth centuries.[39] Some of the early obit founders made explicit stipulations for charitable giving. Elias de Durham, canon, founded an obit around 1228 which provided for 100 poor to be fed on his anniversary day; two poor people were to be fed fish, bread, and ale more regularly.[40] But few obits founded after the mid-thirteenth century

[35] *S. Edmund's Accounts*, esp. 254; D & C, Press II, Procurator's accounts; see Ch. 6; D & C, Press II, Fabric accounts.

[36] *Hemingsby's Reg.* 159, 285; D & C, Press II, Fabric accounts.

[37] *Reg. S. Osmund*, i. 12; *Ceremonies and Processions*, 198, 204, 224–8, 304–5; D & C, Reg. Machon, fo. 89.

[38] E. K. Chambers, *The Medieval Stage* (Oxford, 1903), i. 336–71; J. M. J. Fletcher, *The Boy Bishop at Salisbury and Elsewhere* (Salisbury, 1924); *Statuta et Consuetudines*, 258–61.

[39] *CCR* (1298–1302), 20; *Ceremonies and Processions*, 127.

[40] *Charters and Documents*, 177; D & C, Press IV, Box Ma6.

made such explicit instructions, confining distributions to the cathedral clergy and choristers. Only two of the sixty-three obits mentioned in the *Valor Ecclesiasticus* of 1535 mention hand-outs to the poor.[41] Charitable giving by the cathedral was perhaps hidden from view; some was chan-nelled to more specific outlets, to the 'poor scholars' of Vaux college and a grammar school in Salisbury.[42]

So although it was primarily a clerical institution, with prestigious attach-ments to royalty and aristocracy, Salisbury cathedral was by no means isolated from the pious practices of other lay people. Indeed, it could attract devotional attention in one further way. Other cathedrals (and monasteries) drew in pilgrims to the shrines of their saints.[43] Salisbury cathedral did not originally have its own saint, but as a shrine to Our Lady, to whom it was dedicated, it could attract its share of pilgrims. In the early fifteenth century, in parts of the Low Countries the cathedral was reputed to be one of the principal objectives of pilgrims heading for England.[44] Moreover, the cathedral had a bishop in Osmund (1078–99) who was held in special veneration at an early date: when the old cathedral was widened and extended eastward in the early twelfth century, Osmund's tomb ap-pears to have been moved to the north side of the new high altar.[45]

In the early thirteenth century efforts were made to achieve Osmund's canonization as part of an attempt to encourage the spread of Salisbury liturgies, believed to have been codified by Osmund himself.[46] The timing of the first effort at canonization was no doubt also determined by the financial needs of the dean and chapter. The bones of saints attracted gifts as well as pilgrims and could be used to tap resources from a wide section of society. Relics could be paraded at strategic times to gather

---

[41] Exceptions are Nicholas of York 1260 (*Charters and Documents*, 280); Nicholas of St Quintin 1265 (D & C, Liber Evidentiarum C, fo. 203ᵛ (p. 419), Press IV, C6/10); Robert de Sherwood and Thomas Hotot 1348 (D & C, Press I, Box 21/20); William Okeborne (aug-menting the endowment of Herbert de Bedwynd) 1374 (Press IV, Box O/6, 1); and William Bishop of Winchester 1358 (ibid. 8). *Valor Ecclesiasticus*, ii. 72–86.

[42] *VCH: Wilts*. iii. 369–84; BL Add. MS 28870; D & C, Press IV, EI, 'New Salisbury', 15; Press I, Boxes 9–10, 'Salisbury I', 23, 25; Boxes 11–12, 'Salisbury', 2–6.

[43] See e.g. St Wulfstan canonized 1203 (*VCH: Worcester*, ii, ed. J. W. Willis-Bund and W. Page (London, 1906), 98).

[44] J. de Beer, 'Bedevaart- en Pelgrimplaatjes', in *Gedenkboek Frans Claes Museum 'De Gulden Spoor' te Antwerpen* (Antwerp, 1932), 59–61.

[45] F. J. E. Raby, 'The Tomb of St. Osmund of Salisbury', *Archaeological Journal*, 104 (1947), 146–7.

[46] See Intro. n. 13. A gift recorded in the cathedral inventory of 1222 had been made 'ad tumbam *Sancti* Osmundi', though in another place Osmund is still referred to as just 'bishop' (*Reg. S. Osmund*, ii. 131, 133).

money.[47] The financial advantages to be gained from the relics of saints were obvious: the bishop, dean, and chapter of Salisbury, in the process of rebuilding the cathedral, had the bones of Bishop Osmund brought down from the old cathedral in a ceremony on 14 June 1226 and placed, at the east end of the Lady chapel, in a tomb embellished with a new effigy and later raised on a plinth; in 1228 Pope Gregory IX was petitioned for Osmund's canonization.[48]

But this first attempt to canonize Osmund met with failure. The process of canonization had become much more formal after the twelfth century, often more drawn out and thus more expensive for petitioners.[49] There may not have been enough money for both the rebuilding of the cathedral and a sustained effort to canonize Bishop Osmund; alternatively, there may have been enough money to continue building without recourse to proceeds from a saint's bones. No further effort was made for over 100 years. But in the later fourteenth century a further need for funds arose. The large steeple, constructed by the beginning of that century, was proving to have been a little overambitious. In 1363 the cracked walls of the tower and the belfry were threatening to fall: Bishop Ralph Erghum petitioned the Pope to allow the appropriation of St Thomas's church, Salisbury, to the fabric fund. In 1366 the cathedral acquired a licence to alienate land in mortmain to the fabric fund.[50] It was also under the episcopacy of Bishop Erghum (though he himself had not initially welcomed the idea) that the second attempt to have Osmund canonized was made. The effort was continued by Bishop Robert Hallum in the early ꞏfifteenth century: one reason for this was the hope that offerings to the shrine of a canonized Osmund would aid the cathedral fabric.[51]

The hope of financial gain cannot have been the only reason why the bishop and cathedral wished to pursue the process of canonization. After all, it took until 1457 for the Pope to issue a bull canonizing Osmund, and the expense was always likely to be a disincentive: Nicholas Upton in 1452, then at the papal court, reckoned the likely cost to be £1,000 or more.[52] Moreover, further efforts were being made by the dean and chap-

---

[47] See also St Thomas's cult at Canterbury (C. E. Woodruff, 'The Financial Aspect of the Cult of St. Thomas of Canterbury', *Archaeologia Cantiana*, 44 (1932), 13–22).

[48] D. Stroud, 'The Cult and Tombs of St. Osmund at Salisbury', *WAM* 78 (1984), 49–54; *Reg. S. Osmund*, ii. 55, 85–6, 87–9.

[49] R. C. Finucane, *Miracles and Pilgrims: Popular Beliefs in Medieval England* (London, 1977), 36–8.

[50] *Cal. Papal Reg.* (1362–1404), 89; *CPR* (1364–7), 314.

[51] D & C, Reg. Coman, fos. 70–73; *Canonization of St. Osmund*, p. iv; D & C, Reg. Coman, fo. 77.

[52] *Canonization of St. Osmund*, 115.

ter, in the early fifteenth century, to popularize the Use of Salisbury
associated with Bishop Osmund. The dean may have been aware that
many of the prebendal parishes in 1408 lacked white vestments needed for
the full celebration of the Sarum Use; certainly, in the visitation of 1412
he found that the parishioners of Combe had an ordinal that did not
contain the Salisbury Use.[53] In 1416 Richard Ullerston claimed in a
sermon preached in the cathedral that Osmund's composition of the Use
was 'incomparable in the world'. The Council of Constance that began in
1413 gave an opportunity to promote both cult and Use on a wider stage.
Bishop Hallum was leader of the English nation and about a quarter of the
whole delegation was connected with the chapter. Richard Ullerston had
begun his sermon with a special bidding prayer for the happy outcome of
the Council.[54] There must have been some hope that a new pope would
canonize Bishop Osmund: success would have lent weight to the populari-
zation of the Use of Salisbury.

In the promotion of the cult, the dean and chapter hoped to exploit its
aristocratic connections. Indeed, the establishment of the fraternity of the
cathedral, which admitted lay people of high rank, may have been connected with the effort of canonization. The first admission was made in
1389 and most of the other recorded brothers and sisters were received
into the fraternity in the early fifteenth century. One of the brethren,
Walter Hungerford, wrote a letter to the Pope in 1440, declaring his firm
belief in the sanctity of Osmund because many people, worthy of faith,
had been to his tomb and many cures had been performed.[55] The dean and
chapter were certainly made aware of the pressure that could be exerted
on the Pope by the petitioning of great lords. Simon Huchyns at the papal
curia in 1452 recommended further letters from the lords spiritual and
temporal.[56]

The cult had also been promoted further down the social scale. The
lords who wrote to the Pope were encouraged to testify as to how people
flocked to Osmund's tomb. Huchyns had told Andrew of Sancta Cruce of
the great estimation in which Osmund was held by both high and low
born and how they wished to exhume his body, without the authority of
the Pope, and venerate him as a saint. Sancta Cruce had strongly advised
Huchyns that this should be mentioned in the letters to be written as
it would encourage the Pope to complete the canonization. For the veneration of Osmund without papal authority, he went on to say (in an
interesting comment on the state of Anglo–papal relations), would incline

---

[53] *Reg. Dean Chandler*, 348.   [54] *Canonization of St. Osmund*, 236–42.
[55] D & C, Reg. Hutchings, fo. 124.   [56] *Canonization of St. Osmund*, 108.

England to separate from Rome and 'de hoc multum timet Papa'. More-over, another collection of thirty-three miracles, compiled in 1424, shows a wider audience for the cult than the aristocracy.[57] The group of forty-six witnesses (most of them men) included a knight, but it was also made up of at least one lawyer, ten priests, three villagers, a carpenter, a dyer, a tailor, and a cellarer.[58]

The miracles themselves also suggest that Osmund had become better known since the thirteenth century. The twenty-nine witnesses who had come forward to attest to cures at that time reported that the miracles had all occurred at Osmund's tomb: one woman had to spend four or five nights at the tomb to be cured of madness. But by 1424 Osmund's powers reached well beyond the immediate vicinity of the tomb. Only six of the thirty-three miracles then compiled took place at the shrine: an invocation to Osmund (often coupled with one to Our Lady, the cathedral's patron saint) and a promise of pilgrimage to his tomb was enough now to effect a cure.[59] John atte Berghe, 'armiger', declared that he had been riding with Sir Walter Rouse to Salisbury when the latter was thrown from his horse and dragged along some way in his stirrups: John called out to Osmund, and his companion was released from the stirrups. Robert Levying of Salisbury claimed that five years earlier the small son of Robert Bulke (warden of the prestigious tailors' guild in 1450) had fallen into the river. By prayers and invocations to Osmund the boy was revived.[60]

Nevertheless, Osmund's powers were better known in some areas than in others. Fourteen of the witnesses came from the city of Salisbury. Outside, most came from the nearby villages on the Wiltshire chalklands: from Laverstoke, Durrington, Quidhampton, Amesbury, and Downton. Later miracles in 1440 and 1450 were also recorded at Chitterne All Saints and Great Wishford. Around 1414 in the village of Laverstoke, for instance, a girl had been struck with an iron object used in the game of quoits, and had lain dead for one and a half hours. Friends and spectators had fallen to their knees, promising to go on pilgrimages to Osmund's tomb if the girl was saved.[61] One of the witnesses to the miracle had been

[57] *Canonization of St. Osmund*, 108–10, 55–83.

[58] Compare with other shrines: the suppliants involved in the miracles of St Frideswide of Oxford, St Godric of Finchale, and St Wulfstan of Worcester included large proportions of women, but in general it was mainly men who were the suppliants (Finucane, *Miracles*, 142–3).

[59] *Canonization of St. Osmund*, 35–45, 55–83.

[60] Ibid. 74, 81–2; WRO G23/1/251, fo. 5.

[61] D & C, Reg. Hutchings, fos. 55ᵛ–56; Reg. Burgh, fo. 11; *Canonization of St. Osmund*, 142–3.

Richard Wodewell, a carpenter from Salisbury. The spread of Osmund's cult to these areas may have been promoted by the cathedral: there the estates, prebends, and advowsons of cathedral (and bishop) were abundant (see Map 2). But there is no known bequest to the shrine from Berkshire where there were also large prebends. Economic links may have been more important in disseminating the cult outside the city walls. The powerful attraction of Salisbury as a market centre brought in people with grain, meat, wool, and other trade from surrounding regions.[62] Offerings, worth £19. 5d. in October 1456 (the year before Osmund was canonized), to the 'cista Osmundi' perhaps came mainly from these same areas.[63]

After Osmund was finally canonized in 1457, the dean and chapter no doubt continued to promote the cult. An indulgence was promised to all those who made offerings at his shrine during the following three years. In 1468 a visitation of the cathedral reported scandalous scenes at the shrine around which indecently dressed pilgrims gathered.[64] A more elaborate shrine seems to have been envisaged to house St Osmund's bones in the same year as the canonization. In 1471 a goldsmith from London was being employed on the 'new shrine of St Osmund'. In 1472 a group of twenty-eight canons agreed to collect money from the prebends to replace Osmund's humble tomb with one adorned with gold, silver, gems, and marble. Work on the embellishment of the shrine may have continued for over twenty years: William Swayne left silver in 1484 'to the making of St Osmund's shrine'; in 1493/4 the one account that survives for the shrine recorded a sum of £34 spent on its gilding.[65] The same account roll suggests that the shrine could attract tidy, though not vast, sums in oblations from pilgrims and other benefactors. The sum of £16. 19s. 5d. was collected in offerings. A further £39. 13s. 2d. was raised by selling various goods given to the shrine: pieces of gold, two pax-breads, and an altar piece on which the coronation of the Virgin Mary was painted.

To some extent, the cult was not limited geographically. It was officially promoted: St Osmund's *Depositio* was enjoined for the province of Canterbury in 1480 and his feast days were added to liturgical calendars.[66] The saint's fame is apparent outside the diocese. A group that included the dean of York minster, on its way to Compostela, left precious altar pieces at the shrine in 1473. Miracles had already been reported in 1439 by a man

[62] *Supra*, pp. 13–14.   [63] *Canonization of St. Osmund*, 175.
[64] Ibid. 234; D & C, Reg. Machon, fo. 102.
[65] Ibid., fo. 39; *Canonization of St. Osmund*, 217–18; D & C, Reg. Machon, fos. 107ᵛ–108; PCC 20 Logge; D & C, Press II, Accounts of the shrine of St Osmund, 1493/4.
[66] D. Wilkins, *Concilia Magna Britanniae et Hiberniae* (London, 1737), iii. 613.

from Wherwell, in the diocese of Winchester, and by another from Dunton, in Bedfordshire, in 1453 (though both miracles took place at St Osmund's tomb).[67] Agnes Cole of Phillips Norton, in the diocese of Bath and Wells, accused of heresy in 1460, admitted that she had often reproved those going to the tomb of 'St Oswald' (*sic*) in Salisbury. John Stamford of Thornham in Norfolk had heard of St Osmund's fame: his ship sailing from Newcastle had landed safely in Yorkshire thanks to the intervention of St Osmund and Our Lady of Doncaster.[68]

Nevertheless, the cult enjoyed more attention in the diocese of Salisbury, and particularly within a ten-mile radius of the city itself. Further away at Yatton Keynell a miracle was attested in 1471: blood had poured from the side of one Richard Elmeley until, the parish chaplain and villagers reported, the name of St Osmund had been invoked. The parish was one to which the dean and chapter held the advowson. Most of the bequests to St Osmund's shrine came from areas close to where the miracles of 1424 had been recorded, in those same chalkland regions around Salisbury. Thomas Mapull of Downton gave a total of £66. 13s. 4d. in goods and valuables to the shrine in 1472; Alice Browning, widow of William, a knight, from Melbury Sampford gave six silver dishes to augment the shrine, for which she asked for exequies and mass to be celebrated in the choir on the vigil of St Bartholomew.[69] At Sherborne, with which Osmund had been particularly associated, the parishioners of All Hallows paid a clerk to write down a sermon of St Osmund in 1514/15.[70]

But the cult appears to have been more popular in the city of Salisbury than in the diocese as a whole. Only seven benefactions to the shrine are recorded in wills of 576 testators in the diocese (outside Salisbury) between 1457 and 1520, and none of these came from Berkshire.[71] In the same period nineteen Salisbury testators out of eighty-five left gifts to the shrine of St Osmund. In 1477 John Petevyn, mercer, left a silver dish;

[67] D & C, Reg. Machon, fo. 59; *Canonization of St. Osmund*, 142–3.
[68] Quoted in A. Hudson, *The Premature Reformation: Wyclifite Texts and Lollard History* (Oxford, 1988), 165; *Canonization of St. Osmund*, 142–3.
[69] D & C, Reg. Machon, p. 1; fos. 47ʳ⁻ᵛ, 61ᵛ.
[70] J. Fowler, 'Sherborne All Hallows Church Wardens' Accounts', *NQSD* 23 (1939–42), 252.
[71] For those close to Salisbury: William Beauchámp of Steeple Lavington 1457 (PCC 16 Stockton); Thomas Mapull of Downton 1472; William Stanford of Stratford 1486 (D & C, MS 189, fo. 106ʳ⁻ᵛ); Edward Lamberd of Maiden Bradley 1493 (PCC 3 Vox); John Myllys of Maddington 1516 (19 Holder). For bequests in Dorset: Alice Browning of Melbury Sampford (next to the prebend of Sherborne) 1486 (D & C, Reg. Machon, fo. 61ᵛ); Margery Clement of Lytchett Maltravers 1505 (36 Holgrave); William Chubbe of Spettisbury 1515 (20 Holder) (both next to the prebend of Bere Regis). See also John Mompesson the elder of Bathampton in Langford 1500 (15 Blamyr).

Henry Swayne, esquire, left his sword, silver harness, and two gold rings in 1479. A legacy of 16*s*. 8*d*. was recorded from the widow of William Tanner, merchant of Salisbury, on the account roll of 1493/4. Further miracles were recorded by two Salisbury citizens, John Chamber, tailor, in 1469 and William Holme, tanner, in 1471.[72]

In Salisbury, more than elsewhere, the cult seeped into parochial and civic celebrations. In 1474/5 the churchwardens of St Edmund's paid 17*d*. for the story of St Osmund on parchment; in 1479/80 and 1495/6 further payments were made for St Osmund's feast and story.[73] The doom painting of St Thomas's, carried out some time in the late fifteenth century, includes a life-size mitred bishop in a blue cope, reckoned to be a representation of St Osmund.[74] Moreover, in the city as a whole, the citizens were holding a watch on the eve of St Osmund's day by the end of the fifteenth century. Guilds within the city contributed to the festivities. The tailors' guild required its members to attend the watch; they made annual contributions to the watch (28*s*. in 1531) and at least by 1525 they were performing a pageant for the occasion. The mayor and commonalty were to write to Cromwell in 1540 that

it hath been accustome, upon the eve of St. Osmund, being the eve of St. Osmund, which Saint lieth in the Cathedral church of Sarum, as St. Edward doth in Westminster, on which St. Osmund's eve a solemn watch hath been used, after the order of the watch kept in London and Windsor, even to the which watch much people hath accustomed to resort to.[75]

Despite its propagation, the cult of St Osmund, nevertheless, had not always been able to soften relations between cathedral and citizens. It did not prevent the cathedral from being seen as a clerical institution that could stand in the way of aspirations towards greater independence of government.[76] Nor did it entirely disguise the cathedral's prestigious connections with royalty and aristocracy which could occasionally alienate citizens from cathedral clergy. For the uprising in Salisbury in 1450 was partly directed against those very connections. Some of the canons

---

[72] WRO D4/3, fos. 99ᵛ–100; D & C, Press II, Accounts of the shrine of St Osmund, 1493–4; D & C, Reg. Machon, p. 1.

[73] *S. Edmund's Accounts*, 17, 19, 45, 365.

[74] A. Hollaender, 'The Doom Painting of St. Thomas of Canterbury, Salisbury', *WAM* 50 (1944), 351–70. See Frontispiece.

[75] Benson and Hatcher, *Old and New Sarum*, 126.

[76] See Ch. 7. The chapter act books record the trouble of the bishop with the citizens (John Hall in particular) and applaud the election to the mayoralty in 1470 of William Swayne who had stood out against his fellow citizens (D & C, Reg. Newton, fos. 14, 15; Reg. Machon, fos. 25, 126).

had become closely involved in national politics: Bishop Adam Moleyns, popularly murdered by sailors in 1450, had been dean of Salisbury. Some of the nobles and gentry admitted to the fraternity of the cathedral in the first half of the fifteenth century were also closely connected with the court of Henry VI, and indeed had profited from the disproportionate amount of royal patronage siphoned off by the Suffolk clique. John Stourton, admitted in 1430, had strong links with the Suffolk household and was also connected with the war—or rather, in Henry VI's hands, the peace—effort, keeping the captive duke of Orleans in Somerset and escorting him to Calais in 1439 for the peace negotiations. Eleanor of St Amand was the wife of William Beauchamp, one of the newly created barons of the Suffolk clique in the 1440s who was summoned to Parliament as lord of St Amand, a title specially revived through his wife. Walter Hungerford, admitted in 1413, was to serve in a number of the peace negotiations in France, attending the conference at Arras in 1435 and the Calais negotiations in 1439. He also acquired the wardship of the dower estates of Margaret late Lady Moleyns, whose granddaughter married Walter's grandson Robert, summoned to Parliament as Lord Moleyns in 1445. It was Robert Moleyns who used his influence with the Suffolk clique to seize the Paston manor of Gresham in February 1448 and to set a thousand riotous people on John Paston in January 1449.[77]

There is little evidence to suggest that any of the lay members of the cathedral fraternity were unpopular with the citizens of Salisbury because of their involvement with a divisive clique and a failing war effort. But the citizens were certainly aware of the issues that were affecting the nation. The chamberlain's accounts of 1449/50 register a payment of 20*d.* made to a man to ride to Southampton for 'the tydinges of the Frenchmen'.[78] On the exploits of Robert Hungerford, Lord Moleyns, the citizens may have had more detailed information. At eight o'clock in the evening on Tuesday, 3 June 1449, there was 'a serious rising of the common citizens against Lord de Moleyns in the Inn called the George'. Master Nicholas Upton, precentor of Salisbury, and Walter Bayly, canon, made haste to the inn 'with the body of the Lord', under the protection of which the threatened lord was 'by the grace of God' led safely to the cathedral close.[79]

[77] R. A. Griffiths, *The Reign of Henry VI* (London, 1981), 357, 363, 739, 357, 360, 363, 374, n. 149. Walter Hungerford perhaps should not be identified too closely with the Suffolk clique, having been a feoffee of the duke of York in 1436, but his links with the court did stretch to a congratulation from the king for his help in suppressing a riot in Salisbury in 1443 (*The Complete Peerage*, ed. H. A. Doubleday, D. Warrand, and H. de Walden (London, 1926), 615; Griffiths, *Henry VI*, 587–8, 673).

[78] WRO G23/1/44, Chamberlains' accounts, no. 1.   [79] D & C, Reg. Burgh, fo. 1.

The identification of the cathedral with influential and unpopular courtiers was intensified by the elaborate preparations made for the funeral of Walter Hungerford, who died on 9 August 1449 at Farleigh Hungerford. Nicholas Upton, precentor, with his previous experience as executor of Thomas Montagu, earl of Salisbury, who died in 1428, advised that banners and heraldic arms should surround the funeral procession when the body arrived at Salisbury, that the cathedral bells should sound, and that the dean, precentor, and canons should meet the procession carrying the body at the 'lydegate' by the choristers' school. Walter's son Robert Hungerford and also his grandson, the notorious Robert Moleyns, were to be present, as were the dean, precentor, chancellor, John Passelowe, William Ingram, Richard Langrysh, and two or three other canons who were to bury the body. On 13 August Walter Bayly, one of the executors of Walter Hungerford, gave money to the dean and chapter to distribute to the canons, as the dead man had instructed; on the same day Walter Bayly and Lord Scrope, two of the other executors, agreed with the cathedral treasurer that twenty-four torches and sixty other lights should burn about the body of the dead man on the day of his burial.[80]

Thus the cathedral may have formed the focus of discontent at Salisbury in 1450 because of its connections with the 'false counsellors' of the king. It is perhaps no accident that two of the canons that were particularly singled out for attack during the rising, Nicholas Upton and John Passelowe, were associated with either the saving of Lord Moleyns or the burial of Walter Hungerford, in Nicholas's case with both. Precisely because the cathedral had connections that extended beyond the city, it could, on occasion, find itself alienated from the citizens.

The cathedral occupied an ambiguous place in the religious life of the laity. Even within Salisbury itself the cathedral was an institution set apart from the devotional practices of the citizens. Its fabric fund could attract endowments of land from within the city in the thirteenth century, but by the fifteenth, citizens were more intent on embellishing the fabric of their own parish churches. In 1448 the parishioners of St Thomas's were asking for the dean and chapter's financial help to rebuild and extend their chancel at a time when the cathedral badly needed funds to repair its creaking tower. The cathedral was, of course, primarily a clerical institution: most of the divine services celebrated there during the later Middle Ages were founded by members of the clergy. The activities of dean

[80] Ibid., fos. 23ᵛ–24.

and chapter could also extend beyond city walls and diocesan boundaries. The effort to achieve Osmund's canonization was part of an effort to propagate the Salisbury Use as worthy of national use. The local cult could be presented, so Simon Huchyns hoped, as an English one, enjoying the support of nobility and gentry. The wider involvement with influential courtiers, some of whom were members of the cathedral's fraternity, could occasionally alienate the cathedral from Salisbury citizens.

Even so, alienation on the scale of the 1450 uprising was uncharacteristic. As the mother church of the diocese and the house of St Osmund's relics, the cathedral attracted pilgrims, offerings, and bequests—however 'painful' it may have been for W. Dodsworth in the nineteenth century 'to associate [Osmund's] venerable name with these proofs of popular folly'.[81] J. Hughes suggests that popular support for saints was exclusive to the diocese of York, but the cult of St Osmund was similarly popular in the Salisbury diocese.[82] The influence of the cathedral was stronger in its own prebends. The attested miracles of St Osmund tended to come from estates and parishes in which the lordship, spiritual and temporal, of the dean, chapter, and bishop was exercised. They also took place close to the city of Salisbury which, as an important market centre, drew in produce and people from the surrounding chalkland areas. It was within the city, over which the cathedral towered, that the cult of St Osmund was strongest. As a clerical body with socially exclusive connections, Salisbury cathedral may have seemed, at times, to be somewhat cold and aloof from lay people; yet as an intercessory institution and as the house of Osmund's relics, it offered spiritual services to which citizens and other parishioners were far from indifferent.

---

[81] W. Dodsworth, *An Historical Account of the Episcopal and Cathedral Church of Salisbury* (Salisbury, 1814), 184–5.

[82] Hughes says, for instance, that Osmund's miracles were limited to a period around 1411 (*Pastors and Visionaries: Religion and Secular Life in Late Medieval Yorkshire* (Woodbridge, 1988), 299–319, esp. 319).

3

The Parish and the Living

MONASTERY and cathedral may have touched the devotional lives of
some layfolk some of the time, but the institution that was closest to most,
in theory to all, was the parish. Indeed, twelfth- and thirteenth-century
reformers had sought to make the parish the primary context within
which the laity were to worship. Conciliar and synodal decrees in the
thirteenth century began to spell out the duties of lay people to the parish
in which they dwelt, and to parishes in which they held lands. Tithe and
other customary offerings were to support the parish priest, who was to
administer the seven sacraments, to instruct his flock through preaching
and the confessional. The custody and upkeep of ornaments was settled
on the laity (perhaps with some initial clerical misgivings) and so was a
responsibility towards the church fabric, the nave above all.[1] Lay people
were bound to their parishes, pastorally and financially, from cradle to
grave.

The obligations that the parish framework had come to impose on
parishioners were, broadly speaking, of two kinds. One was an obligation
to the parish structure, a duty to attend and support the mother church.
The other was to corporate worship, maintaining certain standards of
behaviour and contributing to clerical and other parish funds. How far
these obligations were met, whether indeed they were burdens against
which a now 'demoted' laity were forced to struggle, as it is sometimes
claimed,[2] is the subject of this chapter. But attention must be paid to the
variation in parish structure throughout the region. Patterns of settlement, in chalk, cheese, and cloth areas, and of ecclesiastical traditions,
affected both the nature of parochial obligations and the readiness with
which they were met. To concentrate solely on the parish framework,
however, would be to ignore a complexity of devotional loyalties that

---

[1] *Councils and Synods*, i. 82, 512–13; ii, esp. 1008, 1387–8; C. Drew, 'Early Parochial
Organisation in England: Origins of the Office of Churchwarden', *Borthwick Papers*, 7
(1954), 11–12; C. R. Cheney, 'Rules for the Observance of Feast Days in Medieval England',
Bulletin of the Institute of Historical Research, 34 (1961), esp. 119–21, 126, 137.

[2] E. Mason, 'The Role of the English Parishioner 1100–1500', *JEH* 27 (1976), 17–29;
Visitations in the Diocese of Lincoln 1517–31, ed. A. H. Thompson (Lincoln Record Society,
33; Hereford, 1940), pp. xxxviii–xxxix.

existed below and above the parochial level. We shall begin, then, with a closer look at this complexity.

One of the largest parishes in the diocese, eleven miles long at its widest point, was the parish of St Andrew at Sonning, on Berkshire clay vales near the Thames. It had enjoyed an illustrious history, as a minster church, perhaps even as the seat of a bishopric, and in 1091 it was among the endowments of the old cathedral of Salisbury. It remained under the jurisdiction of the cathedral dean throughout the later Middle Ages. Sonning's status as a mother church was no doubt enhanced by its impressive collection of relics, including one of St Cirius, patron saint of children and curer of insanity, which, according to Leland around 1540, was housed in a chapel at the east end of the church, 'whither of late tyme resorted in pilgrimage many folkes of the disease of madness'.[3] As a minster church it had probably once sent out its priests to serve in outlying chapels of the parish; by 1220 eight chapels were counted during the cathedral dean's visitation and each by then had (or was supposed to have) its own stipendiary chaplain.

Throughout the late Middle Ages the mother church exerted a varying gravitational pull on these satellite chapels. In 1220 three had baptismal rights but lacked cemeteries (Arborfield, Hurst, Ruscombe), two were 'almost ready' to make a cemetery (Erleigh St Bartholomew, Erleigh St Nicholas), one (Wokingham) had baptismal rights and a cemetery and had the chapel of Sandhurst dependent on it. Some of these had been founded in the recent past, in response to pastoral need: around 1080 the inhabitants of Whistley (later Hurst), three troublesome miles away from the mother church, acquired a chapel thanks to the efforts of Abbot Athelelm of Abingdon. In 1220 two other chapels, Sindlesham and Erleigh St Nicholas, were allowed to serve the manorial households but not the 'rustici' outside (as the priest at Erleigh had apparently been doing).[4] By 1405 the parochial picture had altered slightly: Sandhurst (now apparently directly dependent on Sonning), Ruscombe, Hurst, and Arborfield had all the sacraments including burial, but the two Erleighs now depended on Sonning for all their sacraments. Sindlesham chapel had disappeared altogether; Erleigh St Nicholas may have been kept going partly as a chantry founded for the soul of John Early in 1314 but was finally

---

[3] *VCH: Berks.* iii. 210–11, 220–3, 227; *The Itinerary of John Leland in or about the Years 1535–1543*, ed. L. Toulmin-Smith (London, 1908–10), i. 109.

[4] *Reg. S. Osmund*, 275–314; *Chronicon Monasterii de Abingdon*, ed. J. Stevenson (2 vols.; Rolls Series; London, 1858), ii. 18–19.

dissolved in 1536; by then, too, only one service a year was held at Erleigh St Bartholomew.[5]

The complexities of Sonning parish raise, first of all, some general points about lay attachment to the parochial structure. As the cult of St Cirius shows, the focus of popular devotion was not always the official patron saint of the parish church. In some parishes the patron saint was neglected. Bishop John Waltham discovered, in 1394, that fifteen parishes out of 140 he visited failed to observe their church's dedication day.[6] In others, it was perhaps the object of a passing fad: the parishioners of St Edmund's in Salisbury made oblations twice annually to 'the hand and ring of St Edmund', apparently because an indulgence had been granted by the Pope, but only for a while, and with declining enthusiasm, between 1473 and around 1501.[7] Parishes could have their own local collections of relics: a little bone from St Blaise's arm and one belonging to St Petroc at Lyme Regis, a tooth and a bone of St Laurence at Hungerford.[8] Such local devotional loyalties, moreover, could cut across parish boundaries. A bridge chapel near Reading housed 'Our Lady of Caversham', which could attract gifts from gentlemen like William Wrottesly (1512), from aristocrats like the countess of Warwick (1439), and from royalty, even Henry VIII himself. In 1536 the reformer Dr London was to report to Cromwell, with evident satisfaction, how he had pulled down the image of Our Lady at Caversham whither there had been 'great pilgremage'.[9] The parish church did not always form the prime focus of devotional allegiance of its parishioners.

Moreover, the parochial structure could not always accommodate such allegiances. Although settlements grew up within Sonning parish, not least Wokingham which was granted its own fair in 1217, none of them gained full parochial status. It had once been easier for lay people to set up chapels and found parish churches. As the minster system gave way to a less centralized system of pastoral care, a myriad of churches had been founded by lay lords, by settlers on newly cleared lands, and by townspeople in their own neighbourhoods.[10] Yet concern to establish the parish

---

[5] *Reg. Dean Chandler*, 102–9; *CPR* (1313–17), 159; PRO E301/51/24.

[6] Reg. Bp. Waltham, fos. 31ᵛ–79.   [7] *S. Edmund Accounts*, 14–53, 360–70.

[8] *Reg. Dean Chandler*, 133, 145, 153, 180, 183.

[9] PCC 21 Luffenham; 10 Fetiplace; and Richard Smith, yeoman of the Robe, 1515 (22 Holder); E. Margrett, 'St. Anne's Well and Chapel, Caversham', *BAJ* 12 (1906), 25–7; see also G. Rosser, 'Parochial Conformity and Voluntary Religion in Late Medieval England', *TRHS* sixth series, 1 (1991), 173–89; W. A. Christian, *Local Religion in Sixteenth-Century Spain* (Princeton, NJ, 1981).

[10] J. Blair, 'Local Churches in Domesday Book and Before', in J. C. Holt (ed.), *Domesday Studies* (Bury St Edmunds, 1987), 265–78; J. Campbell, 'The Church in Anglo-Saxon

as the primary focus of pastoral care made the Church hierarchy fearful of
further unchecked foundation of chapels and fragmentation of parishes,
which would infringe the rights of mother churches and undermine the
financial support of the parish priest. Far fewer parishes were founded in
the later Middle Ages than before, and those that were could be carefully
orchestrated by the Church hierarchy from above. Older towns like
Wilton, Sherborne, and Wallingford could have numerous and tiny parishes founded by local lords or townspeople before the thirteenth century;
but when New Salisbury was founded in the early thirteenth century, the
bishop created only two more parishes.[11] After the twelfth century, then,
the laity's freedom to found churches was much more circumscribed.
Canon law had 'laid its cold hand on the parishes of Europe and froze the
pattern which in many parts subsisted ever since'.[12]

A frozen parish structure did not always adapt to social change. Some
parishioners could find their parishes over-populated or ill served. Dispersed settlements or manor houses could seek additional places of divine
worship. The growth of some towns and villages might have led inhabitants to believe that their local chapel deserved more parochial rights.
Chapelries could sometimes assert a wilful independence of mother
churches. In 1405 and 1409 the villagers of Rockley were refusing to
attend the mother church of Ogbourne St Andrew and provide the holy
loaf. They could also be dissatisfied with the services provided by the
parish vicar: in 1485 they complained that he was not having mass celebrated, or providing the holy water, from the expenses of the vicarage as
he should have done.[13] Between 1360 and 1540 Salisbury bishops recorded
ten complaints in their registers from lay people claiming that parish
vicars or rectors were not fulfilling obligations towards their dependent
chapels (see Map 2).

The social disruption caused by the Black Death and subsequent
plagues after 1348 also distorted the parish structure. The high rate of
mortality may have led communities to demand cemeteries, and sometimes other parochial rights. Between 1360 and 1390, the inhabitants of
three English towns or villages made petitions to the Pope for cemeteries

Towns', in D. Baker (ed.), *The Church in Town and Countryside* (Studies in Church History,
16; Oxford, 1979), 126–7.
    [11] *VCH: Wilts.* vi. 144–51.
    [12] C. N. L. Brooke, 'The Missionary at Home: The Church and the Towns, 1000–1250',
in G. J. Cuming (ed.), *The Mission of the Church and the Propagation of the Faith* (Studies in
Church History, 6; Cambridge, 1970), 72.
    [13] *Reg. Dean Chandler*, 76, 274; D & C, MS 189, fo. 42.

to be attached to their chapels; in the next thirty years, twenty-four communities made similar requests. Only after about 1450 did the number of petitions for cemeteries decrease.[14] At least fifteen places within the diocese of Salisbury petitioned the Pope or bishop for cemeteries between 1384 and 1527 (see Map 2). The disruptions caused by plague could also obscure the relationship of church and dependent chapel. A dispute arose in the late fourteenth century between the rector of Enford church and the dependent chapel of Coombe. After pestilences had carried off a succession of manor lords who had for generations presented priests to the chapel, doubts arose as to whom the right of presentation belonged to. In 1365 the parishioners were judged to have sole right, but in 1387 the vicar of Enford claimed that the right was his. He also complained that parishioners had been attending mass in the chapel early in the morning, before it was celebrated in the mother church.[15]

Nevertheless, the inadequacies of parish structure were exposed in some areas more than others. Here we must return to the particular variations of our region. The problems of outlying chapelries tended to occur in parishes where the structure of old minster *parochiae* was retained—which was more likely to happen where ecclesiastical traditions were strongest. Some of the parishes with multiple chapels (Downton for instance) lay on episcopal manors; many of the others, like Sonning, Great Bedwyn and Broad Chalke were retained as prebends belonging to the cathedral. Sherborne, on Dorset Marshwood vale, once the seat of a bishopric and still a prebendal parish and the site of a wealthy monastic house in the later Middle Ages, had ten dependent chapels in 1405. Two others, Holnest and Castle, had also sprung up, themselves dependent on the chapels of Long Bourton and Oborne. The large parish occasionally creaked at its joints in the face of social change and lay truculence. The villagers of Holnest complained in 1408 at the inadequate services provided by the vicar of Long Bourton and at having to carry their dead to Sherborne. Overcompton chapel actually acquired burial rights in 1431.

---

[14] For 'a perilous and horrible smell' that could emanate from unburied bodies which parishioners were unable to carry to the mother church see *Cal. Papal Reg.* v. 409. For other demands for cemeteries see the following. 1360–90: ibid. i. 354; iv. 77, 166. 1391–1420: iv. 392, 536; v. 94, 205, 300, 317, 370, 371, 374, 390, 401, 402, 405, 443, 587, 609; vi. 108, 229, 245, 248, 441, 492, 500, 501. 1421–50: vii. 198, 261, 280, 394, 521, 524, 579; viii. 173, 505, 581, 602; ix. 63, 112, 480. 1451–98: xi. 144, 116, 630, 661; xii. 222, 784; xiii. 505, 578, 561, 629; xv. 993.

[15] BL Harl. MS 1623, fos. 17, 24; *Historical Manuscripts Commission*, Series 55, iv (London, 1907), 159–60. The dispute also involved another dependent chapel at Compton.

Chalk regions

Clay regions

Cloth regions

Parishes united

Cathedral prebends

Parishes containing concentrations
of episcopal manors

+   Licensed oratories
2   Number of dependent chapels within a parish
B   Chapels given burial rights
⊗   Chapelries raising complaints
      against mother churches

0   5   10   15   20 miles

MAP 2. Parishes, chapels, and oratories

In 1440 it was reported to the bishop that ten chapels were failing to observe the custom of processing with banners to the mother church on the Tuesday of Pentecost week.[16]

Because old minster churches were not exclusive to a particular type of agricultural area, demands for more parochial rights or cemeteries, and complaints from dependent chapelries, could occur all over the diocese. But the nature of settlement in different regions could still affect the strain placed on parochial structure. Dispersed settlements were more a feature of clay regions (though not all) than chalklands. Settlements on the clay vales of Berkshire, especially those thriving from proximity to the busy river Thames, could expand. Near Sonning lay Maidenhead, a growing town but without a parish church because it lay between the two parishes of Cookham and Bray, three miles from the one and over a mile from the other. Only in 1324 were the town's inhabitants able to secure episcopal recognition of their chapel from the bishop. Even so, although the chapel priest's stipend was to be met by the townsfolk and although women could be churched in the chapel, baptism was not to be performed and the townspeople were expected to attend their respective churches on major festivals.[17]

The problem of over-populated parishes, moreover, was one faced by some parishes more than others. It was cloth towns like Salisbury that expanded most in the fifteenth century: the two new parishes in Salisbury had over 1,000 communicants apiece by the sixteenth century. Such problems were less likely to occur in those areas of the chalklands that were not as affected by the cloth industry, where, in any case, settlements tended to be tightly restricted to the river valleys rather than dispersed. In areas outside the cloth regions, and particularly on chalkland, more settlements became deserted and more parishes united during the later Middle Ages.

Yet it is a little misleading, nevertheless, to labour the general woes arising from the static nature of the parish structure. Demands for parochial rights may not, in the end, imply that there was a serious need to increase the number of parishes in the diocese. The problem of a declining population in post-plague years was one that affected even the more densely populated towns. Those with multiple small parishes saw their numbers dwindle: Wallingford may have had eight parishes in the thirteenth century, but it had only four in the fifteenth century, and in 1545 it

---

[16] *Reg. Dean Chandler*, 37–49, 221–34; *Cal. Papal Reg.* vii. 280; Reg. Bp. Neville, second series, fo. 89; D & C, Reg. Hutchings, fo. 63ᵛ (p. 132). Hutchins, *Dorset*, iv. 100, 122–208.

[17] *Reg. Bp. Martival*, ii. 496; *The Cartulary of Cirencester Abbey, Gloucestershire*, ed. C. Ross (3 vols.; London, 1964), iii. 754, 1059–65.

was reported that only one priest was needed to serve them.[18] At
Abingdon in the late fourteenth century, two churches competed for the
attendance of parishioners. The attempt to boost the income of St
Nicholas's church, by allowing people who lived on the monastic granges
to attend its services, led only to a worrying drop in the numbers who
attended St Helen's.[19] Depopulation in most areas meant that the demand
was less for founding new parishes than for combining old ones. In any
case, demands for parochial rights in the Salisbury diocese were fewer
than in other parts of the country: the majority of late medieval petitions
for cemeteries and priests, certainly those made in the papal curia, came
from the dioceses of Lincoln and York, where settlements tended to be
more scattered and parishes larger.[20]

Moreover, the conflicts within parishes show that there were means for
reducing tension. Settlements with dependent chapels could make presentments in visitations and to the bishop himself. Extra parochial rights
could be petitioned for and acquired. Some of the chapels in Sonning
parish quietly secured burial rights, it would seem, between 1222 and
1405. Occasionally, new parishes could even be created.[21] Moreover,
chapelries did not have to acquire full parochial rights to meet pastoral
needs. Nor did they have to resort to rebellion against duties owed to
distant mother churches. The inhabitants of Whistely in Sonning parish
had apparently petitioned for a chapel in the late eleventh century. New
chapels continued to be founded and priests funded to serve in them. The
inhabitants of Preshute endowed a chapel in 1254 for the health of their
souls and in honour of St Martin on new land outside Marlborough but in
the parish of St Mary. The people of Maidenhead or Coombe, as we saw,
were prepared to meet the expenses of the chaplains officiating at their
chapel. And sometimes the payment of a priest's stipend helped to relieve
tensions that might have arisen because chapelries lay at some distance
from the mother church or because social change caused friction between

---

[18] *VCH: Berks.* iii. 539–44; PRO E301/51/36, E301/3/2.

[19] A. E. Preston, *The Church and Parish of St Nicholas, Abingdon* (Oxford Historical
Society, 99; 1935), 30–5.

[20] The villagers of Haxby in Yorkshire complained that they were four miles from one
church and sixteen miles from another (*The Fabric Rolls of York Minster 1362–1550* (Surtees
Society, 35; London, 1859), 254–5).

[21] In the *Valor* of 1535, some thirty parish churches are mentioned in the region that were
'chapels' (or not mentioned at all) in the *Taxatio* of 1291, suggesting, though not con-
clusively, that these places gained greater parochial rights. Most of these were in the more
heavily populated clay and cloth regions (*Valor Ecclesiasticus*; *Taxatio Ecclesiastica Angliae et
Walliae Auctoritate P. Nicholai IV circa A.D. 1291*, ed. T. Astle, S. Ayscough, and J. Caley
(London, 1802)).

the two. In 1405 the inhabitants of Hindon complained to the Pope that the two miles between them and the mother church of Enford were filled with woods in which robberies had been perpetrated, and that in wintry weather access to the church was dangerous. They also added that strangers resorted to their town because it was near the public way and because a weekly market had come to be held there. In consequence, the inhabitants had founded a new chapel with a place adjoining for a cemetery. The Pope mandated that the chapel indeed be licensed and the chaplain appointed by the rector, adding that if the rector refused or neglected to make the appointment, the inhabitants were to do so in his stead. Indeed by 1545 the priest was described as being removable at their pleasure.[22]

Finally, some pastoral needs were met by chapels and oratories licensed primarily for manorial households. New private chapels were certainly being founded from the late twelfth century onwards. They may well have been a mark of social status and, perhaps, a reflection of a desire for a more personal religion away from the corporate celebrations of the parish church (see Chapter 9). But they could also be acquired by households for pastoral convenience. The Foxley family in Bray were granted four licences between 1305 and 1344 for a private oratory in their manor of Woodcriche; in 1341 the licence was granted precisely because of the distance and difficulty of getting to the parish church.[23] The foundation of some of these private oratories may have been influenced by the pattern of local settlement to serve more people than the immediate manorial household. The chapel of Erleigh St Nicholas in Sonning was apparently licensed to admit only the manor household into its services, yet its chaplain had clearly been admitting other parishioners. In 1245 Corsely chapel was referred to as a manor chapel, probably belonging to the Kingston family, yet its distance from the mother church of Warminster may explain why, in 1415, the chapel acquired burial rights. Another private chapel, away from the manor and itself dependent on Corsely chapel, was probably also founded in response to pastoral

---

[22] Preshute: D & C, Press IV, E2, Preshute/1. Hindon: *Cal. Papal Reg.* vi. 51; *VCH: Wilts.* xi. 101; *CPR* (1557–8), 102, 375. Compare the case of St Laurence chapel, Warminster, which inhabitants had endowed because of the distance between chapel and parish church (PRO E301/58/131).

[23] Reg. Bp. Wyvill, fos. 50ᵛ, 62, 62ᵛ, 69, 71ᵛ. See also the manor chapel of Wokefield in Stratfield Mortimer, licensed in 1255 for the use of the manor household—by 1505 the inhabitants of Wokefield were complaining that no divine service was being celebrated there (*VCH: Berks.* iii. 428); Swallowfield in Shinfield (ibid. 274); Heywood in Westbury (*VCH: Wilts.* viii. 177); Upmelcombe in Melcombe Horsey (Hutchins, *Dorset*, iv. 368); and Marlston in Bucklebury (*Reading Carts.* ii. 364). See also J. Blair, *Landholding in Surrey* (London, 1991), 156–7.

need.[24] It is unsurprising, then, to find that licences for oratories recorded in bishops' registers were granted most often—even if not exclusively—during the fourteenth and fifteenth centuries in the largest parishes of the diocese (Sonning, Lambourne, Winkfield, Cookham, Bray, Warminster, Bishops Canning, Enford) and in the more densely populated parishes of the clay vales (see Map 2). The 'failure' of the parish structure to accommodate social changes should not be exaggerated.

The parish structure produced other obligations, financial duties to parish priest and fabric funds. Customary offerings to the parish priest had become enshrined in canon law: mortuary payments; fees at weddings and churching of women; oblations made at the mass during the three main church festivals of Christmas, Easter, Whitsuntide, also at the feast of the church's dedication, and often too at All Saints. The tithe, long compulsory, was becoming much more customary in the twelfth century and being exploited for concerns beyond the support of the parish priest himself. Thirteenth-century ecclesiastical law emphasized the need for fabric funds, to maintain the nave and church ornaments.[25] The response to these duties was not always whole-hearted. Visitational records occasionally reveal rather unedifying glimpses of parish life and even of lay people resenting parochial burdens. At Sonning, once more, the cathedral dean in 1222 and 1224 found some of the priests serving in the dependent chapels woefully inadequate for the task of divine service, not least the one who was blind. Later visitations in 1405 and 1409, to which lay people were summoned to make presentments, uncovered other priestly faults: the vicar of Sonning was accused of adultery, quarrelling with his parishioners, and going about at night with a long sword contrary to clerical decency. Certain lay people also came under visitational scrutiny: two necromancers, ten people failing to pay rents owing to the fabric or altar lights, a man not paying his mortuary fee, and one Thomas Sextauyne at Hurst who withheld tithe of swans.[26]

Before concluding, however, that lay people resented parochial burdens, it is important to recall that these were burdens that the laity themselves were expected to enforce. By the end of the thirteenth century parishioners had a role to play in visitations. These had long been sanc-

[24] *Cal. Papal Reg.* vi. 491; WRO 490, fo. 110a; *VCH: Wilts.* viii. 21.

[25] J. R. H. Moorman, *Church Life in England in the Thirteenth Century* (Cambridge, 1946), 126–31; J. Blair, 'Secular Minster Churches in Domesday Book', in P. Sawyer (ed.), *Domesday Book: A Reassessment* (London, 1985), 119.

[26] *Reg. S. Osmund*, 275–314; *Reg. Dean Chandler*, 105–15, 249–59.

tioned by old canon law and it was in the late twelfth century that bishops, archdeacons, and deans had begun to undertake them more fully to enforce clerical standards. At this stage the laity do not appear to have played much of a role; certainly, the dean of Salisbury in 1222 seems to have uncovered the failings of the Sonning priesthood by asking them questions face to face. In any case these early visitations tended to restrict their enquires to the state of the priesthood, the church fabric, and ornaments.[27] But in 1238/9 Robert Grosseteste, bishop of Lincoln, appears to have widened the scope of the visitation to include more general questions about the moral state of clergy and laity; he also summoned lay people to make presentments. Although his procedure of swearing in laymen initially met with opposition, the practice of summoning several parishioners during visitations seems to have become established by the end of the century.[28] How regularly visitations were undertaken is not clear and there were certainly failings in the system. Bishop John Chandler was to complain in 1420 that archdeacons performed the parish visitation in a perfunctory manner and more often with an eye to the potential yield from procurations than to the defects that required correction.[29] But, in general, the visitation gave the laity a regular role to play in the machinery of Church discipline.

Moreover, the widening scope of the visitation also encouraged the growth of the office of churchwarden, that symbol of lay control within the parish. Early visitations may not have stated which lay people were to be summoned to make presentments, beyond specifying that they be 'trustworthy'. The groups of laity summoned by Dean Chandler in the early fifteenth century are not named as churchwardens but some certainly were. In the records of Dean Davyson's visitation in 1480 the lists of lay people summoned from each parish are headed with the names of two 'yconomi'; indeed, lists of visitational questions of the same period stated that the 'reformation' of the morals of clergy and laity could not ensue without the information that came from church-

---

[27] *Reg. S. Osmund*, i. 305–6; C. R. Cheney, *From Becket to Langton: English Church Government 1170–1223* (Manchester, 1956), 139–41; C. R. Cheney, *Hubert Walter* (London, 1967), 55.

[28] R. W. Southern, *Robert Grosseteste: The Growth of an English Mind in Medieval Europe* (Oxford, 1986), 257–60; *Councils and Synods*, i. 261–5.

[29] Reg. Bp. Chandler, fos. 34ᵛ–36ᵛ. There is only one surviving record of visitations carried out by the Salisbury bishops themselves, in 1394: Reg. Bp. Waltham, fos. 38ᵛ–56ᵛ. The surviving records of the Salisbury deans suggest a regular visitation on cathedral prebends (*Reg. Dean Chandler*, *passim* (1405, 1408, 1412); D & C, Reg. John Netwon (1463), pp. 145–77; D & C, MS 189, fos. 41–94 (1480, 1485/6).

wardens.[30] There were also other reasons for the growth of the office: the obligations imposed on parishioners by legislation in the thirteenth century—the need for separate fabric funds and to maintain liturgical equipment—undoubtedly stimulated the need for regularly elected parish officials.[31] But, more than is sometimes recognized, the rise of the churchwarden may well have been linked with the pastoral efforts of the Church.

Two surviving lists of visitational questions (one from Bishop Waltham's register in 1394, the other a late-fifteenth-century, more detailed, list from cathedral records) show the objects of clerical and lay inquiry.[32] The state of the church formed the first series of questions in the second list: whether the chancel and nave were in good repair, whether dues to church 'stocks' (fabric or altar funds) were being paid, and whether 'the blessed sacrament of the auter which is very God in forme of brede' was being stored in a locked and well-kept pyx. The morals of the laity were considered next: whether there were any heretics, adulterers, slanderers, any who withheld tithes and oblations or who were 'talking and jangeling' in church during divine service. Finally, the questions turned to the state of the clergy. Was the priest resident in the parish? Did he say divine service at the correct time? Did he instruct the laity in the articles of the faith, the Ten Commandments, the seven deadly sins, the four cardinal virtues, and the seven Beatitudes? Was he to be found frequenting taverns or dallying with suspect women? The laity were thus required to ensure that their parish priests performed their duties as the Church required.

Surviving visitation returns show that parishioners at Sonning, as elsewhere, were sometimes keen to present offenders. In fact the type of case they were keenest to present was not a failure to uphold specific parochial obligations, but a failure to conform to more general standards of morality. The bulk of the accusations against lay people in the visitations of Dean Chandler concerned sexual matters, fornication, adultery and related cases such as breaches of marriage contracts, desertions, and scolding by husbands or wives. Punishment might involve a public display of penance, a ritual 'beating' in church, as the penitent walked at the head of the Sunday procession, or even in the market-place; it might also involve a pilgrimage to the cathedral.[33] A 'respectable' concern with upholding

---

[30] *Reg. Dean Chandler*, 191, 197; D & C, MS 189, fos. 49, 54–94.
[31] Drew, 'Early Parochial Organistion', *passim*.
[32] For the following see D & C, Reg. John Coman, p. 102 and MS 189, fos. 49ᵛ–54.
[33] *Reg. Dean Chandler, passim*.

certain standards of morality, sometimes associated with a later and more
'puritan' religion, was already deeply ingrained in late medieval parish
life. Priests were also presented to the visitational court for moral and
pastoral shortcomings. At Thornford in 1405, the parishioners reported
that their priest was often drunk and said services either too quickly or too
slowly. In 1480 the priest at Kingston chapel in Bere Regis was cited for
not administering the sacraments every day, as was customary.[34] There
were certainly more serious contretemps between parish priest and
parishioners. Some time in the late fifteenth century, Sir William Benton,
vicar of Bere Regis, was trapped for a whole weekend in his vicarage by a
malevolent crowd, armed with bows and arrows, and narrowly escaped
death by slipping out through a chamber window.[35] But, in general, the
visitation encouraged the laity to be critical of the clergy in order to
enforce standards set by the Church hierarchy. It is also clear that priestly
failure to provide a certain standard of pastoral care was a failure that
parishioners themselves could be anxious to rectify.

Parishioners also presented lay people for failing to fulfil specifically
parochial duties. Some parishioners were less than willing to pay their
financial dues. There are also hints that some areas harboured more tithe
evaders than others: the visitors at Bere Regis and Hungerford uncovered
refusals to pay tithes more than once during the three visitations of 1405,
1409, and 1412.[36] More frequent were refusals to pay smaller oblations,
like offerings on the day of the church's dedication or for holy loaf
(brought by the parishioners at mass on Sundays, and blessed and distributed).[37] Eight people at the village of Fordington in 1412 were presented
for refusing to provide the holy loaf; Agnes Pokeswell of Netherbury in
1405 was cited for refusing to provide the holy loaf for her houses at
Brimsham and Okebere.[38]

But failures to pay dues were neither uniform nor general. They were
more likely to occur in thriving cloth towns, busy market towns on clay
vales, or in places close by that depended on the markets of these towns,
rather than in smaller rural villages, particularly in chalkland areas.[39]

---

[34] *Reg. Dean Chandler*, 49; see also 20, 43, 45, 48, 52, 77, 208, 228, 234, 242, 248, 255, 377;
D & C, MS 189, fo. 65ᵛ. In the visitation of the prebends in 1480, one priest was cited for
accepting money for divine service, five for not fulfilling the sacraments, three for adultery,
two for celebrating twice in one day, and one for being absent.
[35] PRO C1/48/551. The reasons for this episode are not given.
[36] *Reg. Dean Chandler*, 4, 191, 297; 88, 247.
[37] Reg. Bp. Waltham, fos. 31ᵛ–94.   [38] *Reg. Dean Chandler*, 310, 28.
[39] Reg. Bp. Waltham, fos. 31ᵛ–94 (1390); D & C, Reg. Coman, pp. 103–5 (1394); and *Reg.*

Moreover, there does not appear to have been any general or persistent refusal to pay dues. Bishop Waltham's visitation of 140 parishes uncovered cases of failure to pay tithes in only seven parishes, and failure to pay the holy loaf in only three; Dean Chandler's visitations in 1405, 1408/9, and 1412 brought to light fewer than thirty individual refusals to pay tithes; the visitations of prebends in 1463, 1480, 1483, and 1485/6, though admittedly more cursory, uncovered only two. Agnes Pokeswell of Netherbury appears to have been unusual in her failure to provide the holy loaf: she was told to conform 'like other parishioners'. The obligation to pay tithe does not seem to have been seriously questioned, only when it might be applied: Thomas Ryckeman from Lyme Regis refused to pay tithe on the somewhat ingenious grounds that he had been away sea-fishing during the previous season.[40] The parishioners of St Thomas's in Salisbury made regular offerings to the high altar at Easter of around £45 in the late fifteenth and early sixteenth centuries, a figure that decreased substantially only in the 1530s.[41] In general, tithe disputes seem to have arisen more from within the clerical body than from any lay reaction, and were more often centred around how much was to be paid by whom rather than whether tithe was to be paid at all.[42] Some parishioners, moreover, did more than simply pay their tithes and dues to support the parish priest. When the rector of Castle Combe failed to appoint a priest to the parish in 1406, the parishioners, on their own authority, appointed one themselves, paying him out of the revenues of the church.[43] Support of parish priests was not always restricted to the passive payment of tithe.

Church-going was another obligation that was not always adhered to as much as ecclesiastical legislation required. The enforcement of holy days was not always easy, especially around harvest time. A harvester on the estates of the bishop of Winchester around 1310, when threatened with excommunication by the rector of Harwell for summoning tenants to work on holy days 'with a large horn', retorted that he was going to cart hay whether the rector liked it or not. At the small village of Ryme in 1408,

---

Dean Chandler, *passim* (1405, 1408, 1412). Salisbury and nearby places: Grimstead, Wilsford, and Stratford; Calne, Hungerford, Welford (near Newbury) in cloth areas; Lyme Regis, Roscombe in Sonning, Yatminster in clay regions. There were, nevertheless, other places where tithe defaulters were reported: Donhead St Mary, Frome Whitfield, Charminster, Kingston in Bere Regis, Fordington, Netheravon. These visitations do not cover some of the larger towns in the region (Salisbury excepted) where absenteeism was perhaps more likely.

[40] *Reg. Dean Chandler*, 28, 21.   [41] D & C, Press II, Procurator's accounts.
[42] N. P. Tanner, *The Church in Late Medieval Norwich 1370–1532* (Toronto, 1984), 5–7; J. A. F. Thomson, 'Tithe Disputes in Late Medieval London', *EHR* 78 (1963), 1–2.
[43] *Reg. Bp. Hallum*, 43.

three people were accused of going to harvest corn instead of observing their church's dedication festival.[44] But failure to attend the parish church may not have been as widespread in rural villages as in populous towns (or places near these market centres), where the pace of economic life was brisker and absenteeism less easy to detect and enforce.[45] Bishop Waltham's visitation of the three Salisbury parishes in 1394 revealed a larger number of absentees than visitations in more rural areas.[46]

Despite the failings noted in visitations, church attendance looks as though it was generally high. Dean Chandler's visitations in 1405, 1408, and 1412 uncovered only a dozen people failing to attend church on Sundays and festivals or to go to confession; in only five of the 140 parishes visited and recorded by Bishop Waltham by 1394 were such faults uncovered; and in the visitations of the Salisbury dean in the later fifteenth century no cases of absenteeism were reported. The large number of communicants that some parishes later claimed (in 1545 and 1548) attended their Easter mass may suggest that the majority of the adult population in these small towns came to the service.[47] Preaching could apparently reach a wide audience, occasionally too wide in the dean and chapter's view. In 1461 they took steps to silence a priest who had been inciting the parishioners from the pulpit against Edward IV and the accession of a new Yorkist line to the English throne.[48]

Apart from any pious devotion, in any case, there must have been considerable social pressure to attend church. As some heretics found to their cost, their absence at services was noted. In 1514 John Swayne, or Baynard, a heretical labourer in the village of Willensford, admitted: 'I wold not have comyn unto the churche oft tymes but for the Rumour of

[44] Oxford, Bodley, MS Digby 154, fo. 38 (p. 23); *Reg. Dean Chandler*, 22, 218, 234, 247, 315, 327.

[45] *Reg. Bp. Waltham*, fos. 31ᵛ–94; *Reg. Dean Chandler*, *passim* (1405, 1408, 1412). Salisbury and nearby Grimstead, Newbury and nearby Spene; Chievely, Chardstock, Holnest, Ryme on clay vales; Warminster in the cloth region.

[46] D & C, Reg. Coman, p. 102. Bishop Hallum felt that too many people were frequenting taverns and engaging in business on Sundays and feast days (*Reg. B. Hallum*, 837). For two cases of failure to attend the Easter mass and the confessional in 1487 (though the defendants claimed to have attended mass at another parish church) see WRO D4/3, fos. 94ᵛ, 95, 98ᵛ (1487).

[47] See Ch. 4 n. 50.

[48] D & C, Reg. Newton, fo. 17ᵛ: at Bramshaw (Hants). In 1462 the dean and chapter had to deal with further anti-Yorkist sentiment when another priest, Thomas Adlyngton, proclaimed in the cathedral 'aula' that 'i have be and sayne 4 fals harlottees to Kyng Edward' and 'thou hast a false quart[er] in thy cote' (ibid., fos. 22ᵛ–23). For the importance of pulpits and preaching see BRO D/P 97/5/2, p. 244 (the most prestigious seats at St Laurence's church in Reading by 1544 were in front of the pulpit), and Ch. 9 for heretics listening to sermons.

the people.'[49] Fixed seating in church would have made absence more detectable. Juliane Farman's obvious failure to attend Hungerford church in 1405 would have been all the more glaring because she had her own seat in church.[50] Seating had been known in churches as early as the thirteenth century,[51] but there are indications that fixed seating was becoming more established in the fifteenth century, particularly in the more urbanized parishes. Churchwardens' accounts (at least in Salisbury and Reading, but not in the more rural parish of Winterslow, nor yet in market towns with large rural areas around them like Wimborne Minster or even Calne) began to record charges for pews or seats (see Table 2). As it became more fixed and prevalent, church seating no doubt helped to encourage a certain social conformity. Such communal pressure may explain why, all told, remarkably few cases of failure to fulfil parochial obligations came to light in visitations.[52]

A widespread effort to fulfil obligations towards the church fabric funds might also be the conclusion reached from studying churchwardens' accounts. There are, however, some problems with the suggestion that these funds demonstrate a 'communal' piety. Funds were often kept afloat, in some places more than others, as we shall see in the following chapter, by the property or livestock left by a few dead benefactors. Very occasionally, visitations hint at a less than voluntary effort behind some fund-raising activities. In 1394 two parishioners in Orcheston St George were reported for not contributing to the church ornaments even though they had lands in the parish.[53] The collections made at Easter and Christmas were often so regular that they take on the air of compulsory parish assessments that are said to characterize those of the post-Reformation period. At Poole in 1532 the regular Easter collection was taken at a rate of 1*d*. from every married couple and ½*d*. from single people.[54] Collective effort is more

[49] Reg. Bp. Audley, first series, fo. 155.   [50] *Reg. Dean Chandler*, 88.

[51] *Councils and Synods*, ii. 1006; M. Aston, 'Segregation in Church', in W. J. Sheils and D. Wood (ed.), *Women in the Church* (Studies in Church History, 23; Oxford, 1990), 237–94.

[52] In the dean's visitation of 1485/6, there were no faults to report in twelve churches and chapels out of a total of thirty-four visited (D & C, MS 189, fos. 41–48ᵛ).

[53] Reg. Bp. Waltham, fo. 43ᵛ.

[54] Poole municipal archives, 47 (2). Other accounts used in the survey are as follows. Wilts.: *S. Edmund Accounts* (from 1443); St Mary's, Devizes (from 1499), WRO 189; Calne (from 1527), WRO 2083/1; Winterslow (from 1542), Rectory; Steeple Ashton (from 1543), WRO 697/1; Wanborough (from 1530s), WRO 894/1. Berks.: Reading St Giles (from 1518), BRO D/P 96/5/1; St Laurence (1436, 1440s, 1458, from 1498), BRO D/P 97/5/1, 97/5/2. Dorset: Wimborne Minster (from 1403), DRO PE/WM CW 1/1–40, 41; Sherborne (from 1499), J. Fowler, 'Sherborne All Hallow's Church Wardens' Accounts', *NQSD* 23–4 (1939–44), *passim*.

apparent in collections from plays, church ales, and the ubiquitous Hocktide festivity, on the Monday and Tuesday after Easter (which seems to have involved the men of the parish tying up women with ropes until they paid for their liberty by a contribution to the parish fund—the women getting their revenge on the next day, when the roles were reversed).[55] No doubt at these events, too, communal pressure eased coins from pockets.

There was also a great deal of variation between parishes (see Table 2). Take the churchwardens' accounts of Wimborne Minster that run from 1403 onwards. Wimborne Minster lay on the poor soils of Dorset heathland but it was not a typical rural village: it was a market town, and its parish, containing a large area of the surrounding countryside (claiming 1,700 communicants in 1545), was dominated by a college of secular priests which traced its origins back to a nunnery founded in the eighth century.[56] About 10 per cent (£2 a year) of the parish funds in the early fifteenth century (20 per cent or £6 a year by the 1530s) was raised from renting out property. Small charges came to be made for burials. Around £2 was raised at fairs and markets where stalls were sold to vendors, and in 1496 Henry VII granted the church licence to have two fairs on St Thomas's day and St Luke's day. Larger sums (usually between £4 and £6) were raised at church ales, though after 1498 the ales seem to have been replaced by an apparently less bibulous fund-raising event, the wives from the 'country' competing with wives of the 'town' in bringing cakes to sell. Besides Easter and Pentecost, offerings on saints' days brought in smaller sums. Devotion to the Virgin Mary was certainly present: a Lady chapel had its paintings repaired in 1414/15 and its image of Mary gilded over in 1518. Offerings were made on the feast of Purification throughout the period, and between 1452 and 1501 offerings were also recorded on the other major Marian feast days. St Stephen's day was also an occasion of offerings up to 1512, and St Laurence's between *c.*1465 and 1481. The cult of Henry VI was also no doubt encouraged by the connection of the Tudors to the college (Henry VII made a visit in 1506 for which the cemetery had to be swept clean; and his mother gave two torches to the church in 1495 and later founded a chantry in the college). Between 1495 and 1536 small offerings were made to the pyx of King—sometimes 'Saint'—Henry (around 2*s.* in the 1490s, but thereafter only a few pence).

---

[55] A remnant of the custom seems to have survived at Hungerford in the late 19th cent. (*The Cartulary of St Nicholas's Hospital Salisbury*, ed. C. Wordsworth (WRS; Salisbury, 1902), 97). According to W. L. Barker, 'Hungerford', *WAM* 11 (1868), 150–1, the festivities were supposed to commemorate victory against the Danes.

[56] *VCH: Dorset*, ii. 107–13.

One saint was held in special veneration: St Cuthberga, the patron saint of the original nunnery. On her feast day (31 August) the church was swept clean, lights in the Lady chapel were lit, and a fair was held in the cemetery. Collections were made on her feast day before her image, at her feet (sometimes her head), and in her apron. A piece of worsted was bought by the churchwardens to make a new apron in 1499/1500. Many rings of silver and gold (usually numbering around 100 in church inventories) seem to have been given to her image: 137 rings were counted in 1530 'upon the apron' of St Cuthberga. Individuals could indeed be moved by her cult. Before 1450 Joan Says, a widow, entrusted her executor with a bequest of 'a Tabelet closed in golde a berall' to the image of St Cuthberga 'to sette above her nekke there'; but when the tablet was stolen the executor's wife apparently died of grief. When Thomas Rolle died in London in 1525, he left his largest bequest, 6s. 8d., to the church of Wimborne Minster where he had been born, 'for the devotion I have of the said church and of St Cuthberga'. Finally, in 1538 the order came to remove the image, but such was the association of the parish with the cult that the parishioners could plausibly petition the dean of the college that they might keep the silver from the head of the image.[57]

The corporate activity at Wimborne Minster offers points of comparison and contrast with other parishes. In the larger towns of Salisbury and Reading there were more ceremonies and processions than in Wimborne Minster and certainly more still than in a rural chalkland parish like Winterslow. In the early sixteenth century St Laurence's parish in Reading celebrated a king's play at Whitsuntide, employed morris dancers and plays involving Robin Hood and Maid Marian on May day, put on a Passion play at Easter, a play on Corpus Christi day, and a Cayme's play in the market-place. The wealthier parishes were also more able to fulfil the requirements for ornaments and vestments. A list of vestments and books made in 1472 at St Edmund's parish in Salisbury shows that parishioners had gone well beyond the minimum list of goods required by decree: the parish had one more legend than required, five more antiphonaries, thirteen more processionals, seven more crosses, fourteen more chalices, and a great many more vestments.[58]

The same wealthier parishes were able to respond more effectively to new cults. The newer feast of Corpus Christi was celebrated lavishly at Salisbury and Sherborne, but apparently neither at rural Winterslow nor yet at Wimborne Minster. New feast days were dedicated to the Virgin

[57] PRO C1/19/434; PCC 2 Porche; Hutchins, *Dorset*, iii. 188–9.
[58] *Reg. Dean Chandler*, pp. xxxii–xxxiii; *S. Edmund Accounts*, 3–7. Compared with Archbishop Reynold's list (*Councils and Synods*, ii. 1387–8).

Mary in the late fifteenth century: the feast of the Visitation (2 July) and of the Transfiguration (6 August).[59] The parishioners of Wimborne Minster made collections on all the important Marian feasts, but never, it would seem, responded to the new ones.[60] Their traditional attachment to the older cult of St Cuthberga perhaps proved more resilient in the face of newer practices. But at St Laurence's in Reading emphasis on the Visitation was enhanced by a lavish bequest from Nicholas Nicholas in 1514 who left £40 to make an image of the Visitation to stand in the north part of the church.[61] Bequests to 'Our Lady of Sorrows' increased from the mid-fifteenth century onwards: most of them came from the larger market and cloth towns.[62]

Another cult, that of the Holy Name of Jesus, was given an official feast day of 7 August in 1488/9. In the second half of the fifteenth century parishes all over the diocese seem to have acquired altars, lights, masses, and even guilds dedicated to Jesus, judging from the evidence of wills. Some of these were acquired before an official feast day was proclaimed. Again it was in the more urbanized places that the cult was seized upon more readily or more lavishly. There were certainly Jesus lights in rural parishes like Yatminster, Marnhull, Birton, and Stourpayne; but they were more common in larger market towns like Bridport, Westbury, Wokingham, Wantage, Thatcham, Sherborne, and Shaftesbury, and in some of the most wealthy cloth towns like Trowbridge, Marlborough, Newbury, Reading, and Salisbury.[63] The days of all these new feasts fell in the summer when the Church calendar was comparatively bare. Like another of the newer feast days, that of Corpus Christi, which fell on the Thursday after Trinity Sunday, these newer feasts were perhaps more easily observed in towns than in rural areas, where inhabitants were more

[59] Pfaff, *Feasts*, 13, 38–9, 40–8.

[60] However, the countess of Richmond's chantry chapel at Wimborne Minster was dedicated to Jesus and the Annunciation (1496) (PRO E135/3/21).

[61] PCC 1 Holder.

[62] Pfaff, *Feasts*, 62–83. The first known bequest was in 1457, by William Hous of Marlborough (PCC 11 Stockton). Others were in larger market towns or in cloth regions: Devizes, Malmesbury, Mere, Kingston Deverell, Colerne, and Brinkworth (Wilts.); Windsor and Wokingham (Berks.). But similar bequests can also be found at Highworth, Wyly, and Purton (Wilts.); Stourbridge, Pymperne, Wareham, and Marnhull (Dorset); and Burland (Berks.).

[63] The earliest references to Jesus lights and guilds in these places come from wills (which are not reliable indicators) and are as follows. 1465 Salisbury St Thomas's, 1479 Salisbury St Edmund's, 1470 Reading St Giles', 1493 St Laurence's (see Ch. 6). From other wills: 1469 Yatminster, 1488 Bridport, 1494 Newbury, 1498 Stourpayne, 1502 Sherborne, 1505 Alsforth, 1510 Wantage, 1511 Mere, 1519 Marnhull, 1520 Birton, 1528 Marlborough, 1529 Thatcham, 1534 Westbury, 1535 Wokingham.

affected by the pressures of work around harvest-time. The worlds of town and village were not, of course, isolated from each other: towns-people could be drawn out to the countryside at harvest-time; villagers could be drawn into the Corpus Christi festivities of nearby towns.[64] Yet it tended to be the wealthier and more urbanized parishes that responded to new cults on a more lavish scale than others.

So it was in the larger parishes, particularly in the busy cloth towns, that more ceremonies were laid on, more equipment bought, and newer feasts more easily introduced. Yet this is not the same as saying that there was more communal activity in these parishes. For one thing, there was more social diversity and even fragmentation within larger, thriving towns. Although seating arrangements within these large parish churches may have helped conformity, they also gave expression to the diversity and hierarchies of more urbanized societies. In St Laurence's parish, Reading, in the 1440s it appears that very few seats were charged for, and in the early sixteenth century, when on average ten people a year were charged for seats, these seemed to be mostly elderly women. But the women's surnames suggest strong connections with the top-ranking burgesses. Rulings in 1515/16 made it clear that wives of mayors were to be given precedence; and while 6*d.* was charged for most seats, only 4*d.* was charged for seats in the less prestigious areas in the middle and north range beneath the font. In 1522 £8. 12*s.* 2*d.* was collected as new seats and new occupants were installed. In 1546 it was decreed that the wives of the brethren of the exclusive Jesus mass were to have the highest seats in pews next to the mayor's wife's seat.[65] Village society no doubt had its own rivalries, and certainly the local gentry could be given precedence in pews. But pecking orders tended to be more finely tuned, and sensitive, in thriving towns with their greater diversity of wealth.[66]

Perhaps as a consequence of greater diversity and fragmentation, it was less easy for larger parishes in more urban areas to depend on regular communal events for its finances (see Table 2). A parish like St Giles in bustling Reading was more dependent on rents from land left by dead benefactors than on church ales. Other densely populated parishes that lacked property, like St Edmund's in Salisbury, relied on individual gifts and standard charges. From 1470 to 1547, 17 per cent of the average annual gatherings came from standard charges, for burial and hiring of

[64] M. Rubin, *Corpus Christi: The Eucharist in Late Medieval Culture* (Cambridge, 1991), 164–85.
[65] BRO D/P 97/5/1; D/P 97/5/2, esp. pp. 103–8, 146–7, 244.
[66] Aston, 'Segregation', 266–7.

ornaments, for seats, and for stalls in the cemetery on a market day; 16 per cent came from bequests given, on average, by only six people a year; 45 per cent came from regular collections at Easter and Christmas which were supposed to be from all parishioners—though in 1522/3 it was recorded that the names of those who had contributed were specially written down on a separate bill, suggesting that not all did; a mere 12 per cent came from the festive Hocktide events, and although in some years these could raise proportionally much more, in other years they were not celebrated at all (see Table 2).

In small villages like Winterslow on Wiltshire chalkland, communal fund-raising through ales was conducted virtually every year, arousing images of pastoral nostalgia of Aubreyesque proportions. In 1546 twenty pounds of wool came the parish's way from the shearing done at Milburne.[67] Other pictures of regular rural activity come from Aubrey. A custom of maidens and bachelors exchanging garlands for pennies was held on Trinity Sunday at the Cotswold village of South Newton. The inhabitants of Netherbury claimed in 1566 that they used to stage a play at the Whitsuntide ale, with Robin Hood and Little John, in which the gentlemen of the parish were the chief actors.[68]

Parishes with more regular communal activity were not necessarily restricted to a particular region. Some communal commitment was encouraged by traditional and local objects of devotion, like St Cuthberga at Wimborne Minster, rather than by patterns of settlement. Parishes are also difficult to classify. Those in cloth-producing centres like Calne and Steeple Ashton might be expected to rely little on communal fund-raising and resemble parishes in neighbouring Devizes. Yet, unlike Devizes, their parishes included large areas of rural sheep and corn country: both continued to rely on church ales for most of the sixteenth century. At Calne most of the parish revenue was raised from its annual Pentecost ale. Wimborne Minster, set in a large area of Dorset heathland, produced cloth on a smaller scale than Calne, yet its parish finances relied more heavily on property than Calne's by the sixteenth century. But it, and other more rural parishes, had more regular, communal, fund-raising activities than more densely populated parishes, such as St Edmund's within the cloth town of Salisbury.

Corporate activities within the parish were profuse and varied. Some of them had been imposed by a clerical hierarchy anxious to provide for

---

[67] Winterslow church accounts, fo. 5ᵛ.
[68] Aubrey, *Remaines*, 136–8; Hutchins, *Dorset*, ii. 108.

TABLE 2. Churchwardens' accounts: how money was raised

Parish and dates of accounts	Maximum (£)	Average[1] (£)	From the living (%)				From the dead (%)			
			Standard collections[2]	Events[3]	Pews	Total	Rents[4]	Funeral charges	Bequests	Total
Reading St Giles (1518–47)	17	12	20	15	1	36	52	3	2	57
Reading St Laurence (1500–47)	39	20	27	21	2	50	19	14	2	37
Salisbury St Thomas (1546–8)	20	17	37	18	2	57	0	35	2	37
Salisbury St Edmund (1470–1547)	27	12	45	12	3	60	0	10	16	26
Devizes St Mary (1530s)	9	9	?	?	?	40?	50	?	?	50?
Poole (1530s)	8	8	17	?	0	17?	50	5	2	57
Bridport (c.1442–67)	3	2	40	?	1	41	48		2	50
Wimborne Minster (1403–1547)	24	12								
1403–40			30	48	0	78	10	5	5	20
1500–47			10	40	0	50	30	10	5	40
Sherborne (1500–47)	21	9	7	65	7	79	10	1	5	16
Calne (1527–47)	12	7	?	85	0	85	5	2	1	8
Winterslow (1542–8)	4	2	0	55	0	55	5	0	?	5?

Note: There are several problems with compiling these figures. Proportions of funds raised could vary considerably from year to year and some accounts are unrepresentative. The shortfall in total percentages is partly made up of miscellaneous sales, fines, and occasionally large gifts; but it is also difficult sometimes to distinguish between gifts from the living and bequests from the dead. In Winterslow's case, about 40% of funds came from the annual selling of livestock which could have been acquired from bequest or gift.

[1] Excluding amounts carried over from previous years (which would include combined sums from 'living' and 'dead').
[2] Usually at Christmas and Easter.
[3] Hocktides, ales, and plays.
[4] Property (in Calne's case, acres of land; in Winterslow's, livestock).

pastoral care and to ensure a certain religious uniformity. Thirteenth-century legislation within the diocese, as elsewhere, had enshrined duties and obligations that lay people owed to the parish. Concern to protect clerical income had helped to ensure that the parish system remained static, even frozen. Bishops in the fifteenth century were involved in promoting cults uniformly throughout the diocese. Yet lay people were not rigidly held under any clerical diktat.

A good deal of pious corporate activity continued at a sub-parochial level, around local shrines and chapelries that formed alternative focuses of devotional allegiance. The parish framework in the Salisbury diocese did not always give full expression to these alternatives; yet to some extent it could accommodate them. Lay people could still pay for stipendiary priests and found chapels that did not require full parochial rights to meet changing needs.[69] During the parochial 'ice age' there was room for the occasional thaw. The problem of new settlements clamouring for parish churches was worse in some areas than in others, particularly in parishes with dispersed and thriving settlements in cloth regions or where former minster churches kept a tenacious hold on dependent chapels. In any case, in the period of depopulation after the Black Death there was more demand for combining old parishes than for creating new ones. The extent to which there was any lay pressure to defrost the parish structure can be exaggerated.

Moreover, the parish system in some ways encouraged lay activity in the parish. Thirteenth-century canon law, far from demoting the laity to a tithe-paying beast of burden, officially charged parishioners with duties towards their own pastoral welfare. Above all, these responsibilities, including the payment of tithe, were to be enforced by the laity themselves through the machinery of the visitation. And the criticisms of the clergy that lay people were encouraged to make at visitations were, thus, not so much the product of any lay anticlericalism as the result of a desire to uphold the standards demanded by the Church of the clerical office. Of course, more violent exchanges did take place between parishioners and clergy. But, in general, criticisms of priests show a laity keen to ensure that the priestly services were properly provided.

---

[69] Even by taking the arduous road to Rome: *Cal. Papal. Reg.* iv. 89, 368, 439; v. 243, 275, 277, 319, 495, 527; vi. 29, 51, 131, 247, 795; vii. 83, 441, 521; viii. 84, 522, 600, 675; ix. 461; xi. 92, 534; xii. 530; xiii. 384, 507, 693. The petitions that specifically mention a willingness to pay for priests at the petitioners' own expense are: iv. 421; v. 282, 486, 587; vi. 108, 487; vii. 504; viii. 392; xii. 784, 785.

The positive role that parishioners played in the communal life of the parish helps to explain why lay people were not in constant revolt against parochial obligations. But there are distinctions to be made between different types of parishes in different regions. The distinctions cannot be rigid ones; the invitation to distinguish between parishes on chalk and cheese areas, and between those in cloth-producing and more rural regions, should not be accepted too eagerly. Even within the same region, parishes could be densely concentrated in an urban area (like Devizes) or include large surrounding areas of sheep and corn country (like Calne). The popularity of local saints and cults could cut across regional divisions and parochial boundaries. Yet there are extremes worth distinguishing. At one end were the more urbanized parishes in Reading and Salisbury. With their denser concentration of people and wealth came a greater capacity to adapt to new cults, a richer diversity of ceremonies and processions, in other words, a greater intensity of pious activity. Yet at the same time there was more social fragmentation, more tithe evasion and church absenteeism, fewer regular and corporate fund-raising events, and less reliance on them to balance churchwardens' accounts. At the other extreme were parishes like Winterslow on Wiltshire chalkland, which had fewer ceremonies but more regular ales that apparently involved the whole parish. Within this spectrum, parishes could take on the features of both extremes. Varying degrees of conformity and corporate feeling among living parishioners were also encouraged, as we shall now see, by the requirements of the dead.

4

The Parish and the Dead

A BREVIARY once belonging to Denchworth parish contains a calendar, probably compiled shortly before 1456, which records saints' and feast days. In another hand the established feast day of St Frideswide was added; so too were the feast days of St Osmund, of the Name of Jesus, and of the Transfiguration of the Virgin Mary, all introduced in the later fifteenth century. In 1484, the day before the feast of St Edward, an eclipse of the sun was considered worthy of mention. Equally worthy were the deaths of important people within the parish, notably eleven members of the Hyde family. Names were noted down retrospectively, as far back as that of John Hyde, 'armiger', who had died on 13 July 1139; they continued to be added until 1557, with William Hyde's name. Some of the entries noted that a dirige and mass were to be said for the deceased.[1] The obligations that living parishioners owed the dead, indeed the whole range of services performed for souls in purgatory—burials, chantries, lights, and anniversaries—provide the theme of this chapter. How were these obligations accumulated and what impact did they have on parish life in areas ranging from populous, wealthy cloth towns to smaller villages in chalkland regions?

From the end of the twelfth century (as far back as surviving evidence takes us) certain changes in pious provision for the dead were taking place in the parish church. Endowments within parishes began to be given less to the church as a whole and more to objects within it, in particular to altar lights whose patron saints might intercede for the dead. In some of these early grants the endowment was to merge with the revenue that already sustained the church and its priest. In the mid-thirteenth century Arnold son of Sweyn confirmed a gift made by his father to the vicar of Westbury of two acres of land for the salvation of his soul, from which £1 was to be delivered to the altar of St Thomas on the saint's feast day.[2] But the setting up of funds for altar lights, separate from the church's endowments and fabric funds, was becoming common and even required by synodal de-

---

[1] Oxford Bodley Lat. MS Lit. b.14, fos. 157–162^v.

[2] WRO D1/1/4 p. 160 (fo. 75); for an example at the end of the 12th cent. see PRO C115/L1/6689, fos. 64^v–65.

cree.[3] A rent of two wax candles already belonged to the altar of St Michael at Melksham by the end of the twelfth century, and grants to specific lights multiplied in the thirteenth century. In the 1240s we begin to find grants to the altar and mass of the Virgin Mary in St Helen's church at Abingdon, entrusted to the parishioners 'or their proctors'.[4] Such gifts to altar lights are ubiquitous in the wills of the fourteenth and fifteenth centuries. By the fifteenth century, too, more people than before asked for burial within churches, and at particular altar lights, than outside in the cemetery.[5]

Anniversary services (or obits), long celebrated for benefactors of monastic houses, were also being celebrated in parish churches from the thirteenth century onwards. A very early example comes from Buckland church. In 1235 William the rector gave certain lands to his nephew Robert: from the profits Robert was to distribute bread to the needy on a convenient day of the week in the cemetery of Buckland church and provide a light to burn on Sundays and feast days before the altar of St John the Baptist and another before the statue of the Virgin Mary in the chancel. On William's anniversary a shilling was to be given to the parish priest to celebrate for his soul. If Robert died without an heir, some 'trustworthy man or two' was to be chosen by the parishioners to receive the rent and sustain the alms and anniversary.[6]

The most elaborate and exclusive form of late medieval post-obit celebration—the perpetual chantry—also surfaces in the parish churches of the region in the thirteenth century. Early endowments for masses to be said for the dead in parish churches, like gifts for altar lights, seem to have been given to the parish priest and the endowments that supported him. In the early thirteenth century (and here the intention to set up a separate priest for the perpetual celebration of mass is not yet explicit) one Philip Marmynne left a virgate and messuage to the church of Westbury for a light to be sustained before the altar of St Thomas 'where the divine

---

[3] *Councils and Synods*, i. 271, 310, 318, 407, 430, 520.

[4] D & C, Press IV, E3, Melksham/16; Abingdon Holy Cross hospital muniments, 10a, 11, 17, 21. Other examples are Melksham 1260–80 (*Bradenstoke Cart*. 485); Stoke 1220–2 (WRO D1/1/4, fos. 62ᵛ–63 (pp. 136–7)); Caversham 1240–70 (*Reading Carts*. ii. 913); Atworth in Bradford-on-Avon (BL Harl. MS 61, fo. 57); Southwick manor chapel in North Bradley (BL Lansdowne MS 442, fo. 36).

[5] In the region's wills 65% of testators between 1270 and 1399 asked for burial in the cemetery; in the 15th cent. 61% asked for burial within the church. Very few testators specified the place of burial within the church before 1399; 10% of testators between 1400 and 1449 and 25% of testators between 1450 and 1538 mention specific altars as their burial places.

[6] *Edington Cart*. 547.

offices of the dead were celebrated' and for a chaplain to celebrate mass at the same altar.[7] After 1250 endowments separate from the parish church's were being specifically set up for the perpetual celebration of mass. In 1270 Emily de Lacy, countess of Ulster and widow of Stephen Longspee, earl of Salisbury, endowed a new chapel in her court of Warminster with lands, rents, and certain fines from her tenants, worth £10 a year, which were to support altar lights and two priests to say masses for her soul in perpetuity. By the early fourteenth century large numbers of perpetual chantries were being founded (see Table 3 and Map 3).[8]

One of the consequences of these developments in post-obit gifts and endowments in the parish was the accumulation of souls to commemorate.[9] Later churchwardens' accounts sometimes showed a steady growth in the number of lands and rents from benefactors. In the earliest surviving account from Wimborne Minster parish (1403/4) £2, about 10 per cent of the total receipts, was collected from the rent of ten properties which had probably come from earlier benefactors.[10] Some time before 1437 one Nicholas Mantsiche gave at least one garden, a field, another tenement, and a house later renamed 'St. Mary's house', all of which brought the church an annual profit of around 7s. From 1437/8 until 1477/8 a few pennies were being spent by the parish for his obit. In 1444/5 William Stote had his anniversary celebrated with Nicholas's: from 1442 to 1444 fruit had been sold from his garden for the profit of the church and in 1444/5 the rental included 26s. 8d. from the new house that had belonged to William. In 1449/50 a John Herryng sealed an indenture with the parish, probably for a gift to the church fabric. By 1496/7 a few shillings were being spent on an annual mass for all dead benefactors, or

[7] WRO D1/1/4, fos. 63ᵛ–64; Wood-Legh, *Perpetual Chantries*, 1.

[8] Oxford, Magdalen College, Wanborough deeds, 23–76a. For other early examples of chantry masses founded in detached chapels see: Great Bedwynd 1258 (WRO D1/1/3, fos. 91–92); Canford 1284 (*Bradenstoke Cart.* 379); Abingdon 1288 (*Accounts of Obedientiars*, pp. xxxix–xl); Draycot, late 13th cent. (*Bradenstoke Cart.* 259). For chantry chapels founded in cemeteries see: Potterne *c.*1266 (WRO D1/1/3, fos. 85–86); St Edmund's, Salisbury 1365 (Reg. Bp. Wyvill, i, fos. 226ᵛ–227); Great Faringdon 1478 (PRO E301/51/44). William Chaucey founded a chapel in the cemetery of Charlton church in 1523 for a twenty-year chantry service (PCC 10 Bodefeld).

[9] For an early example of accumulation of services see Thorpe church between the two visitations made by St Paul's cathedral in 1251 and 1297: the 1251 visitation recorded eighty-three sheep and four other animals, maintaining five lights, in the hands of forty-five people; in 1292 there were seven lights maintained by 137 sheep and seventeen other animals hired out to seventy-four people (*Visitations of Churches 1249–52*, 23–6; *Visitations of Churches belonging to St Paul's Cathedral in 1297 and 1458*, ed. W. Sparrow-Simpson (Camden Society, new series, 55; 1895), 29–32).

[10] For the following see DRO, PE/WM CW 1/1–40, 41; and Table 2.

TABLE 3. Perpetual chantry foundations in Wiltshire, Berkshire, and Dorset

	1250–99	1300–49	1350–99	1400–49	1450–99	1500–45
Monastery	9	19	6	2	2	1
Cathedral	10	6	11	5	4	1
Hospital	1	3	1	0	1	0
College	2	2	1	0	0	1
Separate chapel	10	9	2	0	1	1
Parish	6	44	17	12	15	10
Institution	(27)	(42)	(22)	(8)	(7)	(4)
Benefice	(11)	(37)	(15)	(5)	(7)	(1)
Service	(0)	(0)	(1)	(6)	(11)	(9)
TOTAL	38	79	38	19	23	14

Sources: *CPR*, bishops' registers, wills, and other deeds.

'John Herryng and his friends'. Another tenement was given by John Bracy before 1537/8, from which his anniversary was funded. By 1542/3 the rental totalled over £6 a year from about twenty pieces of property and now accounted for over 20 per cent of the money raised for that year.

The rate of accumulation of endowments and souls, however, varied greatly from parish to parish. It might depend simply on need: the flurry of gifts to Wimborne Minster in the mid-fifteenth century was probably stirred up by the effort to rebuild the west tower.[11] It also depended on the wealth and size of the parish. In more rural parishes, like Winterslow and Wanborough on Wiltshire chalkland, endowments were fewer and came in the form of livestock, annually hired out, rather than in the form of property. Wimborne Minster had small endowments of property: it too was rural in its setting on poor Dorset heathland, but was larger, endowed with markets and fairs, and its accounts refer to 'wives of the country' and 'wives from the town'. Calne, though a borough and in the cloth regions, was rather more like rural Winterslow in that it included large areas of rural land, supporting sheep and corn husbandry, within its parish boundaries: only a few acres of land are shown on its church accounts. Parishes in small towns without extensive rural hinterlands, like Sherborne, or like Bridport and Poole (with populations of around 1,000 in the sixteenth century), accumulated more property. St Mary's parish in the busy cloth town of Devizes had amassed about twenty pieces of

[11] See Ch. 5 nn. 20, 21.

property by 1530. In Reading, one of the largest cloth towns in the region, the parishes of St Laurence and St Giles had by the sixteenth century accumulated property worth annually around £2 (from eleven tenants) and £8 (from forty-four) respectively (see Table 2).

It was not always the case, though, that wealthy cloth towns accumulated property rather than livestock. The church of St Edmund's in Salisbury had some altar lights funded from the renting out of sheep and its accounts (like St Thomas's in Salisbury) mention no property at all. But within these parishes, as we shall see, there were guilds with land which contributed to the parish church, and the city did not lack anniversary services. The procurator's accounts of St Thomas's from 1486 onwards show small oblations for obits celebrated every month during the year.[12] In the late fifteenth century the cloth towns of Marlborough and Windsor collected at least twenty obit endowments each from the mid-fifteenth century onwards.[13] Accounts may not show the full number of souls being commemorated, especially since not all endowments for obits were given to the parish. Indeed, in the larger parishes of St Giles and St Laurence in Reading only one general obit for benefactors is recorded in the accounts, though one might have expected many more to have been celebrated in these urban areas.[14] In general, the accumulation of souls and endowments was more likely in populous and more industrialized parishes in the diocese, particularly those profiting from the cloth industry, than in poorer or more rural areas on chalkland areas.

Yet, regardless of the type of parish, the accumulation of services for the dead was neither constant nor unchecked. Not all of them were or could be zealously maintained. Anniversary services for parish benefactors, as in Reading or Wimborne Minster, could be amalgamated into an annual and general service for the dead. Visitations suggest occasional laxity in maintaining other services for souls. At Hungerford in 1405 it was found that William Pyke had left seven marks for a chaplain to say mass for his soul for a year in the church and the residue of his goods to the church fabric, but his executors had refused to pay up. At Little Okeborne in 1412, Nicholas Perys was cited to appear before the visitational court because he had hired a church cow and, for the previous few

---

[12] D & C, Press II, Procurator's accounts.

[13] Marlborough: WRO G22/1/236; PRO E301/59/104. Windsor (1453–1537): Oxford Bodley Ashmole MS 1126, fos. 18–34, 66ᵛ–67; R. R. Tighe and J. E. Davis, *Annals of Windsor* (London, 1858), 125–43.

[14] BRO D/P 97/5/1; D/P 96/5/1. St Mary's Devizes was celebrating two obits in the early 16th cent., one founded by Richard Gobbett in the late 14th cent. and the other by Sir Thomas Newman and Robert Paynter some time later (WRO 189/1).

years, had refused to account for its natural increase which should have been distributed for Thomas Perys' soul on Good Friday. In thirteen of the 140 parishes visited by the bishop in 1394 certain rents owed to the fabric of the church had not been paid, and in seven parishes there had been delays in payments of rents owed to particular altar lights. Eight of the forty or so parishes and large chapels visited by Dean Chandler in 1405 presented defaulters on church rents; eight places had problems in payments for altar lights.[15]

Perpetual chantries were also vulnerable. The declining value of land and profits from rents and perhaps, too, the rise in priests' wages after the Black Death, put paid to a number of chantry endowments. Sometimes sufficient funds could not be found to support a projected chantry.[16] By the time the chantry commissioners made their surveys in 1545 and 1548 (if the returns can be trusted), most of the chantries founded in the thirteenth and fourteenth centuries had disappeared (see Map 3).[17] Bishop Waltham's visitation of 1394 had noted that the new chapel built for the chantry of John Sandehus in an aisle of Gillingham church was partly in ruins.[18] Perpetual chantries had a worse chance of foundation and survival in some parishes than in others. Very few were founded in the poorer chalk and heathland areas of Dorset after the Black Death (the status and courtly connections of Wimborne Minster making this parish an exception). But in areas where the cloth industry began to flourish, chantries continued to be founded. In Salisbury three perpetual chantries were founded before 1350; from then on five were set up in the city parishes. Whereas in the early fourteenth century it had been the local gentry who were most active in founding chantries, in the fifteenth century chantry founders were, more often than not, men like James Terumber of Trowbridge or Thomas Horton of Bradford-on-Avon—merchants who aspired to gentry status by buying up rural estates, but whose wealth was firmly rooted in the cloth trade (see Map 3).

Yet in all areas parishioners could make considerable efforts to keep services for the dead going. Reported cases of failures to provide rents for lights and obits were not numerous, and the visitations made by sub-

---

[15] Reg. Bp. Waltham, fos. 38ᵛ–56; *Reg. Dean Chandler*, 86, 365, and *passim*.

[16] See examples at West Corscombe in 1384 (*NQSD* 14 (1914–15), 191); Heytesbury in 1415 (*Cal. Papal Reg.* 490–1); Aldworth (*CPR* (1350–4), 51; *VCH: Berks.* iv. 7–8); Wantage (*CPR* (1350–4), 108, (1358–61), 44).

[17] See Ch. 10 n. 74. Miles Stapleton's chantry, founded in 1299, survived until 1544, but its endowments were worth only 66s. 8d. a year and no longer supported the daily celebration of mass (*CPR* (1292–1301), 401; PRO E301/51/37).

[18] Reg. Bp. Waltham, fo. 78.

MAP 3. Perpetual chantries founded in parishes

sequent deans (in 1463, 1480, 1483, and 1485/6) reveal only two cases where rents to altar lights were being withheld.[19] Those that were reported at least demonstrate that parishioners could be keen to protect the interests of the dead by presenting offenders who threatened intercessory services. Founders of perpetual chantries might hope that subsequent family members would augment their services' endowments: Christopher Tropenell in 1503 (and his wife Anne in 1517) left small gifts of livestock for his father's chantry in Corsham church.[20] Chantries could also attract bequests from people who were not members of the founding family. The later history of Emily de Lacy's chantry chapel at Warminster saw it collect endowments and souls to commemorate those of the Holland, Hungerford, and Lovel families.[21] In Salisbury efforts were made to sustain the two chantry priests celebrating for the soul of Reginald de Tudworth in the church of St Edmund, the first known perpetual chantry set up in the city in 1318. In 1464 the mayor William Winton conceded one toft in the city to the chantry priests. The churchwardens of St Edmund's occasionally gave small sums to the chantry in the early sixteenth century. The chantry certificates of 1545 show that later chantries founded in the city were helping to keep Tudworth's chantry going: both William Warwick's chantry and William Swayne's contributed rents (16s. and 12s. 12d. respectively) from their tenements.[22] Later generations could sometimes consider it worth while to maintain the services of dead benefactors.

From the thirteenth century onwards, then, parishes (some more than others) received a growing number of specific benefactions such that services for souls in purgatory were accumulated. But the significance of these changes is better appreciated when the difference that these gifts, endowments, and services made to parish life is considered. For none of the services was a private ceremony. The funeral was an activity that involved many. Every parish had a funeral hearse, a wooden framework supported by a bier, over which a pall was draped to shroud the corpse; prickets on the hearse allowed lighted tapers to burn during exequies and mass to remind the living of the deceased. A procession might attend the

[19] D & C, Reg. J. Newton, pp. 145–77; MS 189, fos. 41–94.

[20] PCC 6 Holgrave; 36 Holder.

[21] Oxford, Magdalen College, Wanborough deeds, 3–76a. For contributions to a chantry in Mere see wills of Eleanor Hungerford 1455 and Sir John Stourton 1494 (on condition that the priest sang an obit for his wife Catherine) (PCC 3 Stockton; 23 Doggett).

[22] *CPR* (1317–21), 76; WRO G23/1/215, fo. 6; *S. Edmund Accounts*, 53, 257; and, for 1547/8, WRO 1901/108; PRO E301/58/11.

carrying of a dead person from home to church.[23] In its most lavish form, the late medieval funeral had become a splendid affair. When Sir John Norrys requested burial in the church of Bray in his will of 1463, he asked for 1,000 masses and other observances to be said for his soul in the thirty days after his death; 30*d.* was to be distributed to the poor every day during that time and, 'in encresyng of more devocion and prayours in this behalf to the honour of all myghty god and p[ro]fite of my soule', all the church bells were to be rung for twenty-four hours after his death and at sunrise and sunset for an hour each during the following thirty days.[24] Funeral feasts of the gentry sometimes fed the parish: Sir Henry Esturmey's in 1381, with £7. 7*s.* 7*d.* being spent on sugar, cinnamon, ginger, almonds, cloves, and other spices, would have pleased the more discerning of palates. A rather healthy number of animals had also been slaughtered for the occasion, since a further £27. 3*s.* 8*d.* went on pork, capon, beef, lamb, mutton, mallard, and pigeon.[25] In the busier cloth towns, with their clusters of wealthy merchants, elaborate funerals must have been more frequent. The growing wealth of the cloth trade in Salisbury may even have increased the available expenditure on funeral services, from an average of £2 per testator in the fourteenth century to £3 in the first half of the fifteenth century.[26] The knells rung, the processions carried out, the doles distributed, and the feasts consumed meant that the presence of the dead (particularly in wealthy towns where numbers were greater) made a noticeable if not noisy addition to parish life.

Similarly, only the deaf and the blind could have ignored the anniversary services of benefactors. In essence, the obit involved the repetition of the burial service, placebo in the evening, dirige and requiem mass on the following day, with lights lit round the hearse. But in its most lavish form, particularly among the gentry or the wealthier groups in larger towns, the component observances of the obit advertised, as publicly as possible, the soul's need for intercession—far more than William the rector's anniversary in Buckland had done in the thirteenth century. Bell-ringers or bedemen would announce the imminence of the service and the maximum number of intercessors were sought: priests, poor people, parishioners, churchwardens, and, in borough towns, the civic officials. In 1526 Robert Nuttyng of Marlborough left the reversion of one tenement and two

[23] D. Rock, *The Church of our Fathers*, ed. G. W. Hart and W. H. Frere (London, 1903), ii. 404–5.
[24] PCC 19 Godyn.   [25] WRO 1300/36.
[26] Not that these figures come from large samples: the 14th-cent. figures come from nine wills, those of the first half of the 15th cent. from twenty-three.

cottages to the churchwardens of Sts Peter and Paul's church. Every year the wardens were to spend 13*s*. 4*d*. on five priests, oblations at mass, four tapers, the clerk, the sexton, reading out his name from the parish bede roll (list of benefactors), singing children, farthing bread, and poor people. On the day of the obit itself the parson, the mayor, and the two churchwardens were to offer a penny at the church. The churchwardens were to account to the parson and mayor on the day that the parish accounts were drawn up: any surplus was to be paid into the common coffer until, Robert hopefully added, enough money had accrued to purchase more land for the anniversary or to 'find a priest'.[27] Like the funeral, the anniversary service, especially the more elaborate kind (and particularly in the busier towns), could add to the liturgical life of the parish.[28]

So too did lamps lit at parish altars. They served to keep the memory of their benefactors alive in the minds of living parishioners, not least when they were lit to synchronize with the divine offices of the parish. The sacrament or sepulchre lamp, lit at Eastertide, was often an object of bequest and endowment. In more rural areas livestock was the preferred form of endowment. In 1489 William Thatcham of Warminster gave twenty sheep to sustain the sacrament light and stipulated that all communicants in the church were to say the prayer 'salvatione angelicam' for his soul every Easter.[29] In the rural chapelry of Seend, dependent on Melksham church but containing some wealthy clothiers, a document was compiled shortly after 1500 listing the 'stocks' or endowments (of money, apparently, though some were of sheep or cows) left by thirty-one benefactors.[30] Seven had given lamps to various altars to be lit every holiday at mass. Two others had left endowments for lights to be lit during the offices of the day. But it was the Easter mass that attracted most foundations of lights. Roger Hern had at some time given a cow to maintain the Paschal to be prayed for on Easter day. Moreover, sixteen out of the thirty-one benefactors had anniversary services for their souls. These were not on the scale of Robert Nuttyng's in Marlborough: a few pennies were given to the priest (for dirige and mass), and a smaller sum for bells to be rung and perhaps an altar light to be lit. The dates of the obits were spaced out throughout the year, from the Friday before Epiphany to St Andrew's

[27] PCC 25 Porche; WRO G22/1/236.
[28] C. Burgess, 'A Service for the Dead: The Form and Function of the Anniversary in Late Medieval Bristol', *Transactions of the Bristol and Gloucestershire Archaeological Society*, 105 (1987), 167–91.
[29] WRO 865/64.
[30] For the following see 'The Stoks of Seen' Church', *Wilts. Notes & Queries*, 2 (1898), 528–32.

day (30 November). But there was a marked preference for anniversaries near Easter, four of the obit founders so choosing: the most important festival of the parish calendar was surrounded and liturgically enriched by these other services.

Chantries, of course, provided additional celebrations of mass, the most efficacious of all good works. Even if founded for only a few years, masses for the dead could still add to the offices daily celebrated in the parish church.[31] Special readings and services enhanced the liturgical richness of parish worship, especially if chantry founders demanded different masses to be celebrated for every day of the week. Some of these provided opportunities for the celebration of newer votive feasts. From the early sixteenth century, among several gentry testators (in Berkshire parishes particularly) it was fashionable to ask for temporary chantry priests to celebrate the Mass of the Five Wounds.[32] The perpetual chantry, furthermore, also sought the involvement of the parishioners as a whole, though perhaps not with the clamour of the anniversary service. The daily mass of the chantry priest, after all, was usually celebrated in the quiet of the early morning so as not to disrupt the daily offices of the parish. But James Terumber's chantry in Trowbridge, founded in 1483, was to 'exhort' the people present to say a Pater Noster and an Ave Maria devoutly for the souls of the founder and benefactors.[33] The 'private' mass was intended to involve a wider audience.

Changes in types of chantry foundation also meant that chantry founders tended to rely more heavily on parishioners and their officials. Some of the very early chantries, like Emily de Lacy's at Warminster, formed separate chapels away from the parish church. Fewer examples can be found by the fourteenth century, as more perpetual chantries were founded within parish churches. In 1322 John Alwyne endowed a separate chantry chapel at All Saints Knighton in the parish of Broad Chalke, yet he stressed that after his death the endowment was to be used instead to support a priest to celebrate for his soul within the parish church itself.[34] Moreover, chantries of the thirteenth and fourteenth centuries tended to

[31] C. Burgess, '"For the Increase of Divine Service": Chantries in the Parish in Late Medieval Bristol', *JEH* 36 (1985), 46–65.

[32] From Wilts.: Christopher Tropenell 1503 (PCC 6 Holgrave). From Berks.: Sir Thomas Kyngeston 1505 at Chelrey (3 Adeane); Sir Thomas Englefield 1514 at Englefield (33 Fetiplace); Sir William Fetiplace 1528 at Chievely (6 Jankyn); Elizabeth Willis 1528 at Windsor (Oxford Bodley Ashmole MS 1126, fos. 29ᵛ–30); William Goneld of Cholsey 1530 (PCC 1 Thower); Anne Danvers 1539 (PCC 1 Alenger).

[33] W. H. Jones, 'Terumber's Chantry at Trowbridge', *WAM* 10 (1867), 247–52.

[34] *CPR* (1321–4), 123; see above n. 8 for other examples of free-standing chantry chapels.

be founded in one of two ways. Either the endowments were given to religious houses or secular priests to provide a priest to serve at the parish altar (here the property would merge with the other possessions of the house or rectory), or they were founded as separate benefices that supported priests supervised by the bishop or his officials. Both types required the payment of fines under the provisions of the Statute of Mortmain (1279) because they involved the alienation of land to the 'dead hand' of the church. But a third way, and one increasingly used, avoided the penalties. It involved giving the possession of the endowment to a group of trustees or feoffees and the use of its profits to maintain the chantry priest.[35] These 'service' chantries in the fifteenth century tended to make more obvious use of parishioners and parish officials. James Terumber's chantry at Trowbridge (1483) enfeoffed thirty-six people with the chantry endowment and stipulated that they, with the advice of the churchwardens, were to elect the chantry priest. He also named over forty people whose souls were to benefit from the masses said by his chantry priest.[36] Benefice-type chantries were still founded in the fifteenth century, perhaps because of the legal security they provided; in Salisbury citizens made use of perpetual institutions like the college of St Edmund's and the cathedral. But even these chantries might request the supervision of parish officers. William Swayne acquired a licence to found a benefice chantry, to which the cathedral dean and chapter presented the priest, in St Thomas's church, in 1469. Yet his will of 1484 makes clear that the churchwardens were to check chantry ornaments and vestments when the benefice became vacant.[37]

So services for the dead made an appreciable difference to the liturgical life of the parish, especially in the more densely populated areas and in busier cloth regions, where more were founded. They also benefited parishes in very material ways. Churchwardens could make small profits for the parish funds from funeral services. Burial inside the church, knells for the dead, and hirings of ornaments and vestments could be charged for. This was less common in a chalkland parish like Winterslow and in other small towns. At Wimborne Minster charges for burial inside the church are not mentioned until 1429/30 when they were priced at 3s. 4d.; by 1475/6 the price was 6s. 8d. and in the 1530s additional charges seem to have crept in for hiring crosses and candlesticks at funerals.[38] In larger places like Salisbury or Reading the sheer weight of bodies made

[35] Woodlegh, *Perpetual Chantries*, 8–16.   [36] Jones, 'Terumber's Chantry', 247–52.
[37] *CPR* (1467–77), 90–1; PCC 20 Logge.   [38] DRO, PE/WM CW 1/1–40, 41.

charges more frequent. At St Laurence's in Reading, it was agreed in
1515/16 that anyone who wanted the great bell rung 'at the knyll' at any
burial or anniversary was to be charged 12*d*., and those who wanted it just
'tylled' were to pay 6*d*.; but minds and obits kept for Henry Kelsall were
not to be charged for, presumably because it was he who had paid for the
great bell under the terms of his will in 1493.[39]

Lights that burned around the body at funerals could also contribute to
the lights required for the celebration of the parish offices. The residue of
forty pounds of wax burning about the body of Robert de Wodeford
(1360) was to remain with the provost of St Edmund's college in Salisbury,
as part of Robert's payment for 'forgotten tithes'. The wax would have
contributed to the vicar's (in this case the provost's) obligation to provide
wax for the chancel for the parish mass. Katherine Southend in 1377
requested that, after her burial, the four torches which four poor people
were to carry at her funeral in the church of St Nicholas in Atrio, Wilton,
were to burn in four of the other town churches 'at the raising of the
Host'.[40] Other parishes maintained special lights for the hearse that would
cover the bier of the dead person, to which testators left bequests.[41]
Wanborough church had a stock of sheep and cows managed by separate
wardens for the hearse light.[42]

Bequests to altar lights also contributed to parish fabric funds. Surpluses from the seven altar lights at Wanborough in the 1530s were
handed over by their stewards to the common funds of the parish. In a
large urban church like St Edmund's in Salisbury, some of the altars were
maintained by fraternities, but others were the responsibility of the
churchwardens or other 'stewards', and their accounts were declared at
the annual parochial audit. The twenty sheep that John Ludlow had given
to the light of St Sebastian were hired out by the churchwardens to one
Master Chasye for 6*s*. some time in the 1530s. Gifts of a few shillings were
sometimes made by the stewards of the altar lights of St James, St
Katherine, St Christopher, the Trinity, and of the daughters.[43]

In a similar fashion, anniversary services could also benefit parish life.
The accounts of Wimborne Minster showed that only a fraction of the
profits from obit endowments was actually spent on the service itself,

[39] BRO, D/P 97/5/2, p. 108; PCC 1 Vox. The churchwardens of St Edmund's could
expect 12*d*. (20*d*. after 1494) for the ringing of knells or 'fourthfares' (*S. Edmund Accounts*,
passim).

[40] WRO G23/1/212, fos. 37ʳ–38; Winchester college deeds, 19431.

[41] In 1502 William Borden gave a cow to the church of Staunton 'that the byre might find
a taper upon my hearse forevermore' (PCC 18 Blamyr).

[42] WRO 894/1.   [43] *S. Edmund Accounts*, 367, 72, 61, 366, 14, 27, 369, 42, 363, 47.

especially since by the end of the fifteenth century only one general obit service for benefactors was held annually. The endowments for anniversaries at Seend chapel were small, the lowest 'stock' was worth 7*s.* and the highest only 20*s.* But expenditure on the services never came to more than a shilling. The small outlay required suggests that the surplus from endowments enriched the chapelry's fabric funds. Some of the more lavish provisions for obits made explicit the intention to benefit the parish. Sir John Mompesson left sets of vestments in 1500 to six parish churches in Wiltshire to celebrate his obit; each parish was to have a 'drynkyng of bread, ale and cheese', and the remaining money was to be left to the parish 'as most nede[d]'.[44]

In slightly different ways, chantries were also intended to benefit the parish materially. Founders of temporary chantry could provide vestments and ornaments for their stipendiary priests which, after the completion of the service, could be handed over to the parish.[45] Occasionally, the funds paying for stipendiary priests could also be of more general profit. John Vaughan's priest in Westbury church was required in 1534 to assist 'the divine service of almighty god' in the chancel on holy days for three years, whereupon the 'surplus' of the goods maintaining the service was to be left to the church 'for the use and divine service of God'.[46]

Priests of perpetual chantries could also make valuable contributions to parish life. Their liturgical goods tended not to be used by the parish as those belonging to temporary chantries were (James Terumber's priest was expressly forbidden to use them in 1483). Yet chantry priests can be found contributing to education, musical instruction, and even preaching. They may not always have been applauded for their quality: Sir Edmund Leversedge, as his vision had warned, found the three chantry priests of Frome hopelessly ill-equipped to instruct him. Yet, noticeably in market or larger cloth towns, their contribution was recognized. William Yorke's chantry priest at Ramsbury was called upon to teach the poor students who flocked to the town.[47] Many parishes emphasized to the chantry commissioners in 1545 and 1548 how their chantry priests busied themselves 'in teachyng of children' (Enford), 'in bringinge uppe young children in learninge' (Westport in Malmesbury), in teaching children 'to synge for the maintenance of Divine service' (Bradford-on-Avon), and in

[44] PCC 15 Blamyr.

[45] John Gryce of Malmesbury in 1480 requested that, once his chantry service of three years was completed, the chalice and vestments that he had instructed his wife to buy for the chantry be given over to the use of the parish church (PCC 41 Milles).

[46] PCC 22 Hogen.   [47] PRO E135/17/26.

educating children at schools (Lambourne, Sonning, and at Wimborne Minster 'in the manner used at Eton and Winchester'). At Devizes the inhabitants claimed that the chantry priest of John Cardmaker 'occupies himself in the prechyng of God's word'.[48]

In any case, chantry priests were required by canon law to assist the parish priest at matins and vespers and they were also called upon to lend a helping hand. In large parishes their services were invaluable. When William Westbury, servant of the king, founded a chantry on the north side of Westbury church where he had just built a new chapel in 1437, the justification offered was that there were 1,000 people in the parish who came to the Eucharist at Easter and that, in the absence of the vicar, there were no other chaplains in the church to chant the service on feast and festival days or to administer the sacraments and sacramentals.[49] In 1545 the parishes of Salisbury, Devizes, Malmesbury, Warminster, Chippenham, Corsham, Calne, Bradford-on-Avon, Trowbridge, and Marlborough in Wiltshire, those of Reading, Bray, and Windsor in Berkshire, and of Wimborne Minster in Dorset all contained over 500 people, some well over: they all assured the chantry commissioners that their chantry priests performed an essential role in administering the sacraments at Easter.[50]

In some parishes, particularly sizeable ones dominated by former minster churches, some chantry priests may have helped to serve in outlying chapels. The priests of three chantries in Mere church may have officiated in the dependent chapels of Deverel, Zeals, and Chadenwhych: all of them went rapidly into disuse when the chantries were dissolved in 1548.[51] The ability of the secular canons of Wimborne Minster to serve the four smaller chapels in their parish, by the sixteenth century, was enhanced by large endowments from three chantries. Some chapels that served small communities may have been kept going as chantries with fresh endowments that were to finance a chantry priest (John de Early's at Erleigh St Nicholas, for instance)[52]—increasing divine service where it was needed and thereby helping to ease some of the tensions that arose because of the frozen nature of the parish structure.

In two main ways, then, services for the dead benefited the living: in the provision of ornaments and extra priests and, financially, with the charges

[48] PRO E301/59/26, 59/54, 58/43, 51/40, 3/15; E. Fry, 'Dorset Chantries', *NQSD* 31 (1910), 113 (for Wimborne Minster and Netherbury); PRO E301/59/25.

[49] *CPR* (1436–41), 137, 254.   [50] PRO E301/58, 51, 3.

[51] C. J. Godfrey, 'The Chantries of Mere and their Priests', *WAM* 55 (1953), 153–60.

[52] For references see above n. 8 and Ch. 3 n. 5. For other examples see Hill Deverill (*Reg. Bp. Martival*, ii. 242); St Mary Longcot in Shrivenham (*VCH: Berks.* iv. 541).

or surpluses that could come from gifts and endowments. But let us sharpen the focus on the variations between different types of parishes (see Table 2). At one extreme there was Winterslow, a rural and chalkland village, with endowments of livestock, very few charges for burials, and dependent more on ales for its finances. At the other was a cloth town like Reading near the busy river Thames, with not a few chantry and obit foundations, where its parishes of St Giles and St Laurence relied more heavily on frequent charges on burials, knells, and propertied endowments than they did on their ales and plays. Winterslow relied on the efforts of the living, the Reading parishes rather more on the accumulated gifts of the dead.[53]

Clear distinctions between rural and urban areas, as already indicated, are impossible to make. Parishes in market towns like Wimborne Minster (with its own fulling mills), or even borough towns like Calne, could encompass wide areas of countryside. In the cloth town of Salisbury, St Thomas's and St Edmund's did not rely on property left by the dead like parishes in Reading (although they gleaned much from charges for burial and related services). Even within the same town, as at Reading and Salisbury, there were differences in the amount of property parishes accumulated. But it would not be stretching a point to distinguish between the experience of parishioners within the larger towns, supported by the cloth trade, and that of parishioners in smaller villages, particularly those in chalkland areas. In the former more than the latter there was a greater number of services for souls in purgatory and a greater reliance for finances on endowments left by the dead.

The general picture, then, is of parishes steadily accumulating endowments for the dead and souls to commemorate. The accumulation seems to have developed apace during the thirteenth century: the emphasis on the need for penance for the soul in purgatory encouraged gifts, increasingly specific gifts, to altars and images of saints who could intercede for the dead and before which masses could be said for the soul. Benefactions in parish churches may not have been made entirely at the expense of gifts to monastic orders: it was in the same period, as we saw, that more specific gifts also came the way of religious houses.[54] But the concern of synodal

[53] The stimulating article by C. Burgess and B. Kumin, 'Penitential Bequests and Parish Regimes in Late Medieval England', *JEH* 44 (1993), 610–30, appeared after this was written. For an exception to the pattern they suggest, see the two main parishes of Salisbury which, although within a significant urban centre, did not accumulate any rents of property from the dead. For other difficulties see Table 2 note.

[54] See Ch. 1 n. 41.

and conciliar decrees to make the parish the primary focus of pastoral care, exhorting parishioners to set up separate funds for church fabric and altars, must have helped direct penitential gifts to local parish churches. Perhaps, too, the restrictions placed on founding new churches prompted greater attention to existing parish churches, explaining why very few chantries, for instance, were founded as separate chantry chapels after the end of the thirteenth century.

The accumulation and elaboration of penitential gifts made the presence of the dead all the more significant in parish life. It may well have been another stimulus for the development of the office of churchwarden. In many places there was probably less to do for the dead in the thirteenth century than there was later. William the rector's anniversary foundation at Buckland church in 1235 referred vaguely to the need for 'a trustworthy man or two' to sustain the service.[55] In the fifteenth century churchwardens everywhere were found as trustees of obit endowments, as overseers of endowments not directly given to parish officers, keeping a watchful eye on the performance of an obit and all its component observances, or being rewarded for attendance at the exequies. The annual parish calendar could be crowded with obit celebrations even in a small dependent chapel like Seend. Churchwardens also maintained lights at altars and even chantries of the service type which were more frequently founded in the fifteenth century. A heavy burden of duty came to lie on the shoulders of churchwardens.

The services for the dead also contributed significantly to the corporate life of the parish. Endowments for obits and altar lights fed the common coffers of the parish; chantry priests helped out with pastoral care; services for the dead added colour and depth to the parish liturgy. Living parishioners were continually reminded of the presence of the dead by the bells rung, processions carried out, masses said, and altar lights lit. The dead were remembered in towns by the properties they left, and in more rural areas, where they left livestock as penitential endowments,[56] their memories were perhaps recalled in a more tangible and living sense.

---

[55] *Edington Cart.* 547.

[56] The cow that Robert Martyn left to the parish of Durrington in 1509 to sustain the lamp before the sacrament was to be 'set from man to man so that the cow never dies' (PCC 26 Bennett). The chantry commissioners in Berks. recorded 147 kine, 223 sheep, two mares, and several oxen as endowments supporting post-obit services (PRO E301/3); in Dorset the figures were ninety-two kine, 773 sheep, and thirteen cows (E301/16). The Wilts. commissioners did not record these kinds of endowments, though John Chapman's chantry set up in Maiden Bradley was to be funded from an endowment of 600 sheep (E301/59/27; PCC 10 Bodefeld).

Special days were set aside for the commemoration of parish benefactors:
Sts Simon and Jude at Reading St Giles', Palm Sunday at St Laurence's.
Benefactors continued to serve and play a part in parish life long after they
were dead, drawn into the communal worship of the living.

This accumulation of services was not continual, nor was it ubiquitous.
Obits for several benefactors could be amalgamated to reduce the burden
of celebrations. Not all obits or chantries were maintained by later parishioners; benefactors died a second death as their endowments, which
kept their memory alive, were eaten away and forgotten. Even so, parishioners could make considerable efforts to keep services going, presenting
offenders who failed to pay rents for altar lights and obits at visitations or
by topping up chantry endowments. Failure to continue services was more
likely to happen in more sparsely populated regions, in more rural areas,
often those lying on chalkland soils, where the declining profitability of
land was more keenly felt and the desertion of settlements more frequent.
In areas where the economy was buoyed up by the wealth of the cloth
trade, chantries were more likely to survive and even increase in number
after the Black Death. It was in the larger cloth towns, too, that the impact
of the dead was felt more heavily, where there were more funerals and
more lavish obit services, and where parish revenues relied more heavily
on rents left and services required by the dead. When services for the dead
were finally abolished in 1547, some places, more than others (as we shall
see again in Chapter 10, on the Reformation), were required to sweep
away a great deal of what chantry commissioners called 'purgatory
trasshe'.[57]

[57] As the chantry commissioners in Berks. termed it in 1548 (PRO E301/3).

5

Parish Church-Building

WHEN Dives boasted to Pauper that 'God is in non land so wel servyd in Holy Churche . . . than in this lond', he pointed with pride to the 'many fayre chirchys' that adorned the English landscape.[1] One of the finest in the diocese is St Thomas's in Salisbury; much of the present building belongs to a burst of activity that began soon after May 1448 when the chancel collapsed.[2] On 26 May an elected group of twelve parishioners petitioned the cathedral dean and chapter, rectors of the church since 1399, to rebuild the chancel and the chapels on either side. On 3 June the dean and chapter agreed to rebuild it along the same length and breadth and no further. But the parishioners envisaged something grander, undertaking to build a clerestory above the aisles on the north side of the chancel to match the south side, and determining that the repair of new and old work in the chancel, including the making of the high altar, was to belong to the parishioners and their successors for ever.

How many parishioners contributed to the rebuilding is not known, but the munificence of a select group of benefactors was visibly recorded in the resulting work. William Ludlow, lord of Hill Deverell and 'boteler to iii kynges of England', was buried in the church, 'under a marble tomb at the end of the Hye Auter on the North side thereof; the ile of the whiche the seid William Ludlow hath late new siled and paynted, and sette with scochyn of armes of hymself, his wyf and his children'. The involvement of certain cloth merchants was heavier. Their marks can still be found on tombs, windows, and pillars. The main builder of the south chapel, in which he founded a perpetual chantry, was the cloth merchant William Swayne. The chapel was also used by the tailors' guild, to which William was an important benefactor. His mark was to be seen in the east window of that chapel, and inscriptions of the chapel's roof beams still beseech prayers for the souls of William, his wife Christine, and his father Henry.[3]

---

[1] *Dives and Pauper*, ed. P. H. Barnum (Early English Text Society, 275; London, 1976), i. 188.

[2] For what follows see D & C, Reg. Burgh, fo. 2.

[3] *Tropenell Cart.* i. 36, 274; C. Haskins, 'The Church of St. Thomas of Canterbury, Salisbury', *WAM* 36 (1909), 9; *VCH: Wilts.* vi. 147. *Ancient and Historical Monuments in the City of Salisbury*, i (Royal Commission on Historical Monuments, London, 1980), 30, lists

Church-building unites two themes that were present in Chapters 3
and 4: the efforts of living parishioners and the communal commemoration of the dead. The vast number of churches that were rebuilt or
remodelled in the later Middle Ages are today still the most visible expression of pre-Reformation religion, and provide evidence on which the eyes
of modern historians could focus a little more often. Some 476 churches
in the diocese will be used in this survey. Of course, visual evidence (some
of it now found only through the descriptions of antiquarians) can be
limited; tables showing dates of church-building might almost invite a
derisory curl of an archaeologist's lip. But they may help to test some of
the generalizations made concerning the relative importance of church-
building during the later Middle Ages. The thirteenth century has been
described as 'the time of church building', but so has the fifteenth.[4] R. B.
Dobson suggests with more precision that the last quarter of the fifteenth
century saw a decline in the rate of church-building, pointing out that the
fabric of the four largest parish churches in England—Boston, York,
Coventry, and Hull—were virtually complete by 1450. Yet J. R. Lander
speaks of the decades preceding the Reformation, from 1460 onwards, as
'the great age of church building'.[5] Regional differences may well account
for variety in interpretation,[6] and some account must be taken of local
patronage and economic conditions (bearing in mind Postan's warning
that lavish Perpendicular churches may have little to do with economic
prosperity[7]). So we shall look first at when churches (and parts of them)
were built, who built them, and why.

A broad survey of building activity in the diocese reveals three main
trends. Its sheer scale is striking. Only twenty-four churches in the diocese
(out of 476) remained basically unchanged since the twelfth century and a
further seventy-five from the thirteenth. About 12 per cent were enlarged

one merchant mark as unknown, but it could be John Noyle's. See T. H. Baker, 'Notes on
Some Wiltshire Merchant Marks', *WAM* 36 (1909), 326. For William Swayne see Intro.
n. 77; Ch. 6 n. 68; Ch. 7 n. 38 and Table 10.

  [4] Moorman, *Church Life*, 68; A. H. Thompson, *The English Clergy and their Organisation
in the Later Middle Ages* (London, 1947), 130.
  [5] R. B. Dobson, 'Urban Decline in Late Medieval England', *TRHS*, fifth series, 27
(1977), 9; J. R. Lander, *Government and Community: England 1450–1509* (London, 1980),
148.
  [6] A. K. Wickham, *The Churches of Somerset* (London, 1952), 34; W. G. Hoskins, *The Age
of Plunder: King Henry's England 1500–47* (London, 1976), 26–7, 158–61; G. Williams, *The
Welsh Church from Conquest to Reformation* (Cardiff, 1962), 428 ff.
  [7] M. M. Postan, *Essays on Medieval Agriculture and General Problems of the Medieval
Economy* (Cambridge, 1973), 44–6.

TABLE 4. Changes in church buildings, 1100–1540 (% of 476 churches in Dorset, Berkshire, and Wiltshire)

	12th cent.	13th cent.	14th cent.	15th cent.	1500–40
Building completely unchanged	1	5	4		
Building unchanged apart from windows and towers	4	11	12		
Building enlarged or had aisles built on		12	14	15	5
Building almost completely rebuilt		12	12	23	3
Chancels rebuilt			11	12	
Chapels built on to churches		7	7	15	4
Towers added, heightened, or rebuilt		13	13	44	6

in the twelfth century and a similar percentage of churches were enlarged in each of the following three centuries. More churches seem to have undergone major or complete rebuilding in the thirteenth and fourteenth centuries, and an even larger proportion (23 per cent) thereafter (though perhaps more in the early and mid-fifteenth century than in the decades before the Reformation). But the difference is not marked and may be exaggerated by rebuildings that obscured earlier work. Certainly, in terms of the enlargement of churches, there is little difference from the thirteenth to the sixteenth century (see Table 4).[8]

The work on the fabric of St Thomas's church in Salisbury in the mid-fifteenth century, for instance, was only one episode in a much longer saga of parish church-building in the city.[9] The oldest church, St Martin's, may have been built in the eleventh century; in the thirteenth century the west end of the nave was rebuilt and the south aisle added. The two new parish churches that were founded in the thirteenth century, St Thomas's and St Edmund's, were both cruciform, though St Thomas's had a south chapel, probably dedicated to St Stephen. In the fourteenth century a west tower was added to St Martin's, and a chapel was built on to the north side of the chancel of St Thomas's, probably when Robert

[8] The survey relies on the efforts of Pevsner *et al.*, the Royal Historical Monument Society, 19th-cent. church-crawlers in local society publications, and painters like J. Buckler; the works of antiquarians, Aubrey, Ashmole, and Hutchins; and the present author's observation.
[9] For what follows see *Monuments in Salisbury*, 24, 31–7; *VCH: Wilts.* vi. 144–51; Haskins, 'Church of St Thomas', 1–12.

Godmanstone, mayor in 1380, founded his chantry. In the early fifteenth century a flurry of bequests testifies to the addition of new aisles and chapels to all three churches: at St Edmund's John Barbour requested burial in the new north Lady chapel in 1403 to which he left 40s.[10] Later that century, St Edmund's tower was reconstructed (three bequests for that purpose were recorded by the churchwardens in 1473/4) and in 1497/8 £30. 11s. 10d. was gathered for new windows and other works.[11] At St Thomas's, after the rebuilding of the chancel and chapels in the mid-fifteenth century, the whole body of the nave was remodelled, and in the late fifteenth and early sixteenth century it was heightened with a clerestory and given a richly carved roof and west window. In the same period the south aisle of St Martin's was rebuilt and its north aisle raised; another chapel dedicated to Corpus Christi was added at the west end of the nave in the early sixteenth century. The principal works on all three churches was probably done in the early fifteenth century, but all were added to and embellished throughout the late medieval period. The amount Salisbury testators contributed to the fabric (a rather poor indicator of the total amounts contributed) seems to have been fairly constant from the late thirteenth century onwards, though it increased slightly after 1400, as the following list shows.

	Sum bequeathed (s.)	No. of testators
1270–1349	7	15
1350–1400	7	65
1401–49	15	129
1450–99	17	53
1500–47	14	68

A second feature of late medieval church-building is also suggested by the Salisbury churches: the piecemeal rebuilding of parts of the church. Earlier churches appear to have been built or remodelled as one piece: the naves and chancels of Anglo-Saxon churches like Alton Barnes and St Laurence's at Bradford-on-Avon, or even twelfth-century churches (Knook, Chicklade, Berwick St James, Pertwood, and Highway), seem to have been built at the same time. A great many chancels were rebuilt in the thirteenth century and apsidal extensions were made at the east end. But

---

[10] PCC 6 Marche. See also bequests of Thomas Boyton in 1400 to the 'new fabric' on the south side of St Thomas's (WRO G23/1/213, fos. 30ᵛ–31ᵛ); William Mercer to the 'newly built fabric' in 1407 (ibid., fo. 72); George Meriot in 1410 (ibid., fos. 89ᵛ–91ᵛ); and William Watier in 1417 for the hanging of the bells (WRO G23/1/214, fos. 32ᵛ–33).

[11] *S. Edmund Accounts*, 14, 19, 47.

after about 1350 the chancel remained the least rebuilt part of the church. Moreover, from the late twelfth century onwards we find piecemeal additions to the main body of the church—upwards in the form of clerestories, towers, and pinnacled roofs and outwards with chapels, aisles, and porches (see Table 4).[12]

Thirdly, it is also apparent that church-building was more likely (though not exclusively) to occur in some areas than in others. Not all areas prospered like Salisbury and some churches decayed in this period. At Wilton, not far from Salisbury, one of its churches, St Nicholas in Atrio, was described in 1366 as 'exilis et diruta', and in 1435 it had to be combined with St Nicholas Kingsbury. In 1425 St Nicholas's in West Street was in a ruinous condition, and St Michael's was in decay in the sixteenth century.[13] As we saw, other towns with multiple churches saw parishes disappear; in many areas, particularly the chalklands of the diocese, settlements and churches were abandoned.[14] Moreover, large rebuilding programmes tended to occur particularly in the cloth-producing regions of Wiltshire. The many churches rebuilt in Dorset during the later Middle Ages tended not to be on such a grand scale as in other places in the diocese, and many in the eastern part of the county were not rebuilt at all; they were probably among those 'from Salisbury Plaines inclusively to Middlesex and Surrey . . . [and] . . . all over Hampshire' that John Aubrey chose to describe as 'very mean and despicable'.[15]

Who was responsible for this rebuilding? Before the twelfth century the Church hierarchy had relied heavily on the local lord to found churches which were then regarded as the lord's own property.[16] It had been part of the Gregorian reform movement to wrest the local church and its spiritual endowments from the grip of manorial lords, many of whom gave up parish tithes to religious houses. Even so, local lords continued to impose their stamp on the rebuilding of churches in the countryside. Vestiges of a proprietorial attitude over the local church naturally lingered on, par-

---

[12] For churches cited see *VCH: Wilts*. x. 12; vii. 24; Pevsner, *Wilts*. 282; *VCH: Wilts*. ix. 19; viii. 60; vi. 198. It is rare to find a chancel built at a later date than the nave; but see e.g. Blackland church's 12th-cent. nave, 13th-cent. chancel, and 14th-cent. east window (C. E. Ponting, 'Notes on Churches', *WAM* 24 (1889), 154–6).

[13] *VCH: Wilts*. vi. 29–30; R. Colt-Hoare, *A Modern History of Wiltshire, Branch and Dole* (London, 1832), iv.71.

[14] R. K. Morris, *The Church in British Archaeology* (Council for British Archaeology, Research Report 47; 1983), 86.

[15] Oxford Bodley Aubrey MS 2, fo. 76; see Map 4.

[16] R. Lennard, *Rural England 1086–1135: A Study of Society and Agrarian Conditions* (Oxford, 1959), 290–7.

ticularly where gentry families retained rights of patronage and advowson. The brasses and tombs of the Giffard family, lords of the manor of Boyton, on south Wiltshire chalkland, in the thirteenth and fourteenth centuries, are to be found in the local church: they were probably responsible for the rebuilding of the south chapel and the remodelling of the church executed at the same period in the fourteenth century.[17] Thomas Tropenell of Great Chalfield and Neston (on Wiltshire clay vale), described in 1453 by an enemy in litigation as 'a perilous covetous man', was patron of the churches of Great Chalfield and Corsham. He built the south chapel, decorated with his heraldic arms around 1480, and possibly the chancel of the former, and rebuilt the north chapel of the latter in which he founded a chantry. The Tropenells also became patrons of Great Cheverell church in 1476: the nave of the church was rebuilt in ashlar, with square headed windows, very soon after.[18]

A great many other churches are dominated by the presence of local gentry families, their status proclaimed by brasses, tombs, and armorial bearings—even if these are pushed to the peripheries of churches in chapels and side aisles. The south aisle of Fyfield church (in the Berkshire vale of the White Horse) is dominated by the double effigy, with the hideous cadaver, of Sir John Golafre who died in 1440. Some churches take on the aspect of family mausoleums. Looming large in the church at Aldworth are the effigies of eight members of the Beche family who died in the first half of the fourteenth century. The Englefield family had enjoyed a long tradition of burial at Englefield church when, around 1514, Sir Thomas Englefield was laid to rest in a new chapel on the north side of the chancel.[19] The Estbury family was responsible for additions to Lambourne church. St Mary's chapel south of the chancel may have been the original chantry chapel of John de Estbury who died in 1372; a later Sir John re-endowed the chantry and is commemorated in the chapel as the 'fundator cantarie'. A new chapel dedicated to the Holy Trinity, squeezed in between the angle of St Mary's chapel and the longer south transept, was the work of Sir John Estbury 'armiger', so the inscription on

[17] J. W. Powell, 'A Sketch of the History of Hill Deverell', *WAM* 27 (1894), 245–60; Pevsner, *Wilts.* 126–7. See also the influences of the Russell family in chapels and aisles at Tytherton Kellaways (ibid. 140; *Wiltshire: The Topographical Collections of John Aubrey*, ed. J. E. Jackson (Devizes, 1862), 61); the Bigod family at Box church ('Notes on Places Visited by the Society in 1895', *WAM* 28 (1896), 329–30; Pevsner, *Wilts.* 123–4).

[18] *Tropenell Cart.* i, pp. ii, xii, 269; *VCH: Wilts.* vii. 64; Pevsner, *Wilts.* 257–8; *VCH: Wilts.*, pp. x, 51. The influence of the Hungerfords can be found in at least thirteen Wilts. churches between the 14th and 16th cent.; for six of them see M. A. Hicks, 'Chantries, Obits and Almshouses', 125–6.

[19] *VCH: Berks.* iii. 347; iv. 7–8; iii. 409–12; E. Ashmole, *The Antiquities of Berkshire* (London, 1719), i. 10, 16.

his brass claims, who died in 1502 and was 'fundator istius nove capelle et cantarie'.[20]

Whatever the private concerns of gentry families, building projects of a more communal nature could attract the attention of local lords. When the parishioners of Wimborne Minster began to rebuild their church tower in the mid-fifteenth century, they solicited gentry help. In 1448 they came to an agreement with Sir John Beynton, lord of the manor of Hampreston in the parish, to allow them to draw 200 loads of stone from any part of the common heath of the manor.[21] Judging from the churchwardens' accounts of 1448/9, they also spent not a little effort buttering up Sir John Herryng, lord of the manor of Clenston and of the moiety of the manor of Whitchurch which lay some miles from the parish (and whose initials are on the font of the neighbouring parish of Winterborne Whitchurch). Two pence was paid to Robert Peniston and Nicholas Bere (churchwarden in 1448/9) for riding out to see John Herryng; a total of 17*d*. was given to John's servant William for showing John where the tower was to be built. Two 'pasteys', a cake, and 7*d*. worth of malmsey wine were consumed by John Herryng at the parish's expense; and, as is mentioned straight after the account, an indenture was drawn up in St Mary's chapel in which a suitably relaxed John Herryng presumably agreed to make a gift to the tower. What he gave is not known, but his name crops up in later accounts as among the benefactors for whom an obit was celebrated.[22]

Yet, by the fifteenth century, the local gentry were not always the principal contributors to church-building. In towns besides Salisbury, cloth merchants left their mark on local churches. St Mary's in Devizes was radically altered before the mid-fifteenth century. A stray account dated 1436 records significant contributions of lead, probably for the new roof, made by important individuals, two from the Coventre family and one (44 lb) from William Smyth. The latter also gave two tenements of land in Southbroom for the maintenance of three sepulchre tapers and a font taper for his obit. On the roof of the nave an inscription still reads that William Smyth died on 1 June 1436 and 'ista eccl[es]iam fieri fecit'.[23]

[20] *VCH: Berks.* iv. 260–3; E. Ashmole, *The Antiquities of Berkshire* (London, 1719), ii. 238–41; Reg. Bp. Erghum, fos. 204–205ᵛ.

[21] Hutchins, *Dorset*, iii. 206. Sir John also gave 3*s*. 4*d*. in 1459 (DRO PE/WM CW 1/29).

[22] DRO PE/WM CW 1/26; see Ch. 4 n. 10. There was also a legacy from an 'extranei militi' of 20*s*. in 1445/6; the dean of the college gave 20*s*. in 1459, and work was still being done in 1464 when the churchwardens came to an agreement to collect stones for building (Hutchins, *Dorset*, iii. 206).

[23] *VCH: Wilts.* x. 291; *Wilts. Notes & Queries*, 7 (1917), 196–7. The origins of William Smith's wealth are not known, but he is thought to have been a clothier (*VCH: Wilts.* x. 253).

Journeying through Wiltshire around 1540, Leland was to see a 'very fayre churche havynge been bylded in the mynd of men now lyvinge' in Steeple Ashton, a thriving town that 'standith muche by clothiars'. In the late fifteenth century the church was indeed rebuilt completely in an elaborate Perpendicular style. An inscription records that the work was done between 1480 and 1500. Four benefactors are picked out: 'The North Isle was rebuilt at the cost and charge of Robert Long and Edith his wife. The South Isle for the most part was built at the cost and charge of Walter Leucas and Matilda his wife.' Both men were clothiers, and their help with the building programme continued after their deaths.[24] In his will of 1501 Robert Long, besides leaving a chalice, a printed paper mass book, and two chasubles to the parish, ordered that the works begun on the north side of the church be completed at his expense. Long's widow made an agreement with Thomas Lovell of Trowbridge, freemason, to do the work for £80. Walter Lucas, in his will dated 1495, left a missal, a pair of vestments, and a chalice for the altar of John the Baptist which probably lay in the aisle that he had built.[25] Another Walter Lucas left money in 1514 to buy organs from the church. He also left money to Keevil church, dependent on Steeple Ashton, and which too was remodelled in the early sixteenth century.[26]

Examples of clothiers channelling wealth into church-building are legion: Thomas Horton of Bradford-on-Avon,[27] and the John Winchecombe of Newbury immortalized in a poem in the early sixteenth century,[28] are among the many cases. Sometimes, of course, it is difficult to distinguish between merchant and gentleman. At Trowbridge, both groups contributed to the rebuilding of St James's in the mid-fifteenth century. The 1483 chantry deed of James Terumber, 'the very rich clothier', refers to the church as 'newly built' and lists its benefactors, mer-

---

[24] *Itinerary of Leland*, i. 134; v. 82–3; *VCH: Wilts.* viii. 211–15; Pevsner, *Wilts.* 480–2; *VCH: Wilts.* iv. 143–4.

[25] PCC 4 Blamyr: PRO C1/367/38; PCC 25 Vox. In 1507 Robert Morgan willed that 'suche werkes as be began by Robert Longe in the North Ile . . . be p[er]fourmed' (PCC 6 Bennett); as late as 1524 John Button, a gentleman who requested burial in the church of the Grey Friars in London, left £21 for the making of the church steeple (PCC 20 Bodefeld; *VCH: Wilts.* viii. 213–14).

[26] PCC 21 Fetiplace; Pevsner, *Wilts.* 277.

[27] Thomas Horton founded his chantry in Bradford-on-Avon church *c*.1530 (*Itinerary of Leland*, i. 135; *VCH: Wilts.* vii. 26–7). For Horton's activities in buying demesne land see Hare, 'Lords and Tenants', 217–20. For Horton's contributions to Westwood church see *Itinerary of Leland*, i. 133; *VCH: Wilts.* vii. 26–7; PCC 20 Jankyn; *VCH: Wilts.* xi. 232–4; Pevsner, *Wilts.* 568.

[28] He died around 1520, having helped build the Newbury church west of the pulpit to the tower (*VCH: Berks.* iv. 138, 148–51; see Intro. n. 45).

chants and gentlemen, who 'should be comprised in a table hanging in the high altar of Jhesu exhorting the people present devoutly say *Pater Noster* and *Ave Maria*'.[29] Yet parish building projects by no means relied exclusively on the gifts of gentry and merchants. Other respectable individuals made their contributions, like the lawyer once commemorated in the windows of Broad Chalke church, rebuilt in the early fifteenth century, and the smith or carpenter whose soul was remembered in the sacrament window of Crudwell church.[30]

But there were also more collective forms of munificence, from guilds (as we shall investigate in Chapter 6) and other groups within the parish. The inscription in Steeple Ashton church acknowledging the gifts of two clothiers also states that 'the rest of the work with the steeple was built at the cost and charge of the parishioners'. William Smith and others may have contributed lead to the roof of St Mary's in Devizes in 1436, but much more was given (400 lb) by unnamed parishioners. Occasionally, the collective efforts can be seen in more detail. The parishioners of Wimborne Minster may have needed the support of local gentlemen in 1448 to rebuild their tower, but they had themselves made strenuous efforts to raise enough money throughout the 1440s. The church ales, which had usually raised some £4 or £5, were celebrated with added vigour, and in 1443 the ale raised as much as £9. Careful husbandry and abstemious spending of revenues during that decade ensured that a surplus of £40 had been collected by 1448.[31] Similarly, the rebuilding of the nave and tower of Wanborough shortly before had involved the parish. A brass in the chapel at the east end of the south aisle commemorates the soul of Thomas Polton (who held half a knight's fee in the parish in 1404) and his benefaction of fourteen 'nummos' (pennies) to the church. On the north wall of the tower another inscription can be read: 'Pray for Thomas Polton and Edith his wife deceased, for Master Philip Archdeacon of Gloucester, Agnes and fourteen other of their sons and daughters, for Sir Robert Everard vicar, and all his parishioners who began this tower anno domini 1435.'[32] The building projects of some parishes also marshalled the resources of outlying villages and chapelries. In 1405 Dean Chandler noted in his visitation that twelve people from Bedwyn, Crofton, West and East Grafton, Witton, Wexcombe, and Merton had been appointed by the

[29] *VCH: Wilts.* iv. 32; vii. 153; Jones, 'Terumber's Chantry', 247–52.
[30] *Topographical Collections*, 218, 214–15; G. McN. Rushforth, 'The Sacrament Window in Crudwell Church', *WAM* 45 (1930), 68–72.
[31] DRO PE/WM CW 1.
[32] E. Kite, *The Monumental Brasses of Wiltshire* (London, 1860), 28; *VCH: Wilts.* ix. 182–3.

parishioners of Bedwyn to collect money from these townships and chapelries for the bells of the parish church.[33]

Larger town parishes could also gather their parishioners in times of need. In the parish of St Laurence's in Reading, eighty-six people made contributions to the tune of £5. 16s. 9d. to the works in progress during 1440. Work on the bell tower in 1458 seems to have been paid by a similar number of contributors. When £41 was spent on major works undertaken by the parish in 1519/20, £21. 2s. 1d. was given by 'diverse persons' every Sunday from New Year's day until the Sunday after Michaelmas.[34] Even on works of a smaller scale, considerable activity might be needed. The great bell of St Edmund's in Salisbury was recast in 1474/5 at the cost of £13. 10s. 9d. Gifts made by eight people totalled 38s. 5d.; £4. 19s. 6d. was raised by three 'scoteales' held during the course of the year; a further £2. 4s. 10d. was collected by 'diverse of the parish at diverse tymes'. The money for new windows put in during 1497/8 was raised at Hocktide by the wives of the parish and by gifts from ten individuals; when organs were bought in 1517/18, £5. 0s. 9d. was raised by a special 'gatherynge'.[35]

It would be wise not to overstate the efforts made by the 'whole parish community'. Even in the apparently most collective of building programmes, particularly those in densely populated parishes, only a small proportion of the parishioners may have contributed. The list of eighty-six named contributors to St Laurence's church in 1440 is impressive, but the parish was a large one and, in 1545 at any rate, comprised 1,000 communicants.[36] Moreover, collective efforts sometimes had a competitive edge about them, groups within the parish—wives (from 'town' and 'country' in Wimborne Minster's case), maidens, servants, bachelors, or guilds—striving to outdo each other in fund-raising efforts. Larger town parishes may have found it more difficult to organize regular communal fund-raising efforts. Finally, visitation frequently mentioned dilapidation in church fabrics: parishioners were more reluctant perhaps to contribute to the humdrum upkeep of churches than towards new and glamorous building projects.[37]

---

[33] *Reg. Dean Chandler*, 64.   [34] BRO D/P 97/5/1; 97/5/2, p. 123.
[35] *S. Edmund Accounts*, 19, 47, 59.

[36] PRO 301/51/23. Keene's suggestion (not infrequently seized upon) that pious giving may have increased in 15th-cent. Winchester, because church-building was continued in a period of economic recession, should be taken in the context of his footnote that contributions for the church fabric could have come from just a few wealthy individuals (D. Keene, *A Survey of Medieval Winchester* (2 vols.; Oxford, 1985), i. 126–7).

[37] In Dean Chandler's visitation of 1405 only about a third of the churches and chapels visited were in good order (though things had improved by 1412) (*Reg. Dean Chandler*, p. xxvi).

From how much and by whom, we turn to why so much church-building was undertaken. Both economic and demographic changes no doubt had their effect. The addition of aisles and the widening of naves in the thirteenth century can be partly explained by a growing population and an expanding economy, particularly in the wool trade (although room inside the church provided for much more than congregational space). The worsening conditions of the early fourteenth century and the catastrophic decline in population in the wake of the Black Death was offset, in some places, by wealth generated by the rise of the cloth industry. Parishes in Salisbury, Reading, Devizes, Marlborough, and Trowbridge, with their merchants, tailors, weavers, and dyers, were beneficiaries: some of their wealth was channelled into the fabric of their parish churches. So it is not surprising to find that churches that lay in cloth-producing regions were more likely to be rebuilt, and on a more elaborate scale, than those that lay outside. A high proportion of those that remained unaltered were in more depopulated areas, particularly in the eastern parts of Dorset, near Hampshire, on poor heathland soils, and to some extent on chalkland areas (see Map 4). At least seven of the unaltered churches in Wiltshire and Dorset were described as poor parishes in 1428.[38] The dilapidation of churches in Wilton was one result of economic competition from neighbouring Salisbury.[39] It is difficult, then, to agree entirely with Postan's statement that the architectural evidence of churches 'has nothing to do with the growth and decline of English industry, agriculture and trade'.[40]

Nevertheless, church-building cannot always be neatly correlated with wealth. The cloth-producing areas did not have a monopoly on rebuilt churches. Six of the churches in areas classed as poor parishes in 1428 underwent alterations in the fifteenth century: Figheldean was one of the lowest-rated fiscal areas in Wiltshire in 1377, yet the nave and south aisle of its parish church were entirely rebuilt in the fifteenth century.[41] The townsmen of Lyme Regis complained bitterly about their sufferings, the encroachment of the sea, and the depradations of French pirates in the late fourteenth and early fifteenth centuries, yet were quite capable of extensively rebuilding their church.[42] Even in declining Wilton the churches of St Mary and St Nicholas Kingsbury were apparently rebuilt in the mid-fifteenth century. Gentry patronage, which was not restricted

---

[38] *Feudal Aids 1284–1431: Inquisitions and Assessments* (repr. London, 1973), ii. 82–100; v. 280–98; see Alton Barnes, Chicklade, Pertwood, Ashley, Blacklands, Chisbury, Shorncote.
[39] *VCH: Wilts.* vi. 12–15.   [40] Postan, *Medieval Agriculture*, 46.
[41] *VCH: Wilts.* iv. 314; see also Alton Priors, Ansty, Huish, Rollestone, Edmondsham.
[42] Hutchins, *Dorset*, ii. 44–5.

Chalk regions

Clay regions

Cloth regions

▲   Churches rebuilt in 15th century
+   Churches not rebuilt since 14th century
×   Churches not rebuilt since 12th and 13th
      centuries

0   5   10   15   20 miles

MAP 4. Church-building

Parish Church-Building

to any particular region, explains why certain churches on chalkland and clay vale were rebuilt.

Wealth, moreover, only partly explains why parish churches were rebuilt and altered throughout the later Middle Ages. Once again, the attention devoted to the parish by diocesan statutes in the thirteenth century encouraged a more general lay commitment to the local church. Ecclesiastical attention to the parish also helped to inculcate the sense that parish building was a suitable repository of penitential good works.[43] Thirteenth-century penitentiaries made it clear that a gift to the building of churches was one form of penance.[44] The granting of indulgences, remissions of penance, for parish church-building further encouraged these penitential good works. Already in the late twelfth century, an inscription over the south doorway of St Katherine's chapel at Milton Abbas promised 120 days' indulgence, presumably for those who visited and offered at the chapel. More and more indulgences came to be granted to parish churches. In the thirteenth century archbishops and bishops had granted indulgences to those who contributed to the building of Salisbury cathedral. By the fifteenth century indulgences were being given for the building of parish churches in the diocese.[45] The rebuilding of St Nicholas Kingsbury in declining Wilton must have been encouraged by a licence granted by Bishop Aiscough of Salisbury which included an indulgence of forty days for all those who contributed according to their means.[46] A papal indulgence appears to have been granted to St Edmund's in Salisbury. In 1475/6 1s. was paid out by the churchwardens for the making of six bills (with copies in English) concerning an indulgence granted for all those contributing to the fabric at the Annunciation and at Michaelmas; 4d. was given as a reward for distributing bills and 6d. to a child to 'keep the pardon' at the Annunciation.[47] Donations to the fabric were encouraged by offering and trumpeting the consequent spiritual reward.

[43] See Ch. 3. For earlier examples of more collective church-building see F. M. Stenton, *Documents Illustrative of the Social and Economic History of Danelaw* (London, 1920), p. lxxvii (no. 465); R. L. Lennard, 'Two Peasant Contributions to Church Endowment', *EHR* 67 (1952), 230–3).

[44] J. T. McNeill and H. M. Gamer, *Medieval Handbooks of Penance* (New York, 1938, repr. 1963), 354.

[45] St Katherine's chapel was 300 yards from the monastic church at Milton Abbas (*An Inventory of the Historical Monuments: The County of Dorset* (Royal Commission on Historical Monuments, Edinburgh, 1970), iii. pt. 2, 190–1; Wordsworth, 'Wiltshire Pardons', 22–23).

[46] Colt-Hoare, *Branch and Dole*, 71.   [47] *S. Edmund Accounts*, 361–2.

Various parts of a church, however, could be built at different times and church-building in the later Middle Ages often took the form, as we saw, of piecemeal additions, upwards and outwards, to the church fabric. Thirteenth-century canon law had also formally laid down that, while the chancel was the responsibility of the vicar or rector, the laity of the parish were responsible for the upkeep of the nave.[48] Ecclesiastical patronage accounts for some impressive examples, at Bishops Canning and at Potterne in the thirteenth century, of large chancel extensions with a general rebuilding of the nave to match.[49] But the active involvement of lay parishioners in church-building can partly explain why, after 1350, the nave was more likely to be added to or rebuilt (even kept in a better state of repair) than the chancel. But the distinction between responsibilities for the nave and chancel should not be over-emphasized. The brass in Wanborough tower commemorates the gifts of the vicar and the archdeacon; there were two chaplains who contributed to the new windows placed inside St Edmund's in Salisbury. The clergy did not necessarily consider that their responsibility to the church rested with the chancel alone. Nor did the laity always consider that their duties were solely with the nave. Lay patrons of churches, after all, had a right to be buried in the chancel and some of them, like Thomas Tropenell of Great Chalfield, contributed to their rebuilding. But other parishioners could show concern: the initiative in 1448 for rebuilding the east end of St Thomas's in Salisbury came from the parishioners; the parishioners of St Laurence's in Reading made extensive collections for the chancel windows in the 1520s and 1530s.[50]

Differences in the relative rates of chancel and nave rebuilding, in any case, reflect less on clerical slackness or lay zeal than on liturgical and devotional concerns. The intense rebuilding of parish chancels in the thirteenth century mirrors, in miniature, the work carried out on cathedrals in the same period. The east end of cathedrals saw a growth of shrines and altars, stimulated by a belief in the value of the mass and miracles performed by saints.[51] So too we find chancels of parish churches lengthened and embellished: if such rebuilding slackened after

---

[48] See Ch. 3 n. 1.   [49] See Intro. n. 15.

[50] BRO D/P 97/5/2, pp. 128–215; Cheney, *From Becket to Langton*, 157. It does not appear, however, that lay patrons were more conscientious rebuilders of chancels in the 15th cent. than clerical rectors.

[51] C. R. Cheney, 'Church Building in the Middle Ages', in *Medieval Texts and Studies* (Oxford, 1973), 349–50; C. N. L. Brooke, 'Religious Sentiment and Church Design: The Later Middle Ages', in *Medieval Church and Society: Collected Essays* (London, 1971), 162–82.

1350, it was perhaps because the liturgical needs of a parish had been satisfied.

Liturgy and devotion were also behind the piecemeal additions, outwards and upwards, to the nave. More space may sometimes have been needed simply to accommodate more people, and some of the larger town churches, like St Thomas's Salisbury, were perhaps made roomier to allow large congregations to listen to preachers. But the addition of chapels and aisles often had less to do with the pastoral needs of the living than the liturgical needs of the dead. Altar space at which prayers could be made to saints, and at which masses other than the parochial one could be celebrated, was no doubt encouraged by the endowment of altar lights from the later twelfth century onwards.[52] Some aisles housed relics of saints' bones, particularly on the north side of churches. The north transept of Whitchurch Canonicorum once contained the shrine of St Whyte, whose thirteenth-century reliquary chest was rediscovered in the nineteenth century. The pilgrims who journeyed to the bones of St Ciriac at Sonning found them in a chapel to the north of the chancel.[53]

Some of these altars were established and taken over by fraternities and guilds. But the need for altars was required by individuals as much as by fraternities and parishes as a whole. Many of the additional aisles were clearly intended to house the tombs of gentry and to create new altars for chantry services, perpetual and temporary. One member of the Beche family at Aldworth attempted to found a chantry in the church in 1351; Sir John Golafre endowed a chantry priest who was to serve close to his cadaver effigy at Fyfield in 1440.[54] It is possible that fewer people, knights and gentlemen, were being buried in religious houses in the fifteenth century compared to the twelfth or thirteenth centuries. In the fourteenth century fewer chantries were being founded in monasteries, and more in parish churches, than earlier. Certainly, by the fifteenth century many more of the important parishioners asked for burial inside the parish church, at particular altars, rather than in the cemetery. More altar and burial space, perhaps, was being required.

Moreover, new funereal chapels and chantry aisles were not built in isolation from the rest of the church. Their building could inspire a general rebuilding of other parts of the church. It is no coincidence that

---

[52] See Ch. 4 n. 3.

[53] *An Inventory of the Historical Monuments: The County of Dorset: East Dorset* (Royal Commission on Historical Monuments, London, 1985), v. 78–85; *VCH: Berks.* iii. 219–20; see also J. Blair, 'Saint Beornwald of Bampton', *Oxoniensia*, 49 (1984), 47–55.

[54] *CPR* (1350–4), 51; (1441–6), 53.

the church of Aldworth, littered with the tombs of the Beche family, was almost entirely rebuilt in the fourteenth century. The church of East Shefford was rebuilt in the fifteenth century, helped by Sir John Fetiplace who left £40 in his will of 1460 to repair the church, build new pillars, and erect a timber steeple. But his bequest was bound up with his desire to commemorate the souls of his ancestors: part of the money was to be used to make a closure around the tomb of his father and mother who were buried in the church.[55] Some chantry altars doubled as Easter sepulchres around which much communal ceremony was conducted from Good Friday to Easter day.[56] Once more we find individual chantries contributing to corporate devotional life.

Chantry foundations could also stimulate more extensive rebuilding. At Mere around 1325 a north chapel was built for the chantry of John de Mere, then steward of the manor belonging to the king. Some time after 1350 a south chapel was added in which an inscription mentioning the tomb and chantry of John Bettesthorne is to be found. Soon after, the church was enlarged and the south aisle widened in line with the nave; the exterior of the church is mostly in the Decorated style.[57] In smaller villages a wealthy cloth merchant could dominate the rebuilding of a local church like a manorial lord. Seend chapel was almost entirely rebuilt at the end of the fifteenth century. The brass of John Stokes, clothier, chantry and obit founder, who died in 1498, lies in the north aisle. Indeed, he requested in his will that he be buried in 'my newly built and constructed chapel'. A tradition had it that the Stokes family were the main contributors to the church's rebuilding: a great many painted glasses 'with pictures of some of Stokys children' were to be seen in John Aubrey's day.[58]

The additions outwards of the nave to some extent affected rebuilding upwards. The erection of chantry chapels, with their screens of stone or wood, tended to restrict the passage of light to the central body of the nave. Nave walls raised above the level of aisles and chapels were built with clerestories to allow in more light.[59] More light, too, was let in through the

[55] *VCH: Berks.* ii. 347; iv. 236; PCC 5 Godyn. See also the example of Peter de la Mare's foundation of a chantry in 1349 in a north aisle of Market Lavington church, the chancel and nave of which were rebuilt shortly afterwards (*VCH: Wilts.* x. 103; *CPR* (1343–5), 25, 215).
[56] H. Munro-Cautley, *Suffolk Churches and their Treasures*, fifth edn. (Woodbridge, 1982), 152.
[57] C. E. Ponting, 'The Parish Church of S. Michael, Mere', *WAM* 29 (1896), 20–70; Godfrey, 'Chantries of Mere', 153–60.
[58] *VCH: Wilts.* viii. 106; Pevsner, *Wilts.* 465; *Topographical Collections*, 304; *Wilts. Notes & Queries*, 5 (1906), 196, 349; Kite, *Monumental Brasses*, 38–9.
[59] R. K. Morris, *Churches in the Landscape* (London, 1989), 296–8.

larger windows of Perpendicular churches. It also helped to illuminate other devotional features that were becoming common by the fifteenth century. Clerestories trained sunlight on rood screens above the chancel arch. Older and smaller buildings—for example the Anglo-Saxon church of Bradford-on-Avon, with its low roof and scarcely partitioned-off chancel and nave—may often have lacked this object of veneration with its intercessory group of Christ, the Virgin Mary, and St John. But devotion to the Blessed Sacrament had encouraged the heightening of screens in cathedrals in the thirteenth century, increasing the sense of mystery surrounding the celebration of mass.[60] Chancel screens became increasingly common in parish churches; endowments and bequests were left for the rood light; churchwardens made special collections for the rood at Christmas. In some of the larger town churches the rood loft could accommodate an organ or singers to enrich the liturgical service.[61]

Above the chancel arch and rood screen, doom paintings, depicting the Last Judgement, heaven on the north side, and hell on the south, reminded parishioners of the respective fates of the penitent and the wicked. Early examples can be found from the thirteenth century, and by the fifteenth century surviving examples, like St Thomas's Salisbury, are ever more elaborate and detailed.[62] Extra light no doubt allowed detail to be picked out. Perhaps, too, more light was needed to allow literate parishioners—of which there was a growing number in the fifteenth century, like Robert Long and Walter Lucas at Steeple Ashton—to follow the service in their private mass books. It may also have permitted memorial inscriptions to be read with greater facility. But much glass would have been painted or coloured with images redolent with liturgical meaning and intended for instruction, like the sacrament window at Crudwell, rather than to permit more light for reading.[63]

Upwards, all over the diocese, towers sprouted. Some may have been built by a gentry anxious to demonstrate their lordship over the local area: Sir Thomas Trenchard had his initials stamped on the tower built in the early sixteenth century at Charminster.[64] But as the examples of

[60] Brooke, *Medieval Church*, 162–82.

[61] See Munro-Cautley, *Suffolk Churches*, 138; A. Vallance, *English Church Screens* (London, 1936), esp. 65–85; C. R. Burgess, 'Chantries in Fifteenth-Century Bristol', D.Phil. thesis (Oxford, 1982), 171–82.

[62] Hollaender, 'Doom Painting', 351–70.

[63] The light provided by some of the 15th-cent. windows of St Edmund's church was not sufficient by 1629 to allow the parishioners to read their books; new clear glass had to be installed (*S. Edmund Accounts*, 190).

[64] Pevsner, *Dorset*, 142–3; C. Carpenter, 'The Religion of the Gentry of Fifteenth-Century England', in D. Williams (ed.), *England in the Fifteenth Century: Proceedings of the 1986 Harlaxton Symposium* (Bury St Edmunds, 1987), 66.

Wimborne Minster and Wanborough show, such work could be undertaken by the parish as a whole. Some parishes, like Cranbourne in 1440,
even acquired indulgences to assist tower rebuilding.[65] One purpose may
have been to raise an older tower in line with new heightening of the nave
and clerestories. But another important purpose was intimately linked
with the needs of parishioners both living and dead. When Sir Roger
Caper, esquire, left a bequest of 40*s.* for the building of the tower at
Minety church in 1517 he made clear that it was 'for the bells of the
church':[66] bells summoned parishioners to mass, funerals, and anniversaries. Some towers were fitted with apertures in their east walls for a
sanctus bell to be fitted (some parishes like Wanborough even had special
towers for the purpose): it was rung during mass at ter sanctus at the
elevation of the host and chalice so that it could be heard by townsmen and
villagers unable to attend the service. By the later fifteenth century bells
were becoming larger and more sonorous, and bell towers were required
to cope with the stress of more sophisticated frames which allowed bells to
be rotated through 180 degrees.[67] The rebuilding of St Laurence's tower
in Reading in the later fifteenth century was no doubt better equipped to
accommodate the tenor bell which Henry Kelsall had bequeathed to the
parish in 1493—which did heavy duty, in a populous parish, at burials,
month and year minds.[68] The sound and also the sight of bells reminded
parishioners of their need for intercession. Bells were dedicated to particular saints (Henry Kelsall's was to Jesus) and some were inscribed with
the names of benefactors. In Aldbourne church tower a bell cast in 1416
once rang out for the souls of Richard Goddard and his two wives.[69]

The communal effort of the living and the accumulation of services for the
dead are both aspects of late medieval piety visibly prominent in parish
church-building. The scale of the laity's involvement, in nave and sometimes chancel rebuildings, suggests that, once again, the duties imposed

[65] Reg. Bp. Aiscough, ii, fo. 45.   [66] PCC 32 Holder.
[67] Munro-Cautley, *Suffolk Churches*, 56–7; J. C. Dickinson, *The Later Middle Ages* (London, 1979), 443–4; A Woodger, 'Post-Reformation Mixed Gothic in Huntingdonshire
Church Towers and its Campanological Associations', *Archaeological Journal*, 141 (1984),
269–308.
[68] See Ch. 4 n. 39.
[69] E. D. Webb, 'Notes on Aldbourne Church', *WAM* 28 (1895), 159. It might also be
mentioned that porches were frequently added to churches in the 15th cent. (Munro-
Cautley, *Suffolk Churches*, 59–61). They too had a sacramental purpose, being used for the
preliminary part of the baptismal and marriage services and for the churching of women;
penance could be performed publicly at the entrance to the church by sinners asking for the
prayers of those who went in. Evidence for porch replacement is sketchy, but it appears that
15% of churches had porches added to them in the 15th cent., possibly more than previously.

on them by canon law were not unwelcome burdens with which they were 'saddled'.[70] Willingness to erect chancel screens which served to emphasize the sanctity of the priesthood does not imply a general 'scepticism of clerical pretensions'.[71] Nevertheless, it would be nostalgic to suggest that the whole parish contributed to major works out of pious devotion. There were backsliding and a tendency to contribute to occasional, glamorous, building projects rather than the day-to-day upkeep of the fabric. It is hard to determine how far the duties of the living towards the church fabric were performed out of personal piety or conformist pressure. In any case, even apparently communal efforts could take on a competitive edge. Groups within parishes—perhaps even competing ones—were possibly more responsible for church-building than the collective spirit of some romanticized parish 'community'.

Services for the dead also profoundly affected the character and shape of the parish church: here again there was a creative interplay between individual and collective need. The need for altar space, to set up images and lights dedicated to saints, to permit the celebration of additional masses, even to allow extra space for tombs, seems to have gathered pace from the thirteenth century. Piecemeal additions of chapels and aisles accommodated the liturgical concerns of individuals faced with a purgatorial afterlife. But these additions also benefited the parish at large: by the visual beauty of their decoration, by the extension of the church, even by stimulating the living to undertake a general rebuilding of their parish church. In this context, it is a touch unfair to suggest that the Statute of Mortmain (1279), which restricted the foundation of chantries, helped deflect alms away from landed endowments towards church-building.[72] Parish chantries could assist church-building and it was, after all, the chantry founders themselves, the Tropenells, Swaynes, Longs, and Stokes, who were foremost in the rebuilding and embellishment of their churches.

The belief that church-building was a work of penance helps to explain why churches were rebuilt continually from the thirteenth to the sixteenth centuries. It may also be no accident that from the mid-sixteenth century to the nineteenth, with purgatory abolished, fewer churches seem to have been rebuilt or altered in the diocese.[73] But beliefs and motives are com-

---

[70] Cheney, *Medieval Texts*, 199.   [71] Mason, 'English Parishioner', 27.

[72] K. B. McFarlane, *The Nobility of Late Medieval England* (Oxford, 1973), 95. McFarlane is echoed by Raban, *Mortmain Legislation*, 139.

[73] Work done to churches in the post-Reformation period, however, was carried out in the Perpendicular style, which can lead to the work being wrongly dated to earlier periods (R. K. Morris, 'Church in the Countryside', 78).

plex things, and religious devotion was no doubt mixed with more secular considerations. Pauper hoped that church-building was carried out for the worship of God alone, yet 'I dread me that men do it more for the pomp and pride of this world to have a name and worship therby in the country, or for envy that one town hath against another'.[74] The gentry who daubed their churches with brasses and armorial badges almost certainly wished to advertise their place in local society. Proud William Swayne and 'covetous' Thomas Tropenell no doubt sought to display their worldly honour by founding parish chantries. Feelings of pride and competition were hardly swept away during the Reformation but had to find outlets other than chantry foundation, thereby removing a practice that in some parishes had stimulated more general church-building.

The scale and incidence of building projects must also be set within the context of local conditions. It is true that sometimes rebuilding had had little to do with the distribution of wealth. Much could depend simply on the size of the parish and the number of people within it; parishes large and small can be found in all regions, urban and more rural. In towns that were suffering a decline in overall prosperity and even population levels, the priorities of parishioners were such that their churches could still be rebuilt. The contributions of a local gentry family, of wealthy clothiers retired on country estates, or even of episcopal patronage could compensate for the relative poverty of a particular parish. As the memorials to benefactors of St Thomas's church in Salisbury suggest, it did not need contributions from the whole parish for rebuilding schemes to be funded. But it is not surprising to find that a familiar regional pattern is apparent in church-building. Such activity was most intense during the fifteenth century in parishes that had concentrations of people profiting from the wealth generated by the cloth trade. Churches rebuilt in those parishes, especially in Wiltshire, were rebuilt on a more lavish scale than elsewhere. The parishes that tended to experience least church-building were in poorer areas of Dorset heathland and the depopulated areas on chalk soils that were more remote from the markets of cloth towns.

[74] *Dives and Pauper*, 189. For a case of apparent competitiveness see L. F. Salzman, *Buildings in England: Down to 1540*, second edn. (Oxford, 1967), 24.

6

Parish Fraternities and Craft Guilds

TOO much emphasis on parish life can underrate the importance of other forms of pious practice that had long existed independently of the parochial framework. Fraternities were not new in the later Middle Ages: the burial of dead members, the celebration of masses and anniversaries, so integral to late medieval fraternities, were features present in the tenth century, as guilds at Great Bedwyn (Wiltshire) and Abbotsbury (Dorset) testify. Activities such as the commemoration of the dead and communal feasting reached back to a pagan past.[1] But more and more guilds, providing spiritual intercession for their members, seem to have been founded from the thirteenth century onwards: the fifteenth century has been called their 'golden age'.[2]

The responsibility for the increase in guild foundation has been placed at several doors. The demographic crisis following the destructive visitations of plague after 1348 may have prompted a desire to reconstitute family ties through the artificial means of the fraternity; fear of not being decently buried when so many were dying may have induced men to found 'burial societies'.[3] But a more fundamental reason has been sought to account for a more general movement which began in the thirteenth century and continued into the sixteenth. G. Rosser states that a common stimulus to form fraternities was the desire to 'transcend the limitations, geographical or institutional, of the parish'. The 'freezing' of the

---

[1] *English Historical Documents c.500–1042*, ed. D. Whitelock, second edn. (London, 1979), 605–7; G. Le Bras, 'Les Confréries chrétiennes: problèmes et propositions', *Revue historique du droit français et étranger*, 4th series, 19–21 (1940–2), 362–3; E. Coornaert, 'Les Ghildes médiévales (Vᵉ–XIVᵉ siècle)', *Revue historique*, 199 (1948), 22–35.

[2] G. Rosser, 'The Anglo-Saxon Guilds', in *Minsters and Parish Churches: The Local Church in Transition 950–1200*, ed. J. Blair (Oxford Univ. Committee of Archaeology, Monograph 17; Oxford, 1988), 31–5; E. F. Delaruelle, E.-R. Cabande, and P. Ourilac, *L'Église au temps du grand schisme et la crise conciliaire* (*Histoire de l'église*, xiv, ed. A. Fliche *et al.*) (Paris, 1962–4), 666–8.

[3] H. F. Westlake, *The Parish Gilds of Medieval England* (London, 1919), 19–20; J. Chiffoleau, *La Comptabilité de l'au-delà: les hommes, la mort et la religion dans la région d'Avignon à la fin du moyen âge (vers 1320–vers 1480)* (École Française de Rome, 1980), 273–80; C. M. Barron, 'The Parish Fraternities of Medieval London', in C. M. Barron and C. Harper-Bill (eds.), *The Church in Pre-Reformation Society: Essays in Honour of F. R. H. Du Boulay* (London, 1985), 23–4.

parish structure after the twelfth century made it 'unwieldy in the face of social change': the needs of new and shifting communities were better accommodated within the alternative and voluntary association of the fraternity.[4]

So guilds need to be considered partly within the context of parish life. And the relationship between parish and guild raises other questions. Did a fraternity in any way weaken loyalty to the parish, a loyalty considered primary by the Church? Did not Nicholas of Cusa, attempting reform in Germany in the 1450s, prohibit the erection of new fraternities as detracting from the honour and rights of the parish church?[5] Commentators on English guilds have tended to see them as 'transcending the parish', 'challenging the old order', and 'providing alternatives to the parochial communion'.[6] After all, the merchant tailors' guild in London in the fifteenth century included townsmen from Salisbury and Reading;[7] the palmers' guild of Ludlow collected subscriptions in Salisbury, Marlborough, and Devizes during the early sixteenth century. During the same period a guild of St Clement from the London parish of St Clement Danes was collecting money in Wiltshire.[8] Undoubtedly, a guild could attract gifts from benefactors whose parishes lay far away, but the positive contribution of guild to parish has also to be stressed.

Chapters 6 and 7 will explore the activities of three different, yet often intricately related, types of guild: those that bound together the élite of a town, particularly mayors and burgesses in borough towns; but first of all, those whose membership was based either on the economic ties of a particular craft or on less well-defined criteria, those that were often more closely connected with a particular parish.

---

[4] G. Rosser, 'Communities of Parish and Guild in Late Middle Ages', in S. J. Wright (ed.), *Parish, Church and People: Local Studies in Lay Religion 1350–1750* (London, 1988), 29–55.

[5] Guilds were more likely to be at odds with the parish in northern Europe where the parish framework had become strongly rooted, than in, for instance, Italy where the parish was but a 'feeble plant' (J. Bossy, *Christianity in the West, 1400–1700* (Oxford, 1985), 63).

[6] M. Rubin, *Charity and Community in Medieval Cambridge* (Cambridge, 1987), 258; Tanner, *Church in Late Medieval Norwich*, 68; S. Brigden, 'Religion and Social Obligation in Early Sixteenth-Century London', *Past and Present*, 103 (1984), 96. See also J. Henderson, 'Confraternities and the Church in Late Medieval Florence', in W. J. Sheils and D. Wood (eds.), *Voluntary Religion* (Studies in Church History, 23; Worcester, 1986), 82–3.

[7] John Hunt (tailor) and Symkyn a Kent of Reading, John Griffyth, Richard Gage (weaver), Thomas Mason (draper), John Staveley, and Christina Staveley of Salisbury, were admitted as brothers or sisters into the merchant tailors' in 1410/11, 1431/2, 1413/14, 1422/3, 1425/6, 1434/5, 1436/7 respectively (Merchant Taylors' company accounts, i, fos. 56, 226b, 74b, 134, 161, 258, 280b; I am grateful to Matthew Davies for these references).

[8] E. G. H. Kempson, 'A Shropshire Guild at Work in Wiltshire', *WAM* 57 (1958–60), 50–5; PRO C1/395/55.

By the thirteenth century the small borough town of Bridport had one parish church dedicated to St Mary and a smaller chapel of St Andrew, to the north of the town, where newer tenements had spilled over the old Anglo–Saxon walls.[9] A profusion of fraternities sprang up in the later Middle Ages. Gifts and bequests to two guilds, St Mary and the Holy Trinity, were being made by the mid-thirteenth century. Two more fraternities make their debut in the records during the fourteenth century, one dedicated to the Holy Cross (in existence by 1348) and one to St Katherine (founded around 1360). There are also references to three altar lights within the parish church apparently maintained by the church-wardens rather than by separate guilds. Soon after 1400 five fraternities apparently made their appearance in the parish church, and later two more (including one dedicated to Jesus). Two fraternities, Holy Cross and Sts Mary and James are found worshipping in the chapel of St Andrew.[10]

The guilds of St Mary and St Katherine had strong associations with the bailiffs and burgesses, the élite of the town, and will be discussed in Chapter 7. Some light can be shed on the membership and functions of the other fraternities because, happily, the rules and account books of six of these fraternities survive. Each had slightly different forms of devotion. The Holy Cross fraternity lit lights in honour of Jesus, St Mary, and All Saints as well as the Holy Cross, and its rules ordered that on Sundays and double feasts two candles were to be lit before the Holy Cross altar, especially on the feast of Circumcision. The members of the Two Torches guild were to light torches on Sundays and feast days at the elevation of the host. Four of the guilds, at slightly different rates, were to provide for any member who fell into poverty. Dear to the hearts of all guild members was provision for dead members. The living were all to attend and offer money or wax at the funeral exequies of any member who died. The guild rules of Sts Mary and James, St Nicholas, and Holy Cross specify that if a member perished, on land or at sea, within a certain distance of the

---

[9]   K. J. Penn, *Historic Towns*, 23–7. Bridport had a population of around 1,000 in the early 16th cent.

[10]   Parish lights: DRO DC/BTB D2, CD12, CD13; Lights before the Cross: CD11; St Nicholas: CD14; Torches: CD15; Two Torches: CD16; Sts Mary and James: CD56; Holy Cross: described in *Historical Manuscripts Commission: Sixth Report* (London, 1877), 478–9, since apparently lost, but a transcription was made by Wainwright in the 20th cent.: PQ30 (ii. 96 ff.). All these have brief books, accounts, and lists of members beginning in the early 15th cent. The St Mary guild had accounts of collections from members for 1466–9 (CD31). Also references to St Thomas's guild in 1460 (CD6) and to a Jesus guild in 1522 (CD97).

parish church (one mile, three miles, and seven miles respectively) the body was to be brought back for burial.

The funds of all these guilds came from collections rather than rents, and each had a different day on which their members were to attend the annual accounts. The Sts Mary and James fraternity extracted 1*d.* a year from each of its members; the rules of the other fraternities do not specify a fee. The accounts are never detailed enough to show exactly how much was collected from how many, but there were certainly differences in the amounts each raised. The fraternity of Sts Mary and James gathered least (averaging less than £1 a year) and that of the Torches most (averaging more than £5).

It is difficult to tell how many members these guilds had at any one time. Names were added to and struck off guild lists, which do not appear to be complete (since some of the names of wardens that appear later on in the guild accounts are not mentioned in the membership lists). But a few points about membership are apparent. The clergy were certainly not excluded, though their appearance is only occasional. There are no local gentry figuring in the lists. There were more men than women, and most of the women mentioned were wives of male members. Even so, some women's names appear on their own and one also appears as a warden of a guild. It is also clear that some guilds had a slightly more exclusive membership than others. Aside from the St Mary and St Katherine guilds (which were mainly restricted to the most important townspeople), many of the names in the lists of the other guilds (15 per cent in the case of four guilds) also appear in the account books of the town government, in the rank of town official or even bailiff (see Table 5).[11] Fewer members (7 per cent) of the Sts Mary and James guild are known to have held municipal office. This guild also gathered the least from its members, only retrieved its members' bodies from a mile away, and provided least when its members fell into poverty, so it may have been a guild for the less well-off townsfolk. The Torches fraternity had even fewer, less than 2 per cent, of people who can be identified as town officers. But it did collect more than any other guild—perhaps because its membership was larger as well as less socially exclusive.

Even more apparent is that membership of one guild did not preclude membership of another. Lists of eight fraternities (including, this time, those of St Mary and St Katherine) give the names of 842 people. Four

---

[11] DRO DC/BTB M11, H1, *passim.*

TABLE 5. Fraternities in Bridport

	Lights before the Cross	St Nicholas	Torches	Two Torches	Holy Cross	Sts Mary and James	St Mary	St Katherine
Dates of accounts	c.1420–64	1422–40	1424–58	1420–77	1399–1420	1406–55	1466–9	1428–80
Amount raised annually (s.)	24–32	28–32	>100	50–60	67–118	14–22	80[1]	52–120[2]
Distance guilds prepared to carry dead members' bodies (miles)	?	3	?	?	7	1	?	?
Aid per week given to members fallen into poverty	?	1d.	?	?	3d.	1 farthing	?	?
Members who were also members of other fraternities (%)	68	72	32	52	35	44	26	59
Members known to have served as town officers (%)	15	18	2	19	15	7	25	23
No. of names on guild lists	93	61	119	118	190	91	72	98

[1] In rents.
[2] Plus rents.

hundred and fifty-four names appear only once, but the rest (46 per cent) appear more than once. Fifteen per cent of the names belonged to two fraternities, 14 per cent to three, 11 per cent to four, and 5 per cent to five. The lists of guild members do not overlap in perfect chronology, so that multiple membership may have been greater than these figures suggest. Many people then were not content to place their penitential eggs in one spiritual basket. It was perhaps to avoid any clash of loyalties that guilds performed slightly different services and had their annual meetings on different days. Once again, the fraternities of the Torches and of Sts Mary and James seem to have been for the less wealthy, for those who could not afford multiple guild membership: they had fewest members who were also members of other guilds.[12] That said, even these two guilds had members who enjoyed the suffrages of the other fraternities: we should not over-emphasize the exclusiveness of some guilds over others. The fraternities of Bridport, in the parish of St Mary, were made up of close-knit, overlapping groups of parishioners.

The functions, membership, and rate of foundation of the Bridport guilds are not unusual. References to guilds are ubiquitous throughout the region, in rural and urban areas. But not surprisingly, more are found in heavily populated areas and parishes. Salisbury had, all told, at least ten fraternities in St Thomas's church, six in St Edmund's, and six in St Martin's (though some of these may have been craft guilds and some are difficult to distinguish from altar lights maintained by churchwardens).[13] Accurate plotting of the rise and fall of fraternities is impossible, although scattered references suggest that guilds were founded throughout the later Middle Ages. We find the beginnings of a guild of St Mary at Abingdon in the 1240s;[14] the guild of St Mary at Swanage in 1388 claimed a foundation date of some forty years earlier; a new guild was referred to at Deverell Longbridge in 1405.[15] The incidence of guilds at Bridport suggests, however, that more were founded there in the early fifteenth century than before. Six guild books begin with names and accounts dating from that period, although these guilds may have been in existence

---

[12] Excluding the fraternity of the Holy Cross whose membership lists begin earlier than the other fraternities and therefore are less likely to overlap with the others.

[13] *S. Edmund Accounts*, *passim*; D & C, Press II, Procurators' accounts, *passim*.

[14] Holy Cross hospital, Abingdon, almshouse deeds 10a, 11, 17, 21.

[15] PRO C47/39/92. Only three guild returns from Wilts. Dorset, and Berks. survive from the 1388/9 survey; (Will of Alice Hewytt 1405 (PCC 42 Marche)).

[16] The Lights before the Cross fraternity seems to have begun by 1352/3 (DRO DC/BTB D2, p. 20 (fo. 10ᵛ)).

TABLE 6. Bequests to Salisbury parish altars

	No. of wills	No. of bequests	%
1270–1349	15	0	0
1350–99	65	6	9
1400–49	129	18	14
1450–99	53	26	43
1500–47	68	47	66

earlier.[16] In Salisbury too (though this may again be a trick of the evidence) there were more fraternities in parish churches after 1400 than before; at the very least there were more bequests to guilds from then on (see Table 6). So one cannot avoid questioning whether the Black Death had any immediate impact on the rate of guild foundation.

Details on the intercessory functions of guilds outside Bridport are less plentiful. Certainly, the same concern for a decent burial, altar lights, and obits can be found elsewhere.[17] But some saints were more popular than others. In the region as a whole more guilds were dedicated to the Virgin Mary than any other saint. Some of these Marian altar lights, particularly in a larger town like Salisbury, were maintained by the wives or daughters, though whether these groups of women constituted a separate fraternity, or simply included all the women of the parish, is not clear. Some of the newer feast days stimulated the foundation of guilds: a few were dedicated to Corpus Christi, but by the second half of the fifteenth century there were fewer of these than guilds dedicated to the name of Jesus. In Reading the Jesus fraternities in all three of the town's parishes were the most popular ones as objects of bequest in the wills of townsfolk in the early sixteenth century.[18] Bequests to the guilds of Jesus in the parishes of St Thomas and St Edmund in Salisbury far outnumbered gifts to others by the end of the fifteenth century (see Table 7). Indeed, the Jesus guild of St Edmund's may well have displaced an earlier guild of Holy Cross (just as the Jesus mass had displaced the earlier votive mass of the Holy Cross, celebrated on Fridays, in the liturgical calendar).[19] The first surviving account of the guild in 1476 reveals that one of its tenants was living in the same property that an earlier city rental of 1455 recorded as belonging to

[17] *Reg. Dean Chandler*, 8. Wills do not usually mention guild members attending funerals, though in 1541 Thomas Brownyng of Tolpuddle left a bequest to the brethren of the sepulchre in the parish to have a dinner at his funeral (PCC 17 Spert).

[18] Between 1470 and 1547 twenty-three out of forty-six testators from Reading left bequests to Jesus guilds.

[19] Pfaff, *Feasts*, 66.

TABLE 7. Bequests to particular parish altars in Salisbury

	1350–99	1400–49	1450–99	1500–47
St Thomas's church				
Jesus			10	29
Holy Cross	1	3		
Mary		1		1
Nicholas	1	4	1	
Trinity	1	3		
Christopher		2		
James		4		
Michael		4		
St Edmund's church				
Jesus			6	13
Holy Cross	5	1	2	
James		1		
Trinity	1			
St Martin's church				
Holy Ghost	1	4	5	10
Holy Cross	1		1	
Trinity	1	1		
John	2	1		
Mary	1			

the Holy Cross guild.[20] In St Thomas's, similarly, the first known bequest to the Jesus guild comes in 1465, after which there are no bequests to the parish Holy Cross guild.[21] As popularity for the Holy Name of Jesus increased, so the older Holy Cross guilds in both parishes had been taken over or amalgamated.

Differences of scale and scope also emerged between guilds. The Jesus guilds of Salisbury, Reading, and Marlborough were grander affairs than the parish fraternities of Bridport, since they had chantry priests with endowments of property.[22] When Henry Kelsall, a Reading clothier who had served the town as a member of Parliament in 1483, made his will in

[20] Nevill, 'Salisbury in 1455', 80, 99; *S. Edmund Accounts*, 248. The first extant bequest for the Jesus mass in St Edmund's comes in 1478 (WRO D4/3, fo. 4'). Two testators after 1476, however, still made a distinction between the Jesus and Holy Cross fraternities: William Kensington in 1487 (*S. Edmund Accounts*, 379–80) and Matilda Tuff in 1503 (PCC 21 Vox).

[21] The last extant bequest for the Holy Cross guild in St Thomas's church comes in 1414 (WRO G23/1/214, fo. 14). The first bequest for the Jesus guild was in 1465 (G23/1/215, fo. 13'). The next is in 1476 (WRO D4/3, fo. 81).

[22] Much of the property of the Marlborough Jesus guild was granted between 1519 and 1529 (WRO G22/1/102, 236).

1493, he called himself 'the fyrst Mynder Susteyner and Mayntener of my devocion of the Masse of I[es]hu' in St Laurence's parish. It was reputedly his tombstone, which once lay in the north aisle next to the chancel where the Jesus mass altar was found, that expressed his devotion to the name of Jesus: 'J[es]hu tha in Bethelem was borne | save us that we be not forlorne'. His will also mentions ten other people who were 'sustainers' of the same fraternity and who represented a variety of occupations: one clothier, three drapers, one tanner, one ironmonger, one chandler and fishmonger, one yeoman, and even one gentleman, Richard Smith, who was to become a valet of the king's wardrobe. All ranked high in status within the city: five had been mayors of Reading and the others were burgesses, some of whom had served as town officers.[23] Full membership of the fraternity may also have been restricted to an exalted few, for John Pownser's will in 1517 mentions 'the ten brethren' of the guild. Wives of members were also included, for John's will also stipulates that Isabell his wife was to keep paying 6s. 8d. a year to the guild to remain one of the sisters[24] (a sum far higher than the penny required by the Sts Mary and James guild in Bridport). The Jesus guild's social exclusiveness was made clear by the parish seating arrangements: in 1547 it was agreed that all women of the parish whose husbands were or had been members of the guild were to 'have the highest seats or pewes next unto the Mayor's wifs seate towarde the pulpit'.[25] No *hoi polloi* admitted to this guild then.

Membership of the Jesus guild of St Edmund's in Salisbury may have been similarly, but perhaps not quite so, exclusive. The occupations of those who left bequests to the fraternity (though not the 'brothers and sisters' who made donations four times during the year) are sometimes recorded. Among them, four had been mayors, three were tailors, and one was a merchant: judging from the order of the city processions, all ranked high in the social order. But gifts also came from one tucker or fuller, two brewers, two carpenters, and one chandler, crafts that were less prestigious.[26] A sadler and a smith, belonging to crafts that were least exalted in the city processions, were guild wardens together in 1499.[27]

The accounts of the St Edmund's Jesus guild also furnish some clues as to how such guilds managed their affairs. Like the Bridport fraternities,

---

[23] *CPR* (1494–1509), 452; PCC 1 Vox; BL Harl. MS 965; Kerry, *St. Laurence Reading*, 29–33, 187–8; *Reading Records: Diary of the Corporation*, ed. J. M. Guilding, i (London, 1892).
[24] PCC 1 Ayloffe.   [25] BRO D/P 97/5/2, p. 244.
[26] *S. Edmund Accounts*, 248, 250, 252, 258, 264, 267; WRO 1901/108. Women also made gifts: take e.g. the first year of surviving accounts, 1476/7, where of the fourteen people making gifts or bequests six were women (ibid. 248).
[27] Ibid. 251; see Table 9.

TABLE 8. Amount raised annually by the Jesus guild of St Edmund's, Salisbury

	Amount raised (*s.*)
1470–9	68
1480–9	?
1490–9	99
1500–9	92
1510–19	94
1520–9	?
1530–9	57
1540–9	42

some of the money was raised by collections which peaked at just under £5 in the 1490s. The other major source of revenue was property from benefactors, which (perhaps as an indicator of the guild's growing popularity) increased from four tenements (worth £3. 16*s*. 8*d*.) in 1476 to seven (£10. 8*s*. 8*d*.) by 1538. The revenues paid for a stipendiary priest (£5 a year) and for clerks to look after guild ornaments and vestments.[28] The priest celebrated the first morning mass at the Jesus altar in St Edmund's church, and in winter seems to have been provided with extra torches, presumably to celebrate before the sun rose.[29] On Fridays (the day most commonly associated with the mass of Jesus) more priests and clerks could be paid (22*s*. in 1476/7) during the celebration of the mass and antiphonary of Jesus, when the church bell was also rung. During Lent, Fridays were invested with special celebrations: bread and ale were given to clerics (specified in 1500/1 as being from the cathedral) for singing a 'salve de Jeshu', the antiphon sung in procession with the choir. The fraternity also had an anniversary celebrated for its members: 8*s*. was paid out in 1476/7 for the dirige and mass and for ringing the great bell. The service was held in that year on a special day which the accounts record as the 'die Jeshu Christi'—almost as though the fraternity were treating the day as a feast day before it was officially established by the Church in 1488/9.

---

[28] The accounts from 1476/7 to 1546/7 are not complete (*S. Edmund Accounts*, 248–72); for others not transcribed there see WRO 1901/106 for the years 1513/14, ?1538, 1547/8, and an undated 15th-cent. account.

[29] For the following see *S. Edmund Accounts*, 248, 252–3, 258, 266–8; WRO 1901/108 (years 1539/40 and 1547/8).

Membership of this guild, as at Bridport, did not preclude involvement with another. Of the ninety-nine testators who left bequests to fraternities in Salisbury, forty-four gave to more than one. But fraternities were not just linked by their membership. In 1504/5 the Jesus fraternity of St Edmund's received 13*d.* from the chaplain of the weavers' guild for bread and wine; in 1539/40 it was given £6 from the wives. The Jesus guild also shared the same altar as that of St John the Baptist, just as, elsewhere in the church, the weavers shared the same altar as the wives and daughters.[30] Overlapping membership and co-operation between fraternities must have been more common and varied than these few chance references suggest.

So guilds in small towns like Bridport and larger ones like Salisbury were associations linked by their members, living and dead, and by their activities. They also provided intercessory services that the parish framework may not have entirely satisfied. In a sense, fraternities operated independently of the parish, perhaps even subversively. After all, collections made by the St Edmund's Jesus guild at Easter, Michaelmas, and Christmas clashed with those made by the parish as a whole. Parishioners of one parish could give to fraternities located within another.[31] So how far did guilds draw funds and loyalties away from the parish?

No generalization quite suffices. In a town like Bridport, with just one parish, subversion by a guild was potentially far less likely than in a city such as Salisbury, which had three parishes, or in places with many more. But even within Salisbury gifts to guilds may have followed parish loyalties. The testators who left bequests to guilds tended to leave more to the guilds that lay in the parish church in which they chose to be buried. In any case, testators often left bequests to more than one parish, and were required to do so if they had lands in other parishes.[32] By the same token, they might be expected to remember the fraternities within those other parishes. It is difficult to interpret bequests to guilds in other parishes as 'transcending' the parish structure.

Moreover, there was greater need for guilds in some parishes than in others. In towns with large parishes the parochial framework may have

---

[30] The wives' lights were at the altar of the Blessed Virgin Mary (*S. Edmund Accounts*, 48, 1497/8). The weavers had theirs at the same altar, according to Alice Hamme's will (WRO G23/1/214, fo. 20). For the tailors see the will of John Viresedon/Chapman (PCC 8 Holgrave).

[31] At least five of the forty-four Salisbury testators who left bequests to more than one fraternity left them to fraternities in more than one parish.

[32] See Ch. 3 n. 1.

proved more inadequate than in smaller town parishes or rural areas. The chantry commissioners in 1545 and 1548 reported, as we saw, that several parishes had over 500 people attending the Easter communion: those of St Thomas and St Edmund in Salisbury, of St Laurence, St Giles, and St Mary in Reading, and those in Marlborough, Chippenham, Trowbridge, Windsor, and Bray had guilds that maintained chantry priests.[33] But in places with many more parishes, like Wallingford or Sherborne, fewer fraternities may be found even though they were towns of comparable size.[34] Parishioners of smaller parishes perhaps found their devotional concerns better satisfied by the parochial framework; those in larger parishes may have sought to capture the intimacy of smaller ones by founding fraternities within their parish churches.

But whatever the size of parishes, fraternities within them were not so detached from the parish structure. Guilds that did not have their own priests could apply for the services of the parish priest. At Thornford in 1405 one Stephen Frogpenne was cited before the visitational officials for stealing 4s. 4d. which was owed by the wardens of the St George fraternity to the rector—who prayed every Monday for the fraternity's brothers and sisters.[35] Parish priests could also have their incomes supplemented by other guild contributions. Many of the fraternities in St Thomas's church in Salisbury simply maintained altar lights, but the accounts of the procurator of St Thomas's show that they made annual oblations to the high altar, albeit worth only a handful of shillings, adding to offerings that came from tithes, burials, marriages, and anniversaries.[36] Fraternities that had their own priests, like the Jesus guild of St Edmund's in Salisbury, could help, like the chantries founded by individuals, the pastoral work of the parish priest in large parishes with numerous communicants.[37]

Some of the larger fraternities can be found assisting other institutions of divine service within their parishes. On several occasions the St Edmund's Jesus guild gave payments of 6s. to the priest of Reginald

[33] PRO E301/3, 51, 59.

[34] There was one Jesus guild at Sherborne (J. Fowler, 'Sherborne All Hallows Church Wardens' Accounts', *NQSD* 24 (1943–6), 8). Compare with Bristol where parishes were small and fraternities apparently very few (C. Burgess, ' "By Quick and by Dead": Wills and Pious Provision in Late Medieval Bristol', *EHR* 102 (1987), 839 and nn. 6, 7). But contrast with the fraternities in Cacères (M.-C. Gerbert, 'Les Confréries religieuses à Cacères de 1467 à 1523', *Mélanges de la casa de Velazquez*, 7 (1971), 86–90). Moreover, in smaller villages a fraternity might in any case be synonymous with the parish (P. DuParc, 'Confréries du Saint-Esprit et communautés d'habitants au moyen âge', *Revue historique du droit français et étranger*, fourth series, 37 (1958), 349–67).

[35] *Reg. Dean Chandler*, 49.   [36] D & C, Press II, Procurator's accounts.

[37] PRO E301/59/16, 58/43; see Ch. 4 n. 48.

Tudworth's chantry, which had been founded in the early fourteenth century and whose endowments probably needed topping up.[38] The same fraternity assisted more recent, stipendiary, chantry foundations. In 1496 William Maynard had instructed that after his death nine marks should go every year to a priest to say placebo and dirige twice weekly for ten years at the Holy Rood altar in St Edmund's church. After his death his widowed wife Margaret in 1500/1 gave the Jesus fraternity 2*s*. 4*d*. for bread, wine, and wax that had been granted by the fraternity to a William Harreys, Margaret's and presumably her husband's chaplain. By 1503 Margaret too had gone the way of her husband; one John Selwode gave 4*s*. 8*d*. to the fraternity for bread, wine, and wax used by the two chaplains celebrating for the souls of Margaret and William.[39] The fraternity was supplying materials necessary for other chantry services founded within the same parish.

Parish officials also concerned themselves with guild business. The accounts of the St Edmund's Jesus fraternity were written up at Easter, the same time as those of the parish. So closely were the offices of Jesus steward and churchwarden linked that the former were chosen two or three years after serving as guild officers, to serve as wardens of the whole parish. Similarly, of the twenty-eight known churchwardens of St Mary's in Bridport (between 1405 and 1480) at least fifteen were members of fraternities, and six of these had served as guild officers.[40] Parish officials and guild wardens were here one and the same. Indeed in some instances it is very difficult to distinguish between parish and strictly guild activity. The chantry of St Mary at St Helen's church in Abingdon was sometimes described as belonging to a guild, yet it first appears as one aspect of parish devotional life. Deeds concerning the chantry between 1240 and 1270 refer to lands being given to the proctors of the chantry with the assent of the parishioners, or even to God, the Blessed Virgin Mary, and the parishioners of St Helen's 'or their proctors'.[41]

Where parish and guild were clearly distinguished, churchwardens could keep a critical eye on the activities of fraternities within their parishes. Parishioners summoned to visitations occasionally informed on the deviant behaviour of a guild's brother or sister. In 1405 defects concerning guild activities were found in four of the forty churches and large

[38] *S. Edmund Accounts*, 257, 268, 269, 270; WRO 1901/108 (1547/8).
[39] PCC 4 Horne; *S. Edmund Accounts*, 255, 258, 259.   [40] DRO DC/BTB M11, H1.
[41] Holy Cross hospital, Abingdon, almshouse deeds, 10a, 11, 17, 21, 23, 24, 28, 37, 41, 47, 51b, 57. A gift was also made in 1288 for a clerk to assist the chantry chaplain's services (ibid. 44).

chapels visited by Dean Chandler. At the free chapel of Anderson, where the St Nicholas fraternity helped bury its brethren, one Maud Pycharde had refused to pay the necessary 12*d.* or provide a breakfast at the burial of Jordan the rector, one of the brethren, for whom she was an executrix (perhaps because Jordan had withheld a 'botell' worth 6*d.* and two bushels of barley worth 12*d.* that belonged to the fraternity).[42] So parish officials considered it their responsibility to keep a close check on guilds within their parishes.

Indeed the parish had every incentive to maintain these fraternities: not only did they contribute to clerical funds and assist in the pastoral work of the parish priest, but they also made significant contributions to the fabric funds. The guild at Swanage in 1388 claimed that the surplus from its funds went towards the fabric of the parish church.[43] The Jesus fraternity in St Edmund's Salisbury certainly made occasional donations to the parish church, as much as 57*s.* in 1494/5. The wives of the same parish contributed the exceptional sum of £9 from their lights of the Blessed Virgin Mary.[44] In St Laurence's parish in Reading, the Jesus and Marian guilds appear as lenders and benefactors of the parish. They each gave 15*s.* in 1531/2 towards the repair of the church books; after 1512 both guilds made annual contributions of 33*s.* 4*d.* each for the stipend of the parish sexton. On 18 April 1547, not long before all guilds and chantries were swept away by royal decree, the parish was making formal arrangements for the exact relationship between the parish and the two guilds. The Jesus guild was charged £3 yearly for the payment of the sexton's wages, 3*s.* for the keeping of the clock and scouring the candlesticks, desks, the two priests' and the clerk's chambers. The mass of Our Lady was charged 40*s.* a year for the wages of John Barber, a 'singing man'.[45] At Bridport the Lights before the Cross guild paid 8*s.*, and the Holy Cross guild 26*s.* 8*d.*, for the mending of an antiphoner or 'lydgger' in St Mary's church in 1454. In 1458 £11. 11*s.* 8*d.* was collected from four fraternities for the buying of a parish 'lygger'.[46]

When church-building schemes were in progress, parishes could look to guilds for help. The churchwardens of St Laurence's in Reading borrowed £6. 2*s.* 4*d.* from Our Lady mass for the rebuilding of the chancel.[47] Fraternities that celebrated at parish altars must sometimes have developed a proprietorial attitude towards their area of the church and must

[42] *Reg. Dean Chandler*, 3, 8.   [43] PRO C47/39/52.
[44] *S. Edmund Accounts*, 42, 48, 59, 365, 368.
[45] BRO D/P 97/5/2, pp. 180, 244, and *passim*.
[46] DRO DC/BTB CD6, CD11, PQ30, ii, pp. 96 ff.   [47] BRO D/P 97/5/2, p. 180.

have been willing to contribute to its maintenance. The late-fourteenth-century Lady chapel of St Helen's in Abingdon was the preserve of the Marian guild: its painted ceiling reminded the faithful of an indulgence granted in 1391 by Boniface IX to the chantry and recalled the names of benefactors, one of whom, William Reve, appears as a proctor of the chantry in deeds dated between 1240 and 1270.[48] The needs of guilds for altar space, as with other founders of chantries and devotional lights, undoubtedly contributed to the piecemeal addition of aisles and chapels that was a distinctive feature of late medieval church-building. At Bridport and Salisbury, moreover, there is a correlation—perhaps not coincidental—between major parish church-building projects in the late fourteenth and early fifteenth centuries and an apparent appearance of more fraternities in both places. Parish building efforts and guild foundation could advance hand in glove.

In larger towns, where a diversity of trades could flourish, craft associations formed another layer of guilds. It is tempting to treat them differently from parish fraternities. On the one hand they had clear economic aims. The rise of the tailors' guild in Salisbury (for which the best records survive)[49] at the end of the fourteenth century, reflected the growing wealth of the cloth trade. Protection of their economic interests was a primary aim. A list of eight ordinances laid down in 1479 regulated the practice of their trade. Economic aims were enhanced by the promotion of harmony among guild members. Social drinkings accompanied the election of guild officials and the drawing up of accounts. New wardens had to swear to punish members who disturbed 'the quietness and brotherly love' of the company.[50]

On the other hand, craft guilds were often linked with town government. Status as a burgess could be earned through apprenticeship and attachment to a particular craft.[51] In fifteenth-century Salisbury the city

---

[48] A. E. Preston, 'The Fourteenth-Century Painted Ceiling of St. Helen's Church at Abingdon', *BAJ* 40 (1936), 115–45; Holy Cross hospital, Abingdon, almshouse deeds, 17, 28.

[49] Two guild books survive (WRO G23/1/250, 251), both partially transcribed by C. Haskins, *The Ancient Trade Guilds and Companies of Salisbury* (Salisbury, 1917). References to other craft guilds in the region are as follows. Salisbury—skinners (the first known craft in the city, mentioned in 1380): *VCH: Wilts.* vi. 133; weavers: wills of John Forest 1409 (WRO G23/1/213, fo. 83ʳ⁻ᵛ) and Thomas Child 1413 (G23/1/214, fo. 4ᵛ). Wilton: WRO G25, Wilton general entry book, p. 11. Castle Combe: William Okley 1497 (PCC 6 Horne). Wimborne Minster: Hutchins, *Dorset*, iii. 198. Reading: *VCH: Berks.* iv. 137–9.

[50] Haskins, *Guilds*, 122; WRO G23/1/250, fos. 9ʳ⁻ᵛ, 10ᵛ; G23/1/251, fos. 1ʳ⁻ᵛ, 7ᵛ, 16ᵛ.

[51] S. Reynolds, *An Introduction to the History of English Medieval Towns* (Oxford, 1977), 164–77.

TABLE 9. Salisbury civic processions: the order of the crafts set by the city corporation

1480[1]	1527[2]
Smiths	Smiths
Carpenters	Carpenters, Bowyers, Fletchers, Sawyers
	Masons, Helyers
Butchers, Cooks	Butchers
	Cooks
	Sadlers, Fustours
	Tanners
Dubbers	Dubbers, Glovers, Dyers
Barbers, Chandlers	Barbers, Chandlers, Halliers, Cappers
Fishmongers, Goldsmiths	Fishmongers
	Goldsmiths, Painters, Brasiers
Dyers	
Bakers	Bakers
Brewers	Brewers
	Innholders, Vintners
The two Constables and fellowship	The two Constables and fellowship
Corvisors	Corvisors
	Skinners
Tuckers, Shearmen	Tuckers, Shearmen
Weavers	Weavers with their pageant
Tailors	Tailors with their pageant
Pageant 'if ther be any'	
Mayor and his Brethren	Mayor and his Brethren
Armed men	Armed men
Merchants, Mercers	Merchants with fellowship
The two Constables and fellowship	The two Constables and fellowship

Note: The guilds last in the procession were presumably the most prestigious. The slight changes in precedence and in variety of guilds may well reflect changes of relative standing among the crafts.

Sources: [1] WRO G23/1/2, fo. 139ᵛ.   [2] Ibid., fo. 210.

ledger books referred to nineteen crafts in 1415 and thirty-eight in 1440.[52] In 1480 and 1527 they listed the order of craft guilds in civic processions (see Table 9). Near the back, in the most prestigious places, came the weavers and the tailors. The tailors' guild was the only city craft guild

[52] WRO G23/1/1, fos. 40, 125.

recorded to have had property in Bishop Beauchamp's rental made in
1455.[53] In particular, it had close connections with the city government.
Many of the tailors who were listed as benefactors of the guild can also be
found as mayors of the city; the mayor was also involved, as we shall
see, in the annual procession that the tailors made on 24 June.[54] The
concerns of such craft guilds seem to reach beyond the confines of parish
boundaries.

Yet the religious and parish activities of craft guilds need to be exam-
ined more carefully. If craft guilds were 'primarily concerned with
mundane matters of regulating and protecting the economic interest of
the group concerned', was their 'spiritual well being' so 'secondary in
importance'?[55] Attention has usually been focused on their economic and
social aspects, probably because the Reformation destroyed most of the
religious devotions of these guilds and left their economic interests un-
touched.[56] But harmony among guild members was also aided by the
pursuit of their religious activities. Membership of the Salisbury tailors'
guild meant being 'parterie of the praiers and suffrages of . . . [the]
fraternitie of Seynt John the Baptist'. The first rule book is swamped by
regulations concerning religious activities; a saints' calendar opens the
second book, and five extracts from the four Gospels intrude themselves
into its later pages. The choice of these passages was not perhaps without
design. Two of them (John 1: 1–14, Luke 5: 27–33) were suitable for the
penitential message of the season of Lent. These and the last of the
extracts (John 6: 53–4) were suitable for the votive masses of sinners and
penitents. Indeed the last passage from John was the last reading, according to the Sarum Missal, that was made before the offertory, secretum,
and communion, in a requiem mass. It was therefore suitable also for
anniversaries and masses for benefactors. At the end of these passages are
written the words 'Deo Gracias per evangelia dicta deleantur vestra
delicta'—Thanks be to God! By these gospels may your sins be taken

[53] Neville, 'Salisbury in 1455', 83.

[54] From 1509 to 1546 at least five wardens of the tailors' guild became mayor. The tailors
and the city government had other ties: the mayor and commonalty leased a tenement
adjoining the cemetery of St Thomas's church to the tailors rent-free (WRO G23/1/44, nos.
8 (1508–9), 8a (1509–12), 9 (1512–13)). Also, on one occasion in 1479, the tailors' meeting
was held in the city council house.

[55] J. J. Scarisbrick, *The Reformation and the English People* (Oxford, 1984), 20.

[56] But see G. Unwin, *The Gilds and Companies of London*, fourth edn. (London, 1963), esp.
111–25; Palliser, 'Trade Guilds', 86–116. For an example of a craft guild that grew out of a
purely religious one (in the 12th cent.) see M. de Bouard, 'De la confrérie pieuse au métier
organisé: la fraternité des fèvres de Caen (fin du XIIᵉ siècle)', *Annales de Normandie*, 7
(1957), 165–77.

away.[57] The theme of penance, highlighted by these gospels, was central to the activities of the guild.

The celebration of the craft's feast day on the nativity of St John (24 June) brought the guild members together in honour of their patron saint.[58] The lights and the livery for the procession were prepared in advance. A dinner of beef, mutton, and chicken was held at the chandlers' house, which guild members had to attend. Three days before Midsummer the main feast was held, to which everyone had to make a contribution. On Midsummer's eve the stewards were to bedeck the chapel of St John in St Thomas's church with green straw, and to set before the image of St John a taper of two pounds of wax each and on its head a garland of red roses. They ordered the minstrels to go about the city and at 'viii of the bell' warned the brethren to be ready by nine: the masters and journeymen with their minstrels then carried their lights to the church of St Thomas. They also made an oblation to the high altar. Finally, on Midsummer's day the tailors made another procession (after 1479 attended by the mayor and 'others worshipful with hym') from the chapel of St John on 'Aylewater' bridge to the cathedral, at which the priest would say an evensong 'homwards at the second morrow mass': thence they processed to the 'halle of the Maisters' where the journeymen had 'a drynkyng yn the moste godley wyse' (see Map 5).

The religious activities of the guild did not just involve the living members. The dead brethren could expect a number of services from the living, beginning with burial. In 1479 the guild laid down rules for the provision of torches at funerals.[59] In return for larger gifts, guild members could expect their names to be inscribed on the guild's bede roll to be prayed for in perpetuity.[60] Moreover, the bequest of landed property was often intended to finance the celebration of an obit for the benefactor. On

---

[57] WRO G23/1/250, fos. 9, 10; *Ceremonies and Processions*, 17; Haskins, *Guilds*, pp. xxii–xxiii; *The Sarum Missal*, ed. J. Wickham-Legg (Oxford, 1916), 433; WRO G23/1/251, fo. 12.

[58] For the following see Haskins, *Guilds*, 110–11; WRO G23/1/251, fos. 1–4; D & C, Press II, Procurator's accounts.

[59] Haskins, *Guilds*, 122; WRO G23/1/250, fo. 9ᵛ. For the guilds' pall cloth see Haskins, *Guilds*, 57.

[60] Copies of tailors' bede rolls are found in WRO G23/1/257PC, one probably begun *c*.1444, the other in the 1530s (C. Haskins, 'The Original Bederoll of the Salisbury Tailors' Guild', *WAM* 39 (1916), 375–9); and another in G23/1/250, fo. 206, made from *c*.1495 onwards (Haskins, *Guilds*, 128–30). The numbers of benefactors and gifts recorded are as follows: *c*.1400–49: of 6 benefactors, 4 gave property, 2 gave money or goods; 1450–99: of 17 benefactors, 5 gave property, 12 gave money or goods; 1500–47: of 33 benefactors, 1 gave property, 32 gave money or goods (four of these were gifts for the tailors' hall, completed in 1533).

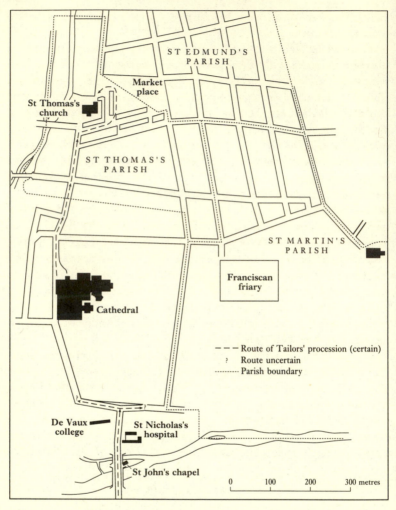

MAP 5. Route of the procession of the tailors' guild in Salisbury on Midsummer's day, according to Tailor's Book 1, fo. 3 (Haskins, *Guilds*, 111)

its bede roll, the first name is John Pinnok, who died some time after 1386. The second name is William More: in 1424 he left twenty marks for the guild to keep his anniversary annually in St Thomas's church on the feast day of St John the Evangelist 'ante portam latinam'.[61] By 1444 obits for

---

[61] John Pinnok arranged in 1386 that William More should dispose of his estate (WRO G23/1/247; G23/1/214, fo. 84).

benefactors had been combined with others and were held on two occasions during the year, on the eve of St John the Evangelist's day and on the feast of the beheading of St John the Baptist. Collective drinkings were held and the attendance of guild members was compulsory.[62] More obits were added in later years. In 1458 John Ashford, a former guild warden, gave a tenement called 'Lokyers' to the guild wardens on condition that they spent 10s. on his anniversary in the church of St Edmund's. Regulations in 1464 show that, by then, two obits and one mind were being held at St Thomas's and two minds at St Edmund's.[63]

The endowments received from benefactors, moreover, also enabled the tailors to support their own chantry priest. Letters patent were acquired in 1446 and 1461 to found a chantry in St Thomas's church.[64] The chantry priest was paid £4 a year (in 1444) and control over him was exercised with care. During the Midsummer procession he was to wear the guild's livery. He was to serve for no longer than the period allotted 'o'lis this good myndes of the craft thim be shewid to hym and optigned' or only 'as long as yt shall plese the wardens'. In 1532 it pleased the guild to allow its priest to continue in service 'from henceforth a whole year'.[65]

The maintenance of the chantry, however, proved a costly undertaking. Bishop Beauchamp's rental of the city in 1455 shows the wardens of the guild in possession of only one tenement. A slump in the cloth trade after 1449 may also have weakened the guild financially. In 1451 a meeting of the tailors decreed that 'alle they that holde shoppe in the Cyte' were to pay the fraternity priest 8d. yearly. In 1464 it was then enacted that every brother and sister was to pay 12d. yearly to the priest's salary. Some effort was being made to increase the number of tenements owned by the guild from the 1450s; yet in 1479 the fraternity admitted that it had 'been att our grete coste and charge to make tariff for money to be levyed amongys us, to pay our channteri preste yerlie, yn ponusshyng and grete hurt to our said crafte'.[66] There is a suggestion, too, that the guild was finding it

[62] G23/1/251, fo. 3ʳ⁻ᵛ; Haskins, *Guilds*, 109–11.

[63] WRO, G23/1/215, fo. 4ʳ⁻ᵛ; Haskins, *Guilds*, 116, 119–20; WRO G23/1/251, fos. 7, 8ᵛ. The three minds were to cost 6s. 8d., the two obits 5s. One of these may have included Edward Goodyer who, according to an inventory of c.1475, left 10s. for obits.

[64] *CPR* (1446–52), 122. On 25 June 1449 the tailors received a new charter from Henry VI revoking one made in 1447 which had moved the chantry from St Thomas's to St Edmund's (D & C, Reg. Burgh, fo. 22). See also PRO C1/108/17; WRO G23/1/258; G23/1/250, fo. 8ʳ⁻ᵛ.

[65] WRO G23/1/251, fo. 2. A livery of four yards of the same cloth as the tailors' own livery (Haskins, *Guilds*, 110; WRO G23/1/251, fos. 2, 19, 20ᵛ, 24, 27ᵛ).

[66] Neville, 'Salisbury in 1455', 88; WRO G23/1/251, fos. 6, 8ᵛ; Haskins, *Guilds*, 21, 121–2; G23/1/250, fos. 7ᵛ, 8ᵛ–10. For gifts of Stephen Hendy, Thomas Danyell, Edward

difficult to fund the anniversary obligations imposed upon them. In 1464 it was agreed that the guild should hold two obits in St Thomas's church, two more minds and another mind in St Edmund's church. If John Ashford's mind was one of those being celebrated in St Edmund's in 1464, then it was only being half funded: 5*s*., not 10*s*., was being allocated for its maintenance. These regulations for the obits and minds were to continue only 'unto such tyme as the lyvelode of the fraternitie encrese'.[67]

Despite financial hardship, however, the guild had clearly made every effort to maintain divine service for the living and dead. And further help was at hand. In 1479 William Swayne, merchant and three times mayor of the city, was able to replenish the guild's stocks; as well as providing for his own obit, he gave nine marks of quit rent a year to maintain the guild's chantry priest. He also gave 40*s*. of quit rent for the guild to celebrate his own obit. This was to be held, so the tailors' rule book went on to state, in conjunction with the guild's main feast-day festivities in St Thomas's church in the chapel of St John the Baptist on the feast of the Nativity of St John (24 June).[68] The tailors' efforts to maintain their chantry and other services suggest that it was not a task that they took lightly.

Clearly, the tailors saw themselves bound together in a religious community with the important duty of maintaining divine service for their living and dead members. It is also clear that contemporaries valued the spiritual services they could provide. William Swayne was not a tailor himself and would have been unaffected by the economic duties owed by other guild members, yet he chose the fraternity as an executor of his good works. Women would not have been masters or journeymen but could be 'sisters' of the fraternity: the names of three, without mention of any husband, appear on the later of the guild's two bede rolls. Furthermore, other testators are found making bequests to more than one craft guild. William Scrop was described as a weaver in his will made in 1462 and he duly left 3*s*. 4*d*. to the guild lights. Yet he reserved his (potentially) largest benefaction to the tailors, the reversion of a tenement, if he had no heirs, for the performance of an obit.[69] Craft guilds could sometimes be considered primarily as religious fraternities dispensing good works for their benefactors.

Goodyer, and John Ashford see Haskins, *Guilds*, 130; WRO G23/1/257PC; G23/1/214, fo. 4^{r-v}.

  [67] G23/1/251, fo. 7.   [68] Haskins, *Guilds*, 121–2; G23/1/250, fos. 8^{v}–10.
  [69] D & C, Reg. Newton, fos. 27^{v}–28; G23/1/250, fo. 206; WRO G23/1/257PC. For other testators see Margaret Cuffe in 1513 (PCC 19 Fetiplace), and her husband William who had in 1500 left £3. 6*s*. 8*d*. to the weavers' altar (PCC 6 Moone).

The spiritual services provided by other craft guilds in the city are less well documented. The weavers certainly maintained altar lights and a chantry priest (though apparently without mortmain licence) in St Edmund's church under the patronage of the Virgin Mary. In the fifteenth century their lights received at least seven bequests, some of which were of land.[70] The barber-surgeons maintained a light in the cathedral and also had property which supported obits.[71] Within St Thomas's church, many guilds made annual oblations to the high altar, probably on the feasts of their patron saints: the barber-surgeons in June, the ironmongers in June or July, the fishermen in July, the glovers in August, the butchers in October, the bakers, merchants, and bell-ringers in November, and the chandlers in December.[72] But only the tailors and the weavers appear to have been wealthy enough to maintain stipendiary priests.

The multiplicity of craft guilds doubtless set up a multitude of different loyalties: some of these may have cut across obligations owed to the parish. In one sense, the activities of a craft guild could transcend parochial boundaries. On days of civic processions, the guilds were reminded of their place in and their obligations towards the whole city rather than one parish. The tailors' assemblies could echo city legislation concerning the obligatory attendance at the watch on St Osmund's night, soon after Midsummer, on 15 July. The guild made annual contributions to the watch, as much as 28s. in 1531; and by 1525 at the latest it had its own pageant or play in the St Osmund's procession (see Table 9).[73] The tailors' activities also spread over more than one parish. Despite having its own chapel in St Thomas's church, the guild invariably held its meetings, until 1533, in the church of the grey friars, located within the parish of St Martin's. In 1447 the guild held a meeting in the chapel of St Katherine in the cemetery of St Edmund's. It was also asked to maintain obits within the parish churches of both St Edmund and St Thomas. And on Midsummer's day the tailors' procession took in the liberty of the close on its way from Aylewater bridge, and halted to hear a mass at one of the cathedral altars.[74] The guild's activities were spread throughout the whole city, regardless of parochial boundaries (see Map 5).

So the religious celebrations of a craft guild like the tailors' could transcend the parish in ways that a 'parish' fraternity like the St Edmund's Jesus guild did not. But despite these extra-parochial activities,

[70] John Forest 1409 (WRO G23/1/213, fo. 83^{r-v}); Richard Gage 1444 (PCC 34 Luffenham); John Briggs 1491 (PCC 1 Doggett).

[71] Haskins, *Guilds*, 361. In 1430 William Harnell left 2s. to the light of the barber-surgeons 'in the Cathedral' (WRO G23/1/214, fo. 124^v).

[72] D & C, Press II, Procurator's accounts.

[73] WRO G23/1/250, fos. 11^v–32^v, esp. fo. 14^v. [74] WRO G23/1/251, *passim*.

the tailors' guild appears to have been more strongly attached to one parish, that of St Thomas. The route of the tailors' procession on Midsummer's day does not seem to have been designed to take in the other two parishes (see Map 5). The guild temporarily shifted its chantry from St Thomas's to St Edmund's in 1447 but it was moved back two years later. On that occasion it may have been necessary to move the chantry to St Edmund's because the chancel of St Thomas's church had collapsed. And tailors were also involved in the process of rebuilding the chancel. Among those deputed by the parishioners of St Thomas to entreat the dean and chapter to help rebuild the chancel in 1448 were Richard Haynes, later present at the tailors' meeting in 1451, and Stephen Hendy, warden of the tailors' guild in 1444. Among them also was William Swayne, later benefactor of the tailors. Swayne may have paid for the building of an enlarged chapel on the south side of the chancel, in which he was to found his own chantry; it was in this chapel, too, the chapel of St John, that the tailors were to have their altar.[75] So perhaps they also contributed to the cost of the new chapel. The tailors' guild, then, helped to embellish the fabric of the parish church in which it maintained its own chantry.

There is also a hint that crafts were involved with other parish fraternities within the parish church. The chaplain of the weavers' guild in St Edmund's in 1504/5 paid a total of 14*d.* to the Jesus guild for bread, wine, and wax throughout the year.[76] The tailors may have made similar arrangements with the parish fraternities within St Thomas's. On occasion, they also employed the same priest as the Jesus guild of St Thomas. In 1535 it was agreed at a meeting that from the feast of St Nicholas, for as long as it pleased the fraternity, Sir Richard, 'last morrow mass priest of St Thomas's should serve as the tailors' own priest'. The morrow mass priest of St Edmund's church was also the priest of the Jesus guild in that church; the same may have been true in St Thomas's church.[77] As has been argued, the devotional fraternities helped to enrich the devotional life of their parishes: by involvement with them, craft guilds were helping to do likewise.

A craft guild like the tailors', moreover, could also supplement the stipends of the parish clergy. It was not just the morrow mass priests who were chosen: in 1531 Sir John Clerk, the parish priest of St Thomas's church, was chosen as the tailors' own priest.[78] Craft guilds that did not maintain their own stipendiary priests could nevertheless contribute to

---

[75] D & C, Reg. Burgh, fo. 2; Haskins, *Guilds*, 131, 136.   [76] *S. Edmund Accounts*, 258.
[77] WRO G23/1/251, fos. 24ᵛ, 27ᵛ; *S. Edmund Accounts*, 252.
[78] WRO G23/1/251, fo. 19.

clerical funds. Regular payments to the high altar of St Thomas's Salisbury came from the altar lights maintained by guilds: in 1509/10 a total of 16s. 8d. was received from nine fraternities. The tailors too gave sums of around 2s. These guild oblations formed part of the funds that the procurator of St Thomas's delivered to the masters of the cathedral fabric (since St Thomas's was appropriated to the cathedral): they, in their turn, used the same funds to maintain other parochial needs and celebrations. The chancel of St Thomas's church was maintained in this way, and so were the celebrations of the parishioners at Pentecost.[79] The funds of craft guilds, then, contributed, directly and indirectly, to divine service, lay and clerical, within the parish church to which they were most strongly attached.

Guild attachment to one parish, however, could cut across parochial obligations in another way. If craft guilds were tied to one parish rather than to several, a conflict of loyalties may have been felt among members who were parishioners of another parish. In 1538 William Williams asked in his will that he be buried in St Edmund's church; yet while giving £3. 6s. 8d. to the fraternity of St John the Baptist, the tailors, he gave only £2 to the fabric of St Edmund's and left nothing to any other fraternity within that church.[80] So perhaps loyalty and generosity to the parish were weakened by membership of a craft that maintained its lights within another parish.

However, it is very difficult to ascertain relative loyalties from the evidence of wills, particularly as they give no indication of spiritual provision made during a testator's lifetime. In fact, only twenty-three Salisbury testators left money to craft guilds between 1409 and 1538: of these only four made the craft guild the object of their largest bequest.[81] Only seven gave to guilds with altar lights in a parish church other than the one in which they chose to be buried;[82] and of these, besides William Williams, only two other testators gave more to the fraternity than to their own parish church.[83] Indeed wills point equally to a concern felt by testators more to provide for the services within their parishes than to maintain

[79] D & C, Press II, Procurator's accounts, no. 7; Accounts of the masters of the fabric from the receipts of St Thomas's.

[80] PCC 25 Dyngeley.

[81] John Forest 1409 (WRO G23/1/213, fo. 83[r-v]); William More 1424 (G23/1/214, fo. 84[r-v]); William Scrop 1462 (D & C, Reg. Newton, fos. 27[v]–28); and William Williams 1538.

[82] Thomas Eir 1410 (WRO G23/1/213, fos. 90[v]–91); Thomas Child 1413 (G23/1/214, fo. 4[v]); William Harnell 1430 (ibid., fo. 124[v]); William Cuffe 1500 (PCC 6 Moone); John Viresdon 1503 (PCC 8 Holgrave); John Wagyn 1524 (PCC 24 Bodefeld). For William Scrop 1462 and William Williams 1538 see above, nn. 80, 81.

[83] Thomas Eir, William Cuffe.

those of their craft guilds. In 1500 William Cuffe, parishioner of St Thomas's, bequeathed £3. 6s. 8d. to 'Our Lady Auter pertaining to the wevers' in St Edmund's church to buy a pair of vestments; but he also left two tenements to the mass of Our Lady in St Thomas's church in which he asked that his body be buried. In any case, the potential danger of such a conflict of loyalties may have been reduced by the possibility that many craft members lived close to one another within the same parish.[84]

Other evidence suggests, moreover, that a guild member did not regularly feel any tension between loyalties to parish or guild. He could be as much involved in the religious life of his own parish as in that of his craft which may have been more strongly attached to another parish. William Garlyk, Harry Goldstone, and Nichols Atkyns were wardens of the tailors' guild in 1481, 1531, and 1527–30 respectively, yet they had all been churchwardens of St Edmund's church in 1477, 1521, and 1523. A number of tailors were also involved in the affairs of other parish fraternities. Richard Sudden was chamberlain of the tailors' guild in 1481, yet had been seneschal of the St Edmund's Jesus mass in 1476 and it was he who gave 40s. to the Jesus fraternity for the souls of two of its members, Thomas Marky, another tailor, and Margaret his wife. John Wagyn was both seneschal of the Jesus mass in 1500/1 and warden of the tailors' guild in 1519 and 1520. William Jeffry was described as a former seneschal of the Jesus mass in 1504/5: his name also appears on the bede roll of the tailors' guild.[85]

But there is one incident that suggests that parish and guild could set up rival loyalties among the tailors. The dating of it presents problems, but the incident appears to have taken place during the chancellorship of Archbishop John Stafford, between May 1443 and January 1450, and probably between 1447 and 1449, when the chantry of the guild was temporarily moved to St Edmund's church.[86] Around that time, a petition was sent to the chancellor by the fraternity of St John the Baptist. It was stated that the king had granted letters patent for the guild to found a perpetual chantry in St John the Baptist's chapel in St Edmund's church.

---

[84] From a rental list made c.1399, the largest number of tailors lived in the New Street chequer, in St Thomas's parish (*VCH: Wilts.* vi. 133).

[85] *S. Edmund Accounts*; WRO G23/1/251. Tailors could also serve as churchwardens of St Thomas's church. The names of four churchwardens from St Thomas's are known for the 15th cent.: one of them, John Wyly (churchwarden 1453/4, WRO G23/1/44, no. 3), was apparently a benefactor of the tailors (*S. Edmund Accounts*, 248, 253, 258; WRO G23/1/251).

[86] PRO C1/108/14. *VCH: Wilts.* vi. 134 refers to this document in the papers of Chancellor John Morton (1486–93) but it should be in those of John Stafford (1443–50). The two men mentioned in the petition, Stephen Hendy and John Staveley, were, respectively, warden of the guild in 1444 and present at a meeting in 1451.

'Diverse vestementes, ornaments and implements' belonged to the chantry in that church 'and nought in the church of St Thomas's'. However, the petition went on to say, two men, Stephen Hendy and John Staveley, both described as parishioners of St Thomas's and both apparently brethren of the tailors' guild, had withheld the vestments, ornaments, implements, deeds, muniments, and letter patents of the guild and were labouring 'with all ther power to destroye the said chaunterie'. The brethren of the guild thus wanted the chancellor to supply them with a subpoena against the two men. The motives of the two are unclear. Perhaps they were objecting to the temporary move of the guild chantry from St Edmund's to St Thomas's which took place between 1447 and 1449. Nothing more appears to have survived concerning the incident, but what it implies is that it was not the guild organization that was subverting the structure of the parish; instead, parochial affiliations were disrupting guild activity.

So fraternities did indeed provide services that the parish did not. They allowed their members a closer control over their devotional lives than did the parishes. They provided additional means of intercession and of expressing attachment to cults, like the Holy Name of Jesus, that were not accommodated by the parish. The activities of craft guilds, too, in many ways duplicated those of parish fraternities. The religious celebrations of craft guilds were quite as important as (and helped to further) their economic aims. As the prayer before the Salisbury tailors' bede roll put it, intercession was required 'for all the brethers and systers quyk and ded, and for all the good doers and well wishers off the present fraternity'. Even in times of economic adversity the tailors' guild made strenuous efforts to preserve its obit and chantry services.

No doubt, convivial celebrations and exclusivity of membership fulfilled a social function that the parish could not. But fraternities did not form independent groups of individuals essentially detached from the parish framework. Members need not have felt the tug of loyalties between their parishes and their guilds. Wardens of parish guilds naturally progressed to become wardens of the whole parish. Individuals do not appear to have found their devotional loyalties strained by membership of several guilds. In a small town like Bridport, and even in larger towns with several parishes like Salisbury or Reading, fraternities seemed well integrated into parish life, not least because parish and guild could contribute much to one another. Guild contributions to the fabric, parish church-building, vestments, and ornaments meant that guilds could be treated as an integral part of parish life—which was why offenders of guild customs could be summoned before parish visitational courts for correction. Even craft guilds need not have sapped loyalty to the parish and could contribute much to the parishes in which they were most firmly based. Indeed the rise of the wealthier cloth crafts in Salisbury was perhaps one facet of a more general investment in parish life in the latter half of the fourteenth century. If the wealth of the cloth trade (rather than fear of mortality after the Black Death) allowed more to be spent on church fabric and chantries, it also allowed investment in guilds which contributed to church-building and even provided additional priests to help in parochial worship. The dissolution of guild chantries in 1548, as many places pointed out, meant that it was not just the guild's members who would suffer, but the other parishioners besides.

7

Guilds of Mayors and Burgesses

In the guild returns of 1388/9, the mayor and burgesses of Malmesbury claimed, somewhat fancifully perhaps, that they and their ancestors had maintained a chapel and a priest since about the year 930, when King Athelstan had granted them land as a reward for their help against the Danes. A chaplain, to be chosen by the burgesses, had sung every day for the souls of king Athelstan, his alleged wife Maud, the burgesses and the benefactors of the town. Gifts to maintain this service had been made, by will or otherwise, 'devant temps de memoire', such that it had accumulated goods worth £10 and an annual rent of £2. 6s. Since this sum was not enough to support a priest, the burgesses had made up the rest of the priest's salary from their own goods.[1]

The corporate solidarity felt among a town's élite could be expressed in a number of ways. Particularly from the eleventh century onwards, many towns had acquired privileges and exemptions which helped the growth of self-government and autonomy. Freedom from tolls, the right to appoint officials, and the ability to hold courts became features that were increasingly known as borough privileges. Another right was to be able to form a guild merchant which could represent the whole town; the guild would include all the enfranchised burgesses, who had often earned membership through apprenticeship to a particular craft. Later privileges of incorporation gave a town the right to a common seal and to be a corporate body in the eyes of the law. By the fifteenth century the term 'guild merchant' had generally lapsed: town government was usually run by common councils, and burgesses gathered collectively as social and religious guilds like those of Malmesbury, even if few towns laid claim to such illustrious pedigrees.[2] As we shall see, however, a desire for collective harmony sometimes reflected a distant ideal rather than any immediate reality. The purpose of this chapter is to examine the function of these guilds, particularly within the context of civic unity, and how they fitted into the structure of devotional life, civic, parochial, and guild.

---

[1] PRO C47/46/413.   [2] S. Reynolds, *English Medieval Towns*, 91–130.

It is important to note, first of all, that structures of government varied widely from town to town. At least thirty towns in the region had acquired borough privileges in the twelfth or thirteenth century but not all had the same degree of autonomy.[3] The most privileged tended to be royal boroughs (Bridport, Dorchester), but there were others dominated by a local lord of the manor (Hungerford) where freedoms were more carefully circumscribed; more regulated still were towns situated on ecclesiastical land, monastic (Abingdon, Reading, and Malmesbury) and episcopal (Salisbury). There were also towns (like Maidenhead) that lacked any borough privileges and an official governing body, but which could nevertheless aspire to some form of self-government. Moreover, there were boroughs with multiple parishes (Wallingford, Wareham, and Wilton), those with just a few (Salisbury and Reading), those with only one parish (Bridport, Poole, and Windsor), and those whose churches lacked parochial status altogether (Weymouth, Melcombe Regis, and Maidenhead). All these differences affected the potential character of the guilds that bound together a town's élite.

The activities of such guilds are, unfortunately, often hidden from sight or only obscurely hinted at.[4] But illuminating evidence comes from Bridport. By the thirteenth century it contained at least two fraternities, one of which, dedicated to the Blessed Virgin Mary, had connections with the bailiffs and burgesses of the town. The fraternity maintained a chantry priest who said mass daily for its benefactors in the chapel of St Andrew, situated in the newer part of the town, which much later became the guild hall of the burgesses.[5] It did, however, maintain connections with the town's one parish church: in 1362 it was agreed with the parish rector that a yearly oblation would also be made in the parish church by all the burgesses and their wives. A new altar was dedicated to the Virgin Mary in the parish church in 1368, and later wills refer to the fraternity as apparently celebrating in the parish church.[6] The fraternity had its own wardens but the supervision of the town bailiffs was ever present. In 1345 the accounts of the fraternity were drawn up at the same time as those of the town government and were recorded in the same 'Old Dome Book'. When John Daber, alias Baker, made his will in 1456 he wished the warden of the Mary guild to keep his obit and gave the reversion of a tenement to

[3] *VCH: Berks.*, *Wilts.*, and *Dorset*, *passim*.

[4] See the chantry of Richard Cardmaker at Devizes in 1392 which the burgesses claimed as their own in 1545 (*CPR* (1391–6), 115; PRO E301/58/39).

[5] For 13th-cent. grants of property to the guild (the earliest in 1268), see DRO DC/BTB CD38, 39, 54, 58, 59, 60; *Historical Manuscripts Commission: Sixth Report*, 480–6.

[6] DRO DC/BTB CD3, Y8, Y9, Y10.

the bailiffs for ninety-nine years for the use of the same fraternity.[7] Membership of the fraternity probably included all those in town office and those who were free burgesses of the town. Certainly, a list of those who paid pennies for the mass of the Blessed Virgin Mary compiled in 1467/8 include nine former or future bailiffs out of a total of fifty-three names; 25 per cent of those on the list, in that one year alone, had served or were to serve as town officers.[8]

The burgesses of Bridport sometimes topped up the endowments of their fraternity.[9] It is possible that by 1337 its endowments had merged with those of the Holy Trinity, the other known thirteenth-century guild, when an account listed the rents of twenty-eight pieces of property, totalling £3. 11s. 5d., belonging to the 'mass of the Virgin Mary and the Holy Trinity'.[10] In 1389/90 the St Mary guild still had some twenty-eight pieces of property which were worth £4.[11] Yet more property had come the way of the bailiff and burgesses for devotional purposes. In 1368 one Robert Bemynstre had given the reversion of certain tenements (worth over £10) to the bailiff and burgesses of the town; he also arranged to bequeath further tenements in 1386 after the death of his wife Alice. But instead of giving these endowments to the pre-existing guild of St Mary, Robert gave them to found a new fraternity dedicated to St Katherine, with a separate chantry priest who was to celebrate in St Mary's church in St Leonard's chapel, for the souls of Robert and all the burgesses. Like the St Mary fraternity, the new guild was to be under the supervision of the bailiffs and burgesses. Indeed, in 1441 it was claimed that the bailiffs were used to hearing the mass of St Katherine at their own good pleasure, without the malicious interference of the incumbent vicar who prevented the chantry chaplain from celebrating mass before the end of the gospel at high mass on Sundays and festival days (probably because of the disturbance caused to the parish mass).[12] Like the St Mary guild, its member-

---

[7] DC/BTB M11, pp. 25–8; DC/BTB Y9.   [8] DC/BTB CD31, 32; H1; see Table 5.

[9] William Mountford gave property in 1424 (DC/BTB CD5).

[10] The Holy Trinity seems to have been a prestigious guild: unlike some of the later guilds, it had property (DC/BTB CD51, 52, 53) and its 13th-cent. rules (now lost) allowed for members' bodies to be carried back to Bridport if they died up to twelve leagues from the town—much further than some of the later guilds (Hutchins, *Dorset*, ii. 23). Like the Mary guild it too celebrated in St Andrew's chapel and there were already links between the properties of the two guilds (DC/BTB CD52). Their endowments seem to have merged by 1337 (DC/BTB G1, pp. 298–9); there are later references to a guild of the Holy Trinity, though no further reference to a priest of the guild supported by endowments (1405/6) (DC/BTB CD4).

[11] DC/BTB M11, pp. 27–8.

[12] DC/BTB CD 18, 20, 22, 23, 31, 32; M11, pp. 30, 59–61; B2, p. 155 (fo. 79); *Historical Manuscripts Commission: Sixth Report*, 495.

ship seems to have been more exclusive than the other fifteenth-century parish fraternities, duplicating that of St Mary's. A list of twenty-three names (one chaplain, nine laymen with their wives, and four widows) seems to have made up the membership of the St Katherine guild in 1466: all of them appear as members of the St Mary guild in 1466/7 or 1468.[13]

The mayor and burgesses of the larger city of Salisbury had similar, but not the same, arrangements. A guild merchant with 303 members was still in existence in 1306.[14] By the end of the fourteenth century a common council seems to have replaced the guild merchant, meeting between four and eight times a year. The mayor and other officers were elected on All Souls' day and the names of about forty people are usually recorded as having attended the meetings. But there were many others, freeholders of the city, who were often said to have attended: ninety-eight people attended the convocation of 1436. After 1412, however, there is mentioned for the first time the existence of a council of twenty-four who attended the meetings; after 1445 we first hear of an outer council of forty-eight citizens.[15]

The city council had its own bede roll, a list of benefactors who gave a good deal of property in the late fourteenth and early fifteenth centuries (see Table 10).[16] In the late fourteenth century too (the first reference is in 1386) we also hear about a guild with St George as its patron saint: it would appear that the twenty-four and the forty-eight, as well as the other enfranchised burgesses or freeholders of the city, were its members.[17] Although the guild had separate officers and funds (records for which are no longer extant), it can nevertheless be identified with the city burgesses.[18] Benefactors of the city apparently saw their gifts as being for the benefit of the commonalty both in its capacity as a secular congregation and in its capacity as guild of St George. When William Ashleigh (a chaplain) gave certain tenements to the mayor and commonalty in 1415,

---

[13] DC/BTB CD22, 32.

[14] *Wilts. Notes & Queries*, 4 (1902), 117–18; *Tropenell Cart.* i. 189–98 (see article 28); Benson and Hatcher, *Old and New Sarum*, 743.

[15] *VCH: Wilts.*, vi. 50; Carr, 'Urban Patriciates', 118–35.

[16] For business of city assemblies see WRO G23/1/1 and 2, legible from *c.*1400 onwards. The chamberlains' accounts are complete for eighteen years between 1409 and 1550 in WRO G23/1/1, fos. 33, 42, 70–71ᵛ; G23/1/2, fos. 184–185ᵛ; G23/1/44, nos. 1–14.

[17] Will of John Prentis (WRO G23/150/111). Benson and Hatcher, *Old and New Sarum*, 100, claim that the earliest mention of the St George guild was in a bequest of William Teynterer, 1376.

[18] Occasional mention is made in the city ledger books of the names of the seneschals of St George: John Wheler was one in 1446 (WRO G23/1/1, fo. 143), and he appears to have become mayor in 1456 (ibid., fo. 123).

TABLE 10. Benefactors of the mayor and commonalty of Salisbury

Benefactor	Date of gift when known	Date of will when known	Source (WRO G23/1)
	[*c.*1350–1399]		
On bede roll			
William Wichford (mayor 1359)*	1369: 30s. rent	1369	/214 Index
Nicholas Taylor (mayor 1372)			
John Upton	1362?: 40s. rent	1380	/214 Index
William Teynterer, elder (mayor 1364)*			
William Teynterer, younger (mayor 1375)*		1376	/214 Index
John Bitterleigh	1393: £100	1395	/1, fo. 3; BL Stowe Ch. 623
John Prentis*	1386: 40s. rent	1386	G23/150/111
John Talbot	1365: reversion		
John Pinnok		1388	/214 Index
Not on bede roll			
Christian Beneyt	1361: messuage		/214 Index
Richard Riborgh	1360: 40s. rent	1360	/213, fo. 39
John Seewyne	1387/8: tenement		/214 Index
	[1400–1449]		
On bede roll			
John Wallop (mayor 1391)*	by 1412: 40s. rent		/1, fo. 48ᵛ
John Baker	by 1419: 40s. rent		/1, fo. 66
Margaret Godmanston		1414	/214, fo. 10
John Newman	by 1409: tenement		/1, fo. 10
William Prentis			
William Salle		1414	/214, fo. 9ᵛ
William Warmwell		1412	/214, fo. 88
William Ashleigh (priest)*	1415: 100s. rent		/1, fo. 56
William Walter*	1412: 40s. rent	1417	/1, fo. 46, /214, fo. 33
John Moner*	by 1419: £4 rent		/1, fo. 66
John Becket*	reversion	1416	/214, fo. 26, /1, fo. 52

TABLE 10. *Continued*

Benefactor	Date of gift when known	Date of will when known	Source (WRO G23/1)
Walter Shirley			
Henry Baron	} by 1442: £4 rent	1424	PCC 3 Luffenham
Christine Lee/Chapman*			
William Warwick (mayor 1430)	1421: 4 cottages	1445	/1, fo. 77
Richard Gage	tenement	1444	PCC 34 Luffenham
Not on bede roll[1]			
William Baly*		1416	PCC 21 Marche
	[1450–1499]		
On bede roll			
William Halstede*	by 1478: tenement		/44, no. 4
Robert Cateston	1453: lands formerly John Nyweman's		
William Swayne	26s. 8d. rent	1484	PCC 20 Logge
Not on bede roll			
John Chafyn	1495: quit claim of tenement		G23/150/12
John Wixhale	tenement		
	[1500–1547]		
On bede roll			
Thomas Birkhead	1533: almshouse	1533	PCC 8 Hogen
Henry Coldstone	6s. rent	1547	PCC 4 Populwell

Note: There were also benefactors known to have given money, one in the 14th cent., six in the 15th cent., and eight in the early 16th cent.

* Anniversary/obit.

[1] The temporary obit of Alice Meriot, 1406, G23/1/213, fos. 73ᵛ–74, appears in the account roll of 1409/10, but not in ensuing ones.

he specified that the profits from them should be used (in part) for the guild of St George.[19] The guild, then, included all the burgesses; but the

[19] WRO G23/1/213, fos. 39–40; G23/1/1, fo. 56. The guild had benefactors who were never involved in city assemblies, like Margaret Godmanston. In general, benefactors of the city did not refer to the guild of St George: for the only two exceptions see wills of William Baly 1407 (PCC 21 Marche) and John Aport 1456 (PCC 6 Stockton).

regulations of the guild in the fifteenth century, as we shall see, were made particularly binding on members of the common council.

On the feast of St George (23 April) the mayor and burgesses had their own celebrations. On that day a large procession took place from and to the church of St Thomas with an image of St George: in 1510 it was set down that all of the twenty-four were to find two men and every member of the forty-eight one man 'wele & clerely harneysed to wayte on the George'. The procession may even have taken in the cathedral, for the fabric accounts of the cathedral record oblations being paid by the guild of St George on the same day. A dinner was also held, to which members of the twenty-four (according to an ordinance of 1492) were to contribute 20*d*. and members of the forty-eight 12*d*.[20] On these occasions too the mayor and his burgesses wore a special livery, different from the one worn at the city procession of the crafts. In 1461 it was ordained that all members of the twenty-four and forty-eight were to receive annually from the 'custodes Sancti George' a (white) hood and livery.[21] One further difference marked out the feast of St George from the other festivals: it was on St George's day that the guild members, the mayor and his burgesses, would attend a mass and dirige for the souls of the dead brothers and benefactors of the guild. They were also to provide, whether present or absent, 1*s*. to the cost of the services and for wax. Provision for dead members was made on other occasions: in 1437 an ordinance was passed commanding that six torches be found on the day of the fraternity to surround the bodies of dead members.[22]

By the fifteenth century the mayor and burgesses, as the fraternity of St George, also maintained their own priest who was to be continually at the mayor's side. The priest was to be paid during illness and enjoyed a tenement, close to St Thomas's cemetery, rent-free.[23] He may have conducted services in the cathedral: when John Prentis made his will in 1386 he gave 3*s*. 4*d*. to the 'Fraternity of St George in the church of the Blessed Mary' (the cathedral). The cathedral fabric accounts record oblations being paid by the guild of St George on the feast day of their patron saint. But the guild may also have had an altar in the parish church of St Thomas.[24] Wherever the altar was,

[20] Haskins, *Guilds*, 40; D & C, Press II, Fabric accounts; WRO G23/1/2, fo. 177.
[21] WRO G23/1/2, fo. 56. For other issues of the same order see ibid., fo. 110ᵛ (1474), fo. 152 (1483), fo. 169ᵛ (1490), fo. 177 (1492). In 1483 two of the forty-eight and of the 'bretherede of Seynt George', John Grey and William Cuffe, refused to receive the hoods and were ordered to do so by the assembly.
[22] WRO G23/1/1, fos. 111ᵛ, 147ᵛ; G23/1/2, fo. 192ᵛ.
[23] Ibid., fo. 148; G23/1/44.   [24] Haskins, *Guilds*, 38.

the priest's chantry celebrations were supported by city endowments that were worth over £50 in 1409/10 (the first extant chamberlains' account).[25] Under the Statutes of Mortmain made in 1279 and 1391 a licence was needed to hold these lands for religious purposes. In 1406 the citizens acquired a charter from Henry IV allowing them to hold lands to the value of 100 marks; in 1412 the bishop, with the agreement of the dean and chapter, conceded the same privilege, for which he was placed on the city bede roll.[26]

Separate anniversaries for individual benefactors, celebrated in the parish churches of the city, also imposed obligations on the city council. Four can be traced back to the fourteenth century, after 1360, and at least seven were set up in the first half of the fifteenth century. For William Walter's obit, founded after 1412, the chamberlains' accounts of 1438 show the expenses of his obit on the morrow of Ascension day: 6d. for a pound of lamb, 8d. for two quarters of sweetened lamb, 8d. for a quarter of wine, 16d. for bread, 2s. ½d. for thirteen gallons of ale, 8d. for cheese; and also 2s. 4d. to fourteen chaplains (2d. each), 1d. for the oblation (mass penny) and 4d. for two bedemen or bellmen 'praying in the street' (see Table 10).[27] Each obit celebration tended to have slightly distinctive features, which may have helped to set it apart from others. Some obits were clearly intended as occasions for feastings: over half the payments for John Moner's anniversary in 1438 went on lamb, bread, cheese, and wine. Some obits advertised the need for intercession by paying the deacon and sacrist for tolling the bells of the parish church: John Moner's obit in 1445 paid out 8d. to those of St Edmund's church. In some of the smaller obits, payments were restricted to priests alone. William Ashleigh's obit payment of 2s. 1d. in 1438 was spent almost entirely on ten priests. The prayers of the poor were sometimes required: the anniversary of Christine Lee saw the payment of 2s. 6d. to poor people.[28] Whatever the precise observance, the attendance of the city aldermen was expected: in 1420 a city assembly ordered the twenty-four to attend the mass of the obit days of benefactors.[29]

The obits were celebrated in all three parish churches in the city and were arranged throughout the year. Separate obits could be combined: in 1409 John Bekot's obit was celebrated with William Teynterer's, founded

---

[25] WRO G23/1/1, fo. 33. In 1419/20 receipts from rents came to £48. 3s. 6d. (ibid., fo. 67ʳ⁻ᵛ). In 1438 they came to £54. 3s. 8d. (G23/1/2, fos. 184–185ᵛ). For the rest of the 15th cent. rents seem to have remained fairly constant.

[26] Raban, *Mortmain Legislation*, 127; Benson and Hatcher, *Old and New Sarum*, 744.

[27] WRO G23/1/44; G23/1/2, fo. 185.

[28] WRO G23/1/44, nos. 2 and 4; G23/1/2, fo. 185.   [29] WRO G23/1/1, fo. 67ᵛ.

TABLE 11. Obits celebrated by the mayor and commonalty of Salisbury before 1480

Date	Name	Church
Lent		
First Sunday	John Wallop	St Edmund's
First Sunday	John Moner	St Edmund's
Second Sunday	John Prentis	St Edmund's
11 April	Christine Lee	St Thomas's
29 June	William Asshley	St Thomas's
Morrow of Ascension day	William Walter	St Edmund's
14 September	William Teynterer	St Thomas's
14 September	John Bekot	St Thomas's
29 September	William Wichford	St Edmund's
?	William Halstede	St Martin's

some forty years previously; in 1419 William Walter's obit was kept at the same time as William Wichford's (see Table 11).[30] The council also made it its duty, according to rules adopted in 1472, to ensure that properties maintaining obits were kept separate from those of the common fund.[31] The vigilance of mayor and aldermen was no doubt encouraged by profits that could be gained from careful management of the properties. Not all of the funds were used up on the obit celebration. The most paid out for the obit of William Walter was 10s. 4d. in 1421, but the property he had given to the city council was worth 40s. annually.[32] So the profits from properties set aside for obits filled the common coffers of the city.

Occasionally, however, the obits could not be financed. On every surviving chamberlains' account roll certain 'rent defects' are recorded: as little as £2. 4s. 6d. in 1449/50 but as much as £16. 14s. 8d. only a few years later in 1453/4. In 1473/4, on top of a £15. 17s. 6d. decrease in rents, a £13. 17s. 6d. default in rents was also recorded. Some of these losses affected the celebration of obits. The 1472 rules concerning rents and obits also stated that if a tenement tied to an obit was unoccupied or in ruinous condition during a particular year, then the obit was not to be

---

[30] Ibid., fos. 33, 39. After 1449/50 William Wichford's obit seems to have been kept with John Wallop's, which was not accounted for in 1412 (WRO G23/1/1, fo. 42), suggesting that the original endowment could no longer sustain the obit.

[31] WRO G23/1/2, fo. 109.

[32] WRO G23/1/44. In 1412 William Walter's property was rented out for £5 (G23/1/1, fo. 70).

kept.[33] Thus John Moner's obit costing 7s. 5d. from a tenement worth £4 in rent was not celebrated in 1473 when the tenement was vacant all that year. William Teynterer's obit was not kept in 1470 and 1474: the George Inn, which supported the obit, is to be found slowly depreciating in value. In 1473/4 too William Walter's obit was not kept: the rent from his former tenement in the market-place had not been paid in full.

There may be particular reasons, as we shall see, for the failure to celebrate these anniversaries, but they are not to be found in any idle neglect on the part of the city council. Precedents had already been set for separate obits to be combined and celebrated on the same day. In 1480 the assembly agreed on a more large-scale solution. Thereafter only three obits a year were to be held for the souls of city benefactors, on 6 January, 3 May, and 23 September.[34] The money was to come from the whole of the city rent receipts, the properties that had once maintained individual obits separately evidently being amalgamated with the rest. This arrangement may have been less burdensome in terms of attendance of obits[35] but it was not so financially. Whereas a maximum of 24s. 6d. was spent on obits in the years preceding the new rule (and the figure could be much less: 19s. in 1444/5 and nothing in 1474), 26s. was spent in 1497/8 and thereafter a regular 24s.

What functions, then, did the guilds of mayors and burgesses serve? There was certainly a social purpose behind their activities. The communal nature of the guild's celebrations served to bind the mayor and his officials in common cause. Unity was clearly a value cherished, but not always attained, by the civic élite.[36] At Salisbury the oath of the twenty-four enjoined obedience on the mayor and prohibited involvement in other 'confederacies or congregations'. Failure to attend council meetings was punished with fines of wax.[37] In 1447, however, after quarrels had

[33] WRO G23/1/44; G23/1/2, fo. 109.

[34] WRO G23/1/2, fo. 135

[35] See C. Phythian-Adams, 'Urban Decay in Late Medieval England', in P. Abrams and E. A. Wrigley (eds.), *Towns and Societies: Essays in Economic History and Historical Sociology* (Cambridge, 1978), 176–8; T. F. Reddway, 'The London Goldsmiths c.1500', *TRHS*, fifth series, 12 (1962), 57.

[36] See Intro. nn. 59, 60; see also C. Phythian-Adams, *Desolation of a City: Coventry and the Urban Crisis of the Late Middle Ages* (Cambridge, 1979), esp. 139; B. McRee, 'Religious Guilds and Regulation of Behaviour in Late Medieval Towns', in J. Rosenthal and C. Richmond (eds.), *People, Politics and Community in the Later Middle Ages* (Gloucester, 1987), 108–22.

[37] WRO G23/1/2, fo. 15ᵛ. The guild merchant of Wilton made it a rule in 1527 that if any 'seditious words about any brother' were said, the offender was to pay 10s. to the common box (WRO G25, General entry book, fo. 116).

disrupted convocations, it was ruled that none of the twenty-four or the forty-eight was to indulge in personal invective or reproach against another, under penalty of 3s. 4d. Two offenders, William Swayne and John Hall, were singled out for special mention: should they disturb the peace again they were to be fined 20s. the first time, 40s. the second, and imprisoned on the third offence.[38] Such was the concern for unity that on other occasions of similar effrontery the punishment might be the provision of a 'iantaculum' (breakfast) for the twenty-four:[39] by this communal act, the fragile social unity of the corporation could be affirmed.

The communal acts of the mayor and burgesses bound together as the guild of St George could achieve the same end. The penalties of wax on non-attendance at convocation were to be levied by the stewards of St George to sustain the lights at the altar of their patron saint.[40] The dinner on St George's day, or at the obits of city benefactors held throughout the year, served to remind the burgesses of their common bonds. In Wilton and Marlborough too the obit days of certain benefactors took place on the day of the mayor's election and drinkings were held for the living burgesses.[41] In Salisbury, where more detail is known, it is also clear that these services took place throughout the year. The anniversary celebrations, whether before 1480 or after, when they were combined into three, took place throughout the year: there does not seem to have been, as C. Phythian-Adams maintained, quite such a divide between a secular and a religious half to the communal year.[42]

[38] WRO G23/1/2, fo. 141a. Remarks made against John Hall's social status may have been particularly pointed. Although a wealthy burgess and mayor of the city on four occasions, he had been accused by the prioress and convent of Amesbury of being their villein (Hare, 'Lords and Tenants', 24).

[39] See the judgment on John Freman, mercer, for certain scandalous remarks touching the mayor's authority (WRO G23/1/1, fo. 92ᵛ). See also the award made between William Swayne, mayor, and Edmund Penstone, gentleman, and one of the twenty-four concerning certain offensive words spoken by the latter about the mayor in the chapter house of the cathedral at vespers on the feast of All Saints 1455: Edmund was to give a pipe of red Gascony wine to the mayor and pay 20s. for a 'iantaculo' for the twenty-four (WRO G23/1/2, fos. 13ᵛ–14). Edmund seems to have been obstructive of Robert Caterton's gift of certain tenements to the mayor and commonalty (PRO C1/54/7).

[40] WRO G23/1/1, fo. 15ᵛ.

[41] The Wilton town ledger mentions seven 15th-cent. benefactors (WRO G25, fo. 12), though not those of the 14th cent. See also WRO G25/1/141/2 (the anniversary of Nicholas Laurens in 1361); and G25/1/128, 129, 130, 133, 136, 138, 139. The Marlborough mayor and burgesses were invited to attend the exequies of James Lowdar in 1519 and then adjourn to 'the tavern in which the mayor and burgesses were used to assemble and drink' (WRO G23/1/246; see also WRO 1230).

[42] C. Phythian-Adams, 'Ceremony and the Citizen: The Communal Year at Coventry 1450–1550', in P. Clark and P. Slack (eds.), *Crisis and Order in English Towns 1500–1700: Essays in Urban History* (London, 1972), esp. 70–7.

In some towns corporate solidarity may have been cultivated for more subversive purposes. Restrictions imposed by ecclesiastical privilege could prove irksome. Laymen in Bridport may have founded fraternities in the thirteenth century to escape the meddling of the parish priest. Both the Holy Trinity and St Mary fraternities were set up, at least initially, in St Andrew's chapel, not the larger parish church, and one benefactor of the St Mary fraternity stipulated that none of the rectors, farmers, or chaplains of the parish church was to interfere with the property he had given the fraternity. Complaints against the rector's provision of pastoral care in the chapel by parishioners sometimes look, in another light, like the efforts of town officials to maintain the status of their guild chapel. In 1362 the bailiffs wished to ensure that the rector fulfilled his obligations towards maintaining the chaplain of St Andrew's; in 1441 they complained to the bishop that the rector had installed a drunkard from Brittany as the chapel's priest.[43]

In towns that lacked full parish churches, burgesses may have founded their own fraternity chantries to boost the status of their main town chapel. Weymouth was a borough town, yet its church was a chapel of ease to Wyke Regis, a mile distant. A feeling of inferiority may have been behind the move to acquire a mortmain licence for a fraternity of St George in the town chapel in 1442 by the mayor and guild wardens.[44] Similarly, Maidenhead borough was split parochially between the churches of Cookham and Bray and also fell between the two royal manors, lacking any communal organization of its own. Efforts to establish its own chapel in the thirteenth and early fourteenth centuries had met with resistance from parish rectors and bishops. The chapel finally established had a chantry founded within it in 1352; in the meantime privileges were being acquired for the town's bridge for 'the bailiffs and good men of Maidenhead'. In 1451 the chaplain of the chantry acquired a licence to found a guild to maintain both chantry and bridge, over which the bailiffs of the town had control.[45] Acquisition of bridge privileges, chapel, chantry, and guild seem part and parcel of a movement to increase the town's autonomy.

Moreover, in towns dominated by an ecclesiastical landlord, fraternities could become focuses for burgesses to assert their independence. Old

---

[43] DRO DC/BTB CD58, 47, 48.

[44] Hutchins, *Dorset*, ii. 445; *CPR* (1452–61), 241. In 1548 the inhabitants claimed that, if they could not have their own chapel of St George, they would have to go to Wyke Regis church, leaving their womenfolk exposed to attacks from invaders (E. Fry, 'Dorset Chantries', *NQSD* 33 (1909), 43).

[45] See Ch. 3 n. 17; *VCH: Berks.*, ii. 30–2; *CPR* (1446–52), 576.

Benedictine abbeys could be particularly fierce in the maintenance of long-established rights. The burgesses of Abingdon certainly found themselves at odds with the abbey, and in 1369 the townspeople attempted to show that Abingdon was a royal borough and that the abbot had no right to tolls, tallages, and other dues. Perhaps as a step towards asserting their independence from the abbey, the townspeople had founded a guild dedicated to the Holy Cross some time in the reign of Henry III. In 1441 the guild acquired a charter of incorporation which officially allowed it to acquire lands in mortmain and the right of pleading as a corporate body in courts of law. Their cause was perhaps helped by the patronage of Sir John Golafre who appears as a member of the guild.[46] Similarly, the burgesses of Reading from the thirteenth century onwards clashed occasionally with Reading abbey. In the late fifteenth century they resisted the abbot's right to select guild officers, and sought to increase their hold over land given to the guild by attempting to prove its status as a body corporate in 1450. It was perhaps in the same defiant spirit that William Colney had founded a chantry to be presented to the mayor and burgesses: in 1450 and 1509 their patronage of the chantry was cited as one of the reasons why the guild merchant was to be considered as a corporation.[47]

Corporate solidarity was also cultivated in Salisbury, not against any monastic house but against the bishop on whose land the city lay. Throughout the later Middle Ages the autonomy of the borough was restricted by episcopal overlordship, and conflicts between bishop and citizens occasionally erupted. In 1306 when Bishop Simon Gandavo attempted to raise tallage in the city on the basis of the 1227 charter, he met with strong, though ultimately fruitless, resistance.[48] The St George guild of Salisbury may well have been formed soon after the conflict over tallage in the early fourteenth century. And when the licence was granted in 1406 for the alienation of land in mortmain, it was said to have been given because two parts of the city were in the hands of clergymen and strangers and scarcely one part in the hands of the citizens. The licence perhaps reflected the citizens' desire to increase their hold over city land.

Other conflicts arose during the later Middle Ages as the citizens sought to weaken the jurisdictional hold of the bishop. A particularly troublesome time was during the episcopates of Bishop Beauchamp

---

[46] See Ch. 1 nn. 57, 58; *CPR* (1441–6), 36–7; (1476–85), 386; Abingdon almshouse deeds, 573, 574.

[47] See Ch. 1 n. 55; BL Add. MS 6214, fo. 7/16; C. F. Slade, 'Reading Records', *BAJ* 61 (1963–4), 48–59. The monks claimed that the burgesses possessed the advowson to the chantry only at the sufferance of the abbey.

[48] See Intro. n. 16.

(1450–81). The citizens seem to have attempted to secure additional privileges for the city and acquire a charter of incorporation. In 1465 Beauchamp was complaining to the king that the city council had been 'daily pretending faithul cheer outward, with feigned language, desceytfully thought of inward malice' to subvert his jurisdiction. The conflict was made more difficult for the burgesses because they were not able to present a united front. It was William Swayne's break from solidarity with his fellow aldermen that weakened the burgesses in their effort to assert their independence from the bishop. Indeed it may have been no accident that the dispute began in 1465 when Swayne's old rival John Hall was mayor. Swayne had obtained a plot of land from the bishop for his chantry house but the city council appears to have claimed the land as its own. When the building of the house had progressed so that 'the walls and chimnies wer of good height', the council, led by John Hall, objected to the bishop's claim to dispose of the land as lord of the manor and to Swayne's possession of it on those terms. In April 1465 the council decided to take forcible possession of the piece of land until Swayne should 'make amends for the trespass done to the said tofte'; this decision was executed by stealth at night. In May, Swayne was summoned before the assembly to answer for his conduct: when he appeared in June he was expelled from the twenty-four until he should submit.[49]

Clearly the aldermen found themselves weakened in their conflict with the bishop when dissension broke their ranks. In a later dispute, the incoming mayor William Easton refused to take the customary oath to the bishop's bailiff in 1473 to assert the status of the mayoralty. It did not help his 'worship' that men like William Boket could insult him to his face.[50] Strict regulations about the conduct of aldermen towards one another could be made, but it was of greater help to inculcate fraternal feeling by involvement in the communal activities of a guild. Duty to one's brethren was a necessary concept in promoting fraternal unity. In Salisbury it needed enforcing if the citizens were to win independence from the bishop.

The same conflict with Bishop Beauchamp had one further ramification. In 1466 the mayor and commonalty were cited before the Exchequer,

[49] Street, 'Bishops and Citizens', 237–45. The commonalty seems to have attempted to lay claim to that plot of land before the dispute began, for they were claiming rent for it in 1438/9, 1444/5, and 1449/50. In 1453/4 they failed to collect the rent (a default of 2s. is recorded), and again during the dispute, 1469/70. See WRO G23/1/44; WRO D1/1/5, Liber Niger, fo. 146, for the bishop's representation to the king; ibid., fo. 164c; WRO G23/1/2, fos. 74b, 76a, 76b.

[50] Street, 'Bishops and Citizens', 251; see Intro. n. 60.

probably at the instigation of the bishop, to show that they were not holding lands in mortmain contrary to the Statute of 1391.[51] Reference was made to similar controversies during the episcopacies of Bishop Chandler, in 1426, and Bishop Aiscough, in 1441 and 1443. The city council may have attempted to avoid paying quit rent owing to the bishop as overlord. A total of ten people were named as having bequeathed or given land from 1406 onwards (and a further twenty messuages or tenements were said to have been acquired by the commonalty) which were cited as being held contrary to the Statutes; the rent owing to the bishop is quoted, along with the holding's value. The citizens were able to acquit themselves in 1473, but not before the protracted dispute had incurred legal expenses and distraint on city property leading to a loss of rents and arrears. And by questioning the legality of gifts of land in mortmain to the commonalty, the dispute also threatened the celebration of obits funded from many of these lands. That almost none were kept in 1469/70 and 1473/4 (the year the dispute was settled) may not be coincidental. William Walter's obit, regularly celebrated up to 1454 (the date of the last extant account roll before 1469) was not observed in 1470 and 1474: the tenement from which part of the rent was drawn to maintain the obit was one whose alienation to the mayor and commonalty was in question. Christine Lee's messuage which supported her anniversary was similarly disputed: in 1474 expenditure on her obit (the only one celebrated in that year) was cut back. The threat posed to these celebrations, which involved the fraternity of St George, may have been one reason why the city assembly decided a few years later to amalgamate the obits: alienations of individual properties may have been questioned, but obits could still be celebrated from the common fund of the city.

Yet too much stress can be placed on the subversive potential of guild foundations. Borough towns that were not situated on ecclesiastical land, like Devizes, Windsor, and Bridport (all royal boroughs), acquired chantries to serve their mayors and burgesses just as readily, and Windsor secured a charter of incorporation in 1462.[52] The townsmen of Malmesbury appear to have had fewer disputes with its abbey than those of Reading and Abingdon; in 1507 the mayor, aldermen, burgesses, and bridge officers of Wallingford agreed to celebrate an obit for the dean of

[51] For what follows see PRO E368/240 and E159/250. There are ten benefactors specifically mentioned who left property to the mayor and commonalty between 1407 and 1448: George Meriot, Richard Pinnok, John Tenterelles, John Asshley, William Walter, Walter Shirley, John Halstede, Christine At Lee, Walter Short, John Aparke. Not all the names appear on the city bede roll (see Table 10).

[52] *CPR* (1461–7), 248, 551.

the college of secular priests within the town.[53] The impetus behind other guild foundations, the penitential concern for the soul in a purgatorial afterlife, was at the back of those founded by mayors and burgesses as well. How this concern was expressed varied from place to place. At Wilton, celebrations were on a more meagre scale than at Salisbury: one John Broune in 1468 gave only a silver bowl, for which he was to be prayed for with '*de profundis, pater, noster* and *ave maria*' by the rector of Trinity church, to whom one penny was given from the seneschal of the guild merchant.[54] Some burgesses (like those at Malmesbury) did not acquire mortmain licences to accumulate land, but those of Bridport acquired two fraternities and chantry priests to serve their intercessory needs. However, all found themselves in a reciprocal relationship with their dead brethren.

Although the élites of borough towns had their own celebrations, they were far from existing in splendid isolation from the religious activities of other guilds and parishes. As individuals, burgesses were frequently involved in the affairs of their parishes and other fraternities. The town officers of Bridport may have had two fraternities of their own, yet most of the bailiffs of Bridport between 1400 and 1480 can be found belonging to one or more of the parish fraternities within the town.[55] Wardens of the Jesus guild in St Edmund's Salisbury are likewise to be found, further on in their careers, not only as wardens of the parish and members of craft guilds but also as mayors of the whole city.[56]

As heads of town governments, mayors and bailiffs were expected to perform a number of religious duties within the town as a whole. In a large city like Salisbury, processions of craft guilds like the tailors' requested the presence of the mayor. Civic processions required the attendance of mayor and city council: dressed in a livery of scarlet or crimson—not the white garb required on the feast of St George—they took part in the processions of the craft guilds. Civic processions may well have been the occasion of fractious disputes over precedence, as changes could be made in the order of craft guilds. The overseeing presence of the mayor perhaps kept a delicate civic unity intact. The processions at least pro-

---

[53] J. M. Moffat, *The History of the Town and Abbey of Malmesbury* (Tetbury, 1805), 106–7; BRO W/ACa 1, fo. 1r–v.

[54] See above n. 41.

[55] Thirty-five out of fifty-five bailiffs between 1400 and 1480 were members of guilds, as were a further nineteen out of forty-two other town officers—comparing lists in DRO DC/BTB M11 and H1 with guild lists, see Table 5.

[56] See Ch. 6 n. 26.

claimed the ideal of unity which was why mayors ensured that all crafts
were to appear in the best manner possible 'to the honour of the city'.[57]

As corporate bodies, moreover, mayors and burgesses kept a watchful
eye on town parishes. The Salisbury mayor could be called upon to
supervise the annual accounts of the Jesus fraternity in St Edmund's.
Occasionally the mayor and members of the inner council were paid to
attend anniversary services, the endowments of which had not been entrusted to them.[58] This practice is much more evident in Marlborough: of
the nineteen people known to have left property for obits in the sixteenth
century, four gave their endowments directly to the mayor and burgesses,
but five others required the mayor to attend the obit mass.[59] Individual
chantries founded in borough town parishes could also be supervised by
town officers, though less so in Salisbury, perhaps, where other corporate
bodies like the college of St Edmund's and the cathedral were more often
chosen to present chantry priests or supervise the services.[60] But in other
towns borough officials had more clearly defined duties. In Bridport the
bailiffs were brought into the supervision of the chantry of Michael
Munden as soon as it was founded in 1361. If the rector failed to present
a priest when the chantry fell vacant, it was laid down, the bailiff was to
present one of his own choice. Indeed, in 1450 the bailiff reported that the
rector, John Heliar, had failed to appoint a priest within a month of a
vacancy and had finally presented John Chipping who, the bailiff claimed,
was a fornicator and adulterer. The burgesses had their own candidate
who was a man of 'good discretion and honest conversation'. In 1477/8
the chantry chaplains refused to let the bailiffs visit the chantry and its
house, so the burgesses denied them their salary. Normally, though, relations with the chantry priests seem to have been peaceable. Munden's
priests sometimes entertained the bailiff in their household and the burgesses occasionally augmented the chantry's endowments.[61]

---

[57] WRO G23/1/2, fos. 139ᵛ (1480), 210 (1503), 254 (1524). For contributions of the city
treasury to the fire at St Osmund's watch in the market-place see G23/1/44, no. 8 (1508–9).
The livery worn by the civic élite during craft processions was potentially more hierarchical
and divisive than the uniform white livery worn on the feast of St George: the 'mayor and
his brethren' were to wear scarlet (if they were former mayors) or crimson gowns (if they
were members of the twenty-four but not former mayors). On civic processions—the
tensions they created or the unity they inspired—see Rubin, *Corpus Christi* 243–71 and
references cited there.
[58] Will of Joan Peerse, widow, 1536 (PCC 15 Dyngeley).
[59] WRO G23/1/246; WRO 1250.   [60] See Ch. 4 n. 37.
[61] *A Small Household of the XVth Century, being the Account Book of Munden's Chantry,
Bridport*, ed. K. L. Wood-Legh (Manchester, 1956), pp. xxx, 85 ff.; DRO DC/BTB H1, pp.
60, 708–4 (*sic*).

The links between town officials and parishes may have given rise to a complexity of loyalties for individuals. In towns with more than one parish, those who were parishioners of one parish might find themselves, as town officials, involved in the affairs of another. In Reading the possibility was recognized. At St Laurence's in 1532/3 it was agreed that the mayor was to be given custody of a cup that had been given to the parish, but only if he was a parishioner of that church.[62] But in towns like Bridport, Windsor, and Poole, where the parish was virtually coterminous with the borough, links between parish and town government were sometimes so close as to make it difficult to distinguish between the two.

On the one hand, the municipal coffers of these towns could contribute directly to those of the parish. In 1518 the scribe of the town book of Poole made a careful note that one Master Stroude owed £8 towards the making of the new rood loft in the church.[63] In Windsor, in the early sixteenth century the corporation accounts record occasional gifts to the churchwardens of St John's and to the parish rood loft.[64] When St Mary's at Bridport was rebuilt at the beginning of the fifteenth century, the bailiff and burgesses (whatever their attachment to the chapel of St Andrew) paid for work on the church and for its rededication by the bishop. When £15. 16s. 8d. was collected for the church bells in 1405/6, some of the money was raised by parish fraternities, but £10 of it came from the town coffers. The £62. 16s. 6d. raised by Christmas 1408 for the bell tower was accounted for in the presence of the bailiffs.[65]

On the other hand, the parish could contribute to civic projects. When a new windmill was built at Baiter in Poole in 1542, church money was used to make up the necessary sum.[66] When rebuilding began on the town harbour of Bridport in 1447, collectors were sent out far and wide, to Berkshire, Somerset, Devon, and Cornwall. Some of the efforts were disappointing. One of the collectors, John Greyve, had a woeful tale to report: whereas in the previous year he had been able to gather large quantities of groats, pennies, wool, broken silver, and rings for the works of Mary Magdalen hospital near the town, he could scarcely collect a dishful of wheat, malt, or barley, or even a piece of bacon, for the harbour works. Another collector had even run off with some of the funds. But the townspeople of Bridport had been assiduous in their efforts, and the

---

[62] BRO D/P 97/5/2, p. 190. The mayors of Salisbury and Wallingford celebrated obits in all their respective town parishes (see Table 11; BRO W/ACa 1, fo. 1ʳ⁻ᵛ).

[63] Poole municipal archives, Old Town Book 23 (1), pp. 10, 95.

[64] BRO WI/FAc 1, fos. 21, 22.

[65] *Historical Manuscripts Commission: Sixth Report*, 492; DRO DC/BTB CD4.

[66] Poole municipal archives, Old Town Book, 23 (1), pp. 68, 70.

money they collected was recorded in the town book. They had also acquired indulgences for contributions to the project and had made clear how the priests of the parish could contribute. The rector, the chaplains of the chantries of St Katherine, St Mary, and St Nicholas of Munden's chantry, and the hospital chaplain were all to celebrate masses for the benefactors of the harbour.[67] Town contributed to parish as parish to town: so close-knit were the two in some places that it is difficult to disentangle the activities of the one from the other.

Thus the fraternities of burgesses performed functions different from other kinds of guilds. They catered for a certain social exclusiveness and served to engineer a social harmony among the town's officials. A few of them (Abingdon, Hungerford, but not Salisbury) counted local lords of the manor among their membership which no doubt added prestige. Some of these guilds helped to boost the status of the borough élite, who, in places dominated by an ecclesiastical landlord, may have sought to increase their autonomy and independence. Even in royal boroughs like Bridport, the town élite emphasized its autonomy by holding its main fraternity's celebrations in a chapel separate from the parish church. In towns that lacked borough privileges, these guilds could act as surrogate town councils. But guilds of burgesses do not need to be seen as fundamentally confrontational in intent, which was why they flourished equally well in towns that were not faced with irksome restrictions to their local government. Common to all of them, indeed to other kinds of fraternities as well, if one might labour a point, was the provision for their dead members in purgatory.

The interconnectedness of guilds of burgesses with other guilds leads to some general conclusions. There are, for instance, common features in the timing of guild foundation in many places. Unless the evidence deceives us, there was an apparent rise in the number of guilds from the end of the fourteenth century in a small town like Bridport and in a much larger one like Salisbury. If plague and a horrifying death rate was responsible—and certainly the rules of the Bridport guilds make plain the concern for a decent burial—one should note that its effect was not immediate. It may well be that the increasing wealth per capita, which was one result of plague in some areas, allowed the surviving townsfolk of Bridport and the citizens of Salisbury to spend more on penitential good works. Moreover, the dramatic decline in population after the Black

---

[67] *Historical Manuscripts Commission: Sixth Report*, 496; DRO DC/BTB H1, pp. 713–16.

Death may well have increased the number of vacant holdings and decreased the profitability of rents.[68] Corporate bodies like town guilds stood to benefit from these changes and could step into the holdings of individual townsmen who were heirless or reluctant to acquire more tenements. The Bridport burgesses amassed enough property to found a new fraternity in 1368. Most of the land belonging to the city council of Salisbury by the end of the fifteenth century seems to have been acquired in the fifty or so years after 1360. But in Salisbury too the chronology of guild foundation seems to synchronize with the rise of the cloth trade, most obviously in the beginnings of the tailors' and weavers' guilds. Growing wealth may also have allowed others to dispose of property and money for religious purposes more readily.

If there were connections between guilds, there were also links between guilds and parishes. To some extent, it may have been the inadequacies of the parochial framework that prompted guild foundation. In large parishes particularly, like St Edmund's in Salisbury, parishioners may have found that fraternities like the Jesus guild were more adaptable to their devotional needs. In towns like Weymouth, Wyke Regis, and Maidenhead, which lacked their own parish churches, a guild might have lent added status felt to be lacking, perhaps, with the absence of full parochial rights. A guild like St George's in Salisbury gave expression to a sense of solidarity among the borough élite that reached beyond the boundaries of the city's three parishes. Moreover, guilds can be seen as potentially subversive of the parish structure. They could cut across parish boundaries, drawing parishioners away from their own parish churches. But it is important to recognize the contribution that guilds could make, to church-building, ornaments, and vestments, to the colour and depth of parish life. And as we saw with the tailors' guild, parish ties could be stronger than guild loyalties.

As G. Rosser writes, there is no need to see the relationship between guild and parish as one of conflict. A common impetus to form guilds may well have been to 'transcend the limitations, geographical or institutional, of the parish'.[69] Of course, there were many ways, other than founding guilds, to relieve any tensions caused by the inadequacies of the parochial framework. Places that lacked their own parish churches could set up dependent chapels; parishioners who found fault with the pastoral care of the parish priest could seek redress at visitations. So perhaps the history of parish and guild can also be tied in another way. The insistence of

[68] R. H. Hilton, *The English Peasantry in the Later Middle Ages* (Oxford, 1975), 210–12.
[69] Rosser, 'Parish and Guild', 33.

thirteenth-century canon law on the importance of the parish may not only have encouraged the growth of fabric funds, churchwardens, and chantries. It may also have stimulated the foundation of fraternities within the parish churches by parishioners who wished further to increase the divine service of the parish. The wealth that eased the foundation of guilds in Bridport and Salisbury was also channelled, as we saw, into the building and embellishment of their churches. Major church-building was undertaken in both places in the early fifteenth century and some of the additional chapels and altar space may have been taken up by new fraternities. The apparent rise of fraternities was, arguably, one facet of a wider interest and investment in the religious life of the parish.

There was, of course, a myriad of differing patterns of guild and parish structures. Naturally, a closer relationship between the parish, fraternities, and civic government existed in towns like Bridport and Poole where the parish boundaries all but matched those of the borough. In the larger city of Salisbury some of the guilds appear to have been more detached from the city parishes or to have transcended their boundaries. There is apparently less interest in the affairs of the parishes in the Salisbury town ledger books than in those of Poole and Bridport; the guild of St George maintained obits in all three parishes and seems to have had its own altar in the cathedral. The Salisbury mayor and burgesses had responsibilities over some chantries within the city but not as obviously as the town officials of Bridport.

Yet, whatever the detail, one common pattern emerges: in all these towns there was a honeycomb of interlinking devotional structures. Parish guilds within the same town shared the same or similar membership; their priest might share the same altars; they might even contribute to each other's celebrations. They could also find their activities subsumed by the devotional needs of the parish within which they worshipped. In larger towns, with a greater diversity in economic life, another level of craft guilds linked up with other fraternities, the parish framework, and the town government. Civic processions, even if they allowed tensions between craft guilds over precedence to surface, could assert the ideal of harmony within the town. A final layer on the devotional edifice in borough towns was the assemblies of mayors and burgesses who turned, chameleon-like, with a mere change of livery, into religious fraternities in their own right. Town council meetings may well have been the forums of much dissent, where festering disputes poisoned the civic air. But the guild framework supplied a healing ideal of unity, an ideal to which quarrelling burgesses could aspire. And as well as being a member of an élite town guild, a burgess could find himself bound up in a multiplicity of devotional loyalties, as a parishioner and a member of other fraternities. It is difficult to tell whether the bailiffs of Bridport, for instance, considered it their duty to contribute to parish church-building in their capacity as parishioners, whose concern it was to maintain the church fabric, or as members of parish fraternities, which contributed to parish life; as members of the St Mary and St Katherine guilds, who held their celebrations within the parish church, or even as heads of the town government, responsible for civic works. Such a multiplicity of loyalties, far from leading to disunity and fragmentation, could contribute much to the social cohesion of late medieval towns.

8

Hospitals, Almshouses, and Charity

IN 1415 William Ashleigh of Salisbury left several tenements for the use of the mayor and commonalty, half of which were to sustain the fraternity of St George, the other half the Holy Trinity hospital. Like the St George fraternity, the hospital had been set up in the second half of the fourteenth century. An indulgence granted in 1379, which relaxed forty days of penance for all who gave alms to the poor inmates, recalled that the hospital had been founded next to Black bridge by Agnes Bottenham: in place of what had hitherto been a common brothel 'where lewdness, murders and other mortal sins were carried on', the foundress had established a house for twelve permanently resident poor and a further eighteen 'poor strangers' who were to be given lodging for three days and nights. Every day two priests were to celebrate the canonical hours in the hospital chapel, and twice daily the poor were to say the psalter of the Virgin Mary and pray for the benefactors of the hospital. In 1396 John Chandler the elder, one of Agnes Bottenham's executors, apparently re-endowed the hospital and entrusted its supervision to the city mayor.[1]

The clear links between the Trinity hospital, the St George guild, and the town government show that yet another layer should be added to the devotional structures within certain late medieval towns. But hospitals and almshouses also raise wider issues about charitable giving. Provision for the poor was inseparable from pious expression; it was, as canonists had emphasized since the twelfth century, one of the seven works of mercy in the penitential process of making satisfaction for sin.[2] In return, the poor were expected to pray for the souls of the benefactors in a regular regime of prayer. As a form of institutionalized charity, hospitals were founded throughout the later Middle Ages, either with chapels and burial rights or as houses that simply provided poor relief.[3] Other forms of charitable relief came through doles to the poor, including at funeral and

---

[1] WRO G23/1/1, fo. 56; 1446/34, 43; G23/1/213, fo. 33ᵛ; *VCH: Wilts.* iii. 357. The accounts run 1407–11, 1452–3, 1457, 1460–1, and from 1478 onwards (WRO 1446, Box 'Accounts').

[2] Rubin, *Charity and Community*, 54–74.

[3] R. M. Clay, *The Medieval Hospitals of England* (London, 1909).

TABLE 12. Hospital and almshouse foundations

Date of foundation or first mention	No. of foundations		
	Wilts.	Berks.	Dorset
12th cent.	4	3	
13th cent.	15	5	7
14th cent.	3	3	2
15th cent.	6	8	3
16th cent. (to 1545)	2	4	

Sources: *VCH: Wilts.* iii. 334–68; *VCH: Berks.* ii. 92–102; iii. 328, 378; iv. 265; *VCH: Dorset* ii. 98–107; R. M. Clay, *The Medieval Hospitals of England* (London, 1909). To these may be added: Wilts.: Salisbury (Harnham) 1310 (WRO G23/150/94); Salisbury 1410 (WRO G23/1/1, fo. 147); Dauntsey 1418 (*Reg. Bp. Hallum*, 224) and see also will of Sir John Stourton 1494 (PCC 23 Doggett); Devizes *c.*1451 (will of Thomas Coventry, PCC 17 Rous); Salisbury, St Edmund's 1445 (will of William Warwick, Reg. Abp. Stafford, fo. 137); East Lavington 1505 (Lord Beauchamp's will, PCC 2 Bennett). Berks.: Marshill 1494 (will of Thomas Colyns, PCC 11 Doggett); Windsor, Shert street 1503 (BRO D/EB 7B); Wantage 1530 (will of Stephen Fordeham, PCC 29 Alenger); Wokingham 1537 (will of Jeronius Lambold, PCC 11 Dyngeley).

other services. But was there more change than continuity in the patterns of hospital foundation and other charitable relief? As we shall see, M. Rubin has argued that there were changes for the worse. The difficulty is knowing how far hospital foundation is a 'sensitive indicator'[4] of changing attitudes to the poor, or how far it reflects other pressures. It is important to relate hospital history to that of other institutions: religious houses, parishes, and, as the Trinity hospital suggests, guilds.

In the sketchiest terms, hospital foundation in the diocese seems to have undergone three changes in the later Middle Ages. The first is that fewer hospitals were founded and endowed from the mid-thirteenth century onwards (see Table 12). Indeed, not all the earlier hospitals survived after the fourteenth century. That of Southbroom is not heard of again after 1337, nor are those at Marlborough (St Thomas's) after 1340, Great Bedwyn after 1360, Wootton Basset after 1406, Malmesbury (Mary Magdalen) after 1439.[5] By the time the chantry commissioners had made

[4] 'The history of endowment and changes of [hospitals'] functions within society can be sensitive indicators of changing ideas and expectations related to charitable giving' (Rubin, *Charity and Community*, 183).

[5] *VCH: Wilts.* iii. 340–3, 362, 369.

their survey in 1545, the role of hospitals founded in Devizes (St John's), Cricklade, Marlborough (St John's), Calne, Old Sarum, and Sherborne St Thomas had apparently altered: they were all described as free chapels which no longer supported any poor people.[6] Faltering hospital endowment seems to have been matched by a steady decline in the proportion of testators leaving bequests to almshouses in the fourteenth and fifteenth centuries (see Tables 12 and 13(b)).

A change in the type of foundation also seems to have occurred from the end of the fourteenth century. Earlier hospitals were generally endowed with one priest or more, and a separate chapel and staff to look after the inmates. The occupants of almshouses in the fifteenth century, however, were expected to live without assistance apart from the help of their neighbours and to attend the local parish church rather than their own separate chapel. There were some notable and lavish exceptions at Sherborne, Abingdon, and Salisbury, all of which were founded with priests and chapels in the late fourteenth or fifteenth century. But more typical of the period was James Terumber's almshouse at Trowbridge (1483) whose six inmates were required to attend the parish church twice a day, at seven or eight in the morning and at five or six in the evening depending on the season.[7]

One might, more tentatively, relate a change in the type of hospital foundation to changes in the type of poor admitted. Early hospitals needed a staff to cope with the sick. St Nicholas's hospital in Salisbury was to admit the infirm as well as the poor.[8] Indeed a number of these hospitals were founded specifically for lepers. Leprosy seems to have abated in England by 1350, hence a decline (in general) in the need for such houses.[9] And many later almshouses appear to have been intended not for the sick but for the poor alone, usually the 'old and impotent'.[10]

Nor were some of these later almshouses intended to cater for temporary inmates and travellers merely passing through. The early statutes of St Nicholas's hospital in Salisbury in 1229 mention a concern to succour the pilgrim or traveller, a concern given material expression by

[6] PRO E301/58/54, 69, 29, 87, 57; E301/59/54, 9, 10, 8, 39.

[7] DRO D/SHA CH2 (1437) and J. Fowler, *Medieval Sherborne* (Dorchester, 1951), 231 ff.; *CPR* (1441–6), 36–7 and Abingdon, almshouse deeds, 616; Jones, 'Terumber's Chantry', 232–42.

[8] *St. Nicholas's Cart.* 1–2.

[9] Clay, *Medieval Hospitals*, 35–47; L. De Maitre, 'The Description and Diagnosis of Leprosy by Fourteenth-Century Physicians', *Bulletin of the History of Medicine*, 59 (1985), 327–44.

[10] The hospital of Abingdon St John once served as an infirmary for the sick, but in the 15th cent. it had become a home for work people of the abbey (Preston, *St. Nicholas*, 64).

the house's situation on Ayleward bridge on the road leading to the city. But few of the fifteenth-century almshouses were intended to give temporary relief, and by 1478, when Bishop Beauchamp refashioned the statutes of St Nicholas's hospital, no other relief seems to have been provided save for the permanent residents. Moreover, rules governing admission to later almshouses were sometimes quite specific as to the groups of poor to be admitted. Cricklade hospital was said to have been established for poor wayfarers in the thirteenth century, but in 1415, while still ostensibly providing such relief, it was reconstituted as a house specifically for the use of poor infirm priests who were not to consort with laymen and who were to be dressed in regular habit. Margaret Hungerford's almshouse in 1472 was to give preference to the poor tenants of Hungerford estates, and none of them (here a moralistic tone is adopted) was to be lecherous, adulterous, or a tavern-goer. In other areas, usually larger towns, measures were taken to exclude strangers from almshouses. At Sherborne in 1437, the hospital rules allowed admission only for those who had been living continually in the town. The Trinity almshouse in Salisbury may have initially admitted temporary travellers, but in 1456 and 1492 the mayor and burgesses agreed not to let in any stranger 'but the pore pepull such as hath been dwelling in the cyte longe tyme'.[11]

Indeed some of these town almshouses seem to have been admitting a rather exclusive clientele. In 1479 the burgesses of Reading reported that the hospital of St John had admitted women who had been 'onest mennys wyvys that had born offyce in the town before, and in age were fall in poverti'.[12] At Sherborne the almshouse was supervised by twenty brethren of worthy townsmen who looked after their own members as much as the truly poor. If any of the twenty brethren fell into poverty, he was to receive 20*d*. a week, and if he died his widow was to receive 10*d*. a week. As for the twelve 'poor, feeble and impotent' men and four women, they were to receive 10*s*. a week for meat and drink. New inmates were expected to give all their goods to the house; accounts between 1468 and 1540 register ten people entering who had only a few shillings to give. But accounts of the same period also report that sixteen people paid around 40*s*. or 50*s*. to take up residence in one of the almshouse's tenements and receive food and clothing. Three of them could afford to pay the additional £5 needed to join the fraternity, and one almshouse inmate had goods worth £40.[13] So, while the almshouse catered for the poorer towns-

---

[11] *St. Nicholas's Cart.*, pp. lxiv, 1–2, 7–8; *Reg. Bp. Hallum*, 1020; Jackson, 'Ancient Statutes', 289–308; DRO D/SHA CH2; WRO G23/1/2, fos. 32, 192ᵛ.

[12] BL Add. MS 6214, fo. 14.

[13] DRO D/SHA CH2; D/SHA A1–79 (esp. nos. 37–45, 54–60); PRO C1/158/16.

people, it also provided a kind of pensioned security for the members of its own fraternity.

All three changes might tempt depressing conclusions about the nature of charitable giving in the later Middle Ages: that it was declining and that it was becoming more discriminatory, towards a respectable poor. M. Rubin has argued that attitudes to the poor had altered by the late fourteenth century: the pauper had come to be seen as a menace in the mind of the employer and entrepreneur suffering the problems of labour shortages in the wake of the Black Death. Thirteenth-century communities had been open-handed in their generosity in alms-giving and in the foundation of hospitals; by the later fourteenth century, suspicion of the poor had so increased that hospitals were left to decay, or were transformed into chantries that provided less for the poor (a specified and respectable poor at that) and more for the hectic accumulation of prayers for the souls of benefactors.[14]

But evidence for growing discrimination is not always clear-cut. Very little is known about what kind of people were admitted as permanent inmates of earlier hospitals beyond the vague wording of foundation charters. Compared with Margaret Hungerford's moralistic specifications in 1478, Bishop Bingham in 1229 stressed only that the inmates of St Nicholas's were to be 'Christ's poor', yet one assumes that he would not have placed the lascivious or bibulous in that category any more than Margaret. In any case, some earlier hospitals were specific about the kind of poor they admitted: Walter le Bret's foundation at Wootton Basset (1266) apparently made provision only for the poor of the parish.[15] The late-thirteenth-century rules of the Mary Magdalen hospital of Reading listed adultery as the 'first and greatest' sin for which an inmate could be expelled. If there was a movement towards favouring a respectable poor, it may well have begun before the Black Death. In 1337 one of the inmates of St John's hospital in Reading (founded to admit 'Christ's poor') came from the worthy craft of shoemakers who maintained an altar light in St Laurence's church.[16]

Later almshouses did not entirely depart from earlier practices. Not all of them neglected provision for the sick. Leprosy seems to have lingered longer in southern regions of England, Dorset included: the pardoners of Allington hospital near Bridport in 1467 were collecting for the lepers 'in

[14] Rubin, *Charity and Community*, esp. 50–3, 71, 98, 289–97; M. Mollat, *Les Pauvres au Moyen Âge* (Paris, 1978), 192–232.
[15] WRO D1/1/2, Liber Evidentiarum B, no. 397 (pp. 144–5).
[16] BL Cott. Vesp. Ev, fos. 39, 80ᵛ.

their horrible disease and infirmity'.[17] That Margaret Hungerford had to
exclude lepers explicitly from her house at Heytesbury suggests that
leprosy still lurked in rural Wiltshire.[18] Some later almshouses, moreover,
may not have been as choosy about their inmates as others: James
Terumber's detailed provision for his almshouse at Trowbridge did not
specify what kind of poor people were to be admitted save that they should
not be disruptive. Some of the inmates at Sherborne almshouse, those
who had means, might have found themselves turned away from the
portals of Heytesbury almshouse, which was intended to admit only the
poor man who was 'destitute of temporal goods where with he myght lyve
ellis where'.[19]

Temporary relief for the traveller was not always forgotten. Robert
Clarke is supposed to have granted land for the gathering of firewood to
the almshouse at Thatcham for the poor dwelling there and for poor
travellers and lame soldiers returning home, some time in the mid-
fifteenth century—perhaps in more benevolent days before 1450 when
vagrant soldiers returning after the loss of Normandy achieved notoriety
for the part they played in Jack Cade's rebellion.[20] The Trinity hospital in
Salisbury may have closed off relief towards the temporary poor only in
response to royal statutes against vagabondage in 1452 and 1493 (which
the citizens had copied into the ledger books), and perhaps with the
disturbing memory of Jack Cade's rebels—indeed the image of pieces of
Cade's carcass which had been carried to the city—still fresh in their
minds.[21]

As to the apparent decline in hospital foundation, two qualifications
stand out. First, the overall decline seems to have come well before the
Black Death, indeed before the end of the thirteenth century. And secondly, decline was more apparent in some areas than others. Instead of
reflecting a change in attitude to the poor, almshouse foundation might
simply have reflected economic need or the level of poverty. In some areas
new opportunities for surviving labourers and artisans after the Black
Death stimulated a rise in the standard of living and a decline in the need
for institutions catering for poor relief. Apart from the hospital founded
in prosperous, cloth-producing Sherborne, no other almshouse seems
to have been founded in Dorset from the mid-fourteenth to the mid-

[17] DRO DC/BTB AB/44.   [18] Jackson, 'Ancient Statutes', 289–308.
[19] Jones, 'Terumber's Chantry', 247–52; Jackson, 'Ancient Statutes', 289–308.
[20] *VCH: Berks.* iii. 328; S. Barfield, *Thatcham, Berkshire, and its Manors* (London, 1901),
i. 154; I. M. W. Harvey, *Jack Cade's Rebellion*, 68.
[21] See Intro. n. 53; WRO G23/1/1, fo. 159; G23/1/2, p. ii. Relief for vagabonds does not
seem to have been denied in 1438, as *VCH: Wilts.* claims (ii. 348).

sixteenth century. Perhaps rural parts of Dorset simply did not have a problem with a labouring poor. In Berkshire, on the other hand, there was a bumper crop of almshouses sown from the mid-fifteenth century onwards, almost as many as had been founded in the previous three centuries. Almshouses may have been needed in the county, with its more populous towns and market centres which attracted immigrants. Moreover, the Trinity almshouse in Salisbury reflected economic conditions at the end of the fourteenth century: the population of Salisbury in a time of demographic recession was kept buoyant by immigrants from the countryside, some of whom perhaps needed the initial support of a new almshouse. In any case, the city authorities, thriving on a boom in the cloth industry, need not have felt insecure at the sight of idle artisans demanding higher wages. In contrast to elsewhere, bequests to almshouses in Salisbury did not decline in the fifteenth century (see Table 13).

A closer look at the founders and patrons of hospitals also suggests that certain groups in society were becoming more, rather than less, charitable during the later Middle Ages. There had been a strong clerical flavour, monastic and episcopal, to the foundation of hospitals set up before the mid-thirteenth century. Royals and aristocrats also figured prominently as hospital founders or patrons. But in the mid-thirteenth century members of the knightly class, like Sir Philip Basset at Wootton Basset, had also begun to emulate their social superiors in hospital foundation. Knightly families continued to found hospitals after the thirteenth century, particularly in Berkshire, where the Hungerfords, Golafres, Estburys, and Fetiplaces founded their own almshouses. Even bishops could still be active benefactors: William Aiscough was a principal benefactor of the refounded house at Sherborne in 1437, where inmates were required to wear a 'bishopehuyter' on the right breast of their woollen gowns. But the most active founders of later hospitals (not that they had been inactive before) were townspeople, particularly in towns made wealthy by the cloth trade—at Sherborne (run by the townsfolk rather than the bishop), Reading, Wokingham, Devizes, and Abingdon.[22]

Hospital foundation in Salisbury illustrates this trend more amply. The first hospital founder in the city, in fact, had been a bishop, Richard Poore, and the foundation had involved the citizens but little. The cartulary of St

---

[22] Of twenty-four known founders in the diocese in the twelfth and thirteenth centuries, fourteen were clerical, five royal, and five aristocratic or gentry; from the fourteenth to the sixteenth centuries, of eighteen known founders, nine were town burgesses, seven gentry, one clerical, and one aristocratic.

TABLE 13. Bequests to hospitals

(a) Salisbury

	No. of testators	No. of hospital bequests	St Nicholas	Holy Trinity	'Bede rowe'	Other hospitals
1270–1349	15	2 (13%)	1			1
1350–1399	65	7 (11%)	3	4		2
1400–1449	129	41 (31%)	9	39	3	4
1450–1499	53	10 (19%)	2	7	4	0
1500–1547	68	15 (22%)	6	15		2

(b) Wiltshire, Berkshire, and Dorset

	No. of testators	No. of hospital bequests
1260–1349	19	4 (21%)
1350–1399	49	8 (16%)
1400–1449	163	13 (8%)
1450–1499	224	20 (9%)
1500–1545	774	34 (4%)

Nicholas's records a steady flow of rents and landed gifts, usually no more than a few acres, until 1289. A few of these gifts came from townspeople, but most came from landowners outside the city, even from aristocratic and knightly donors.[23] But the benefactors of the later Trinity almshouse were usually citizens who left property inside the city. The first surviving account of the hospital in 1407 records an income of £12. 14s. 8d. from the rents of eighteen properties, an income which steadily increased to over £18 by 1546. The accounts record extra gifts in times of need: Thomas Coke left 40s. to the almshouse in 1523, and it was probably the same Thomas Coke who had given £10 in 1512 to rebuild one of the almshouse's tenements.[24] Fifteenth-century citizens were also more likely to leave bequests to the almshouse that their fellow citizens had endowed than to the hospital of St Nicholas which was founded by the bishop (see Table 13(a)). Evidence for other fifteenth-century almshouses alludes to the involvement of the citizens. In 1410 John Moner, in full convocation

[23] *St. Nicholas's Cart.* 12–13, 15–16, 56, 71, 81–2, 83, 89, 91, 93, 95–6, 146–7, 151, 153, 154–6, 164, 167, 168, 173–5, 187, 193, 195, 199, 201.
[24] WRO 1446: Box 'Accounts'; 35, 64, 80; Box 'City records'.

of the citizens, gave his tenement by Upper Fisherton bridge for almshouses.[25] Mention is made in the will of William Warwick in 1445 and in later wills to the poor in 'beden rewe' of St Edmund's parish.[26] And in 1534 Thomas Brickett or Birkhed stated in his will that 'the five almshouses I have bilded in Dragon Streete should be given to the use of 5 poore men or women . . . and that the gift over to be doon by the mayor of the city'.[27] There was perhaps a certain communal pride taken by the citizens of Salisbury in the fortunes of the Trinity hospital and their other almshouses.

In other borough towns mayors were also asked to play a role. Thomas Coventry in his will of 1451 asked that the reversion of rents that supported his almshouse go to the mayor of Devizes.[28] But parish officials could also supervise these later almshouses. The distinction between town and parish government cannot, of course, be laboured, not least because many mayors or burgesses had served as churchwardens. But not all almshouses in Salisbury were under the direct jurisdiction of the mayor. The churchwardens of St Edmund's may have had some involvement with the 'bedenrewe' in that parish: in 1500/1 the accounts record a gift of 4*d.*, which the churchwardens were presumably to administer, to 'cuidam pauperis in le bedredyn rowe'.[29] Trowbridge and Heytesbury were not borough towns with their own mayors, and almshouses within them relied on the partial supervision of the parish officials.[30] In some places, like Thatcham, the churchwardens seem to have taken over the supervision of the almshouse by the fifteenth century; in others, like Wimborne Minster, the parish seems to have increased its interest in local hospitals, beginning to make occasional small payments to the house of St Margaret from the late fifteenth century onwards.[31] Some towns and parishes, then, had apparently become more charitable in the fifteenth century than before.

Changes in hospital foundation also look less depressing if they are related to trends other than any shift in attitude to the poor. Hospitals were very like other institutions of divine service. As with monasteries, inmates were

---

[25] WRO G23/1/1, fo. 147.

[26] Reg. Abp. Stafford, fo. 137. See also wills of Edith Payne 1456 (PCC 8 Stockton); William Maynard 1496 (4 Horne); Thomas Coke 1523 (10 Bodefeld); Alice More 1530 (11 Thower); Stephen Beche 1531 (8 Thower); Thomas Martyn 1536 (1 Dyngeley).

[27] PCC 8 Hogen; WRO G23/1/2, fo. 278.   [28] PCC 17 Rous.

[29] *S. Edmund Accounts*, 53.

[30] Jones, 'Terumber's Chantry', 250; Jackson, 'Ancient Statutes', 291–2.

[31] *VCH: Berks.* iii. 328; DRO PE/WM CW 1/41, pp. 3 (1475–6), 6 (1476–7), 73 (1528–9). See also the Poole churchwardens' accounts in 1532 (Poole municipal archives, 47 (2) (1530–2)).

required to celebrate a daily ritual of prayer: the priests of St Nicholas's in Salisbury celebrated the canonical hours (except midnight matins) and the poor inmates were to say the Lady psalter twice a day, dressed in russet habits. Like monasteries, hospitals acquired indulgences to encourage penitential gifts from the faithful. The Salisbury Trinity almshouse acquired at least four separate indulgences to send out pardoners throughout the diocese, who collected on average several shillings a year (46s. in 1516/17) between 1410 and 1533. The letter of indulgence owned by Allington hospital in 1467, which was to be carried around by its pardoners, listed indulgences, rather improbably, from eight popes, thirty cardinals, two archbishops, nine bishops, adding up to fourteen years and 215 days' remission of days in purgatory.[32] Like monasteries too, hospitals also began to attract gifts for specific spiritual services in the thirteenth century. Some benefactors began to be received into the spiritual benefits of the house, others gave land to sustain lamps in hospital churches, and some entrusted chantry endowments to hospitals in the early fourteenth century.[33] Two hospitals in the diocese, Maiden Bradley and Easton, even became houses of regular orders.[34] So in certain respects, the foundation and endowment of hospitals might be expected to follow the pattern of monastic houses. Fewer monasteries and hospitals (in general) were founded after 1250; just as gifts to some monasteries began to peter out in the later thirteenth century, so too did gifts to hospitals like St Nicholas's Salisbury, and ones at Wilton and Wallingford.[35] To some extent, hospital endowment was affected less by a change in attitude to the poor than by the pressures that also affected monastic houses.

In other respects, hospitals with their own chapels and secular priests were not dissimilar to, and were even potential rivals of, parish churches. Parish and hospital churches could attract visitors to their altars and

---

[32] Salisbury: *St. Nicholas's Cart.* 1–2; WRO 1446/34, Box 'City records', Reg. Bp. Chandler, fo. 3; Reg. Bp. Waltham. fo. 12; Reg. Bp. Mitford, fo. 119ᵛ; Reg. Bp. Hallum, fo. 47; Reg. Bp. Audley, fo. 172; WRO 1446/58, Boxes 'City records' and 'Accounts'. Allington: DRO DC/BTB/46.

[33] *St. Nicholas's Cart.* 57, 151, 195. Wallingford: BRO W/T Acc. 901 THa 19, 28, 42 (1265–1325). Malmesbury St John: PRO CP25 (1) 251/15/42. Salisbury Trinity: WRO 1446/34. See also the gifts of John de Harnham and William Chitterne (1403) for obit and lights at St Giles Wilton (*CPR* (1330–4), 21; (1401–5), 189); John Cammel 1399 (WRO G23/1/214, fo. 87); Table 3.

[34] *VCH: Wilts.* iii. 296, 324.

[35] See Ch. 1; *St. Nicholas's Cart.*, *passim*; WRO G25/1/107; BRO W/T Acc. 901 THa 1–53. Gifts to the hospital of St John in Cambridge also petered out in the 13th cent., well before the Black Death (Rubin, *Charity and Community*, 208, 212, 235).

images. The Salisbury Trinity almshouse collected around 2s. from offerings to the Trinity image in its chapel; the women of Newbury were supposed to have been churched after childbirth in the hospital chapel of St Bartholomew.[36] But hospital chapels were not supposed to provide an alternative to the parish mass, and ecclesiastical authorities from the thirteenth century onwards saw to it that the rights of the parish church were not infringed by hospital foundations. Some parishioners may have been attending mass in the chapel of St John's hospital in Malmesbury until the mid-thirteenth century when the practice was forbidden to all except those wearing the habit of the hospital.[37] Permission was given to Allington hospital to have two chaplains celebrating in its chapel who were to enjoy oblations given to the house except those, it had to be explicitly stated, from the parishioners of Adlington and Allington.[38] The same concern that the founding of new parishes might damage the rights of older parish churches may well have inhibited the founding of hospitals with their own chapels—and encouraged the movement towards almshouses without staff and priests.[39]

In still other ways, early hospitals and later almshouses were like chantries or were integrated with chantry foundations. In fact, one of the earliest known chantries in the diocese, at Wanborough in 1270, was originally intended as a hospital: because funds were insufficient, the intended hospital was replaced by two chantry priests who were to distribute £1 to the poor every year.[40] The Hungerford almshouse at Heytesbury was originally endowed from the union of chantries at Upton Scudmore and Calne and the free chapels of Corston and Hilmarton, which were said to be 'too poor to support incumbents'.[41] Some later almshouses—James Terumber's at Trowbridge, Sir John Estbury's at Lambourne, and Sir John Golafre's at Fyfield—were established at the same time as the founders' chantries in their parish churches. Ecclesiastical concern, mortmain restrictions, and the declining profitability and availability of land had gradually made it more difficult to found chantries as separate chapels and to endow perpetual chantries: the same pressures might help to explain why fewer well-endowed hospitals, and proportionally more smaller almshouses without chapels, were being founded in the fifteenth century (see Chapters 3 and 4).

---

[36] WRO 1446, Box 'Accounts'; PRO E133/10/1541, E133/3/407, 413, 416.

[37] *Reg. Malmesburiense*, ii. 75–8.

[38] DRO DC/BTB/AB46; AB/43; G1, Old Dome Book, pp. 311–13.

[39] See Ch. 3 n. 11.   [40] Oxford, Magdalen College, Wanborough deeds, 65a.

[41] Reg. Neville, second series, fos. 55–56ᵛ.

Finally, certain town almshouses should be seen as an aspect of guild activity, and therefore integrated into the social and devotional structures of town life. Burgesses not only exercised patronage over hospitals but also contributed to their maintenance. Part of the oath of the Wilton burgesses, certainly by 1532, was the promise to 'pay the poor men of St. Gyles 12d by the year every quarter 4d'. At Bridport the bailiffs and burgesses had exercised patronage over the hospital of Allington and of St John within the town since the thirteenth century. When the harbour was rebuilt in the late 1440s, it was not just the parish priests, chantry, and guild chaplains who were asked to pray for the benefactors to the harbour, but also the hospital chaplains.[42] The welfare of hospitals and of the town as a whole were interlinked.

The foundation and endowment of some almshouses can be associated very closely with town and guild concerns. The St George guild at Salisbury was founded or heavily endowed after 1360, in the same period as the Trinity hospital. Indeed, many of the citizens who were members of the St George guild were also members of a fraternity that supported the Trinity almshouse by making contributions four times a year. At a convocation of the mayor and burgesses held on the Friday before the feast of St George in 1424, some thirty-six people out of forty-five present 'agreed to be brothers of the hospital or fraternity of St. Trinity' by paying 4d. a year to support the hospital.[43] So, apart from any need to provide for the poor, the Trinity almshouse was founded as part of a general movement to increase the divine service of the city—seen also in church-building and guild foundation, including that of St George—near the end of the fourteenth century. Its foundation, supervised by the city authorities, may also reflect the longer-term efforts of the citizens to increase their own powers of self-government. If they felt the need to regulate town life, including moral matters such as the practice of prostitution in the city, the same need may have encouraged the foundation of a hospital on a site once notorious for its common brothel.[44]

In other towns hospital foundation, like certain guilds, appears closely bound up with town councils seeking to assert their independence against ecclesiastical overlords. At Abingdon the foundation of the hospital of St Cross was part and parcel of the effort of the Holy Cross guild to establish itself as an incorporated body. In 1441 it acquired a charter of incorpor-

[42] WRO G25, General entry book, p. 120; Hutchins, *Dorset*, ii. 15–16.

[43] WRO 1446, Box 'Accounts'; WRO G23/1/1, fo. 89ᵛ. Some of them pledged 8d. rather than 4d.; some of the names are obscured.

[44] See above n. 1 and Intro. n. 54.

ation and licence to alienate land in mortmain worth up to £40 a year: the guild's object was not only to maintain two chantry chaplains in St Helen's church and to repair the road to Dorchester, but also to support the thirteen poor men and women set up in its almshouse.[45] At Reading the burgesses acquired various powers which they used to claim the status of their guild merchant as a body corporate against the lordship of the abbey. They were seised of certain stalls, shops, and messuages; they sent representatives to Parliament; they had freedom from tolls; and they were patrons of the chantry founded by John Colney. But unlike other towns (Salisbury, Abingdon, and Wilton included), they lacked patronage over the town's two almshouses, both of which were the responsibility of the abbey. Even so, the burgesses clearly considered the affairs of the almshouses to fall within their remit: in 1479 they complained to the king about the abbot's neglect of the almshouses. Meanwhile, another almshouse for five people was founded around 1449 by John Leche, or A'Larder, on land purchased from the abbey, who in 1477 made provision for three more poor people in his will. It is not clear who originally supervised the charity, but it is clear that the mayor and guild merchant came to do so. In 1501, along with the other members of the guild, the mayor Richard Cleche, involved in several confrontations with the abbey, was enfeoffed with the almshouse's property. The acquisition of this patronage looks like part of the longer-term effort of the guild merchant to widen its powers of government and assert its independence from monkish overlordship.[46]

At Sherborne twenty brethren supervised the town's almshouse, refounded in 1437. The twenty included three priests, but most were substantial members of the town. Some of them had found themselves at odds with the abbey in the previous year when they attempted to move the baptismal font into the section of the abbey church set aside from the parishioners. The bishop singled out four men as ringleaders: one, John Baret, was to be a principal benefactor of the almshouse, and two, John Kayleway and Richard Rochett, were to be among the first twenty brethren. The townsmen were anxious to assert their control over parochial matters, regardless of the wishes of the abbey; their willingness to refound the almshouse, governed by a new fraternity of their own, reflects a similar desire for government over local affairs. Sherborne was not a borough, like Abingdon, Reading, or Salisbury, with its own mayor or bailiffs:

[45] *CPR* (1441–6), 37; see Ch. 1 n. 57.
[46] See Ch. 1 n. 60; BL Add. MS 6214, fo. 22; PCC 12 Logge; Coates, *History and Antiquities*, 133–4; *VCH: Berks.* iii. 378.

the almshouse fraternity provided the townsmen with a surrogate town council.[47]

So the rise and decline of almshouses reflects concerns other than just changing attitudes to the poor. But the nature of charitable giving should not be judged merely by the incidence and functions of hospitals. The number of poor people admitted was seldom large, generally twelve or thirteen for the earlier hospitals (to signify the number of disciples with Jesus at the Last Supper) and smaller groups of five or six for some later almshouses.[48] There were other forms of charitable giving which have also been seen as changing during the later Middle Ages. M. Rubin has seen a threatening poor being regarded, by the later fourteenth century, less as objects of charity in their own right and more as liturgical appendages hired at funeral and other services to amass merit for the souls of individual benefactors.[49] Other historians have discerned a greater discrimination in alms-giving in the fifteenth century and a greater specificity in benefaction to the poor.[50]

We shall now turn to other forms of charity. For the clergy, care for the poor was mandatory as well as virtuous. Monasteries were supposed to follow St Benedict's own admonition to receive the poor stranger and visitor and some, like Reading and Abingdon, had their own almshouses. As we saw, the level of support they provided may not have been high in proportion to their revenues, yet in absolute terms it may have been substantial, particularly from some monasteries in Dorset. But the scope of monastic charity may have been gradually narrowing in the later Middle Ages: abbeys began to build inns which charged their guests for lodging; distributions tended to become restricted to certain times of the year. But growing discrimination, if such it was, may have begun at an early date. In the thirteenth century some monasteries could be rigidly discriminatory as to the type of poor that qualified for their charity; others

[47] See Ch. 1 n. 59.

[48] Numbers above thirteen were rare (Clay, *Medieval Hospitals*, 136–46). For the numbers in the St Edmund's parish almshouse see the will of Thomas Martyn 1536, who left 6*d*. to be spent on the day of his obit on 'the bedyn rowe of the said town . . . that is to saye to every house an ob[olus]' (PCC 1 Dyngeley).

[49] Rubin, *Charity and Community*, 184–92, 292, following Mollat, *Les Pauvres*, 187–9, and Chiffoleau, *La Comptabilité de l'au-delà*, 302–55.

[50] M. G. Vale, 'Piety, Charity and Literacy among the Yorkshire Gentry 1370–1480', *Borthwick Papers*, 50 (1976), 26–7; P. W. Fleming, 'Charity, Faith and the Gentry of Kent 1422–1529', in A. J. Pollard (ed.), *Property and Politics: Essays in Late Medieval English History* (Gloucester, 1984), 45–6; W. K. Jordan, *Philanthropy in England 1480–1660: A Study of the Changing Pattern of English Social Aspirations* (London, 1959).

gave up daily distributions and became more systematic in their dispensing of alms, on certain feast and anniversary days, which tended to exclude the casual beggar and favour the local poor. Perhaps a less open-handed form of alms-giving was all that was expected: relative lack of criticism about monastic charity may suggest that religious houses were performing their charitable duties acceptably in the eyes of contemporaries.[51]

Institutions of secular clergy also provided some support for the poor in an equally controlled manner. Salisbury cathedral made distributions, and some of the earliest obits made provision for large groups of poor on the anniversary day. But by the mid-thirteenth century most chantry and obit founders specified only the canons, vicars-choral, and choristers as the objects of their alms-giving. Most of the distributions from the cathedral's sixty-three anniversaries listed in the *Valor* in 1535 were to ministers of the cathedral, and only two to the poor. Some alms-giving may be hidden from view, but a good deal of it may have been dispensed, as early as the thirteenth century, on narrower lines: to the poor scholars of Vaux college and the grammar school for 'poor children' in the city.[52] Other colleges of secular priests, like Wimborne Minster, provided similarly selective charity. According to the chantry commissioners' report of 1545, the college annually distributed £5 to the poor, and one of its chantry endowments provided for a school for the poor children of the town.[53] Again this form of charity tended to favour the local poor rather than the vagrant beggar.

It had long been a stipulation of canon law, in any case, that the secular clergy were to distribute a proportion of their income to the local parish poor. A provincial decree in 1281 insisted that clerical hospitality was to be provided 'so that at least extreme necessity among poor parishioners is relieved'.[54] Although the poor stranger was also to benefit, priority was given to the local poor. Once more, the level of priestly charity is difficult to determine and later canonists could emphasize the importance of local circumstance in determining patterns of giving. It is doubtful whether a third of the tithe was ever distributed to the poor, as legislation hopefully required, especially in the later fourteenth century when profits from benefices tended to shrink. But the level of charity dispensed by the local clergy may have been significant, significant enough for parishioners to make the occasional complaint that their priest was not helping the parish

---

[51] See Ch. 1 nn. 80–7. For an example of 13th-cent. 'discriminatory' charity see the Cistercian abbey of Beaulieu in Hampshire: during harvest-time alms were given only to pilgrims, old people, children, and those incapable of work (*The Account Book of Beaulieu Abbey*, ed. S. E. Hockey (Camden Society, fourth series, 16; 1975), 172–82, 269–81).

[52] See Ch. 2 n. 42.   [53] PRO E301/16/110.   [54] *Councils and Synods*, 906–7.

poor.[55] Vicars and rectors were reminded of this duty when their churches were appropriated to religious institutions. St Thomas's in Salisbury was appropriated to the cathedral in 1399 with the permission of Bishop Mitford, for whom the cathedral was to distribute alms to the parish poor on his anniversary. In the late fifteenth century some £2, or 5 per cent of the receipts from tithes and other oblations in the parish, was being distributed to the poor.[56] The secular clergy also remembered their duties to the poor in parishes they had served far more often than lay people in their wills.[57]

Clerical alms-giving, then, had an in-built bias towards the local poor and it may have been discriminatory at any early date, that is, earlier than the Black Death. The laity also dispensed charity in ways other than through almshouses. Many manor courts served to supervise traditional forms of support for the poor, helping widows and younger children, and even elderly tenants no longer able to work their holdings. Margaret Hungerford's support of her tenants in the almshouse she founded at Heytesbury in 1472 was presaged by her ancestors: in 1386/7 Thomas Hungerford was supporting ten paupers at Farleigh Hungerford on pensions of ¾d. a day and between 1428 and 1431 Walter Hungerford was paying thirteen paupers on his estates 17s. 4d. annually.[58] Families, households, and individuals in authority dispensed charity in ways not often revealed by surviving records. And although begging in a public place was increasingly frowned upon in late medieval legislation, private begging—going from door to door—was never proscribed and must have been resorted to.[59] The importance of these less-institutionalized forms of charity may even explain why almshouses were relatively scarce.

Other forms of giving can be detected in wills. Individual doles to the poor could be made at funerals and anniversary and chantry services, or as separate bequests not tied to a particular service. Once again, the level of support these gifts could provide is almost unknowable and probably

[55] At Fisherton Delamere, South Newton, and Sutton Courtenay (Reg. Bp. Waltham, fos. 43, 47, 69 (1393)).

[56] D & C, Press II, Procurators' accounts (1486–1538) and Fabric accounts (1487–1538).

[57] Twenty-six out of 122 wills made by the clergy in the region from 1360 to 1547 left bequests to the poor apparently outside funeral services, a proportion (21%) above that of lay people (see below n. 66).

[58] C. C. Dyer, *Standards of Living in the Later Middle Ages: Social Change in England c.1200–1520* (Cambridge, 1989), 120–4, 254–5; M. A. Hicks, 'St. Katherine's Hospital Heytesbury: Prehistory, Foundations and the Refoundation 1408–1472', *WAM* 78 (1984), 64–5.

[59] C. C. Dyer, *Standards of Living*, 252; M. K. McIntosh, 'Local Responses to the Poor in Late Medieval and Tudor England', *Continuity and Change*, 3/2 (1988), 209–45.

varied wildly from place to place. The household accounts of Munden's chantry priests at Bridport show very modest and occasional payments to the poor in the mid-fifteenth century; some chantries, so the commissioners reported in 1545 and 1548, dispensed no charity at all.[60] But others could provide more than £1 annually to the poor, usually on the anniversary of the founder. The priest of William Yorke's chantry at Ramsbury in 1476 was supposed to distribute 1*d.* to each of twenty poor people at least every month after celebrating exequies and mass.[61] Rich pickings could be had at the funeral and obit doles of gentry in rural areas and of merchants in towns like Salisbury. In 1412 William Warmwell willed that thirteen poor men and women were to attend the exequies and mass of his funeral service in the church of St Thomas; he also wished that 3,500 pence be distributed to the poor in the two years after his death.[62] Indeed the sheer number of wealthy people in the larger town parishes meant that such doles could be a more regular source of support for the local poor than in more rural areas.[63]

Patterns in this kind of charitable giving can be made out only dimly. Like the clergy, lay people probably gave priority to the local poor in their doles. Regular obit services in parish churches favoured the local parish poor rather than the stranger or traveller, who would have been ignorant as to when doles might be had. Some parishes may have made further efforts to help their poor. If we can trust John Aubrey's rather picturesque descriptions of church ales at South Newton and Kington St Michael, some of the money collected on feast days, even before the Reformation, went to the poor. In the late fifteenth century some parishes like Wimborne Minster seem to have extended their interest into care for the local poor, not just in keeping an eye on local 'bede' almshouses, but also by giving small distributions to poor people. Well before the introduction of poor rates, the parish provided a measure of charitable relief.[64]

Was the charity favouring the local poor part of a wider attitude that discriminated between particular types of poor people? From the last two decades of the fourteenth century onwards, a growing number of wills

[60] *Small Household*, 16, 30.   [61] PRO E135/17/26.   [62] WRO G23/150/94.

[63] See B. Geremeck, *The Margins of Society in Late Medieval Paris* (Cambridge, 1987), esp. 188. Some contemporaries even complained that the poor could live off the relief provided by funerals and anniversaries (ibid. 192–210; J. Sanchez-Herrero, *Las Diocesis del Reino de León, Siglos XIV y XV* (León, 1978), 405).

[64] See Intro. n. 37 and above n. 31; S. and B. Webb, *English Local Government in English Poor Law History*, i. *The Old Poor Law* (London, 1927), 8–14; Rubin, *Charity and Community*, 237–45; Mollat, *Les Pauvres*, 329–38; P. Bonenfant, *Hôpitaux et bienfaisance publique dans les anciens Pays-Bas des origines à la fin du XVIIIe siècle* (Brussels, 1965), 45.

TABLE 14. Bequests to bridges and roads

	No. of testators	No. of bequests
1260–1349	34	3 (9%)
1350–1399	114	3 (3%)
1400–1449	292	31 (11%)
1450–1499	277	34 (12%)
1500–1545	842	69 (8%)

seem to suggest that testators were becoming rather choosy about their objects of charity. Gentry singled out poor tenants in their wills. Yeoman or wealthy townsfolk, gentry too, specified the local poor in their bequests: poor householders, those without ploughs, neighbours, unmarried maidens. In the latter part of the fifteenth century, testators (particularly the gentry) singled out poor scholars as worthy of bequest. More tended to give to charitable works like bridges and roads (Table 14). Some testators left food and clothing rather—one might hazard a guess—than entrust a profligate poor with money to spend on themselves. There is even a whiff of the soup kitchen about some of the bequests. Richard Gage, Salisbury weaver and merchant tailor of London, left a relation £24 in 1443 to distribute a bowl of soup to the poor every Friday for twenty years.[65]

Yet the notion that greater specification in bequests to the poor indicates a growing fear of the unemployed or vagrant poor in the wake of labour shortages is not easy to substantiate. Wills made in the city of Salisbury before the Black Death do not show testators handing out doles to large numbers of poor with gay abandon. It was in the later fourteenth century that more testators, as well as specifying certain types of poor, left money for distributions that were unspecific.[66] One of the earliest seems to have been Richard Riborgh in 1361 who left fifty marks to the poor and ill-shod in the city where need was greatest.[67] Perhaps executors of these wills were expected to discriminate as to who received the doles, but this may have been nothing new.

Wills made before the mid-fourteenth century also show that the use of the poor as liturgical appendages at funeral and anniversary services was

[65] PCC 34 Luffenham.

[66] The proportion of Salisbury testators making doles to the poor apparently outside funeral/obit was as follows. 1270–1349: 6%; 1350–99: 11%; 1400–49: 12%; 1450–99: 7%; 1500–38: 13%; 1539–47: 14%.

[67] WRO G23/1/212, fo. 39.

TABLE 15. The poor at funerals

	No. of wills	No. specifying funerals	No. mentioning poor at funerals
Salisbury			
1270–1349	15	11	5
1350–99	65	32	13
1400–49	129	66	45
1450–99	53	15	7
1500–47	68	19	7
Rest of region			
1260–1349	19	5	5
1350–99	114	14	10
1400–49	66	48	31
1450–99	113	40	31
1500–38	358	96	43
1539–47	194	38	20

a well-established practice. Before 1348, 45 per cent of Salisbury testators who mentioned burial arrangements required doles to the poor at their funerals. During the rest of the century fewer, 40 per cent, actually mentioned such doles. In the first half of the fifteenth century this figure increased to 66 per cent before dropping off during the following century (see Table 15). The apparently greater concern to make liturgical use of the poor at burials around 1400 (and from the evidence of wills alone this concern may be more apparent than real) had little to do with any changing attitude to the poor. It was in the same period that more church-building was begun, more fraternities and almshouses founded, indeed that funerals (like William Warmwell's) were more lavish. Wealthy citizens simply had more to give to the poor and seemed unruffled at the prospect of large numbers of poor assembling at the parish church door for funeral doles.

In the late medieval diocese of Salisbury, fewer hospitals were being founded in the fifteenth century than in the twelfth or thirteenth centuries; fewer were founded with priests and staff to look after the sick or passing traveller, and some older hospitals saw their endowments shrivel up or converted to other uses. By the fifteenth century too it is possible to discern a greater selectivity in charitable giving: almshouses seemed to cater for the old and respectable poor and testators specified certain groups of poor people in their wills. But had charitable giving become less open-handed and more discriminatory? The level of charitable provision could have depended on a number of things: the extent of poverty, a response to a particular need, or the wealth of the charitable donors, the ability to respond to poverty. Gifts to the poor might reflect an attitude to the poor or mirror concerns that had little to do with poverty. The evidence itself is not clear-cut.

If there was a discriminatory or wary attitude to the poor in the fifteenth century, it was beginning before the social unrest that followed the Black Death. Some religious houses had become more calculating in their charitable provision in the thirteenth century. Early hospitals, founded before the Black Death, may not have been quite the undiscriminating places of refuge they have sometimes been perceived to be. In any case, after the Black Death wills do not reveal (if they reveal anything at all) a sudden change in attitudes to the poor. The concern to harness the poor to liturgical services seems a well-established practice before the mid-fourteenth century, and if there came to be more bequests to specific groups of poor, there were also more bequests that appear undiscriminatory.

In any case, the number of hospital foundations and endowments was dwindling as early as the mid-thirteenth century. In many respects, this had less to do with attitudes to the poor and more with the pressures that restricted the endowment of other similar institutions of divine service. The 1279 Statute of Mortmain helped to make the foundation of religious houses a more expensive and drawn-out undertaking. The Church hierarchy's suspicion of chapels that could exercise parochial functions perhaps encouraged a growing preference for almshouses without staff and separate chapel. The declining value of landed rents in the late fourteenth century put paid to the endowments of many chantries and chapels: the apparent cut-back in charitable relief made by some hospitals was probably as much to do with decreasing returns from its rents as with a fear of attracting the wrong sort of poor.

It is also possible to paint a rather brighter picture of late medieval charity, to some extent in general, but certainly in particular areas. Some groups in society—gentry, townspeople, and other parishioners—seem to have become more rather than less generous in founding almshouses in the fifteenth century. To some extent, their charitable concerns blended with other considerations. In Sherborne, Reading, and Abingdon the desire of the towns' élite to extend their powers of self-government dovetailed nicely with almshouse foundations, over which they exercised control. But charitable giving was also, to some extent, a response to need. There may have been few complaints about a decline in hospital, priestly, or monastic charity because the level of support they provided met the expectations of contemporaries. Fewer almshouses, perhaps, needed founding in rural Dorset in the fifteenth century, when labourers' wages were higher, than in the thirteenth century. But in parts of Berkshire, where more almshouses were founded in the fifteenth century than before, a certain kind of poverty—an immigrant poor attracted to thriving market towns—may have needed tackling. It was perhaps only in the sixteenth century, with a rising population and prices, that problems of poverty and vagrancy became of more serious concern to authorities.[68]

Back in late-fourteenth-century Salisbury, a healthy measure of that open-handed charity sometimes said to characterize earlier centuries can be discerned. The Trinity almshouse was the work exclusively of the citizens, unlike the thirteenth-century foundation of the St Nicholas's hospital. It was the product of the city's growing wealth which was also channelled into church-building, chantry or guild foundation, and lavish funerals which also employed the poor. It was also a response to a particular need, admitting strangers who might have been attracted to the wealth of the city. Policies of admittance became stricter only in the mid-fifteenth century, at a time of brief economic depression and social unrest. But the Trinity's foundation was also bound up with the efforts of the city council, and its guild of St George, to strengthen its hand against episcopal overlordship. The hospital's history is related not only to the need for poor relief but also to other devotional concerns and institutions within the city.

[68] P. Slack, *Poverty and Policy in Tudor and Stuart England* (London, 1988), 17–18.

9
Private Devotion and Lollardy

GIVEN the overwhelming evidence for the strength of orthodox and corporate forms of religion in the region, Capgrave's claim that the Lollard heresy 'began first in the diocyse of Salesbury' is rather surprising.[1] By 1382 the chancellor of Salisbury cathedral was being alerted to the preaching of heretics. In 1388 an edict was passed empowering the chancellor, Hugh Cheney, knight, and John Bitterle to search all books, schedules, and quires written in English or Latin in the city of Salisbury for the unsound doctrines of John Wyclif.[2] During the 1370s Wyclif had questioned the spiritual authority of the Pope, the right of unworthy priests to receive tithes, and the need for priestly exegesis of the Bible. He had denounced the abuses of the contemporary Church and demanded its reformation: a true Church of the elect was to spread the message of the Scriptures to all men. On scriptural, metaphysical, and moral grounds, Wyclif had denied transubstantiation at the Eucharist, for which he had finally been condemned in 1382.[3]

A heresy that reduced priestly mediation and encouraged the reading of the Bible in the vernacular might well have appealed to lay people. On the one hand, criticisms of the priestly hierarchy were voiced ever more strongly in the fourteenth century, partly because the failings of the Church were made glaringly obvious by the 'Babylonish captivity' of the papacy at Avignon and the scandal of the Schism after 1378. But it was also because the Church had been too successful. The accumulation of endowments and tithes, and the centralization of papal government and jurisdiction, had already led academics, preachers, and friars to contrast the simple precepts of the Christian faith in the time of the Apostles with

---

[1] *The Chronicle of England by John Capgrave*, ed. F. C. Hingeston (Rolls Series, London, 1858), 252. Capgrave probably had in mind one William Ramsbury whom Walsingham mentions as an early Lollard preacher in the region (see below n. 45).

[2] *Wykeham's Register*, ed. T. F. Kirby (2 vols.; Hampshire Record Society; 1896–9), i. 238; ii. 337–8; *CPR* (1385–9), 468. The decree also applied to Leicester and Nottingham.

[3] McFarlane, *John Wycliffe*, 89–97; M. H. Keen, 'Wyclif, the Bible and Transubstantiation', in A. Kenny (ed.), *Wyclif in his Times* (Oxford, 1986), 1–16; J. I. Catto, 'John Wyclif and the Cult of the Eucharist', in K. Walsh and D. Wood (eds.), *The Bible in the Medieval World* (Studies in Church History, subsidia 4; Oxford, 1985), 269–86.

the practices and wealth of the late medieval Church.[4] On the other hand, the growth of a 'devout and literate laity', demanding devotional books, personal confessors, altars, and oratories, is also apparent. The ravages of plague in the second half of the fourteenth century, the influence of mystics and hermits, and the pastoral efforts of archbishops promoted a more personalized, penitential devotion.[5] But not all demands were satisfied and fear of heresy may have made that satisfaction less easy to deliver: access to the Bible in the vernacular was placed under much stricter supervision after 1408.[6]

The inadequacies of the Church and more corporate forms of devotion, however, do not mean that Lollardy became a popular and easily identifiable movement. Yet A. Hudson's analysis of over 250 manuscripts of Wyclifite scriptural translations and thirty-one English sermon cycles makes it difficult to sustain the view that Lollardy was merely the exaggerated product of post-Reformation propaganda or a series of 'heterogeneous and ill-assorted conclusions' scarcely deserving the name of 'creed'.[7] Attempts to judge the coherence of Lollardy based on the evidence of heresy trials alone are certainly flawed.[8] Yet trials do provide names of heretics and indicate the incidence of heresy and occasionally its strength in local society. Some areas may have been more susceptible to Lollardy than others. Were there features encouraging heresy in the diocese of Salisbury that serve to make Capgrave's comment less surprising?

Let us turn first to the background of orthodox private devotion. Over a small group of people, from the late fourteenth century onwards, there hung a mood of introspection, even morbid austerity. Edmund Leversedge's emphatic confession of sinfulness and denunciation of those proud 'gallants' was given visual expression in the gloomy murals that were once to be found in Margaret Hungerford's chantry chapel in

[4] G. Leff, *Heresy in the Later Middle Ages* (Manchester, 1967), 1–30.
[5] J. I. Catto, 'Religion and the English Nobility in the Later Fourteenth Century', in H. Lloyd-Jones, V. Pearl, and B. Worden (eds.), *History and Imagination: Essays in Honour of H. R. Trevor-Roper* (London, 1981), 43–55; Hughes, *Pastors and Visionaries*, esp. 258–98.
[6] A. Hudson, *Lollards and their Books* (London, 1985), 161–2; M. Aston, *Lollards and Reformers: Images and Literacy in Late Medieval Religion* (London, 1984), 212.
[7] Hudson, *Premature Reformation, passim*, esp. 251, 515; Aston, *Lollards and Reformers*, 9; McFarlane, *John Wycliffe*, 186.
[8] Hudson, *Premature Reformation*, 32–8. Cases of excommunication are another possible source, for they may include instances of the penalty for suspected heresy, but without confirmatory evidence of a suspect's heresy the information is of little value: no such cases have been found for the diocese of Salisbury (PRO C85/147, 148, 149). See also F. D. Logan, *Excommunication and the Secular Arm in Medieval England* (Toronto, 1968), 68–71, 189–94.

Salisbury cathedral.[9] A certain sepulchral fashion among courtly clerics
and knights for tombs with double effigies (stately figure above, putrid
cadaver below) influenced Sir John Golafre at Fyfield (1440). Some inscriptions on monuments and brasses, like John Bettesthorne's at Mere
(1396), spelled out uncomfortable warnings to the faithful: 'what I am so
you will be also.'[10]

Evidence for a more penitential devotion might also be found in wills.
Two Salisbury citizens in the early fifteenth century included lengthy
preambles in their wills which spoke of the transitory nature of this 'vale
of misery'.[11] A few gentry testators in the late fourteenth century struck a
morbid note by rejecting some of the suffrages available after death. Alice
West in 1395 required that her body be buried 'with right littel cost or
solemnity'. Elizabeth de Loudres in 1396 specifically stressed that no alms
should be given out on the day of her burial.[12] In 1390 John Dauntsey
asked his executors that his 'body be carried into the church of Dauntsey
wyth little cost and ther be bured wyth the first masse wythoute eny other
coste or solempnte. And afterward and this I will that I be layde on the
erthe ryghnaked as I came in to the herthe.'[13] Others were still more
extreme. William Stourton in 1410 asked for his 'putrid body' to be buried
naked. In 1415 Sir Thomas Broke, 'wycked sinner' to be saved from
damnation only by the Passion of Jesus Christ, dismissed his body as
'foule caryon' and restricted his bequests to poor people. His son Thomas
in 1439 left money only for the poor and followed his father's austerity,
denouncing himself as a wretched sinner whose soul would reach salvation only if found 'clene and worthy of true repentance'.[14]

Such expressions of austerity were not common, but they fed on other
forms of personal devotion that were more so. John Dauntsey's sense of
unworthiness may have been the result of private prayer, encouraged by
the licence for an oratory he acquired from the bishop in the year before
he made his will.[15] Private chapels were not a new feature of devotional
life. The acquisition of domestic chapels in manor houses had been regarded as a mark of gentry status by the end of the thirteenth century.[16] In

---

[9] See Intro. n. 1; M. A. Hicks, 'The Piety of Margaret Lady Hungerford', *JEH* 38 (1987),
28–9.

[10] Kite, *Monumental Brasses*, 22–3.

[11] Thomas Sextayn 1401 and John Barbour 1403 (WRO G23/1/213, fo. 43; PCC 6
Marche); see Intro. n. 72.

[12] PCC 4 Rous; Reg. Bp. Mitford, fo. 16ᵛ.   [13] Reg. Bp. Waltham, fo. 228ᵛ.

[14] PCC Marche, fos. 216, 316ᵛ–317; Luffenham, fo. 217ᵛ; C. Kightly, 'The Early Lollards:
A Survey of Popular Lollard Activity in England, 1382–1428', Ph.D. thesis (York, 1975),
341–3.

[15] Reg. Bp. Waltham, fo. 94ᵛ.   [16] Hughes, *Pastors and Visionaries*, 10.

1235 Geoffrey Esturmey came to an agreement with the rector of Burbage church to maintain his own manor chapel with books and ornaments as long as he continued to hear a sermon in the mother church on the five principal feast days.[17] It is difficult to say how far the demand for private chapels or oratories increased in the fourteenth century, when the registers of bishops start to present a more detailed picture. Between 1300 and 1350, 144 licences were granted for oratories by bishops in the diocese of Salisbury as a whole; between 1350 and 1399 there were a further 187.[18] By the second half of the fourteenth century, it was not just the nobility and gentry who were seeking licences for oratories: thirteen citizens of Salisbury also acquired them.[19] From the fourteenth century onwards, too, licences from the Pope were acquired in the diocese for portable altars: two between 1300 and 1349, seven from 1350 to 1399, thirty-six from 1400 to 1449 and seven from 1450 to 1499. Among these were six citizens from Salisbury.[20] A demand for private confessors, already encouraged by the friars in the thirteenth century, seems to have been increasing in the later fourteenth century as well: eighteen licences were granted by the bishops of Salisbury between 1350 and 1399 whereas only one had been before 1350.[21]

Those who acquired a private oratory and personal confessor may have possessed devotional books. Thomas Boyton, one of the Salisbury citizens to acquire a licence for an oratory, made his will in 1400. He left Nicholas Touker, his chaplain, one red-bound portiforium and a white temporale; he also left a black psalter to his son William and a red psalter to William Okeden, both of whom were to be given their psalters when they reached the age of 7.[22] Other testators, usually gentry, in the fifteenth and early

---

[17] WRO 1300 Ailesbury MS, 'Rough lists', sect. 7, nos. 1, 2, 3. For other 13th-cent. examples of private chapels see Radulf de Chany (WRO D1/1/2, fo. 118ᵛ (no. 330)); Walter de Pavely, knight (WRO D1/1/4, fo. 74 (p. 158)); Thomas Maudit (Longleat MS 8968, 8972); William of Calne, knight, at Warminster and Lord Hugh of Hinton (*St. Nicholas's Cart.* 58, 65–6); Thomas of Purton, knight, and Roger of Cherlton (*Reg. Malmesburiense,* ii. 161, 454).

[18] The recording of licences seems to vary from register to register: under Bishop Gandavo (1298–1315) three were granted; under Bishop Martival (1315–30) none, but under Bishop Wyvill (1330–75) 141. Between 1350 and 1355 eleven were granted, between 1355 and 1374 none, but 175 are recorded between 1375 and 1399.

[19] Reg. Bp. Erghum. fos. 2ᵛ, 6ᵛ; Reg. Bp. Waltham, fos. 93ᵛ, 94ᵛ, 95; Reg. Bp. Mitford, fos. 11, 115ᵛ, 120ᵛ, 123ᵛ.

[20] *Cal. Papal Reg., passim.* For Salisbury citizens see iv. 495; v. 56; vii. 534; ix. 316, 584; x. 386; xii, part 2, 822.

[21] Only one licence for a private confessor was recorded after 1400 (*Reg. Bp. Hallam,* 815 (1412)).

[22] WRO G23/1/213, fos. 30ᵛ–31ᵛ.

sixteenth centuries, mentioned the possession of psalters, missals, and mass books in their wills. Alice West, so humble with her funeral arrangements in her will of 1395, mentioned a mass book, a matins book, and books in English and French.[23]

Approval of a more penitential devotion and personal holiness is to be found, too, in the support of those who followed an austere calling. The Carthusian order netted a considerable proportion of the bequests to monastic houses in the later Middle Ages. William Stourton wished his 'putrid body' to be buried in the charterhouse of Witham, and Edmund Leversedge found his penitential devotion compatible with bequests to Witham and Hinton.[24] Individual hermits and anchorites who chose a life of enclosure in cells next to parish churches and religious houses or by bridges also attracted the support of the more penitentially inclined. Alice West and Elizabeth de Loudres, who rejected sumptuous funerals, left bequests to individual anchorites. The eremitic movement was certainly not new in the later Middle Ages, but it may well have been re-emerging in the fourteenth century. The number of hermits was greater in Yorkshire than elsewhere, possibly because of an abundance of aristocratic patrons who were important in the spreading of the eremitic movement.[25] But there were certainly hermits to be found in the diocese of Salisbury. Some of them were in remote places near the coast or (more frequently) in forested areas.[26] Some were attached to religious houses, such as the Black Friars at Fisherton-Anger and the Benedictines at Malmesbury.[27] The gentry sometimes had their own tame hermits: in 1420 one hermit at Little Horningsham received a plot of land from Isabel de Bonham.[28] But there was also a fashion among the élite of some of the cloth towns to act

---

[23] PCC 4 Rous. Sixty-seven out of about 1,600 lay testators in the region mentioned books in their wills (from 1377 onwards); fifteen of these were Salisbury citizens and most of the rest gentry. Between them they mentioned thirty-seven missals or mass books, ten breviaries, nine psalters, six matins books, six antiphonaries, two ordinals, one 'pupilla oculi', one 'pilgrimage of souls', one 'legend sanctorum', two decretals. Secular works mentioned were: two books of law, three Gowers, 'Higden's Pollicronicon', and the 'Great chronicles'. For Bible owners see Ch. 10 nn. 23, 24.

[24] See Intro. nn. 1, 82.

[25] Hughes, *Pastors and Visionaries*, 64–126. R. M. Clay, *The Hermits and Anchorites of England* (London, 1914).

[26] Blackmoor, Bentley Wood, Woodby Hill, Burton Hill, Stanton St Quintin, Poole. See ibid. 204–5, 212–13, 252–3; *VCH: Wilts.* iii. 152–3. To the twelve known places with hermits in Berks. listed by Clay may be added Wallingford (*VCH: Berks.* iii. 542) and Thatcham (Reg. Bp. Waltham, fo. 98ᵛ). To the seventeen listed for Wilts. may be added Codford St Mary (*VCH: Wilts.* iii. 152); Little Horningsham (Longleat MS 7514); Old Sarum, where two hermits were excommunicated in 1388 (PRO C85/147/53), and Ramsbury (*Reg. Bp. Langton*, 450).

[27] See also Poughley, Sherborne, Edington (Reg. Bp. Beauchamp, second series, fo. 15ᵛ).

[28] Longleat MS 7514.

as patrons of hermits. Richard Ludlow at Maidenhead vowed before Bishop Beauchamp, the mayor, and the principal men of the district in 1423 to 'lede my lyf to my lyves ende in trewe continentz and chastite and to eschewe alle open spectacles, scotales and tavernys . . . and alle other suspecte places of synne'.[29] The hermit living in the Black Friars of Fisherton-Anger attracted bequests from Salisbury citizens from 1498 onwards.[30] A hermitage established in Marlborough in the early sixteenth century enjoyed the patronage of the mayor and burgesses.[31]

There is evidence, then, for new forms of piety in the diocese, an interest in more personal forms of devotion, and an admiration for an austere piety. But 'private' devotion did not necessarily mean a movement away from the more public forms of devotion. Patronage for hermitages may suggest a growing respect for the holiness of the inner life but, besides contemplation, hermits often performed intercessory services. The hermit at Marlborough, rather like a chantry priest, was to pray for the souls of his benefactors. Rather like the inmates of almshouses, Richard Ludlow vowed in 1423 to hear mass every day and to say the Lady psalter (twice on Sundays and other holidays), fifteen Pater Nosters and Aves 'in the worschip and mynde of the woundys that oure lord suffrid for me and for alle mankynde'. The difference in services demanded of hermit, monk, chantry priest, and almsman should not be overdrawn.

The more private forms of devotion practised by rural gentry, urban merchants, and burgesses may well have been increasing by the end of the fourteenth century, but interest in them is difficult to quantify. The level of interest in private oratories and confessors cannot be perfectly ascertained from bishops' registers. Fewer people apparently required licences from the bishop in the later fifteenth century, yet there is no reason to assume that interest in private devotion had declined. Perhaps, by then, bishops were more loath, in face of heretical subversion, to grant licences for worship away from the corporate life of the parish. But it is more likely that incompleteness of bishops' registers prevents accurate assessment of demand.

In any case, 'private' forms of religion need not be viewed as a movement away from more outward pious practice. Apparently private chapels could serve the pastoral needs of a wider community.[32] Many of those who

[29] Reg. Bp. Chandler, second series, fo. 40ᵛ.
[30] John Chafyne 1498 (PPC 28 Horne); Nicholas Martyn merchant 1512 (PCC 18 Fetiplace); John Stone 1535 (PCC 30 Hogen); Joan Peerse 1536 (PCC 15 Dyngeley); Anne Stone 1536 (PCC 38 Hogen); Thomas Martyn merchant 1536 (PCC 1 Dyngeley).
[31] WRO G22/1/102. [32] See Ch. 3 nn. 23, 24.

possessed private oratories or devotional books apparently had little difficulty in conforming to the demands of parish or guild. Thomas Boyton of
Salisbury had a private oratory, personal confessor, and devotional literature but in 1400 he asked for burial in the middle of St Thomas's church
and willed that twenty marks be given to the new south aisle. Three of the
Salisbury citizens who asked for licences for oratories in the late fourteenth century, John Upton, John Baker, and Nicholas Taylor, had their
names recorded on the bede roll of the guild of St George.[33] Books that
might have nourished the inner life of their owners were often left to
enrich the devotional life of a wider audience: Cecily Cheney in 1430 left
a missal from her own chapel to her parish church of Westbury.[34] Even
testators who expressed more extreme sentiments in their wills did not
entirely depart from more conformist practices: Elizabeth de Loudres did
not permit alms to be given out on the day of her burial, but she did allow
forty pounds of wax to burn about her body; John Dauntsey ensured that
whatever his funeral lacked for in the way of suffrages was made up in the
days following: he left £10. 10s. for the singing of 100 masses after his
death 'in the hastiest man[ner] that may be done'. William Stourton
mentions missals in his will and a bequest to Archbishop Arundel
of Canterbury. The apparent growth of interest in private piety was
compatible with, and did not generally subvert, the requirements of
public orthodoxy.[35]

Nevertheless, private devotion could encourage deviation from the
path of orthodoxy. Introspection, the habit of private prayer, or devotional
study could encourage withdrawal from and even criticism of outward
conformity. The line between orthodoxy and heresy, particularly in the
late fourteenth century, was not a boundary clearly staked out by the
authorities but a shifting no man's land of opinions that were not always
easily identifiable as heretical.[36] The support of Lollardy among the Wiltshire gentry is difficult to gauge: the more austere or penitential feelings
expressed in the wills of John Dauntsey and Elizabeth de Loudres may
indicate a moderate dissent which was sympathetic to the more radical
tendencies of Lollardy. The harsher passages in the wills of Sir Thomas
Broke and son, William Stourton, and John Dauntsey are strikingly similar to those of the so-called Lollard knights identified at the royal court in

---

[33] WRO G23/1/213, fos. 30ᵛ–31ᵛ; see Table 10.
[34] PCC 14 Luffenham.   [35] See also Duffy, *Stripping of the Altars*, 233–65.
[36] Hudson, *Premature Reformation*, esp. 429; Catto, 'Religion and the English Nobility',
55; K. B. McFarlane, *Lancastrian Kings and Lollard Knights* (Oxford, 1972), 207–20; Vale,
'Piety, Charity and Literacy', 12–14.

the late fourteenth century. William Stourton is found in association with John Montagu earl of Salisbury, Sir Thomas Latimer, Sir John Cheyne, and William Beauchamp. In 1410 Sir Thomas Broke arranged with the infamous John Oldcastle the marriage of his son with Joan Braybrooke, the only daughter of Oldcastle's wife, Joan Lady Cobham. The same son, he of the 'putrid cadaver', was associated with Oldcastle's rebellion in 1414.[37]

The influence of Lollard knights may not have been restricted to the court. William Stourton and Sir Thomas Broke (the elder) must have known each other at a local level. In 1381 Sir William served as justice of the peace in Wiltshire, and in 1401 he and Sir Thomas served on the bench together.[38] Another knight who served as justice of the peace in the county, as well as sheriff and member of Parliament in January 1380, was Laurence of St Martin. Thomas Walsingham reported with some horror that Laurence became 'seduced' by Wyclif's teaching. In 1381 at the Easter mass, instead of swallowing the consecrated host, he kept it in his hand, returned home, and proceeded to divide the host in three. He ate one part with his oysters, another with his onions, and the remaining part with his wine. The consecrated bread, he declared, was on a par with any other bread. Laurence did not go unpunished: he was condemned to do penance in a public place every 'feriis sextis' for the rest of his life before a stone cross carved with representations of his misdeeds. He also appears to have been dismissed from the office of sheriff in May of the same year.[39] How Laurence became aware of Wyclif's teachings is not clear, but possible links with knights like Stourton and Broke suggest a wider network of connections between the locality and the Lollard clique at court.[40]

The influence of powerful patrons perhaps allowed heresy to become established in the localities. Lollard knights are known to have presented heretical priests to benefices and established Lollard scriptoria on their manors in areas that subsequently became centres of heresy.[41] Such links, although tenuous, might be detected in the case of Salisbury diocese. Perhaps Lollardy at Newbury, where heretics were known as early as 1402,

[37] McFarlane, *Lancastrian Kings*, 215–16.

[38] *CPR* (1381–5), 141; *CCR* (1399–1402), 388.

[39] *Chronica Monasteri S. Albani: Thomae Walsingham, Quondam Monachi S. Albani, Historia Anglicana*, ed. H. T. Riley (2 vols.; Rolls Series, London, 1863), i. 450–1; M. Aston, 'Wyclif and the Vernacular', in A. Hudson and M. Wilks (eds.), *From Ockham to Wyclif* (Studies in Church History, subsidia 5; Oxford, 1987), 294–5.

[40] To R. G. Davies, however, the Lollard knights formed a clique and 'cliques do not make new friends' ('Lollardy and Locality', *TRHS*, sixth series, 1 (1991), 198–9).

[41] A. K. McHardy, 'The Dissemination of Wyclif's Ideas', in Hudson and Wilks (eds.), *From Ockham to Wyclif*, 361–8.

had been encouraged by Sir Lewis Clifford's landed interests in the area
and his presentation of John Malden, an Oxford graduate, to the benefice
in 1393.[42] John Montagu had manors at Letcombe Regis, Bisham, and
Thatcham; the Cobhams and Braybrookes had manors at Clyffe Pypard,
Great Somerford, and Broughton Giffard.[43] All these places produced
cases of heresy in later years. Heresy was also found in Wilsford where
John Dauntsey had practised his more austere form of piety, and at Shaw,
where Richard de Abberbury, who was an executor of John Montagu's
will with Thomas Clanvowe and John Cheyne, had founded a hospital for
thirteen poor people in 1393.[44]

As a proselytizing creed, however, Lollardy did not have to rely on the
powerful to spread from Oxford. Itinerant preachers, according to
Walsingham, practised their perfidy in the diocese. There was indeed a
Lollard preacher active in Wiltshire, who was tried before Bishop John
Waltham in 1389. The preacher, William Ramsbury, asserted that he had
been tonsured and given a habit, a russet tunic 'cum mantelo de eadem
secta', by a certain Thomas Fishburn. He denied that after the consecration the bread became the body of Christ: he was also accused of conducting a mass ceremony that retained the elevation of the host but without the
words of consecration. There is enough to suggest William's familiarity
with Wyclifite teachings. He rejected the powers of popes, bishops, and
priests to excommunicate and absolve. Their status was to be brought
down closer to that of lay people by permission to marry. Tithes, mortuary
fees, and payments made at purification and marriage were not to be
made. More positively, William stressed that the role of the priest was to

[42] *CPR* (1401–5), 198. The *VCH* suspects the men arrested of Lollardy (*Berks*. iv. 137).
Certainly Lollardy was found in the town after 1490 (*CPR* (1388–92), 306; Reg. Bp.
Waltham, fo. 88ᵛ; *BRUO*, 1208). However, John Malden was provost of Oriel and is not
known to have supported Wyclif; Sir Lewis Clifford also owned manors in places in which
Lollardy is not known to have taken root.

[43] *VCH: Berks*. 218; *Wilts*. iv. 218; ix. 28; xiv. 197. Direct connections of later Lollardy
with Wyclif's Oxford are more tenuous. There was a vicar of Bere Regis who had been at
Oxford in the 1380s, at Exeter college (where one Laurence Stephen had supported Wyclif
for a time), and was obliged to clear himself of the charge of heresy in 1412. But there are no
known cases of Lollardy appearing in that parish later on (although there were several cases
of non-payment of tithes) (*BRUO*, 1772, 1917; *Reg. Bp. Hallum*, 1113, 1126; see Ch. 3 n. 36).
At Letcombe Basset (where later Lollards were found) William Selby, a known associate of
Wyclif, was an absentee rector in the 1380s; Oxford graduates of the late 14th cent. can also
be found at Locking and Marlborough St Peter's (where later Lollards were discovered) but
none of them is known as a heretic (*BRUO*, 1185, 1341).

[44] McFarlane, *Lancastrian Kings*, 25; T. F. Tout, *Chapters in Medieval Administrative
History*, iv (Manchester, 1928), 344–6; *VCH: Berks*. ii. 93–4, 99; *CPR* (1391–6), 369; W.
Dugdale, *Monasticon Anglicanum* (6 vols.; London, 1817), vi. 715. There is no evidence to
prove, however, that Sir Richard was a Lollard knight.

preach the people to 'transire per patriam cum biblia'; he stated that it was enough to confess to God and that he and his followers were 'in vera fide et nulli alii'.[45]

Quite what impact the preaching and support of a Ramsbury or a Laurence of St Martin had is not easy to discern. The surviving evidence from trials would not immediately suggest that heresy became a serious problem for the Church. Only one heretic (in 1405) was denounced to the authorities in the visitations conducted by the dean of Salisbury cathedral into the prebends in 1405, 1408, 1412, 1464, 1480, and 1485.[46] Between 1390 and 1450, apart from an incident at Edington in 1428 and the rising of 1431, there are only ten known cases of heresy recorded in bishops' registers for the whole diocese. No Wiltshire Lollard is known to have been involved in Oldcastle's rebellion in 1414 though prosecutions were made in Dorset and Berkshire. In Reading, Lollard schedules are known to have been posted up in 1416. Only a further seven cases of heresy received the attention of bishops before 1486.[47]

Some opinions uncovered by prosecutors would not imply the existence of a coherent Lollard sect. William Wakeham was supposed to have said, according to a weaver, John Lytull, that the land was above the sky.[48] Other beliefs were inconsistent. It is difficult to square those Lollards who spoke of Wyclif as a saint, like Robert Stilman in 1518, with those who attacked the whole cult of sainthood.[49] Wyclif and later heretics asserted the primacy of Scripture: John Brewer of Aldbourne considered that there was more good in a cask of ale than in the four Evangelists. Whereas John Okeford of Bishopstone near Salisbury claimed in 1516 that the 'cristen soul' was never damned, the soul ascending to bliss while the 'caren body' remained, Thomas Tailor affirmed in 1486 that when the

---

[45] *Chronica Monasteri S. Albani*, ii. 188; Reg. Bp. Waltham, fos. 222–223ᵛ. See A. Hudson, 'A Lollard Mass', *Journal of Theological Studies*, 23 (1972), 407–19. William Ramsbury is not known to have been at Oxford.

[46] *Reg. Dean Chandler*, 31.

[47] PRO KB9/209/63–9; *Chronica Monasteri S. Albani*, ii. 317; *Reg. Bp. Hallum*, nos. 908, 1113, 1133, 1142. The cases of 1428 and 1431 are described below. For the others see Reg. Bp. Chandler, fos. 17ᵛ–18, 25 (1418); Reg. Bp. Neville, second series, fos. 48ᵛ (1431), 52 (1437), 57ᵛ (1434); Reg. Bp. Aiscough, second series, fos. 52ᵛ (1440), 53ᵛ, 54ᵛ (1443); Reg. Bp. Beauchamp, ii, series 2, fo. 17ᵛ (1478).

[48] Reg. Bp. Neville, second series, fo. 52.

[49] *The Acts and Monuments of John Foxe*, ed. S. R. Cautely and J. Pratt (8 vols.; London, 1853–70), iv. 207–8. C. von Nocklen makes a case for consistency concerning the Lollard position on saints, but has to give them 'the benefit of the doubt' and admit that 'the pressures of popular piety were strong' ('Another Kind of Saint: A Lollard Perception of John Wyclif', in Hudson and Wilks (eds.), *From Ockham to Wyclif*, 429–43).

body died so did the soul, like the blowing-out of a candle.[50] Different nuances of belief were also expressed: some Lollards scorned the whole ceremony of the Eucharist, but to John Bever at least the words spoken by the priest at the time of consecration were 'good and holy'.[51] Of course these inconsistencies of belief may have been more apparent than real: the words of heretics were not always recorded in full and may have been reported second-hand from the testimony of hostile witnesses.[52] Yet it is still likely that some of the sharpness and coherence of Wyclif's ideas was lost as Lollardy spread from Oxford.

Furthermore, it is not always clear how 'Lollard' those accused of heresy were. In the no man's land between heresy and orthodoxy, the authorities sometimes found it difficult to determine which opinions were truly heretical. Richard Woodhill of Durnford had refused to appear before the bishop to answer charges of heresy and in 1459 he appealed to Rome. Some of the charges, particularly his refusal to receive the Eucharist, look suspiciously like hard-line Lollardy; yet the heretical content of other charges is more questionable. He was accused of failing to go to the parish mass and of saying that fornication was not a sin and that tithes were not due on lambs born after the feast of St Mark.[53] Many other people were denounced at visitations, even excommunicated, for not paying certain dues or not attending the parish services, yet the charges of heresy had not been made against them.[54] Take the case of Juliana Farman and Margery Coterell of Hungerford, excommunicated in 1409 and imprisoned in Sherborne castle. Neither had attended church for five years, received the Eucharist, or eaten 'flesh on Easter date'. Juliana had also taken a chalice, ornaments, vestments, sixteen sheep, and ten marks from St Katherine's light within her church. But no charge of heresy seems to have been brought against either of them.[55] What constituted heresy was sometimes decided less by the beliefs expressed by the accused than by the opinion of the accuser.

In 1428 John Upton, a parishioner of Edington, was made to abjure certain 'heretical' opinions. With several other parishioners, eleven of whom are named, he had met before a cross in the hamlet of Tinhead on the feast of Pentecost. At the command of John Rous of Baynton, they

[50] Reg. Bp. Neville, second series, fo. 48ᵛ; Reg. Bp. Audley, first series, fo. 160; *Reg. Bp. Langton*, no. 484.
[51] Reg. Bp. Audley, first series, fo. 147ᵛ. On the various nuances of beliefs expressed about the Eucharist see Hudson, *Premature Reformation*, 281–90.
[52] Ibid. 33.　　[53] *Cal. Papal Reg.* xi (1455–64), 536–7.
[54] See Ch. 3 n. 36. For a case of excommunication for the non-payment of tithes see PRO C85/149/24: John Hooke of Damerham in 1442.
[55] *Reg. Dean Chandler*, 88, 247, 553; PRO C85/148/22.

pledged, under penalty of 40s., not to pay more than 1d. at funeral exequies, marriages, purifications, and anniversaries.[56] As A. Hudson points
out when citing this case, refusal to pay tithes and other offerings had been
made by previous Lollards, not least by William Ramsbury.[57] Yet in this
instance it is difficult to know whether the rejection of customary offerings sprang from attachment to any Lollard creed. John Rous was the
younger son of John Rous, senior, and had been given the manor of
Baynton in 1413. The dispute over the tithes of Baynton chapel had
involved John Rous's ancestors. In 1339 a quarrel between the collegiate
church of Romsey and the prebendary of Edington on one side and the
chapel's rector Thomas and patron John Rous, knight, on the other, about
the great tithes from the hamlet of Baynton, had led to an affray in which
a man had been killed. In 1364 the rector and John's successor Richard
were summoned before the bishop to answer for their withdrawal of tithes
of corn and hay, mortuary fees, and other parochial rights. The root of the
problem was not whether tithes should be paid at all but to whom they
should be paid. The same problem may have been at the back of John
Rous's protest in 1428. After all, his later actions do not suggest that he
was a full-blooded Lollard, who rejected all the suffrages of the Church:
in 1444 he conferred the manor and advowson of Baynton on the
Bonhommes of Edington and, according to the Tropenell cartulary,
'yerely hath an obit kept in the rectory church of Edington for his manner
of Baynton'.[58] Perhaps John Rous was using the others, who may have
been more deeply steeped in Lollardy than he, to rally support for his
dispute. But it is also possible that the authorities were using the charge of
heresy as a weapon against a less serious offence. Whereas in the fourteenth century the dispute over tithes had not led to the charge of heresy,
by 1428 refusal to pay offerings due to the Church had become associated
with heresy in the minds of the Church hierarchy. Lollardy could be
defined as much by the persecutors as by the heretics themselves.

One further example may illustrate the point. In 1431 a group of rebels
under the leadership of a weaver, William Manderville, alias Jack Sharpe
of Wigmorland, caused trouble in London, the Midlands, and parts of the
West Country.[59] Bills and schedules were distributed which called for a

[56] Reg. Bp. Neville, fos. 32ᵛ–33. There were nineteen people named altogether in the trial, twelve of whom 'with several others of the parish' were said to have met with John Rous.
[57] Hudson, *Premature Reformation*, 293.
[58] *VCH: Wilts.* viii. 248–9; *CCR* (1339–41), 257, 263; *Edington Cart.*, nos. 31, 32; *Tropenell Cart.* i. 271; *VCH: Wilts.* iii. 322; Colt-Hoare, *A Modern History of Wiltshire: Hundred of Heytesbury* (London, 1827), 161–2.
[59] For the following see Harvey, *Jack Cade's Rebellion*, 26; Aston, *Lollards and Reformers*, 33–4; J. A. F. Thomson, *The Later Lollards 1414–1520* (London, 1965), 58–60.

wholesale replacement of great prelates and peers of the realm with members of their own group. On 9 May a group of men in Salisbury, which included a clerk, a weaver from Westbury, and a fuller from Abingdon, had put up posters in Salisbury urging an assault on the cathedral in order to raze its buildings to the ground and carry off its goods and relics. The theme of religious disendowment had appeared in Wyclif's teachings in the Lollard petitions to Parliament in 1395 and 1410, and in Oldcastle's rising of 1415, so the revolt of 1431 was in one sense a Lollard revolt.[60] Yet no rebel was charged with heresy. The bringing to trial of people whose attachment to Lollardy was questionable might also indicate that the authorities could exaggerate the depth of heresy.

Some Lollards, moreover, expressed fear of discovery. Certainly, some were not denounced straight away: the parson of Northmoor and the abbot of Abingdon had reasoned with Philip Broune of Hinton Waldrist and had persuaded him, temporarily, to believe in the sacrament of the altar. But although other Lollards could remain successfully hidden for a long time, it was usually by dint of secrecy and outward conformity.[61] Thomas Broughton of Hungerford may not have been to confession or believed in the sacrament of the Eucharist for twenty-five years, yet he said:

I have ev[er]y yere receyved the said holy sacrament not for that I had any stedfast byleve therin: but that I should not be noted and knowen of the people. And beyng in the Church or ellyswher whan the said hold sacrament was present I feyned with myn handes to honour it as cristen men use to do, but my mind and entent was nothyng therto but to god almighty above in heven thinkyng that he was not ther p[re]sent in the blessyd sacrament.[62]

Other heretics expressed a similar fear of detection. In 1514 John Swayne, or Barnard, labourer of Wilsford, and his wife Margery both 'wold not have comyn unto the churche oft tymes but for the Rumor of the pepull'. Thomas Smyth, husbandman of Chirton, considered going to church 'avayleth not but of the avoydyng the rumor of the people'.[63] Clearly, what concerned these heretics was less being detected by the inquisitorial powers of the Church hierarchy than being denounced by an orthodox populace.

Finally, a number of Lollards were unearthed because they had publicly denounced popular practices. Michael Gamare of Wimborne St Giles in

[60] Hudson, *Premature Reformation*, 114–15, 337–46; McFarlane, *John Wycliffe*, 177.
[61] *Reg. Bp. Langton*, no. 419.   [62] Reg. Bp. Blythe, fo. 74.
[63] Reg. Bp. Audley, first series, fo. 155ᵛ.

1516 had presumably voiced his opinion that it was 'alewde thyng and amadde condition or use occupied in his contree or paryshe that wemen will cum and sette their ca[n]dles a fore atree, the Image of Saynt Gyles'. Roger Parker of Letcombe Regis in 1499 had scorned those men and women that went 'barefote and offer Images of wex or money to the reliques of Saint Bernold [Bearnwold]' in Bampton (Oxfordshire).[64] Alice Tailor of Bisham admitted in 1502 that 'I did rebuke oon Agnes Miller because she did kneale uppon her kneys afore the crosse in the proucession tyme saying too here "Stonde up olde foole! Whertoo knelist thow?"' Alice Hignell of Newbury was driven to more violent thoughts: 'when devote Cristen people be offering their candel to the ymage of seint Erasme I have wold I had a hatchet in my hand And wer behynde theim to knoke theim on their heddis.'[65] The attacks of all these Lollards were directed at the pious practices of the majority.

Nevertheless, attempts to belittle the significance of Lollardy from the fragmentary record of heresy trials require caution. Despite the diversity of opinions deemed to be Lollard, it is possible to disentangle, using the impressive corpus of surviving Lollard literature, a core of beliefs that unified a distinct sect. Even the negative utterances of Lollards against popular piety reflect beliefs first expressed by Wyclif: over half the heretics tried in the diocese from 1390 to 1540 denied the doctrine of transubstantiation as Wyclif had done, and over a third shared Wyclif's distrust of images and pilgrims. Furthermore, Lollardy was not simply a knee-jerk reaction to orthodox piety. The apparent predominance of negative beliefs in the registers may simply reflect the nature of questions by the persecutors.[66] There were also more positive doctrines expressed. Thomas Broughton in 1498 expressed a concern for preaching in the delight he took in listening to sermons. William Carpenter alias Harford alias Daniell of Newbury denied the need for priestly mediation in confession: 'it were as goode for eny cristen man to shrive of his felowe as of a priste.'[67] Above all, there were those like Wyclif who stood for a Church separate from the 'carnal' ecclesiastical hierarchy: Thomas Bikenore defined

[64] Ibid., fo. 158ᵛ; Reg. Bp. Blythe, fo. 73ᵛ.

[65] Reg. Bp. Audley, first series, fo. 169; *Reg. Bp. Langton*, 495.

[66] Hudson, *Premature Reformation*, 301. In 1428 a questionnaire seems to have been produced by which Lollard beliefs could be tested systematically (A. Hudson, 'The Examination of Lollards', *Bulletin of the Institute of Historical Research*, 46 (1973), 145–59).

[67] *Reg. Bp. Langton*, 497; see also Reg. Bp. Aiscough, fo. 53ᵛ; Reg. Bp. Blythe, fo. 74; Reg. Bp. Audley, first series, fos. 163ʳ⁻ᵛ. To Augustyn Stere in 1491, the Eucharist was a profit-making rite closer to the treachery of Judas than to the Last Supper (*Reg. Bp. Langton*, 486).

'holichurche' in 1443 as the 'Congregacion of trewe men whiche only shul be saved'.[68]

Two features of Lollardy helped to maintain the heresy as a coherent sect. There are suggestions that a network of heresy operated over a wide geographical area. Thomas Bikenore, living in the diocese of Salisbury at the time of his trial in 1443, had been born in Bristol, had preached in Wallingford and Windsor, and was in touch with the Chiltern group of Lollards and possibly with the East Anglian group led by William White. John Whithorn, rector of the parish of Letcombe Basset, had links with heretics in London: in 1508 he was accused of bringing gifts for two men imprisoned in the 'Lollers Tower'.[69] Other heretics were also found to have crossed diocesan boundaries. In 1475 the bishop of Bath and Wells warned Bishop Beauchamp that a suspect, Thomas Warve of Marston Bigot, had moved to the city of Salisbury. John Gough, tried in 1499, was active in Chipping Faringdon, but was known to be 'late of Bristol'.[70] Contact with other Lollard groups may well have lent some cohesion to Lollardy as a whole. Richard Petefyn claimed, with appropriate medieval disregard for numerical accuracy, that he had converted forty people to heresy and that 20,000 people were of his opinions.[71]

More importantly, Lollards had books in English which they could read for themselves or have read to them. William Wakeham, tried in 1437, had met with others in private houses in Devizes and Marlborough to hear and read the Bible in English; he was also heard to say that it was 'no better for a layman to say the lord's prayer in latin than to say Bibull Babull'.[72] Much later, in 1486, Thomas Tailor of Newbury and Augustyn Stere of Speen both confessed to having 'a boke of commaundements' (possibly one of the Lollard commentaries on the Decalogue) which taught against the worship of images.[73] Thomas Broughton of Hungerford likewise spoke of an English book 'that we calle the commaundement boke', from which he had 'herd redd dyvers times' that images ought not to be honoured.[74] Thomas had also put his bookish learning to more discriminating use:

---

[68] Reg. Bp. Aiscough, second series, fo. 53ᵛ.

[69] Hudson, *Premature Reformation*, 141–2; Reg. Bp. Audley, first series, fos. 143–6; Hudson, *Premature Reformation*, 157, 167.

[70] Reg. Bp. Beauchamp, i, second series, fo. 3; Reg. Bp. Blythe, fo. 78ʳ⁻ᵛ.

[71] Thomson, *Later Lollards*, 78.

[72] Reg. Bp. Neville, second series, fo. 52ᵛ. See also Reg. Bp. Aiscough, second series, fo. 52ᵛ.

[73] *Reg. Bp. Langton*, nos. 484, 486; Hudson, *Lollards and their Books*, 162.

[74] Reg. Bp. Blythe, fo. 74. See also the trial of Richard Lyllington of Castle Combe who preached openly in the alehouses of Marlborough and Devizes (*Reg. Bp. Langton*, no. 499).

sith the tyme of my first acqueyntance with the said heretickes I have had a great mynde to here sermouns and prechynges of doctours and lerned men of the church. And as long as they spack the veray wordys of the gospels and the epistles such as I had herd afore in our english bokkys, I herked wele unto theym and had great delight to here them.

Attention to the written word, especially if it was scripturally based and in the vernacular, was a constant feature of Lollardy after Wyclif—even though after about 1440 there was a rapid decline in the number of surviving Lollard texts actually produced.[75]

The survival of a coherent set of beliefs suggests that it would be unwise to dismiss Lollardy as insignificant simply because it was not detected. The dearth of recorded heretics between 1440 and 1480 that is apparent all over England does not imply that heresy had disappeared. Some Lollards who were later rooted out had remained undetected for many years: Philip Broune (tried in 1486) for twelve years, Thomas Loryng (1486) for sixteen or seventeen, Thomas Broughton (1498) for twenty-five.[76] Bishop Beauchamp (1450–81) may not have recorded the discovery of many heretics in his diocese, yet he did launch a commission to find heretics in 1475, the results of which are not known.[77] Trials after 1480 indeed suggest that heresy had merely been concealed rather than extinguished. Whereas sixteen cases of heresy were recorded between 1380 and 1480, seventeen people were tried under Bishop Langton (1485–93), twenty-five under Bishop Blythe (1493–6), and seventy under Bishop Audley (1502–24).[78] The difference may only indicate increasing success in detection rates or better-kept records rather than a growing number of heretics; but it also suggests that Lollardy was in no danger of extinction.

Some of these later Lollards were also influential people. A wide spectrum of society is revealed, with occupations of twenty-six Lollards given in the bishops' registers between 1485 and 1524. The lower orders are certainly represented: one tanner, one cooper, one carpenter, one shoemaker or 'wullwynder', and three labourers. Slightly wealthier, perhaps, were the two fullers, three weavers, and four tailors. There were also one

---

[75] Hudson, *Premature Reformation*, 451–3.

[76] *Reg. Bp. Langton*, 419; Reg. Bp. Blythe, fos. 73ᵛ, 74.

[77] Reg. Bp. Beauchamp, ii, second series, fo. 17ᵛ.

[78] The increase in the number of heretics brought to trial seems to have been a national phenomenon (Hudson, *Premature Reformation*, 447–8). It is difficult to put the relative fewness of heretics brought to trial between 1440 and 1480 down to a reluctance of bishops during that time to prosecute. Bishops Aiscough (1438–50) and Beauchamp (1450–81) were no different from their predecessors (*VCH: Wilts.* iii. 14).

rector, two millers, and seven husbandmen.[79] Some of the later Lollards described by John Foxe were comfortably well-off. Robert Collins of East Hendred owned six horses, four acres of wheat, and thirty acres of barley, worth just under £20 altogether, in 1543.[80] Others in the same parish, like William White and John Collins, were churchwardens.[81] Within Reading, John Lewis, weaver, and Thomas Scochyn, tailor, who were brought to trial for heresy in 1499, were burgesses of the guild merchant.[82]

Moreover, none of these men was isolated from the activities of local society. Robert Collins did not ignore some of the communal activities of his local parish church, contributing to the new casting of the great bell in 1543. As churchwardens, William White and John Collins enforced the decisions of ecclesiastical courts. In 1507 one John Passemar, yeoman or husbandman, admitted to rejecting many of the suffrages of the Church, the worship of images and the sacrament of the altar, the offering of candles, and the need for baptism and fasting, but he was by no means detached from the affairs of his local parish in Bray. He can be found as the plaintiff and defendant in cases of debt in the local manor court, and his rejection of the Church's sacraments had not extended to passing up the subtenancy of the parsonage.[83] Perhaps it was essential for Lollards to be integrated into local life, if only to deflect suspicion. But perhaps, too, detection and abjuration of their heretical views did not always damage their social position. Long after Thomas Scochyn of Reading was tried for heresy, he remained a burgess. In 1509 he gave 8s. to the works on the guild-hall, although he was not among the twenty who, early in the following year, contributed to the renewal of letters patent for the guild chantry. Later in the year he was listed as 'mortuus', but his name (if it is his) also appears credited in the churchwardens' accounts of St Giles, where he was a parishioner, with the gift to the lights of the rood loft in 1512.[84] There may have been considerably more prominent people with private, but known, Lollard sympathies who were tolerated because they conformed outwardly.

[79] *Reg. Bp. Langton*, 48–83; Reg. Bp. Blythe, fos. 70–79ᵛ; Reg. Bp. Audley, fos. 108ʳ⁻ᵛ, 130–183ᵛ.

[80] *Acts and Monuments*, iv. 233–43; BRO D/A1 6, fo. 170.

[81] BRO Archdeaconry MS c3, fo. 40b. For other examples see D. J. Plumb, 'John Foxe and the Later Lollards of the Thames Valley', Ph.D. thesis (Cambridge, 1987), Ch. 3.

[82] Reg. Bp. Blythe, fo. 70; *Reading Records*, i. 87, 93–4, 96–100.

[83] Reg. Bp. Audley, first series, fo. 147; BRO D/EG M44, 48 (1500–2, 1504, 1508); PRO C1/317/22.

[84] *Reading Records*, i. 111, 114, 116, 119; BRO D/P 96/5/1.

The integration of Lollards into all sections of local society may suggest that the original Lollard preachers had been successful in their mission. Perhaps Lollardy became, temporarily, more difficult to detect after 1440 because the missionaries had established local 'schools' of heresy.[85] The seeds of heresy that the early preacher William Ramsbury had sown may well have produced forbidden fruit. He was said to have performed his mass ceremony in ten Wiltshire towns and villages; he had also preached in the churches, cemeteries, and alehouses of a further eighteen.[86] Many of the places through which he had passed produced further cases of heresy in the century and a half following his trial.

It is also possible that some areas were more susceptible to Lollardy than others. In some parishes, ecclesiastical discipline had been less easy to impose. It may not be coincidental that a number of places in which Lollardy flourished—Abingdon, Wallingford, Reading, Bisham, Thatcham, and Cookham—lay along the diocesan boundary, over which itinerant heretics might flit, creating jurisdictional difficulties for prosecuting bishops. Pastoral provision in other parishes may have encouraged traditions of dissent. Wokingham, Maidenhead, and Newbury were busy towns that did not have their own parish churches and where parishioners had chafed at the lack of parochial rights. Parishioners in Ogbourne St Andrew and Urchfont had complained at the rector's neglect of adequate supervision for dependent chapels: some of them were later denounced as Lollards. Some heretics, indeed, were found in places remote from the mother church of the parish: Bulkington in Keevil; Upton in Blewbury; and Turleigh, half a mile from the chapelry of Winsley, itself dependent on the church of Bradford-on-Avon. Most of these places lay on the clay vales, where dispersed settlements were more likely, but the potential problems of outlying chapelries were not just caused by the nature of settlement. Former minster churches, like Bradford-on-Avon, which lay on clay and chalklands, also kept chapelries that developed full parochial rights.[87] But whatever the cause, pastoral needs that gave rise to problems were fertile seed-beds for heresy.

Still more obvious Lollard breeding-grounds were the cloth-producing regions. Indeed, William Ramsbury seems to have been drawn to them as places perhaps more likely to harbour subversion. Devizes, Marlborough, Hungerford, and Castle Combe all disclosed a significant cache of heretics in the fifteenth century. Some of the heretics later brought to trial were

---

[85] Hudson, *Premature Reformation*, 447–9.
[86] Reg. Bp. Waltham, fos. 222–223ᵛ.   [87] See Ch. 3 n. 16.

MAP 6. Lollardy

associated with the cloth trade: weavers, tailors, fullers, and even a 'woolwinder'. Rather than a predilection of cloth workers for heresy, the influences of the cloth trade were probably more subtle. Some Lollard cloth workers must have been reported to the authorities by members of their own trade: William Wakeham was shopped in 1437 by a weaver in Devizes or Marlborough.[88] Even so, it was within cloth towns, where the pace of economic life was quicker and more precarious, that disorder of all kinds was more likely to flourish, and discipline, secular and ecclesiastical, was less easy to enforce. Where failure to pay tithes and to attend church was higher, so were the chances of sedition and heresy.[89]

Yet if heresy and dissent were more intense in these towns, so was the practice of orthodox piety. The wealthier townsmen could afford devotional books, and petition for private altars and oratories: there were certainly links between a more personal approach to sin and penance and an interest in radical heresy. It was in the same towns too that the more outward corporate forms of devotion blossomed, where more guilds, chantries, and obits were founded, more lavish funerals and processions undertaken, and more churches rebuilt. Most of the places in the diocese where Lollardy was found after Wyclif also saw their parish churches extensively rebuilt.[90] Lollardy may have been a coherent creed and even a distinct sect, but some of its venom flowed from a disgust at the overwhelmingly orthodox practices of the majority. The heresy of Wyclif himself had partly been kindled by a strong antipathy towards the 'fides laica', especially the way in which it had entangled the sacrament of the Eucharist with a morass of additional ceremonies.[91] Later Lollardy was similarly fuelled by a continuing opposition to the pious practices of the majority. The intensity of orthodox devotional activity in certain places encouraged a heretical reaction: it is not surprising, to amend Capgrave's statement, to find Lollardy emerging in some places within the diocese.

---

[88] Reg. Bp. Neville, second series, fo. 52.
[89] See Ch. 3 nn. 40, 45, 46.   [90] Compare Map 4 with Map 6.
[91] Catto, 'John Wyclif and the Cult of the Eucharist', 275.

10

The Reformation

ON the morning of 25 April in 1517, Thomas Poyntz, esquire, and Thomas Manselston set out for the abbey of Kingswood to meet with the abbot who was 'welbeloved with all the goode & sadde men that dwelled within v myles of the said monasterie'. To their dismay, they arrived only to find that their abbot had been deposed. They demanded to know the charges, that a fair trial be held, but were stilled when told that the orders had come from the king. Thomas Poyntz promptly declared that he was the king's servant 'sworn to hys grace & wold be glad & also was bound to assyste & further hym or eny other in alle thynges that he knowe to be done by the kynges high commaundment and pleasure'. He spoke, it was said, 'lyke a sadde gentilman'.[1]

Two decades later the king's subjects were required to obey orders that were more far-reaching. Henry VIII's break with Rome culminated in the Act of Supremacy in 1534, and between 1535 and 1540 the monasteries were completely dissolved. In 1536 pilgrimages were abolished and in September 1538 royal injunctions forbade the practice of burning candles before images as things 'not understood or minded on'. Between 1535 and 1539 the diocese of Salisbury had a bishop in Nicholas Shaxton who was more than anxious to press on with more radical reform that emanated from the royal court.[2] He forbade the decking of images, night-watching in porches, and pilgrimage. More destructive of Catholic practices were the orders of Edward VI from 1547: all images were to be destroyed, and endowments supporting chantries, obits, and lights for souls in purgatory were to be sold off by the Crown.

It is still a puzzle why these changes were not resisted with more violence. The opponents of a somewhat pugilistic debate tend to square up along two broad lines. Some historians have detected a weakening in Catholic enthusiasm in the sixteenth century;[3] others have seen the Refor-

---

[1] PRO STAC2/34/97.

[2] *VCH: Wilts.* iii. 27; *LP* xiii (1), 93; Benson and Hatcher, *Old and New Sarum*, 238–9.

[3] A. G. Dickens, *The English Reformation* (London, 1964); Elton, *Reform and Reformation*.

mation as destroying a still very popular faith.[4] Qualifications have been
introduced to both views: acceptance of change was swifter in some regions than in others, particularly in the south-east of the country and in
ports with access to the Continent.[5] Perhaps, too, the popularity of the old
faith mattered little in face of royal power.[6] There may well have been
other 'sadde gentilmen', like Thomas Poyntz, who were prepared to bow
to royal commands. Yet evidence for the popularity of new and old faiths
can be equivocal. Professions of loyalty to the king cannot be taken at face
value: Thomas Poyntz's was, intended for royal consumption, in a Star
Chamber case, and glosses over the part he played in causing a riot.
Indeed, attitudes to the destruction of Catholic practices are sometimes
difficult to fathom, and evidence for them is contradictory. In seeking
reasons for the acceptance of change, moreover, we must also gauge attitudes towards the less destructive aspects of the Reformation. The reforms under Edward VI, as we shall see, were intended to establish a godly
commonwealth, morally and socially reformed, in which the scriptural
Word of God was preached from the pulpit. Acquiescence in these reforms may have depended neither on immediate conversion to Protestantism nor on a full appreciation of all the theological issues at stake. Some
forms of pious practice survived the Reformation and some of the concerns of reformers may have reached across any theological divide. We
shall look, first, at signs for the growing interest in reform in the early
sixteenth century, showing that these signs too can be misleading; then
more closely at the difficult passage of the Reformation; and, finally, at the
reasons for its acceptance in the region.

There is quite plausible evidence to suggest that, by the early sixteenth
century, more lay people were prepared to welcome radical change. Protestant heresy could feed off a long and active tradition of Lollard dissent.
More Lollards, some of whom possessed Wyclifite texts, were being
brought to trial (though this may not, of course, indicate a rise in the real
number of heretics). Others who were tried as Lutherans came from areas
in which Lollards had once been found: Salisbury, Windsor, Newbury,

---

[4] C. Haigh (ed.), *The English Reformation Revised* (Cambridge, 1987); Scarisbrick, *Reformation*; Duffy, *Stripping of the Altars*.

[5] A. G. Dickens, 'The Early Experience of Protestantism in England 1520–1558', *Archiv
für Reformationsgeschichte*, 78 (1987), 187–222; R. Whiting, *The Blind Devotion of the People:
Popular Religion and the English Reformation* (Cambridge, 1989).

[6] R. Whiting, 'Abominable Idols: Images and Image-Breaking under Henry VIII', *JEH* 33
(1982), 30–47.

and Reading.[7] John Mandrel, a husbandman, who finally went to the stake in Queen Mary's reign, had originally come from the parish of Keevil where one Robert Makam, or Bragge, had been tried for heresy in 1504. He found audiences for his preaching in Edington and Devizes, where Lollard preachers had once roamed. Much of what he taught did not differ markedly from earlier Lollardy: the attack on the worship of images ('they were as good to roast a shoulder of mutton'), on the Church hierarchy, the Eucharist, pardons, and suffrages from the Church.[8] The people steeped in an older tradition of heresy perhaps relished the new Protestant regime when it came. The churchwarden of Locking in 1553 was one John Colyns who probably belonged to the same family that had formed something of a Lollard mafia in the area during the 1530s.[9]

If the progress of heresy was helped in the 1530s and 1540s by a native tradition of dissent, it nevertheless drew more inspiration from the Continent. John Mandrel, according to John Foxe, became 'a diligent hearer and fervent embracer of God's true religion' only after the Scriptures had been translated into English by William Tyndale. The accusation brought against John Forsett, a priest of St Edmund's in Salisbury, was not one of Lollardy but of a fondness for the books of Melanchthon and the words of Luther. He had connections with Londoners, certain 'christian bretheren', who collected subscriptions from members like some kind of heretical book club: John had asked them to send 'some goodly mater in ryme or mytre, to give currage unto lytle chylder to rede the word of God'.[10] Foxe's early martyrs in Windsor in the 1540s, Henry Filmer, Robert Testwood, and Anthony Peerson, were similarly inspired by new learning. Some of the early Protestants, like former Lollards, were prominent in local society. Henry Filmer was described as churchwarden of Holy Trinity church in Windsor. In Reading, there were men like Stephen Carwood who was a burgess and churchwarden of St Laurence's church in 1536, and who was involved with radical Protestants in

[7] See Map 6. Robert Stilman was condemned in 1518 for declaring that the book 'Wycliffes Wicket' was 'good and holy', and that John Wyclif was a saint in heaven; in 1530 Richard Johnson possessed a copy of the same book (*Acts and Monuments*, iv. 207–8; v. 41, 467–73).

[8] Ibid. viii. 102–3; Reg. Bp. Audley, first series, fos. 130ᵛ–131.

[9] WRO D1/43/1 fo. 43ᵛ; *Acts and Monuments*, iv. 234–42. However, Collins was a common name: for other Collinses who were churchwardens in the same year see WRO D1/43/1, fos. 37ᵛ (Newbury), 45 (Cumnor).

[10] PRO STAC2/34/28; Brigden, *London and the Reformation*, 124–6; Hudson, *Premature Reformation*, 482–3.

TABLE 16. Bequests for masses 1500–1547

	No. of wills		Chantries (%)		Anniversaries (%)		Lights (%)	
	S	W	S	W	S	W	S	W
1500–29	41	417	59	32	12	13	68	39
1530–8	22	170	68	28	32	15	50	35
1539–47	7	210	42	8	14	11	0	13

Note: S = Salisbury. W = Wilts., Dorset, and Berks.

London.[11] There were indeed men in place, known for their opinions, who would readily execute radical reform when the time came.

Reform was not expedited, however, merely through the actions of a hard core of fifth columnists. There were also those who were not converts but may have been sympathetic to reformist views. Some evidence suggests a more general susceptibility to Protestant change. The preambles of some wills display definite signs of Protestantism. Others, which avoided the traditional invocation to God, the Virgin Mary, and the saints, might suggest reformist tendencies, and there were more of these in the 1530s and 1540s.[12] Some evidence suggests there may have been a waning interest in old practices. There was an apparent decline in the proportion of testators leaving bequests to monasteries and friaries in the early sixteenth century (see Table 1). Some of the final beneficiaries of dissolved monastic lands were Protestants. Sir Nicholas Poyntz had encouraged reformist preachers on his estates. The Poyntz family were already stewards and lessees of Kingswood monastery before the Dissolution, when they acquired many of its lands and used the stones of its buildings to rebuild their mansion at Newark. In Malmesbury there was no better example of a 'flint-faced' Protestant capitalist than William Stumpe, who after the Dissolution was to fill the town's monastic buildings with looms for his cloth-weaving enterprises.[13]

There was, moreover, a decided drop in bequests to altar lights and fraternities after the 1538 injunction against such offerings (see Table 16).

[11] *Acts and Monuments*, v. 464; J. Martin, 'The People of Reading and the Reformation 1520–1570', Ph.D. thesis (Reading, 1987), 89–90.

[12] Between 1539 and 1547 about half of all testators in the region began their wills without the traditional invocation.

[13] J. H. Bettey, *The Suppression of the Monasteries in the West Country* (Gloucester, 1989), 25, 124, 133–46; *VCH: Wilts.* iv. 146–7; *Itinerary of Leland*, i. 132.

A growing reluctance to hand over property for chantries and guilds may be discerned. In Salisbury the last perpetual chantry founded was William Swayne's in the second half of the fifteenth century. The bede roll of the town council's St George guild records the names of twenty-five benefactors who gave property to the guild before 1450, but only three for the rest of the century and only two in the early sixteenth century—and one of these required an almshouse to be set up (see Table 10). Far fewer benefactors of the tailors' guild in Salisbury gave land after 1479, and some of the names on the bede roll in the sixteenth century were not entered for overtly religious purposes but for the building of a guild-hall, for which contributors were entitled to attend the guild's dinners. The Jesus fraternity of St Edmund's parish was apparently losing members: there was a slow haemorrhaging of amounts collected at the four customary times of the year in the early sixteenth century (see Table 8). Bequests to the shrine of St Osmund, after initial interest shown by Salisbury testators in the late fifteenth century, are much harder to come by in wills after 1510.[14] Oblations made to the pyx of the Holy Trinity almshouse had been worth, on average, 26s. in the 1490s, but by the 1520s they amounted to less than 10s. and in the 1530s and 1540s to less than 5s. Offerings to the almshouse's image of Holy Trinity disappear from the accounts after 1521; offerings for indulgences were no longer collected after 1533.[15]

Conversely, there were more bequests to concerns of which reformers could approve. The dissolution of monastic and chantry lands was ostensibly part of a programme of social and even moral reform for the benefit of education and also for the relief of poverty. Rising population, inflation, and enclosures in the middle years of the sixteenth century had made vagrancy an even more pressing problem: there were others besides radical Protestants who could sympathize with the Edwardian concern for poor relief.[16] There had already been a rise in the proportion of testators who gave to the poor at times unconnected with intercessory burial or post-obit services.[17] We find a Robert Beryatt in Dorset in 1545 devoting most of his bequests to selected groups of poor people, prisoners, poor householders, the oldest people who could not come to church, and the very poorest. In 1538 William Williams, a Salisbury draper, asked that as many poor people as possible be brought to him *before* his burial so that he

[14] In Salisbury only one testator made a bequest to the shrine after 1513: Thomas Martyn of Salisbury 1536 (PCC 1 Dyngeley). Outside the city, the last known bequest comes in 1516, from John Myllys of Maddington (PCC 19 Holder).

[15] WRO 1446, Box 'Accounts'.　　[16] Brigden, *London and the Reformation*, 475–83.

[17] Between 1538 and 1547, 26% of all testators in the region left bequests to charitable concerns (outside the funeral), a higher proportion than earlier (see Table 15).

could distribute £30. He also asked that, if his children died, his sheep be sold and the money used to 'sette poor creatures a worke' in making woollen cloth for twelve years[18]—a bequest satisfactory to the keenest advocate of the Protestant work ethic.

It would, of course, be an over-simplification to suggest that these charitable efforts mark a shift to a more Protestant mentality, which purportedly gave greater attention than a Catholic one to the object of charity rather than to divine reward for the donor.[19] Both Robert Beryatt and William Williams left bequests to fraternities and altar lights, and both used the traditional invocation to God, the Virgin Mary, and all the saints in the preambles of their wills. In any case, concern for the poor also represented a response to new problems of poverty. The inhabitants of Newbury in 1547 were claiming that the poverty and indigence of the town's poor people 'dyd daily increase' such that relief provided by their almshouse was under strain.[20] But the heightened problem of poverty may have increased sympathy to the more radical plans of reformers. Charles Bulkley informed Cromwell in 1536 that he would convert the friary in Salisbury into a place which would house twice as many poor people as there had been friars, who would work rather than beg for their living.[21] It was perhaps a scheme that accorded with contemporary assessments of social need.

In the early sixteenth century, moreover, some testators were also leaving bequests for Bibles and sermons. The Protestant emphasis on the Word of God, preached and read, had already been promoted in the 1530s: Bishop Shaxton had sought to encourage the reading of the Scriptures in the vernacular, to ensure that all benefices worth over £10 possessed an English Bible, and that sermons were preached in his diocese.[22] A few of the gentry were well placed to read parts of the Bible in English for themselves. Sir John Mompesson in 1500 left his son his 'fair little bible'; in 1504 Sir Edward Hungerford mentioned a book of two parts of the Bible kept in his chapel. Lady Anne Danvers had her own copy of the New Testament in English in 1517 which she donated to the abbey of Syon.[23] Some townsmen were keen that their parishes should possess the Scriptures: William Page of Devizes, by a will made in 1533 though proved in 1542, left St John's church 'one hole byble of the best and largest volume'.[24]

[18] PCC 41 Pynnyng, 25 Dyngeley.   [19] Slack, *Poverty and Politics*, 8–9.
[20] PRO C1/1276/75.   [21] *LP* xiii (2), 156.
[22] Benson and Hatcher, *Old and New Sarum*, 238–9.
[23] PCC 15 Blamyr; 17 Holgrave; Barfield, *Thatcham, Berkshire*, ii. 246–8.
[24] PCC 4 Spert.

For the 'devout and literate laity' the Protestant emphasis on the Word was not unacceptable.

A more critical appreciation of the words of reformers among the literate was sharpened by education. From the end of the fifteenth century more gentry wills evince a concern that their children be placed in a school, and that bequests be given to scholars in Oxford.[25] Some of the later chantry founders intended that their priests should teach the children of the area. Hospital priests, too, as at Newbury, were instructing 'ignorant youths'.[26] Rising standards of education for the gentry and wealthier townspeople need not have encouraged susceptibility to Protestantism, but some schools were open to new learning and to humanistic influences which could be critical of the Church hierarchy. In Reading during the early sixteenth century, it was the abbey school that attained local fame in instructing the sons of gentry from the surrounding area, but it was run by one Leonard Cox, a humanist who was a friend of both Erasmus and Melanchthon.[27]

Yet an acceptance of the Protestant emphasis on the Word of God did not have to depend on literacy. The spoken word used in sermons, preached in a language rich with biblical imagery, could make the new faith accessible to a much wider audience.[28] There may also have been a growing taste for the preaching of sermons. John Diot of Trowbridge in 1538 asked for three 'goodly' sermons at his burial and his fellow townsman Walter Long left a bequest for one 'goodly' sermon in 1545.[29] Some town councils were making special provision for sermons: at Poole in 1542 Dr Bartlett was paid for two sermons in one day out of the town coffers.[30] There are also hints that radical preachers could find an audience. A dozen blows were meted out to one John Popley when he spoke out against a certain Latimer, undoubtedly Hugh Latimer, who had preached 'many erroneous wordes' at West Kington near Bristol.[31] According to John Foxe, the Protestant Anthony Peerson in Windsor was 'greatly esteemed amongst the people who flocked . . . to his sermons'. And in 1541

[25] Four testators from Dorset 1505–46, six from Wilts. 1492–1539, and eight from Berks. 1467–1528.
[26] PRO E301/59/8 (Heytesbury), 36/91 (Sherborne), 51/41 (Childrey).
[27] Coates, *History and Antiquities*, 322; *VCH: Berks.* ii. 70; Martin, 'People of Reading', 61–4.
[28] P. Collinson, *The Birthpangs of Protestant England: Religious and Cultural Changes in the Sixteenth and Seventeenth Centuries* (Cambridge, 1988), 120–5.
[29] PCC 26 Dyngeley; 11 Alen.   [30] Poole municipal archives, 48 (3), p. 2.
[31] PRO C1/872/51. Hugh Latimer was rector of West Kington, and had been criticizing certain practices, like the pilgrims passing along the Fosse Way *en route* to Hailes abbey (*Hugh Latimer: Works*, ed. G. E. Corrie (Parker Society, Cambridge, 1845), ii. 364).

Henry Filmer actually gained the sympathy of the Windsor town council, and the bishop, for his attack on a vicar who preached 'fond and fairish tales' about the Virgin Mary holding out her breast to nourish St Bernard.[32] Some townsmen were taking offence at religious tales that did not have a biblical foundation.

Moreover, from the 1520s the Church and certain Catholic practices were attracting a good deal of criticism, even, to follow R. Whiting, a rising tide of criticism.[33] Chantries were being dissolved prematurely in the 1530s.[34] Cases came before the Chancery court that reveal an apparent carelessness in keeping post-obit services going: Sir William Carrant wrongfully entering into a mill at Sherborne which supported the celebration of an obit; stewards of John Seyntloo's chantry at Calne damaging the celebrations of mass by withholding the profits of certain endowments.[35] Tithes were a source of contention, if not on the scale seen in London, as priests found their incomes declining relative to the rise in prices. Humphrey Watkyns was complaining at the exorbitant distress caused by the demands for tithes of Simon Bell, parson of Bradipole. Resistance to the collection of tithes seems to have stiffened within Salisbury. The procurators of St Thomas's church were able to account for over £40 in oblations delivered to the high altar at Easter in the 1480s; by the late 1530s this figure had been reduced by half.[36] There are suggestions of a certain readiness to remove images from churches. A case came before court of Star Chamber inquiring whether Brown and Jack, servants of Benet Joy, had removed an image of St George from Purton church, and whether one of the churchwardens had commanded them so to do.[37]

Some areas, moreover, may have responded to reform more swiftly than others. Visitations were undertaken throughout the diocese (now comprising just Berkshire and Wiltshire) in 1550 and 1553 to enforce Edwardian reform, and in 1556, under Queen Mary, to reverse Protestant change. The visitors in Edward's reign were intent on ensuring that, among other things, every parish had sermons preached at least four times a year, possessed a copy of the Paraphrases, and had a carpet for every

[32] *Acts and Monuments*, v. 470–2.

[33] Whiting, *Blind Devotion*, esp. 26–32, 67–8, 127–44.

[34] Free chapels and chantries were found in Whittenham, Early Whiteknights, East Hendred, Binfield, Englefield, North Standen, Chadelworty, Fylberd, and Witham in Berks. (PRO E301/3, E301/51); and at Highworth, Chippenham, Bromham, Ramsbury, East Lavington, and Chute in Wilts. (E301/58, E301/59).

[35] PRO C1/1034/38, 401/17; see also C1/445/44, 801/15, 335/89, 1059/71.

[36] Brigden, *London and the Reformation*, 51–2, 167–8, 201–4; PRO C1/929/9–10; D & C, Press II, Procurator's accounts.

[37] PRO STAC2/25/272.

altar. Their findings suggest that these reforms were more likely to have been undertaken in the cloth towns and clay areas than in chalkland and rural parishes. The Catholic visitors of 1556, moreover, found that the rood screen and side altars were less likely to have been put back in those same cloth and clay areas. Chalkland parishes tended to have been either less destructive of roods and altars or quicker to replace them in Mary's reign (see Map 7).[38]

Now the division between chalk and cheese, cloth and less industrialized regions, is not clear-cut, nor is it perfectly represented in the visitational findings. Parishes were too variegated to be squeezed into this framework, and the approximate division apparent in the visitations is not entirely explained by religious preference. Some of the parishes in Edward's reign that lacked sermons and Paraphrases perhaps could not afford the expense of preachers and new books. Perhaps propinquity to Buckinghamshire, a known hot spot for Lollard and Protestant activity, affected northern parts of Berkshire in Mary's reign. Moreover, conformity to royal decree is testified to in churchwardens' accounts of all kinds of parishes. None the less, some were quicker to conform than others. The parish of St Laurence's in Reading rapidly stripped the images from the church in advance of royal orders, and the accounts of 1547/8 show a massive removal or even destruction of stained glass and images. Rood loft and church plate were sold off in the same year for £60. New service books were bought during the following year. The chalkland parish of Winterslow in rural Wiltshire was rather slower to implement change. Only in the year after October 1548 did it 'rid' the church of images and sell a chalice. A painted hearse cloth was sold a year later still. The pulling down of altars was carried out in advance of the orders in the autumn of 1550 (as in a great many other parishes), but it was only after October 1551 that a book of Common Prayer and the Paraphrases were bought. Even so, in 1553 the visitors reported that the parish lacked the latter. In the first year and a half of Mary's reign the same parish was also very quick to remake altars and the rood and re-establish its May day and Easter celebrations. St Laurence's in Reading had to wait until 1556 for some of the trappings of Catholic worship (the sepulchre, 'morrow mass', Hocktide festivals) to be replaced.[39] It is not implausible that reform had

[38] WRO D1/43/1, fos. 6–168; D1/43/2 fos. 1–36ᵛ. For the cautious return of some Catholic practices in the diocese see I. T. Sheild, 'The Reformation in the Diocese of Salisbury, 1547–62', B.Litt. thesis (Oxford, 1960), 132 ff.

[39] BRO D/P 97/5/2; Winterslow rectory, Churchwardens' accounts, fos. 9ᵛ–16ᵛ; see also R. Hutton, 'The Local Impact of the Tudor Reformations', in Haigh (ed.), *Reformation Revised*, 114–38.

MAP 7. Visitations 1551, 1553, and 1556

a greater chance of acceptance in the more economically advanced areas of the region.

However, it is as well to avoid being deterministic about the passage of reform. It is also difficult to avoid the impression that Protestants were very much in the minority even in the 1540s. The very signs that Protestant reform was becoming more acceptable often seem equivocal. A rising tide of criticism need not indicate a sea change. The growing number of cases in Chancery and Star Chamber suggests not so much an increase in criticism as a more general expansion of litigation in these courts. There had, in any case, always been criticism; obits and chantries had been allowed to disappear into oblivion in the fourteenth and fifteenth centuries, their endowments sometimes amalgamated into others or their founders even forgotten.[40] Moreover, the dissolution of some chantries in the 1530s need not indicate eager Protestant anticipation. Some chantry endowments simply could no longer support their stipendiary priests. The chantry of St Mary at Englefield, worth only 60s. a year, was dissolved by Sir Francis Englefield—who was subsequently imprisoned in the Tower in 1551 for his sympathies towards the Catholic Princess Mary.[41] Some of the main beneficiaries of dissolved monastic lands in the region, like Sir Thomas Arundel and Sir John Tregonwell, were also conservative in their religious tastes.[42]

Premature removal or selling of Church goods is sometimes capable of explanations other than incipient iconoclasm. Many must have been aware of the imminence of royal spoliation of Church goods and disposed of them before they fell into the hands of royal commissioners. Robert Gryffyths, steward of the Salisbury tailors' guild, bought a silver chalice from the guild in the year before the guild's chantry was dissolved.[43] There is also plenty of evidence to suggest that reports by guilds and parishes on their post-obit endowments to the royal commissioners in 1545 and 1548 were modest with the truth. In 1550 John Knight, gentleman, was accused of earnestly exhorting the tenants of the Newbury hospital lands to 'sticke fast together and declare unto the commissioners [that the hospital was] no chantry or free chapel'.[44] The inquiry into the concealment of chantry lands was still a lively one in the late sixteenth

[40] See Ch. 4 nn. 15–17.   [41] PRO E301/3/16; *VCH: Berks.* iii. 407.
[42] Bettey, *Suppression*, 138.   [43] 'Wiltshire Chantry Furniture', *WAM* 22 (1885), 221.
[44] PRO E315/8/124, fos. 70–3. The churchwardens of Trowbridge claimed in 1545 and 1547 that the revenues of the Corpus Christi fraternity had been spent on the mending of highways during the previous five years (PRO E301/58/46; E301/59/46). Yet the fraternity still possessed vestments in 1545 (WRO 865/314).

century.[45] In 1576 an investigation in Devizes was being conducted into the lands held, since the late fourteenth century, by the mayor's priest in St John's church and by the churchwardens of St Mary's for the performance of Richard Gobbet's dole.[46] The fulfilment of royal orders was sometimes more apparent than real.

Far from conclusive, too, are indications of religious preference based on wills. Some do indeed make explicit statements of Lutheran faith but others leave no doubt about their commitment to Catholicism: Sighert Peche, a gentleman of Cookham, in 1540 referred to the Sacrament as the 'very body of Christ'. Preambles in the 1530s and 1540s that begin with an invocation to God alone need not be seen as secretly Protestant or warily non-committal. In fact, most of the preambles of wills made at Salisbury before the 1470s, for instance, likewise contained no invocations to the Virgin Mary and the saints, for which scribal fashion must have been partly responsible.[47] The pattern of pious giving in wills is also equivocal. There is little sign that the proportion of bequests to altar lights was decreasing before the 1538 proclamation against such offerings or that bequests for anniversaries were falling. Bequests for temporary chantries even seem to have been increasing in the early sixteenth century and for longer periods, perhaps to compensate for the tightening financial restrictions on perpetual chantry foundations, and their final prohibition in 1532 for periods longer than twenty years (see Table 17). In the year that gifts to saints' images were prohibited, the parishioners of Wimborne Minster bought a new 'legend' for their cherished St Cuthberga.[48] There was still in the 1530s a large reservoir of penitential giving on which the Church could draw.

By the 1540s, however, it was a reservoir less easy to tap. Prohibition on the offerings to images had an immediate effect: less because the desire to give was waning, perhaps, and more because testators could not be sure that executors would or even could fulfil their bequests. Some would-be donors were evidently aware that other pious practices might shortly meet the fate of offerings to images. In 1539 William Seyman, barber, left vestments and a mass book to the Jesus altar in St Mary's church, Marlborough, but carefully directed that these goods were to go to the church's high altar if the guild 'be not maynteyned'. Richard Tubervyle,

[45] C. J. Kitching, 'The Quest for Concealed Lands in the Reign of Elizabeth I', *TRHS* 24 (1974), 63–78.
[46] PRO E133/2/347.
[47] PCC 37 Alenger: see Intro. n. 74 and Duffy, *Stripping of the Altars*, 504–23.
[48] DRO PE/WM CW 1/40, p. 116; see Ch. 3 n. 57.

TABLE 17. Bequests for temporary chantries
1270–1545

	No. of wills	No. of years requested			
		1	2–5	6–10	11–20
1270–1349	35	5	1		
1350–99	117	8	2		
1400–49	279	15	19	8	1
1450–99	275	30	29	10	4
1500–45	797	96	60	23	17

gentleman, left bequests to several fraternities in 1545, as long as, he added (perhaps ruefully), they were allowed to survive.[49] Moreover, this cautious attitude may have some bearing on the apparent rise in the proportion of bequests to charity and the poor in the late 1530s and 1540s. These need not indicate a shift to a Protestant attitude to charitable giving. As offerings to images were banned, so penitential gifts were diverted to the less contentious use of the poor. Richard Betelcombe of Poole left £6 in 1546 to be given annually for ten years to the parish chantry, but 'in case the parish will not have the service of the church meynteyned', a reduced sum of 8s. a year was to be given to the poor.[50]

Even within Salisbury, signs of susceptibility to reform and attachment to the old faith existed side by side. Caution seems to have been exercised in the execution of bequests. Joanne Peerse's elaborate bequest to gild the image of St Anne in St Thomas's church in 1538 was partially converted into an extra donation to the Trinity almshouse by her executors.[51] Not all evidence can be taken to suggest a decline in Catholic belief. There were still benefactors of the St George guild in the 1540s who, if they did not give land, certainly left money to be included in anniversary services. Fewer testators remembered St Osmund in their wills, but the town council was still ordering the St Osmund procession in 1545.[52] There were more names added to the tailors' bede roll in the sixteenth century than

[49] WRO G22/1/247; PCC 15 Alen; see also land in Shaftesbury given by Elyn Mathew for intercessory purposes, but only on condition that 'the Kynges lawes wold suffer that they remain for ev[er]' (PRO E301/16/104 (in 1545)).

[50] PCC 28 Alen.   [51] See Intro. n. 79.

[52] In 1540 Henry Wrastely left 20s. to the city chamber, and Thomas Southe remitted money owed by his father in 1543, to be prayed for in the bede roll (WRO G23/1/2, fos. 293, 296, 229ᵛ).

before and, even if landed endowments were scarcer, some gifts left no doubt of an attachment to old religious practice. William Middleton (a steward of the guild in 1519) finally earned a place on the bede roll for bequeathing 'the blak vestments to requie[m] mass'.[53] And testators in the city before 1538 left as much for temporary chantries, obits, and altar lights—and even monastic houses—as their predecessors had done in the fifteenth century (see Tables 1 and 17).

Moreover, reformers met with opposition, even within the more economically advanced towns. Foxe's martyrs of Windsor in the 1540s may have attracted crowds to sermons but they also encountered entrenched Catholic attitudes. Henry Filmer had to upbraid a labourer at Clewar, just outside Windsor, for going to church on Sunday to worship images, to 'see your God', and do 'as other men do'. Robert Testwood had to speak out against the practices of Relic Sunday and the cult of Henry VI which attracted pilgrims from distant Devon and Cornwall; he outraged one William Symonds, later mayor of the town, by striking the nose off an image of the Virgin Mary.[54] Some dissatisfaction with the king's dissolution of the monasteries also emerged: a butcher near Windsor declared his sympathies for the Pilgrimage of Grace in 1536; the vicar of Bradford-on-Avon, William Byrde, was attainted for expressing similar sympathies.[55] Cherished forms of pious practice could still be defended. At Brimpton in 1535 the rector Ralph Shaw was reported by his parishioners for apparently ridiculing their incomprehension of the Latin mass: 'what can ye tell', he was reported to have said, 'whether I dyd pray for you or whether I asked a vengeance on you all.'[56]

In many towns, reform and royal policy were both promoted and resisted. Newbury had a long history of Lollard dissent but an active tradition of chantry foundation and church-building that was still flourishing in the 1520s when the parish church was substantially rebuilt. In 1539 Miles Coverdale reported that popish books, with the Pope's name undeleted, still abounded in that town. Yet there were those who wished for Protestant reform. In 1550 'certayne of the parishioners' were to complain that their parson was not able to preach God's Word, and did not follow the king's orders for he taught that the Sacrament was indeed

[53] WRO G23/1/257PC, G23/1/250, fo. 206.   [54] *Acts and Monuments*, v. 467–8.
[55] Tighe and Davis, *Annals of Windsor*, 139; *LP* xv. 498.
[56] BRO D/A2 C3, Liber Actorum, fo. 46. A change of regime, however, did not improve the relations of Ralph Shaw with his parishioners. In 1553 he was reported for not teaching the catechism and for being absent from church on Sundays (WRO D1/43/1, fo. 167).

Christ's true body.[57] At Poole the town council may have been interested in sermons but they also supported traditional Catholic practices: in 1539 they paid for a new rood loft in the parish church. When Thomas Hancock arrived to preach against idolatry in 1548, he met with the violent opposition of Thomas White, John Nothered, and William Havilland, all of whom had been mayors of the town in the 1540s and before. William came from a merchant family who had played a prime role in the rebuilding of the parish church in the early sixteenth century and had its own chantry priest: small wonder, then, that he with the other two demanded that Thomas Hancock say a dirige for all souls. Their confrontation with the preacher became ugly, and Thomas Hancock was saved from having his 'guts drawn out' only by the intervention of Morgan Reade, then mayor (and mayor once before in 1541), who thrust him into the chancel out of harm's way. Reform was carried out in Poole and Church goods sold, but opposition lingered. At the beginning of Mary's reign the same three opponents of Thomas Hancock attempted to set up an altar in the church for the celebration of a papist mass, but had to resort to the privacy of their own homes when the altar was pulled down.[58]

In other towns, royal orders were carried out with almost indecent haste by some in the teeth of apparent opposition from others. At Reading the ascendancy of a group of reformers in the guild merchant in the 1530s helps to explain why the order in 1547 to strip parish churches of all images was quickly complied with in St Laurence's church, two weeks before the official proclamation was made. Yet on 18 April 1547, not long before chantries and guilds were dissolved, the same parish calmly established rulings about the contributions to be made by their doomed Jesus and Mary guilds.[59] Clearly, at the beginning of Edward VI's reign there were parishioners who neither envisaged nor desired wholesale Protestant reform. In Devizes some reform seems to have been carried out by stealth. In Mary's reign (it would seem) a complaint was made to the bishop that certain churchwardens had sold off Church goods including a rood cross worth £30 and five chalices worth £20: 'nowe of late they have crafteleye used such days of metyng or reconnynge when they are sure that the

[57] *Remains of Miles Coverdale*, ed. G. Pearson (Parker Society, Cambridge, 1846), 498–500; WRO D1/43/1, fos. 39ᵛ–40.

[58] *Narratives of the Days of the Reformation*, ed. J. G. Nichols (Camden Society, 1859), 72–84. Thomas White was mayor in 1531, 1538, and 1545; William Havilland in 1523, 1533, and 1544; John Nothered in 1540, 1547, and 1552 (Poole municipal archives, 23 (1); Hutchins, *Dorset*, i. 47).

[59] Martin, 'People of Reading', 113–61, 90; BRO D/P 97/5/2, p. 244.

welthest and cheffest of the paryshe be from home, as they did on Monday market day at Salisbury.'[60]

Within Salisbury there was even some heated resistance to change during the episcopacy of the radical Nicholas Shaxton. The bishop's Scottish chaplain, John Madowell, had preached against the old ways, but in February 1537 he felt it expedient to appeal to Cromwell to cover himself from complaints by the citizens. He claimed that the people of Salisbury had torn down proclamations that relaxed fasting at Lent, had failed to remove the Pope's name from books as ordered, and had imprisoned a man who had protested against the preaching of one Dr Wattes, an old-fashioned friar. The city burgesses were repeatedly behind opposition to reform policies pursued by the bishop and his under-bailiff, John Goodall. In 1537 the bishop was bringing a case to Chancery about the mayor's refusal to answer to the under-bailiff. In August 1538 Goodall complained that certain priests in confession had forbidden white meats in Lent, the reading of the New Testament in English, and the company of those of the new learning. One priest, Master Lovell, was preaching seditiously against the king, and Giles Hakluyt (who had rebuked several scholars for not being at evensong on the eve of the Exaltation of the Holy Cross) was protected from imprisonment by the mayor.[61] Goodall also brought a case before Star Chamber against two priests who in the same year had encouraged people to kiss and kneel before an image of the resurrection on Easter day in a chapel within St Martin's church. But it was the mayor and burgesses who, in turn, accused Goodall of sacrilege: the picture of the resurrection (unbeknownst to Goodall) contained the consecrated host, which fell out when the image was being removed.[62]

Furthermore, although services for the dead were abolished in Edward VI's reign, citizens used the Catholic reaction in Mary's reign to resurrect them. In 1556 the tailors' guild agreed once more to 'cause a solemne dirige to be kept at St Thomas's church accordyng to the olde custom and the Sunday shalbe kepte the obit masse and the same daye they shall bryng in the lyght and make good an honest dyner to the wardens and masters'. In an assembly in March 1555, the mayor and burgesses had already

[60] WRO 189/10.

[61] See G. R. Elton, *Policy and Police: The Enforcement of the Reformation in the Age of Cromwell* (Cambridge, 1972), 100–7; *LP* xii (1), 746; PRO C1/890/1–4; *LP* xiii (1), 141, 237, 606.

[62] PRO STAC2/16/91; *LP* xiv (1), 777. On this incident see M. Aston, *England's Iconoclasts*, i. *Laws against Images* (Oxford, 1988), 230, and Duffy, *Stripping of the Altars*, 421, both of whom, strangely, believe it to have taken place in the cathedral.

reinstated the three diriges in St Thomas's church for the city's benefactors, which 'for certain causes lett downe ever sithers the begynnyng of King Edward VIth until this time'. In October 1556 they agreed that the mayor's priest should celebrate in St Thomas's church according to old custom.[63] The religious preferences of the city élite appear steadfastly conservative.

So the passage of Protestant reform, even in a flourishing cloth town, was neither inevitable nor smooth. Yet it came to be accepted none the less. And peaceably at that. The citizens of Salisbury resisted the radical Shaxton and revived old practices in Mary's reign, yet the Protestant reforms ordered under Edward VI do not seem to have been greeted with a conservative backlash similar to that in the 1530s. Salisbury does not seem to have been involved in the rising of 1549, and the region as a whole, in contrast to Devon and Cornwall or Norfolk, was the scene of only isolated outbreaks against Protestant reform or landlord enclosures.[64] Throughout the 1540s and 1550s, moreover, the Salisbury city council does not appear to have been destructively split between Protestants and Catholics. Factions there must have been, but there was no radical change in the composition of the inner council between 1546 and 1556. Soon after Edward's succession, in September 1547 only three of the thirteen attending the council session had not served at some point during the previous reign. Among them was Henry Coldstone, who made a will in the same year revealing a traditional taste for obit services, chantries, and fraternities.[65] At the end of Edward's reign, still, half of the principal councillors had served before 1547. Mary's reign did not alter these proportions. The revival of obits and chantry priest was undertaken in assemblies that included an equal number of councillors who were new, and who had served first in Edward's reign or in Henry's.

Some must have found their position ambiguous. Thomas Chaffyn, senior, was one burgess who attended assemblies right through the three reigns. In 1547 he was berated by the Protestant Thomas Hancock for threatening the preacher with imprisonment on account of his reformist preaching against the Sacrament. He served in the council meetings that

[63] WRO G23/1/250, fo. 145ᵛ; G23/1/2, fo. 315ᵛ.
[64] Three artisans at Newbury were indicted for plotting the king's death; at Wilton there was a rising against enclosure (B. L. Beer, *Rebellion and Riot: Popular Disorder in England during the Reign of Edward VI* (Kent, Ohio, 1982), 152, 158). Dorset may have been preserved from violence, but the Sherborne parish register recorded an 'Insurrection in the West' in 1549 between 17 and 26 July (DRO PE/SH/RE 1/1, fo. 3).
[65] WRO G23/1/2, fos. 282–316ᵛ; PCC 4 Populwell.

abolished obits and chantries in Edward's reign, yet was prominent in
their revival under Queen Mary. His will in 1558 reveals a reformatory
concern for the poor, with bequests to the city almshouses, to his own
almshouse, and to the poor dwelling in Salisbury and Warminster. But it
also discloses an attachment to 'ancient customs used in times past': he left
£6. 13s. 4d. as a 'stock' for the renewed Jesus Mass in St Thomas's church,
so that its stewards and their successors 'shalbe the better willing' to
remain in office.⁶⁶

Acceptance of change sprang from many a complex motive. It may not
be fair to characterize the behaviour of burgesses like Thomas Chaffyn as
an opportunistic exercise in clinging to power, a cynical bending to the
wind. There are other lights in which such behaviour has to be seen, and
other contexts in which apparent religious conservatism (just as apparent
Protestantism) appears more ambiguous. The city burgesses resisted
Bishop Shaxton's changes in the 1530s, yet it was a resistance that should
be viewed from the perspective of the old dispute against episcopal
overlordship. John Goodall certainly considered the mayor and his brethren's conservative stance to be tinged with hypocrisy. John Madowell
mentioned in his complaint about the citizens that there 'was variance
between the Bishop and the City because the Mayor would be the king's
officer and not the bishop's'.⁶⁷ In June 1537 the city fathers had petitioned
Cromwell against the possible renewal by Bishop Shaxton of the charter
that kept the mayor subservient to the bishop and his bailiff. In the same
year Thomas Chaffyn was singled out by the bishop for refusing to obey
the orders of the bailiff; despite 'haveing the personage of a sober man
[Thomas was] nevertheless the most importune and seditious person of
them all'. With the backing of the bishop, Goodall did little to soothe the
burgesses' sensitive self-esteem when he denounced the mayor as a mere
officer of the bishop, like the catchpole or bellman, and, rather un-
pleasantly, wished 'a turd . . . in the mayor's teeth'. Later, in 1538,
Goodall found himself imprisoned by the mayor. Denouncing Goodall to
the Star Chamber for sacrilege was a useful means of undermining the
episcopal official's presumed authority. The bishop's attempt to enforce
religious change was being used by the burgesses to mount another campaign to assert their independence from episcopal jurisdiction. It was not
until 1612 that the citizens gained a charter of incorporation, yet hopes

⁶⁶ WRO G23/1/2, fos. 282–316ᵛ. Thomas also willed priests to be paid on the day of his
'departure' and for a chantry service to be endowed (PCC 64 Noodes).
⁶⁷ See Intro. n. 16; Ch. 7 nn. 48, 49, 51; Street, 'Bishops and Citizens', 322–8; *LP* xiv (1),
778; *LP* x. 623.

must have been raised during Edwardian and Elizabethan reform that they would finally win independence from the bishop.[68]

Their attitude to Edwardian reform may also have been ambivalent, particularly towards the destruction of chantry and obit services for the dead. It was not as if the relationship between the living and the dead had always been a happy one. The efforts required of the living to ensure the survival of chantry and other services had sometimes been considerable. Even wealthy guilds like that of St George or of the tailors in Salisbury had run into difficulties when supporting the services demanded by their dead benefactors. These services could indeed contribute to the worship of the living, and the parishioners of St Thomas's and St Edmund's in Salisbury (along with many others) certainly petitioned for the survival of their chantry priests.[69] Yet there were also incentives for the living to relieve themselves of obligations to the dead and for churchwardens and municipal officers to jettison the sometimes heavy duties imposed by post-obit services and endowments.[70] In towns faced with more acute economic difficulties, energy to keep other ceremonies going had been further sapped: in 1540 the Wallingford burgesses had already stopped their Hocktide revels to escape the 'sumptuous costs' they entailed. Even in Salisbury efforts were made in 1520 and 1522 to reduce the numbers of craft guild feasts held in the city.[71]

But it also worth considering whether services for the dead affected the living in another way. The accumulation of property and rents by parishes affected parochial funding. As we saw, the proportion of funds raised from the rents of dead benefactors at Wimborne Minster between 1400 and 1500 rose from 20 to 40 per cent (see Table 2). In other parishes, especially in larger urban centres, the proportion was much higher. The management of such funds possibly encouraged corporate confidence,[72] at least among the parish élite, but it may also have meant that commitment to parish life among other parishioners became more diluted. Whereas rural parishes like Winterslow still relied on the regular and collective celebration of ales, larger market centres came to depend more heavily on rents left by the dead.[73] By 1547, the living in these parishes did proportionally less to keep parish finances afloat than they had done in 1400.

[68] Benson and Hatcher, *Old and New Sarum*, 237–8; *LP* xii (2), 1026; *LP* xiii (2), 1178; Street, 'Bishops and Citizens', 328–61.
[69] See Ch. 4 n. 50.   [70] Burgess, '"By Quick and by Dead"', 857.
[71] *VCH: Berks*. iii. 535; WRO G23/1/2, fos. 245, 248; Phythian-Adams, *Desolation of a City*, esp. 287.
[72] Burgess and Kumin, 'Penitential Bequests', 628; see also Ch. 4.
[73] See Ch. 4 (and for exceptions, esp. Salisbury).

It was not, furthermore, as if the living had always been vigilant about keeping services going. In their surveys of 1545 and 1547, the chantry commissioners did not record as many of the chantries founded before 1400 as of those founded later on (see Map 3).[74] Parishioners and guildsmen had sometimes neglected services when endowments diminished or problems arose. To some extent, the living were prepared to serve the dead only so long as the dead were able to pay their way. Moreover, by 1547 many of the dead people for whom services were still being maintained had died rather a long time ago. Four-fifths of the perpetual chantries founded in parishes that survived until royal destruction had been set up before 1480, beyond the reach of living memory (see Map 3). In Salisbury most of the endowments for services maintained by the tailors' and St George's guilds had been made by benefactors who had died by 1450 (see Table 10). Late medieval religion was indeed a cult of living friends in the service of dead ones,[75] and in the widest sense of the word, these former chantry and obit founders were 'friends' benefiting parish and guild—but ones no longer fresh in the memory of the living. It was rather hard to remain on intimate terms of friendship with people who had been dead for over a century. There were both precedents and incentives for the living to accept the consequences of the abolition of purgatory.

But a willingness to abandon certain religious practices is not an entirely convincing explanation for the acceptance of change. Processions, pageants, and obit services had served social functions, not least the fostering of civic harmony and unity, goals not so easily abandoned. The spectre of social disorder had certainly loomed during the passage of religious reform.[76] Even during the 1530s, although the burgesses resisted certain changes, they did not applaud the consequences of others: some were troubled by the disruption that opposition to royal policy could cause. In August 1538 the mayor, Henry Coldstone, and several other prominent burgesses, including Thomas Chaffyn, were examining the perpetrators of a subversive rumour that an angel had appeared before Henry VIII at Portsmouth and that the king was planning to go on pilgrimage again.[77] Social stability had always been more difficult to

[74] 60% of the perpetual chantries known to have been founded before 1400 were not recorded by the commissioners in 1545; 20% of those founded after 1400 were not recorded.
[75] See Intro. n. 5.
[76] W. K. Jordan, *Edward VI: The Young King* (London, 1968), 433–93; J. A. Youings, 'The South-western Rebellion of 1549', *Southern History*, 1 (1979), 99–122.
[77] *LP* xiii (2), 62. See also the case of two reactionary Spaniards spreading treason in 1541 (ibid. xvi. 1032).

achieve in towns where economic life was vigorous. Social unrest could
feed on the vagaries of the cloth trade. Quarrels within a town's élite broke
out over considerations of status that were enlivened by growing wealth.
Faction was always more likely in these places, and the Reformation
certainly divided opinion even within the same town. Some must have felt
it sensible to chart a careful course through troubled waters, following the
ship of state without rocking the boat. Social harmony would be the better
preserved, and after the Reformation the problems of public order continued to tax town and parish authorities. The avoidance of faction within
a town council was also an attempt to ensure continuity and stability
within the council and city during a very unsettling period.

It would still, however, be a crude distortion to suppose that burgesses
accepted reform merely to ensure social stability. Preservation of a social
order was also inseparable from the articulation of a moral one. The
Edwardian Reformation aimed not just at a reformation of religion, but at
a reform of morals. In pursuit of the godly commonwealth, reformatory
decrees were accompanied by an extraordinary burst of moral outrage
against all forms of sin: preachers like Hugh Latimer inveighed against
corruption at court and the rapacity of the landowning class, bent on the
covetous acquisition of dissolved monastic and chantry lands. The sweat-
ing sickness in 1551 seemed to be the external outpouring of inner deprav-
ity. Church ales were condemned as bucolic immorality. Moral attitudes
hardened still further in the later sixteenth century with the worrying
growth in the number of vagrants and other poor. Sexual delinquency was
prosecuted more stringently than ever by Church courts and lay magis-
trates, by a 'godly' laity, and by the practically minded disturbed by the
spectacle of disorder.[78]

Some of the denunciations of moral turpitude were linked to criticisms
of the Catholic Church. Yet the appeal of enforcing moral behaviour also
drew on values, deeply embedded in Christian society, that did not depend for their expression on precise theological doctrines.[79] It had long

[78] W. K. Jordan, *Edward VI: The Threshold of Power* (London, 1970), 280–92, 358–67,
466–71; Brigden, *London and the Reformation*, 108–18, 458–83; I. W. Archer, *The Pursuit of
Stability: Social Relations in Elizabethan London* (Cambridge, 1991), esp. 251–8; M. Ingram,
Church Courts, Sex and Marriage in England 1570–1640 (Cambridge, 1987), esp. 94–101, 163,
166–7; P. Collinson, *The Religion of Protestants: The Church in English Society 1559–1625*
(Oxford, 1982), 158–61, 230–8.

[79] M. Spufford, 'Puritanism and the Social Order?', in A. Fletcher and J. Stevenson
(eds.), *Order and Disorder in Early Modern England* (Cambridge, 1989), esp. 51–3; M. S.
Byford, 'The Price of Protestantism: Assessing the Impact of Religious Change in Elizabethan Essex: The Case of Heydon and Colchester 1558–1594', D.Phil. thesis (Oxford,
1988), Ch. 1.

been the concern of the Salisbury city fathers to control the moral and social behaviour of citizens, to legislate on the activities of vagrants and even prostitutes.[80] The appeal of enforcing moral values was not restricted merely to a 'respectable' élite.[81] Certain moral values and behaviour—attendance at church, the punishment of drunkenness, fornication, and adultery—were rooted in the vision of an ordered Christian society. A concern for moral reform had frequently surged into ecclesiastical courts and town legislation before the Reformation. The public parading of adulterers through the streets of Devizes in the late sixteenth century had been presaged by the public penances and 'beatings' imposed by late medieval courts.[82] In cloth towns like Calne, Devizes, and Salisbury, the godly and practical sought to legislate against brothels and regulate ale-houses, powerful rival attractions to Church and sermon, much as they had done before the Reformation.[83] Churchwardens retained their traditional role of moral watchdogs; those of St Edmund's in Salisbury continued to present wayward priests to the ecclesiastical courts.[84] Part of the Reformation message had been to establish a religious and moral revival: it was a message that had informed a vision of an ordered Christian society well before the Reformation. It made the passage of reform more palatable.

In other respects, too, the Reformation did not represent a complete uprooting of the past. The ordering of a Protestant religious life could be grafted on to traditional structures. Long after the abolition of purgatory, the civic élite of Salisbury continued to commemorate their dead benefactors in a civic context. Miraculously, the burgesses had managed to salvage the endowments of the St George's guild and the Trinity almshouse, presumably because they were able to claim that these lands served secular and municipal purposes. Names continued to be added to the bede roll of city benefactors. In the later sixteenth century endowments were being given to the mayor and commonalty for the partial use of the poor in almshouses. Thomas Abyn, mayor in 1551, finally gave £20 for the yearly distribution of corn to the poor; Henry Tirrel left twelve tenements to

[80] See Intro. n. 54.

[81] P. Collinson, *Godly People: Essays on English Protestantism and Puritanism* (London, 1983), 407–8; Collinson, *Religion of Protestants*, 189–241.

[82] See Ch. 3 n. 33; B. H. Cunnington, *Some Annals of the Borough of Devizes 1555–1791* (2 vols.; Devizes, 1925), i. 35; ii. 3, 12.

[83] Ingram, *Church Courts*, 94–5; P. Slack, 'Poverty and Politics in Salisbury, 1597–1666', in P. Clark and P. Slack (eds.), *Crisis and Order in English Towns 1500–1700: Essays in Urban History* (London, 1972), 163–9; P. Clark, *The English Alehouse: A Social History 1200–1830* (London, 1983), esp. 127, 145, 152, 160 ff.

[84] See Ch. 3 nn. 28, 30, 32; *S. Edmund Accounts*, 153.

support almshouses. Gifts to the mayor and commonalty for the management of almshouses had already been foreshadowed by Thomas Brickett's
gift in 1536, and perhaps by the foundation of the Trinity almshouse itself
in the late fourteenth century. By the end of the sixteenth century the city
bede roll included names that reached back more than two centuries.
Former benefactors were no longer offered intercession for their souls in
purgatory, yet were still commemorated for the good service they had
performed for the city. Their gifts, the bede roll prayer began, helped to
increase 'love and charity' among the citizens so that they might 'after this
life . . . be partakers of the liefe everlasting'.[85]

The new religious order was made less alien by the survival of other
ceremonies. Civic processions continued, no longer held on St Osmund's
day, but as Midsummer feasts, processions, pageants, and plays—with
giants and hobby-horses—in which craft guilds continued to be involved.
In the late sixteenth century, too, the tailors' annual procession to the
cathedral and to St Thomas's church no longer involved witnessing the
miracle of the mass but, instead, attendance at evening prayer.[86] Collective
activity by burgesses and members of craft guilds continued to allow
displays of status and authority, and to encourage harmony within the city
and among themselves.

At parish level, certain traditions were kept alive. The destruction of
purely religious guilds may have temporarily reduced the number of
channels open for the laity to exercise control over their devotional lives,
yet the rapid expansion of parish offices in many places, and the civic and
parochial funding of preachers, ensured that such habits of control continued to find outlets.[87] In St Edmund's and St Thomas's churches,
Salisbury, communal feast-day celebrations, like Corpus Christi day, may
have been discarded. Yet Hocktide gatherings continued for a few decades
more, Rogation week went on being celebrated, and a Whitsuntide 'danc-

---

[85] WRO G23/1/2, fo. 188[r-v]. At Abingdon the reconstituted Christ's hospital continued
to remember benefactors in dedicatory prayers (Abingdon almshouse deeds). The Bridport
bailiff and burgesses lost the endowments of their prestigious Marian guild, but took over the
guild's chapel of St Andrew as their meeting place (see Ch. 7).

[86] Haskins, *Guilds*, 184–5, 170–5. The attempt to preserve the St Osmund feast had a
competitive edge to it: Salisbury wished to preserve its Midsummer feast like Westminster
and Windsor (see Ch. 2 n. 75).

[87] Compare Scarisbrick, *Reformation*, 164–8, with N. Allridge, 'Loyalty and Identity in
Chester Parishes', in S. J. Wright (ed.), *Parish, Church and People: Local Studies in Lay
Religion 1350–1750* (London, 1988), 104. From an English perspective, the vitality of the late
medieval parish community and fraternities could be 'the seed bed of the Reformation'; but
those same fraternities on the Continent might have been preparing the ground for the
'spiritual activities of small groups of the Tridentine and Baroque period' (Barron, 'Parish
Fraternities', 36–7; Chiffoleau, *La Comptabilité*, 286).

ing' (until around 1611) raised money for the church fabric. Easter collections and charges for pew seating continued on from pre-Reformation practices; charges for knells became charges for burials, banns, weddings, and christenings.[88] Elsewhere many parishes were able to hold on to property left by dead benefactors. By 1547, rents from such property did not always fund specific services: benefactors could be commemorated collectively on a general obit day from common parish funds rather than individually (as they may once have been) from their original endowment. In such parishes the claim could quite legitimately be made that these rents funded parochial needs, not 'superstitious' uses.[89] In some places too Hocktides and ales were celebrated into the late sixteenth century, and longer in more rural areas, at least until they were attacked by the more puritan of moralists.[90] Continuity in parish life and the salvaging of parochial funds perhaps made it easier for the traditionally minded to reconcile themselves to more destructive changes.

Other ceremonies survived in different forms, helping to maintain a rhythm of worship in parochial life. Rites of passage—baptism, marriage, burial—continued to mark parochial ceremony. Protestant theology removed any need for intercession after death; puritan moralists sought to strip funeral ritual of any eschatological purpose; knells at burials were no longer rung. But prayers for the dead were never forbidden and traditional practices at burial continued. John Aubrey recorded the survival of wakes, dirges, watchings, and 'soul cakes'; distributions to the poor at the funeral continued to be made; charges for burials continued to profit parish coffers.[91] Elaborate burial and anniversary services no longer marked the parish calendar, but sermons at funerals were already being asked for in wills in the 1530s,[92] and funeral orations, replete with commemorative biographical detail about the deceased, became one of the distinguishing marks of English Protestantism in the reign of Elizabeth. To some, even so, funeral sermons remained suspiciously like 'popish trentals'.[93] And many testators preferred to mark their burial not with funeral orations but with traditional social drinkings.

[88] *S. Edmund Accounts, passim.*

[89] See Ch. 4 n. 9. Compare with guilds and their practice of amalgamating obits (above n. 85, Ch. 6 n. 62, and Ch. 7 nn. 34, 51). The detaching of specific rents from the specific 'superstitious' services may help to explain the 'puzzle' (Burgess and Kumin, 'Penitential Bequests', 630) as to why parishes were able to hold on to such property during the Reformation.

[90] Underdown, *Revel, Riot and Rebellion*, 47–105; Ingram, *Church Courts*, 101–2.

[91] Aubrey, *Remaines*; C. Gittings, *Death, Burial and the Individual in Early Modern England* (London, 1984), 42, 49–50, 107–10, 121.

[92] See above n. 29.   [93] Collinson, *Godly People*, 519–20, 413–14.

Ritual involvement in parish life, moreover, could be structured around regular sermons and enforced attendance at church, around feasting and fasting, fund-raising, and charitable giving. Bell-ringing continued to remind parishioners of their obligations, if not to attend feast days, to attend sermons or morning prayer.[94] And habits of 'voluntary' religious and collective behaviour, independent of the parochial framework, found expression in other forms. Pilgrim shrines were abolished, yet could survive as goals of a different kind—such that the gathering that 'gadded' to hear the 'trental of sermons' held at Pilton (Somerset) in 1586 could be likened to the pilgrims who had once journeyed to the same spot to make offerings to its shrine.[95] Above all, the Prayer Book, with its saints' and feast days, kneelings and signings with the cross, preserved more than an echo of older rituals.[96]

The progress of Protestant reform was slow and difficult, and was not simply the result of the ascendancy of Protestant groups over Catholic opposition. Ultimately, the acceptance of reform may tell us more about the strength of royal power than the popularity of either faith. It was proper to behave, as Thomas Poyntz had done, like 'sadde gentlemen'. But acceptance did spring from a multitude of other motives that could vary from place to place. Within the region, bustling cloth towns perhaps accepted reform more quickly than smaller communities in chalkland areas. Cloth towns had long experienced Lollard dissent; some Lollards occupied prominent positions in the social hierarchy. Early Protestant proselytizing, even if inspired by Continental heresy rather than native dissent, found a response in the same areas and among the influential. If, during the reigns of Henry VIII and Edward VI, England resembled a child force-fed spoonfuls of ever more radical reform, to use C. Haigh's analogy, there was a significant number of people who found the fare rather tasty.[97] It is not so surprising that the visitation officials of 1556 found that the band of parish churches in Berkshire from Sparsholt to East Hendred did not have a rood, that most blatant symbol of the intercessory function of the Catholic Church: the same parishes had long harboured traditions of anti-Catholic dissent.

Yet the areas where Lollardy had been found were also areas marked by a vigorous indulgence in very orthodox practices. Lollardy had been

---

[94] *S. Edmund Accounts*, 97, 105, 927.
[95] Cited in Collinson, *Religion of Protestants*, 262–3.
[96] As Duffy resignedly concedes (*Stripping of the Altars*, 589–91).
[97] Haigh (ed.), *Reformation Revised*, 15.

partly fuelled by a reaction to orthodox activity. Heretics in Newbury were found in significant numbers in the early sixteenth century when the parish church was being completely rebuilt. Where the cloth industry in particular had brought prosperity, more guilds, chantries, and obits had been founded and more processions and ceremonies, civic and parochial, established. Perhaps the abolition of purgatory provided a release, even for the more orthodox, from certain ceremonies and from the services for long-dead benefactors that had accumulated most heavily in the more densely populated cloth towns.

Even so, some of the same parishes and towns tentatively chose to shoulder the same burdens in Mary's reign. In any case, the response to reform could be more complex and sophisticated. Protestant emphasis on the Word of God may have been more acceptable to the educated and literate, who were more numerous in the more economically advanced towns. The élite burgesses of Windsor certainly approved of Henry Filmer's denunciation of the superstitious tales preached by the parish vicar. The same towns had generally been more responsive to new cults and liturgies, especially ones that emphasized the figure of Christ more than other saints.[98] Many of these were obliterated during the Reformation, but the vigorous adoption of new feasts of the Virgin Mary and of Jesus at the end of the fifteenth century was not incompatible with a readiness to consider reforms in the sixteenth.[99] Moreover, the Reformation was also underpinned by a moral message that was not lost in towns facing more acute problems of order. Harmony and authority were goals perennially striven for, with difficulty, by civic and parish authorities. It was the more industrialized areas that continued to experience the greater social problems, and it was towns like Salisbury and Calne that saw a 'godly' laity, more stringently than elsewhere, enforcing the moral standards necessary for social stability in the later sixteenth century.

Social conditions, however, did not exclusively determine the acceptance of reform. Other variables altered responses. In Salisbury attitudes were coloured by episcopal lordship: the contrast between stiff resistance to reform in the 1530s and acceptance in the 1540s and 1550s seems less contradictory in the context of the long-standing struggle against the bishop. Secular lordship in a region might decide religious affiliation: the recusancy that lingered in southern parts of Wiltshire was no doubt sustained by the Catholic Edward Lord Stourton.[100]

---

[98] See the way in which the Jesus guilds in Salisbury seem to eclipse all other parish altars in the late 15th cent. (see Ch. 3 n. 63 and Table 7).

[99] See Ch. 6; G. Rosser, *Medieval Westminster 1200–1540* (Oxford, 1989), 274–8.

[100] Ingram, *Church Courts*, 86.

And finally, even in the economically more advanced towns, acceptance of Protestantism did not entirely depend on literacy and a sophisticated response to the theological issues. There was much about the Reformation that was syncretic: Protestant reform could be grafted on to accepted moral values and even (initially) on to traditional ceremonies. Patterns of pious practice within parishes kept a rhythm that did not have to be entirely disrupted by the imposition of a new religion. Customary church-going on feast days could be converted into the habit of attending sermons. Sacraments like baptism, marriage, and burial could continue to mark the clock face of parochial life. By the second half of the sixteenth century, destruction of Catholic doctrines had been great; but continuity in pious practices and devotional habits ultimately made religious change more acceptable.

Conclusion

A BROAD change in pious practice from the thirteenth to the early sixteenth century appears to present itself. A book that begins with religious houses, proceeds through parishes and guilds, and reaches heresy and Reformation might harbour the assumption that lay devotional concerns shifted—away from an attachment to religious houses and the giving of land to monasteries and nunneries, and towards the parish, guilds, and almshouses, over which they exercised greater 'control', culminating in an anticlericalism that paved the way for the Reformation.

To some extent, a new sort of lay person had emerged during this period, one who seemed to encroach on priestly territory. Parish, guild, stipendiary priests, and chantry and altar funds were accumulated and managed by lay people. Devotional services could be harnessed for purposes of which the clerical hierarchy did not approve. The St George guild and processions in Salisbury provided a focal point of opposition to episcopal overlordship. Some lay people presumed to sit in chancels during divine service.[1] Others seem to have taken on the clerical voice of a preacher, denouncing sin, worldly luxury, and even the clergy. The moralizing of mystics, of gentry like Edmund Leversedge, even of some guild and almshouse legislation was akin to the more subversive utterances of 'Lollard knights'. Other members of the laity could retreat from the strictures of parochial life into private chapels where they might consort with hermits or interpret the Scriptures for themselves.

If a new 'pious' creature was emerging, the Church hierarchy had been partly responsible for its creation. An informed laity, involved in the pastoral cares of the Church, had been a goal of ecclesiastical reform in the thirteenth century. Synodal and diocesan legislation had established the primary importance of the parish, the need for fabric and altar funds and for churchwardens to manage them. It had required parishioners to voice complaints against lay people and clergy during visitations. Bishops like Grosseteste had pronounced on the need for a pastoral mission to preach in the vernacular and inculcate a knowledge of the Scriptures. By

---

[1] Churchwardens were required to report this offence (D & C, MS 189, fo. 54).

the early fifteenth century the mission had become only too successful. The activities of some lay people seemed to have slipped beyond clerical control; faced with the Lollard threat, the Church attempted to curb preaching in the vernacular and the translation of the Bible.[2] The Reformation was to make a layman supreme head of the Church.

Nevertheless, it is best to avoid the Shelleyesque image, however tempting, of a lay monster destroying its clerical creator. The view on late medieval piety from the vantage point of the Reformation can be distorting. There was as much continuity as change from the thirteenth to the sixteenth century. Religious houses, particularly ones that enshrined the relics of venerated saints, continued to perform an intercessory role throughout the later Middle Ages. Lay people had always exercised a certain 'control' in their religious lives, founding chapels and fraternities, at a subparochial level and at a level that cut across parish boundaries. The need for the priesthood was made stronger by the successful propagation of the doctrines of penance and purgatory which stimulated the accumulation of endowments for services that interceded for souls. Heresy was the reaction of a minority against this need, the doctrines, and their accumulation. And the Reformation was accepted with a relative lack of violence less because the cry for reform had become stronger and more because it did not represent a complete break with the past.

It need not be assumed, moreover, that the Church found itself in opposition to the needs of 'popular piety'. Bishops could accommodate the desire of some lay people for a more private devotion with the dissemination of approved books and the advocacy of a 'mixed life'. The propagation of new cults like that of St Osmund by the Salisbury bishop, dean, and chapter met a willing response among lay people. The promotion of the Name of Jesus into a fixed feast day seems to have emerged from a groundswell of popular feeling for the cult as much as from official encouragement. Clerics did not always relish the use to which feasts and cults were put: the vicar of St Helen's in Abingdon complained to Bishop Neville in 1437 about a 'carnal and diabolical effigy' that accompanied the parishioners' procession on the feast of the Holy Cross.[3] Yet there was no constant confrontation between popular practices and clerical concerns. The wills of the clergy are not obviously different from those of lay people. They refer more frequently to books (mainly liturgical ones) and bequests to the poor, as befitted the clerical

[2] Hudson, *Lollards and their Books*, 161–2. For Grosseteste's posthumous popularity among Lollards see Southern, *Robert Grosseteste*, 298–309.

[3] Reg. Bp. Neville, fo. 109.

office and duties. But as in the wills of lay people, bequests to church fabrics and altar lights abound.

From a local level, moreover, broad changes in pious practices are made more complex by a variety of influences. This study has emphasized institutional and regional influences, but there are other distinctions that have been touched on. Some implications can be drawn out concerning the effect of 'class' on religious life. To an individual like Edmund Leversedge, religious experience transcended corporate worship and regional boundaries. But his individuality may also have been the product of social context, of his place in society and his position as gentleman.[4] Other members of the gentry sported the religious habits in which Edmund chose to dress; indeed, one devotional practice that tended to mark out the gentry from other groups in society was an attachment to monastic houses. Edmund had connections with the Carthusians; the gentry, more than other social groups, maintained abiding connections with the older orders. A lingering attachment to monastic houses emphasized a social detachment from local society that was also reflected in a tendency to retreat from the pressures of more corporate forms of worship. Private chapels spared many a gentleman and woman from the obligation of attending the local parish church save on important feast days. They also provided the means of pursuing a more private religion. In 1530 Lady Anne Danvers had a private chapel in her 'Chamberhouse' in which she required a chaplain to say mass for her soul; within its confines she had no doubt studied her copy of the New Testament which she was to give to the confessor at the abbey of Syon.

Other interests pursued by the gentry suggest a certain fashionable sophistication, a readiness to respond to new devotional trends. Edmund's professed morbidity had been occasionally found in the wills of other gentlemen, particularly among the so-called Lollard knights. The occasionally gentry testators continued to express a wish for a puritan simplicity in their post-obit arrangements: Thomas Say in 1498, who possessed a book called *Pilgrimage of Souls* (reminiscent of Edmund Leversedge's experiences), did not wish his funeral to be a 'sumptuous one'.[5] Some preambles of wills (also mainly from the gentry) refer to the miserable vale, the wretched world, even their wretched bodies. Other

---

[4] See, most recently, C. Richmond, 'Religion and the Fifteenth-Century English Gentleman', in R. B. Dobson (ed.), *The Church, Politics and Patronage in the Fifteenth Century* (Gloucester, 1984), 193–208; C. Richmond, 'The English Gentry and Religion c.1500', in C. Harper-Bill (ed.), *Religious Belief and Ecclesiastical Careers in Late Medieval England* (Woodbridge, 1991), 121–50; C. Carpenter, 'Religion of the Gentry', 53–74.

[5] PCC 14 Moone.

TABLE 18. Choice of burial places by gentry and
others 1350–1538 (%)

	Gentry	Others
Parish nave	35	50
Parish cemetery	3	18.
Parish chapels/aisles	16	28
Parish chancel	12	
Monasteries	16	2
Friaries	10	
'In the ground'	8	2

Note: Sample of 144 gentry testators in the region, and
103 yeomen, husbandmen, merchants, clothiers, mercers,
drapers, tailors, and fullers.

wills evince a concern to keep abreast with the most up-to-date
elaborations of the liturgy. Edmund's attachment to Corpus Christi, the
sacrament and feast, found corporate expression in all groups of society,
but response to newer or incipient feasts, like the mass of the Five
Wounds, is more apparent in the wills of gentlemen than other social
groups.[6] A taste for novelty and sophistication was also developed by
education. Edmund Leversedge's intended period of study in Oxford was
matched by the concerns of other gentlemen. William Fetiplace, esquire,
in 1528 left £12 to scholars of divinity in Oxford for them to preach the
Word of God for a whole year. Certainly, from the end of the fifteenth
century, gentry testators seem to reveal a concern for an educated up-
bringing for their offspring. Thomas Dauntsey in 1503 was intent on his
son finding an exhibition to a school 'where gentlemen ought to learn'.[7]

Education, fashionable sophistication, and privacy could distance the
gentry from the more corporate forms of devotion of parish and guild.
Fewer members of the gentry chose to be buried within the parish church
than other social groups, and those that did, particularly where they had
rights of patronage, might select the relative seclusion of the chancel as
their burial site (see Table 18). Fewer too left bequests to the fabric of
parish churches, and a still smaller proportion left bequests to parish altar
lights and fraternities than yeomen, husbandmen, or craftsmen, lower
down the social scale.[8] Gentry involvement in parish church-building

[6] See Ch. 4 n. 32.   [7] PCC 6 Jankyn, 40 Holgrave.
[8] 22% of the same sample of gentry left bequests to altar lights; 40% from the other non-
gentry group did leave such bequests.

tended to centre on the building of chapels and aisles in which they chose
to be buried and set up altars for their chantries. Some even built chapels
detached from the main body of the church. To the parish church of St
Peter, Charlton, in 1523 William Chaucey left ten marks for mending the
chalice, six sheep to the rood light (to top up an endowment he had already
given of twenty-four sheep), and a pair of vestments of black velvet with
his arms to be set within them. But during the next ten years his chantry
priest was to celebrate for his soul in a chapel to be built with £20 in the
cemetery of the church. William Filliol, knight, in 1527 was anxious to
instruct the parishioners of Horton of 'the dome to come' by his unusual
bequest to have the figure of Jesus sitting on a rainbow painted on to a
background of 'playster of parys' on the wall above the high altar; yet he
wished his 'wretched body' to be laid to rest in the church of the grey
friars of Salisbury.[9]

Detachment from parochial life was perhaps inevitable among a certain
kind of gentry, particularly the wealthier sort, who had landed interests in
more than one parish. Indeed some gave a passing nod of recognition to
their multiple parish obligations: Edmund Mompesson in 1500 left vestments for obits to be celebrated in seven Wiltshire churches; John Estbury
in 1508 bequeathed twenty chalices to ten parish churches in Berkshire.[10]
From the late fourteenth to the early sixteenth century the Hungerford
family left bequests to, or their marks on, at least thirteen churches in
Wiltshire. The involvement of such gentry families in building projects
had perhaps to be carefully enticed, in the manner that Sir John Herryng's
help was sought by the parishioners of Wimborne Minster in 1448/9.[11]
Occasionally some gentlemen were even disruptive of communal parish
life. In about 1416 such was the noise created by the canons, armed men,
and archers in Sir John Drayton's 'fortress' in a wood close to Culham that
herons, egrets, and other birds refused to nest there, and the vicar and
parishioners dared not make their customary Rogationtide procession
around the parish and manor.[12] It is not surprising that this sort of
gentleman was not found as guild- or churchwarden.

Among the gentry, then, there was a certain isolation from the more
corporate pious practices found in the parishes and guilds of town and
countryside. It was, perhaps, the same detachment that helped ensure the
passage of the Reformation which swept away so many of those corporate
practices. Education, personal devotion, and the private reading of books
and Bibles arguably allowed a more sophisticated response to the novel

[9] PCC 10 Bodefeld, 23 Porche.   [10] PCC 15 Blamyr, 9 Bennett.
[11] See Ch. 5 n. 22.   [12] PRO C1/6/219.

doctrines of Protestant reformers and a distaste for the superstitious extremes of some of the illiterate. Aloofness from parish life might have led some of the gentry to view the destruction of some of its corporate practices, such as the funding of altar lights and fraternities, with a certain equanimity. Gentlemen like Thomas Seke, Hughe Powlett, John Saintlowe, John Rogers, and Thomas Dyer served on the commissions in Dorset that saw to the dismantling of chantries and guilds.[13]

Yet it is clear that affiliation to Protestantism was not decided on class grounds.[14] Active gentry reformers can be contrasted with families like the Englefields, supporters of erstwhile nuns and even the Catholic Princess Mary. In any case, the grouping of the gentry together as a class can be distorting. The more important gentlemen, with estates in many parishes, can be contrasted with the plethora of minor gentry who might have few lands in only one parish. Perhaps many such gentlemen were regularly involved, as they were said to be at Netherbury, in the corporate efforts that raised money for the whole parish. It is obvious too that the distinction between gentlemen and other members of society can be a blurred one. Wealthy cloth merchants displayed similar devotional concerns to the gentry: an interest in books, oratories, even bequests to religious houses which might shelter members of their own family. And some gentlemen had closer connections with the activities of townsmen: Sir George Meriot, much like the wealthier citizens of Salisbury, contributed £10 to the rebuilding of St Thomas's in 1410.

Some of the 'private' concerns of the gentry, moreover, had a deliberately public intention. The 'worship' of a gentleman in his local society, it hardly needs pointing out, was dependent on the conspicuous display of power. Burial in chancels, the building of family chapels, and seating in pews served the needs not so much of inward piety as of outward status. The aim of the gentry was less to be isolated, or even detached, from local society than to impress their stamp on its communal life. Fewer of the gentry than other social groups left general bequests of money to the fabric of the parish church. Yet proportionally more provided parishes with costly ornaments and vestments upon which their names and coats of arms could be inscribed.[15] Private oratories could occasionally serve the pastoral needs of a wider group in a parish than the immediate household of a particular lord. The perpetual chantries of the gentry founded in local churches served not only the private interests of their own souls but also

[13] PRO E301/16.
[14] See M. Weber, *The Sociology of Religion*, trans. M. Fischoff (London, 1965).
[15] 20% of gentry left bequests of ornaments; 5% of non-gentry.

the wider ones of the parish, marking out their founders as parish benefactors of a distinctive kind.

The Reformation, therefore, was also destructive of practices to which the gentry had contributed. The wholesale selling of plate and liturgical ornaments disposed of benefactions left by local gentlemen and gentlewomen. The suppressing of chantries swept away the services that supported the intercessory needs of many a gentry family. After all, in 1557 William Hyde had his name placed in the calendar of Denchworth Breviary, where the souls of his ancestors, as far back as the twelfth century, were commemorated.[16] And the dissolution of monasteries destroyed institutions with which the gentry, more than any other social group, had traditionally retained stronger links. Perhaps their support for traditional forms of piety was declining: proportionally fewer left bequests to religious houses in the sixteenth century than before.[17] Some even gained by the massive dispossession of monastic lands, although the gentry families who gained most from the Dissolution seem to have been those from outside local society rather than those from within. Others stood to lose from Protestant reform and perhaps acquiesced to the king's 'high commaundment and pleasure' only from a sense of obedience, akin to Sir Thomas Poyntz's, like 'sadde gentlemen'.

A certain sophistication, an aloofness from the concerns of other parishioners, a penchant for socially exclusive monastic houses: all these characteristics tended to mark out some of the gentry from other social groups. But they were not characteristics alien to other aspirants of social status like wealthy merchants and burgesses. Nor did they detach the gentry entirely from the communal concerns of other parishioners. The pious gentleman or gentlewoman was not a particularly distinctive creature. In the sea of late medieval piety, the species that 'the religion of the gentry' most resembles is perhaps the red herring.

Gender is another distinction that could potentially affect pious practices. Differences between men and women in parish life were encouraged by canon law and by social custom. John Myrc wrote of a different liturgy required for boy and girl, man and woman, at baptism, purification, and death.[18] The old belief that women were naturally more impure seems to have come to the surface at Lyme Regis in 1405 when the vicar was

---

[16] See Ch. 4 n. 1.

[17] Between 1350 and 1499 60% of the gentry in the region left bequests to monasteries, and between 1500 and 1535 50% did so.

[18] *Instructions for Parish Priests by John Mirc*, ed. E. Peacock and F. J. Furnivall (Early English Text Society, 31; London, 1868).

reprimanded for allowing women to approach the high altar.[19] Churching was a ceremony after childbirth that naturally involved women alone: in 1576 an old witness at Newbury recalled how the wives of the parish used to make offerings before the image of St Leonard in the old hospital chapel after childbirth.[20] The sufferings of some saints, like the holy maidens, were ones with which women were best able to identify.[21] The distinctiveness of women was encouraged by role reversals in Hocktide festivities, when women might 'tie up' men and extract money for the fabric funds. It was also encouraged by fixed seating which at first (though not always) seems to have been made for women alone. Not till 1522 at St Laurence's in Reading, when new seats were put in, did men begin to be charged for seats. Often women seem to have been seated on the north side of the church, perhaps because they would be furthest from the perils of hell usually depicted on Doom paintings on the south side above the chancel arch, or because they would face the image of the Virgin Mary to the left of the figure of Christ on the rood screen (though in St Laurence's the women sat on the south side, perhaps in order to face the chancel chapel dedicated to the Virgin Mary). As rules in St Laurence's church also make clear, the positioning of women, wives, and widows on their side of the church was determined by social ranking.[22] A sense of social distinctiveness among women was encouraged by secular custom and ecclesiastical law.

The activity and role of women in parish life is also clear. There are no known women serving as churchwardens in the region, but some did become wardens of parish guilds and altar lights. Women were often the most active group in the parish in promoting cults and raising funds. The cake-selling by the wives of Wimborne Minster was the single most profitable source of revenue for the parish in the early sixteenth century. At the Hocktide festivals elsewhere it was the women of the parish, whether at St Giles' or St Laurence's in Reading, at Sherborne, or at St Edmund's in Salisbury, who gathered more than the men or bachelors and who had their own supper paid for by the parish after the festivities. Women are often to be found washing and repairing church vestments and the wives of the parish sometimes acted as guilds who looked after the altars and images of the Virgin Mary, the protectoress of women.[23] In 1573

---

[19] *Reg. Dean Chandler*, 21.   [20] E133/3/407.

[21] E. Duffy, 'Holy Maydens, Holy Wyfes: The Cult of Women Saints in Fifteenth- and Sixteenth-Century England', in W. J. Sheils and D. Wood (eds.), *Women in the Church* (Studies in Church History, 23, Oxford, 1990), 175–96.

[22] BRO D/P 97/5/2, pp. 146, 244; Aston, 'Segregation', in 257–94.   [23] E133/3/07.

an old man in Plush remembered that it was the women who used to give 'diverse silver rings' to the image of Our Lady.[24] Michael Gamare, accused of heresy in 1519, inveighed against the custom of the women at Wimborne St Giles who set their candles before the image of St Giles.[25] If the Church made 'little specific provision for women',[26] the role that women played in parish life meant that many did not have to seek a devotional outlet in heresy.

Perhaps more women than men were vigorous in their pious practices. But it is difficult to discern any pious practices that were distinctively 'feminine'. Attempts to find a feminine piety through wills is potentially fruitless: women (particularly widows) who made wills may have been executing the plans of husbands. Alice Meriot's concern in her own will for the fulfilment of her late husband's is apparent only because of the unusual denunciation of his executors in 1406.[27] One may seek in certain aspects of late medieval devotion—touching, feeling, and kissing images and ornaments—a bias towards activities more readily associated with women than men.[28] But this association may be too stereotypical. The activities of women described by the old man of Plush may have been highlighted to belittle their significance, at a time when concealment of former chantry lands was being hunted down. In any case, by no means were all women orthodox in their piety: bishops had to root out some stoutly heretical women from the diocese, some of whom complained against excessive veneration of images, by men as much as women.[29] During the Reformation, moreover, there are no instances in the region, such as the episode in Exeter (when certain women tried in vain to prevent the destruction of their rood screen),[30] of women being more protective of the old faith than men.

Issues of both class and gender, however, have not been made the focus of this study. The emphasis has been on the institutional and regional influences affecting the expression of pious practices. One of these influences was the pattern of ecclesiastical lordship. Pastoral traditions might sometimes preserve an archaic, minster form of parish structure. Monastic lordship in certain towns (episcopal lordship in the case of Salisbury) affected the character of certain pious practices: some guilds functioned as rallying-points for the struggles of townsmen for greater autonomy. In

---

[24] PRO E133/1/191. [25] See Ch. 9 n. 64.
[26] C. Cross, '"Great Reasoners in Scripture": The Activities of Women Lollards 1380–1530', in D. Baker (ed.), *Medieval Women* (Studies in Church History, subsidia 1; Oxford, 1978), 378.
[27] See Intro. n. 80. [28] Richmond, 'English Gentry', 140–2.
[29] See Ch. 9 n. 65. [30] Youings, *Dissolution*, 164–5.

other areas, nevertheless, religious houses could still attract penitential bequests. Moreover, the region as a whole, in the eyes of bishops, was a uniform diocese. New cults were propagated in the diocese as a whole, even if the response, to the cult of St Osmund for instance, was more immediate in areas where episcopal and cathedral manors and parishes lay thickest on the ground.

More importantly, the landscape itself could also determine pious practice: differences do emerge between settlements or parishes that grew up on chalkland soil and those that flourished in clay regions. John Aubrey's picturesque imagery of communal sheep-shearing and bucolic ales in chalkland parishes was conjured from a fertile, post-Civil War nostalgia but also from acute observation: the nucleated settlement, where manorial influence remained strong, was a feature more likely (though not exclusively) found along the river valleys in chalk soil. The clay and wood–pasture parishes, in Wiltshire at any rate, were more densely populated, and within them settlements, sometimes with their own chapelries, were more dispersed. Within them too, manorial control was potentially weaker and parochial ties looser, allowing subversion and heresy to grow more easily.

The chalk–cheese division is too glib a classification, however, to be an entirely satisfying explanation of religious differences in regions and parishes. There is a more obvious contrast to be drawn between the cloth-producing towns and less industrialized areas. To some extent this division tended to reinforce the clay–chalk divide since the main cloth-producing areas fell on clay soils. The wealth and markets of the cloth towns helped keep their populations buoyant by attracting migrants into them, whereas parishes in chalkland areas tended to become depopulated in the wake of the Black Death. The wealth generated by cloth allowed a greater capacity to invest in penitential good works: church-building, chantry and guild foundation. It also generated social problems, dissension, and heresy. The continuing provision of almshouses in the cloth areas of Wiltshire and Berkshire during the fifteenth and early sixteenth centuries and beyond was a response to the unsettling effect of immigration and social problems. Heresy too, before and after the Reformation, flourished more readily in the same areas: the puritans and separatists lurking in the cloth-weaving parishes from the late sixteenth century were the spiritual successors of the heretics who had been unearthed in the same parishes during the late medieval period.

Nevertheless, the contrasts between chalk and clay, cloth towns and more rural villages, cannot be rigidly drawn. Only in extreme cases can contrasts in religious life be made. In the rural village of Winterslow parishioners could not perhaps afford some of the more elaborate ceremonies characteristic of late medieval society. The parish had an obit day for benefactors, but the accumulation of endowments, in the form of livestock, had not been extensive by the 1540s; no perpetual chantry or fraternity seems to have been founded in the parish. The more populous parishes of Salisbury or Reading, however, offered a different experience for their parishioners. Wealth and sheer numbers meant that ceremonies were more elaborate and frequent, that more guilds and chantries were founded, and that new cults and liturgies were more readily seized on. There was a steadier accumulation of property and liturgical goods from dead benefactors, and more anniversaries were founded and chantries set up.

However, a greater intensity of ceremonies did not mean that parishioners were as closely bound in communal effort as those in Winterslow. There, parish finances were kept afloat by the regular efforts of living parishioners, particularly by the annual church ale. In Reading or Salisbury, by contrast, church ales or other collective fund-raising activities were not organized as frequently. Parish finances relied more heavily on the accumulated property from the dead, or on charges for services rendered for them, than on the corporate effort of the living. In such towns there were many focuses of collective loyalty other than the parochial one: in parish fraternities, craft guilds, guilds of mayors and burgesses, and almshouses. To some extent these groupings reflect a more fragmented society. Indeed, efforts to maintain cohesion had to be made because peaceful unity was more fragile, even among the burgesses in town councils. Society in Salisbury was potentially more fragmented and unstable, more likely to attract the poor to its gates and almshouses. Tithe evasion or church absenteeism was perhaps more frequent; so was sedition and heresy which fed off a reaction to the accumulated wealth of churches and fraternities. The city authorities felt the need to quell riots, regulate its level of poor relief, and even legislate on issues of moral welfare like prostitution. A sense of corporate identity was less easy to achieve in such an 'urbanized' society.

Yet we have also seen that a diversity of devotional loyalties was not necessarily a source of social fragmentation. To some extent it made for social cohesion. Multiple obligations could produce a honeycomb of complementary loyalties that bound townspeople closer to their parishes, guilds, and town. Rebuilding a parish church could, at one and the same time, be a parochial, guild, or even civic project. Town processions bound the members of craft guilds into closer civic unity and, by taking in the boundaries of town parishes along their routes, reminded those involved of their parochial attachments. The social and religious cohesion of a thriving cloth-producing town like Salisbury, and even of smaller towns like Bridport, could be kept intact by the devotional groupings, which, however various and diverse, were interlocked with each other and with the town as a whole. Nevertheless, such a cohesion was less easy to keep intact.

Conditions and needs within different places partly explain responses to religious change. It is not surprising to find a more sluggish response to reformational decrees in the relatively cohesive parish of Winterslow, with no (apparent) history of dissent, with little accumulated lumber from dead benefactors to shed, and with a tradition of collective parish activity. Salisbury, however, had a longer history of dissent and heresy, even if it had never been a serious danger to social stability and orthodox piety. The city's living citizens, the wealthier sort, had been been capable of responding to religious novelty, whether to new liturgical feasts or to a more personal approach to devotion. Its dead citizens made demands on the living that could be burden-some and were occasionally ignored: the abolition of purgatory and the removal of any need to intercede for the dead did not prove to be entirely unacceptable.

Ultimately, however, it would be too deterministic to attribute acceptance of reform to socio-economic conditions. Even within Salisbury, our paradigm of a cloth town, response to change was multifaceted and the passage of reform far from smooth. Moreover, the Reformation did not destroy all preceding religious practices. In the end, it was made palatable by what it preserved and continued from late medieval practices. Civic processions and guild activity still fulfilled a social function. City benefactors could still be commemorated, and incorporated into civic traditions. Corporate parish life could be structured around regular sermons rather than traditional feast days. The citizens' eventual acquisition of official independence from episcopal lordship was the culmination of an effort that reached back to well before the Reformation divide. In the post-Reformation world, the Salisbury mayors and burgesses exercised a moral rigour in its social legislation, which progressed naturally on from their pre-Reformation concerns. And in the region as a whole, the floodgates opened in Edward VI's reign, releasing a tide of sermonizing and legislation on manners and morals, were fed by late medieval channels: the concern of Church courts to prosecute sexual misconduct, and of city legislation to contain prostitution; the moralistic rulings imposed on almshouse inmates by a Margaret Hungerford; and even the morbid attacks on pride and greed by an Edmund Leversedge.

The Reformation was immensely destructive of long-cherished practices, which was why it was, at times, resisted just as much in cloth towns as elsewhere. By the end of the sixteenth century, religious life could seem very different. The parish church was no longer a place in which the visual senses were focused on the elevation of the host at mass and enriched by an abundance of painted symbols and images filling corners, chapels, and aisles. It had become an open space in which the minds of pew-seated congregation were fixed on the pulpit and cerebrally engaged by biblical texts on whitewashed walls.[31] Yet the contrast can be drawn too extremely. In the new order there were practices preserved from the old, rituals that survived even if transformed, a moral vigour that tapped into an earlier tradition. There were pious practices in the new order that a parishioner, faced with change but brought up in an older faith, could recognize and ultimately accept.

[31] R. W. Scribner, *For the Sake of Simple Folk: Popular Propaganda for the German Reformation* (Cambridge, 1981), 3–4; Scarisbrick, 164–5.

Bibliography

I MANUSCRIPTS

London

British Library

Add. MS 6214, 28206, 28870, 34193, 36390–3
Add. Ch. 5691, 15174, 18182, 18226, 18479, 40046, 40637, 40638
Cott. MS Claud. Eiv, MSS Vesp. Ev, xxv
Harl. Ch. 57, E41
Harl. MS 61, 965, 1623, 6716
Lansdowne MS 231, 442
Stowe Ch. 623

Public Record Office

Ancient deeds from Catalogue of Ancient Deeds
   C146/206, 536, 605, 5161, 6194, 9531, 9561, 9582, 9583, 9609
   E40/4619, 4829, 4868, 6552, 8529, 9360, 9371, 9375, 9377, 9382, 9390, 9535,
      11972, 12097
   E42/391
   E210/126, 308, 467, 1742, 1932, 1948, 2006, 2061, 2159, 2160, 2168, 2798,
      2985, 3067, 3206, 3226, 3411, 3516, 3519, 4588, 5396, 5478, 5676, 6494,
      7187, 7202, 7220, 7271, 7344, 7420, 7525, 7540, 7658, 8817, 9077
   C1/6/219, 9/434, 48/551, 54/7, 108/17, 158/16, 317/22, 335/89, 367/38, 385/
      89, 395/55, 401/17, 445/44, 801/15, 872/51, 890/1–4, 929/9–10, 1034/
      38, 1059/71, 1276/75
C47/39/52, 46/413, 158/16
C85/142/53, 147–9
C115/LI/6689
C142/51
C143/215/20
C270/309/72
CP25 (1) 251/15/42, 40/270
E40/9375, 9535
E42/150
E133/1/191, 2/347, 3/407, 3/413, 3/416 10/1541
E135/3/21, 17/26
E159/250

E301/3, 16, 36/91, 51/41, 58, 59/8
E315/8/124
E368/240, 250
KB9
PCC Rous-Noodes (PROB11/1–26)
SC8/37/1829–31, 93/4613, 239/11943, 10470–5
STAC2/16/91, 24/408, 25/272, 34/28, 34/97

Abingdon

Almshouse deeds 1–861

Dorchester

Dorset Record Office

Bridport: DC/BTB C1– Court rolls, 1277–
    D2 Register 1327–1456
    G1 'Old Dome Book'
    G2
    H1 Red Book Town accounts 1444–
    M1 Bailiffs' accounts 1307–1404
    M6
    M7 Cofferers' accounts
    M11 Town and churchwardens' accounts 1389–1457
    Q1 2 Cofferers' rentals 1440, 1480–1
    S1 ff. Deeds
    Y1–11 Wills 1313–1480
    AB26, 42, 43, 44, 46 (CD 62) Hospital deeds
    CD1–100 Fraternity books and deeds
    PQ30 Transcript of rules and accounts of Holy Cross
D10 Bundle T310 'Weld of Lulworth'
Sherborne: D/SHA CH2, 3, A1–79 (Almshouse), PE/SH/RE 1/1
Wimborne Minster: PE/WM CW 1/1–40, 41

Longleat

Longleat House
Deeds: 6830, 7514, 8018, 8032, 8966, 8968, 8972, 8974

Oxford

Bodleian Library
Ashmole MS 1125, 1126

Aubrey MS 1, 2
Lat. MS Lit. b.14
Digby MS 145

Magdalen College

Corton MS
Wanborough deeds

Poole

Municipal Archives

23 (1) Old Town Book 1493–
46 (1) Town accounts 1524–
47 (2) Churchwardens' accounts 1530–2
48 (3)

Reading

Berkshire Record Office

Archdeacon of Berkshire Liber Actorum 1535–6 D/A2 C3
   MS C3
   D/A1 233/1–425 Wills and inventories 1530–
   D/ED F 134, 140 Other wills
Bray: D/EG M1–50 Manor court rolls
Chipping Lambourne: D/Q1 25 Almshouse *c.*1532
Cookham: D/E SK M8 Court rolls
Lambourne: D/QI Almshouse 1468–
Reading: D/P 96/5/1 St Giles' churchwardens' accounts
   D/P 97/5/1, 2 St Laurence's churchwardens' accounts
Wallingford: W/ACa 1 Corporation minutes 1507–
   W/FAd Acc 901 Bridgemen's accounts 1532–8
   W/T Acc 901, THa 1–53 Hospital St John, *c.*1225–70
Windsor: D/EB T3, 4 (Almshouse), 7B
   D/XP 149/1/1 Churchwardens' accounts 1530–
   WI/FAc 1 Town accounts 1514–

Salisbury

Cathedral Archive

Mss 103, 189
Press I, Boxes 7, 9–15, 21

Press II, Accounts of the collectors of rent of the chapel of St Thomas
    Accounts of the procurator of St Thomas's with the masters of the fabric
        (1486–1539)
    Accounts of the masters of the fabric from the receipts of St Thomas's (1487–
        1538)
    Accounts of the shrine of St Osmund 1493–4
    Box 'Chancellor'
    Communar account rolls, from 1329
    Chapter act books: Register Corffe 1348–56
        Register Coman 1385–7
        Register Dunham 1387–94
        Register Holmes 1395–1402
        Register Draper 1402–5
        Register Viring 1408–13
        Register Harding 1419–35
        Register Hutchings 1440–6
        Register Burgh 1447–57
        Register Newton 1461–3
        Register Machon 1468–75
        Register Harwards 1497–1535
        Register Holt and Blacher 1538–63
    Fabric accounts 1464–1531
    Liber Evidentiarum C
Press III, Box 'Chancellor'
Press IV, C3, C4, C6, E1, E2, E3, 'Mixed', Boxes 13–15, Box 'Literae', Box O, Box
    'Testamenta', Box 'W'
Press V, 2, Inventory of the chantry of William Warwick

Trowbridge

Wiltshire Record Office

Episcopal registers
    Register Robert Wyvill 1330–75
    Register Ralph Erghum 1375–88
    Register John Waltham 1388–95
    Register Richard Mitford 1395–1407
    Register John Chandler 1417–26
    Register Robert Neville 1427–38
    Register William Aiscough 1438–50
    Register Richard Beauchamp 1450–81
    Register John Blythe 1494–9
    Register Edmund Audley 1502–24

Register Lorenzo Campeggio 1524–34
Liber Evidentiarum B D1/1/2
Registrum Rubrum D1/1/3
Statuta Ecclesia Sarum D1/1/4
Liber Niger D1/1/5
Visitations 1551, 1553, 1556, D1/43/1, 2
Subdean's register act book (1476–8) D4/3
Register Dean Chandler and Dean Sydenham D5/1

Borough records
  G22 Marlborough
    Court and general entry books: 1/12–16
    Deeds and wills: 1/102, 1/218, 1/236, 1/245, 1/246, 1/247
  G23 Salisbury corporation muniments
    Ledger A and B 1/1, 1/2
    Domesday Books 1/212–215: 1 (1350–66), 2 (1396–1413), 3 (1413–33), 4
      (1459–79)
    Chamberlains' accounts 1/44
    Tailors' guild 1/250, 1/251, 1/257, 1/258PC
    Deeds and wills: 1/96, 1/246, 150/11, 150/12, 150/88, 150/94, 150/98,
      150/103, 150/111
  G25 Wilton
    General entry book
    Accounts of the guild merchant 1/20
    Deeds and wills: 1/107, 1/216, 1/198–9, 1/128–9, 1/133, 1/136, 1/138, 1/
      139, 1/141/2, 1/205, 1/219
    Wilton abbey: 1/202–5
    Hospital St Giles and Anthony: 1/167
Other deeds and parish records
  Calne 2083/1
  Devizes 189, 1556
  Eston 1300 (Ailesbury MS)
  Maiden Bradley priory 1332
  Marlborough 1197/21, 1230/1, 1250
  Mere 865/313–316
  Salisbury 1446 (Trinity hospital), 1900, 1901
  Sherston 59
  Stanley abbey 473, 1213/1–17
  Steeple Ashton 697/1
  Wanborough 894/1
  Warminster 865/64, 1206
  Wilton nunnery 1422
Hungerford cartulary 490/1470
Other wills: 144/73, 212A/16, 492/284, 492/285, 1178/242

Winchester

Winchester college

Deeds: 1393, 4932, 4934, 4957, 5363, 5407, 19431, 19444, 19466/3, 20294

Winterslow

Rectory

Churchwardens' accounts 1542–

II PRINTED SOURCES

Abstracts of Feet of Fines relating to Wiltshire for the Reigns of Edward I and Edward II, ed. R. B. Pugh (WRS 1; Devizes, 1939).

Abstracts of Wiltshire Inquisitions Post Mortem, 1242–1326, ed. E. A. Fry (British Record Society, Index Library, 37, 1902–8).

Abstracts of Wiltshire Inquisitions Post Mortem, 1327–1377, ed. E. Stokes (British Record Society, Index Library, 48, 1909–14).

The Account Book of Beaulieu Abbey, ed. S. E. Hockey (Camden Society, fourth series, 16, 1975).

Accounts of the Obedientiars of Abingdon Abbey, ed. R. E. G. Kirk (Camden Society, 1892).

The Acts and Monuments of John Foxe, ed. S. R. Cautely and J. Pratt (8 vols.; London, 1853–70).

The Anglo-Saxon Chronicle, iv, ed. S. Taylor (Cambridge, 1983).

Annales Monastici, ed. H. R. Luard (Rolls Series; London, 1869).

Aubrey's Natural History of Wiltshire, ed. J. Britton (London, 1847).

A Biographical Register of the University of Oxford to A.D. 1500, ed. A. B. Emden (Oxford, 1957–9).

Calendar of Antrobus Deeds before 1625, ed. R. B. Pugh (WRS 3; Devizes, 1947).

Calendar of the Close Rolls Preserved in the Public Record Office 1227–1550 (62 vols.; London, 1902–55).

Calendar of Entries in the Papal Registers relating to Great Britain and Ireland: Papal Letters, 1198–1492, ed. W. H. Bliss, C. Johnson, J. A. Twemlow, and M. J. Haren (15 vols.; London, 1893–1978).

Calendar of the Patent Rolls Preserved in the Public Record Office 1216–1509 (54 vols.; London, 1891–1916).

The Canonization of St. Osmund, ed. A. R. Malden (WRS; Salisbury, 1901).

The Cartulary of Bradenstoke Priory, ed. V. C. M. London (WRS 35; Devizes, 1979).

The Cartulary of Cirencester Abbey, Gloucestershire, ed. C. Ross (3 vols.; London, 1964).

The Cartulary of St. Nicholas's Hospital Salisbury, ed. C. Wordsworth (WRS; Salisbury, 1902).

Ceremonies and Processions of the Cathedral of Salisbury, ed. C. Wordsworth (Cambridge, 1901).

Charters and Custumals of the Abbey of Holy Trinity of Caen, ed. M. Chibnall (London, 1982).

Charters and Documents Illustrating the History of the Cathedral City and Diocese of Salisbury in the Twelfth and Thirteenth Centuries, ed. W. Rich-Jones and W. D. Macray (Rolls Series; London, 1891).

Chronica Monasteri S. Albani: Thomae Walsingham, Quondam Monachi S. Albani, Historia Anglicana, ed. H. T. Riley (2 vols.; Rolls Series; London, 1863).

The Chronicle of England by John Capgrave, ed. F. C. Hingeston (Rolls Series; London, 1858).

The Chronicles of Stephen, Henry II and Richard, ed. R. Howlett (Rolls Series; London, 1885).

Chronicon Monasterii de Abingdon, ed. J. Stevenson (2 vols.; Rolls Series; London, 1858).

Chronicon Vilodunense, ed. W. H. Black and R. Colt-Hoare (London, 1830).

Churchwardens' Accounts of S. Edmund and S. Thomas, Sarum 1443–1702, ed. H. J. F. Swayne (WRS; Salisbury, 1896).

Councils and Synods with Other Documents relating to the English Church II (1205–1313), ed. F. M. Powicke and C. R. Cheney (2 vols.; Oxford, 1964).

Dives and Pauper, ed. P. H. Barnum (Early English Text Society, 275; London, 1976–80).

The Edington Cartulary, ed. J. H. Stevenson (WRS 42; Devizes, 1987).

English Historical Documents c.500–1042, ed. D. Whitelock, second edn. (London, 1979).

The Fabric Rolls of York Minster 1362–1550 (Surtees Society, 35; London, 1859).

Feudal Aids 1284–1431 (6 vols.; repr. London, 1973).

FOWLER, J., 'Sherborne All Hallows Church Wardens' Accounts', *NQSD* 23 (1939–42); 24 (1943–6).

FRY, E., 'Dorset Chantries', NQSD 27 (1906), 216–33; 28 (1907), 12–29; 30 (1909), 13–57; 31 (1909), 15–114.

Hemingsby's Register, ed. H. M. Chew (WRS 18; Devizes, 1962).

Historical Manuscripts Commission: Sixth Report (London, 1877).

Historical Manuscripts Commission (Series 55, 4; London, 1907).

Hugh Latimer: Works, ed. G. E. Corrie (Parker Society, Cambridge, 1845).

Instructions for Parish Priests by John Mirc, ed. E. Peacock and F. J. Furnivall (Early English Text Society, 31; London, 1868).

The Itinerary of John Leland in or about the Years 1535–1543, ed. L. Toulmin-Smith (11 parts in 6 vols.; London, 1908–10).

Jacob's Well: An English Treatise on the Cleansing of Man's Conscience (Early English Text Society, 75; London, 1900–1).

John Aubrey: Remaines of Gentilisme and Judaisme 1667–87, ed. J. Britten (London, 1881).

Lacock Charters, ed. K. Rogers (WRS 34; Devizes, 1977).

Letters and Papers, Foreign and Domestic, of the Reign of Henry VIII, ed. J. S. J. Brewer, J. Gairdner, and R. H. Brodie (21 vols. and addenda; London, 1862–1932).

Narratives of the Days of the Reformation, ed. J. G. Nichols (Camden Society, 1859).

A Perambulation of Kent by William Lambard 1570, new edn. (London, 1827).

Reading Abbey Cartularies, ed. B. R. Kemp (2 vols.; Camden Society, fourth series, 31, 33; 1986–7).

Reading Records: Diary of the Corporation, ed. J. M. Guilding, i (London, 1892).

The Register of Henry Chichele, ed. E. F. Jacob, ii (Canterbury and York Society, 42; Oxford, 1937).

The Register of John Chandler Dean of Salisbury 1404–17, ed. T. C. B. Timmins (WRS 39; Devizes, 1984).

The Register of John Pecham, Archbishop of Canterbury 1279–92, ed. F. M. Davis (Canterbury and York Society, 44; Torquay, 1976).

The Register of Robert Hallum, Bishop of Salisbury 1407–17, ed. J. M. Horn (Canterbury and York Society, 72; Torquay, 1982).

The Registers of Roger Martival Bishop of Salisbury 1315–30, Canterbury and York Society (55), vol. i, ed. K. Edwards (Oxford, 1969); (57) vol. ii, ed. C. R. Elrington (Oxford, 1973); (59) vol. iii, ed. S. Reynolds (Torquay, 1965); (141) vol. iv, ed. K. Edwards and D. M. Owen (Torquay, 1975); (138) vol. v (vol. ii *bis*), ed. C. R. Elrington (Torquay, 1972).

The Register of S. Osmund, ed. W. H. Rich-Jones (2 vols.; Rolls Series; London, 1883).

The Register of Thomas Langton, Bishop of Salisbury 1485–93, ed. D. P. Wright (Canterbury and York Society, 74; 1985).

Registrum Epistolarum Fratris Johannis Peckham Archiepiscopi Cantuarensis, ed. C. T. Martin (3 vols.; Rolls Series, 77; London, 1882–5).

Registrum Malmesburiense, ed. J. S. Brewer and C. T. Martin (2 vols.; Rolls Series; London, 1879–80).

Registrum Simonis de Gandavo, ed. C. T. Flower and M. C. B. Dawes (2 vols.; Canterbury and York Society, 40, 41; Oxford, 1934).

Registrum Wiltoniense, ed. R. Colt-Hoare (London, 1927).

Remains of Miles Coverdale, ed. G. Pearson (Parker Society, Cambridge, 1846).

S. Editha sive Chronicon Vilodunense im Wiltshire Dialekt, ed. C. Horstmann (Heilbronn, 1883).

The Sarum Missal, ed. J. Wickham-Legg (Oxford, 1916).

A Small Household of the XVth Century, being the Account Book of Munden's Chantry, Bridport, ed. K. L. Wood-Legh (Manchester, 1956).

Somerset Medieval Wills 1383–1500, ed. F. W. Weaver (Somerset Record Society, 16; 1901); *1501–1530* (19; 1903); *1531–1558* (21; 1905).

The Stacions of Rome, ed. F. J. Furnivall (Early English Text Society, 13; London, 1867).

Statuta et Consuetudines Ecclesiae Cathedralis Sarisburiense, ed. C. Wordsworth and D. Macleane (Salisbury, 1915).

'The Stoks of Seen' Church', *Wilts. Notes & Queries*, 2 (1898), 528–32.

Taxatio Ecclesiastica Angliae et Walliae Auctoritate P. Nicholai IV circa A.D. 1291, ed. T. Astle, S. Ayscough, and J. Caley (London, 1802).

Thomas Gascoigne: Loci e Libro Veritatum, ed. J. E. T. Rogers (Oxford, 1881).

The Tropenell Cartulary, ed. J. S. Davies (2 vols.; WRS, 1908).

Tudor Economic Documents, ed. R. H. Tawney and E. Power, iii (London, 1924).

The Use of Sarum, ed. W. Frere (Cambridge, 1898).

Valor Ecclesiasticus temp. Henrici VIII Auctoritate Regia Institutio, i and ii, ed. J. Caley and J. Hunter (Record Commission; London, 1814).

Visitations of Churches belonging to St. Paul's Cathedral 1249–52, ed. W. Sparrow-Simpson (Camden Society, new series, 53; Camden Miscellany, 9; 1895).

Visitations of Churches belonging to St. Paul's Cathedral in 1297 and 1458, ed. W. Sparrow-Simpson (Camden Society, new series, 55; 1895).

Visitations in the Diocese of Lincoln 1517–31, ed. A. H. Thompson, i (Lincoln Record Society, 33; Hereford, 1940).

Willelmi Malmesbiriensis Monachi: De Gestis Pontificum Anglorum, ed. N. E. S. A. Hamilton (Rolls Series; London, 1870).

William Langland: The Vision of Piers Plowman, ed. A. V. C. Schmidt (London, 1982).

Wiltshire: The Topographical Collections of John Aubrey, ed. J. E. Jackson (Devizes, 1862).

The Works of Thomas Deloney, ed. F. O. Man (Oxford, 1912).

Wykeham's Register, ed. T. F. Kirby (2 vols.; Hampshire Record Society; 1896–9).

III SECONDARY WORKS

ALLRIDGE, N., 'Loyalty and Identity in Chester Parishes', in S. J. Wright (ed.), *Parish, Church and People: Local Studies in Lay Religion 1350–1750* (London, 1988), 85–124.

ARCHER, I. W., *The Pursuit of Stability: Social Relations in Elizabethan London* (Cambridge, 1991).

ASHMOLE, E. *The Antiquities of Berkshire* (3 vols.; London, 1719).

ASTON, M., *Lollards and Reformers: Images and Literacy in Late Medieval Religion* (London, 1984).

—— 'Wyclif and the Vernacular', in A. Hudson and M. Wilks (eds.), *From Ockham to Wyclif* (Studies in Church History, subsidia 5; Oxford, 1987), 281–330.

—— *England's Iconoclasts*, i. *Laws against Images* (Oxford, 1988).

ASTON, M., 'Segregation in Church', in W. J. Sheils and D. Wood (eds.), *Women in the Church* (Studies in Church History, 23; Oxford, 1990), 237–94.

BAKER, T. H., 'Notes on Some Wiltshire Merchant Marks', *WAM* 36 (1909), 324–8.

BARFIELD, S., *Thatcham, Berkshire, and its Manors* (2 vols.; London, 1901).

BARKER, W. L., 'Hungerford', *WAM* 11 (1868), 140–59.

BARRON, C. M., 'The Parish Fraternities of Medieval London', in C. M. Barron and C. Harper-Bill (eds.), *The Church in Pre-Reformation Society: Essays in Honour of F. R. H. Du Boulay* (London, 1985), 13–37.

BEER, B. L., *Rebellion and Riot: Popular Disorder in England during the Reign of Edward VI* (Kent, Ohio, 1982).

BEER, J. DE, 'Bedevaart- en Pelgrimplaatjes', in *Gedenkboek Frans Claes Museum 'De Gulden Spoor' te Antwerpen* (Antwerp, 1932), 53–69.

BENSON, R., and HATCHER, H., *Old and New Sarum or Salisbury* (London, 1834).

BERESFORD, M., *The Lost Villages of Medieval England*, fourth edn. (London, 1963).

BETTEY, J. H., *The Suppression of the Monasteries in the West Country* (Gloucester, 1989).

BIRCH, W. DE G., 'Collections towards the History of the Cistercian Abbey of Stanley', *WAM* 15 (1875), 239–307.

BLAIR, J., 'Saint Beornwald of Bampton', *Oxoniensia*, 49 (1984), 47–55.

—— 'Secular Minster Churches in Domesday Book', in P. Sawyer (ed.), *Domesday Book: A Reassessment* (London, 1985), 104–42.

—— 'Local Churches in Domesday Book and Before', in J. C. Holt (ed.), *Domesday Studies* (Bury St Edmunds, 1987), 265–78.

—— *Landholding in Surrey* (London, 1991).

—— (ed.), *Minsters and Parish Churches: The Local Church in Transition 950–1200* (Oxford Univ. Committee for Archaeology, Monograph 17; 1988).

BOLTON, J. L., *The Medieval English Economy 1150–1500* (London, 1980).

BONENFANT, P., *Hôpitaux et bienfaisance publique dans les anciens Pays-Bas des origines à la fin du XVIIIᵉ siècle* (Brussels, 1965).

BOSSY, J., 'The Mass as a Social Institution 1200–1700', *Past and Present*, 100 (1983), 29–61.

—— *Christianity in the West, 1400–1700* (Oxford, 1985).

BOUARD, M. DE, 'De la confrérie pieuse au métier organisé: la fraternité des fèvres de Caen (fin du XIIᵉ siècle)', *Annales de Normandie*, 7 (1957), 165–77.

BOWLES, W. L., and NICHOLS, J. G., *Annals and Antiquities of Lacock Abbey* (London, 1835).

BRAKESPEAR, H., 'Lacock Abbey', *WAM* 31 (1900–1), 197–240.

—— 'Malmesbury Abbey', *WAM* 38 (1914), 458–97.

BRIDBURY, A. R., *Economic Growth: England in the Later Middle Ages* (London, 1962).

BRIDGEN, S., 'Religion and Social Obligation in Early Sixteenth-Century London', *Past and Present*, 103 (1984), 67–112.

—— *London and the Reformation* (Oxford, 1989).

BROOKE, C. N. L., 'The Missionary at Home: The Church and the Towns, 1000–1250', in G. J. Cuming (ed.), *The Mission of the Church and the Propagation of the Faith* (Studies in Church History, 6; Cambridge, 1970), 59–83.

—— *Medieval Church and Society: Collected Essays* (London, 1971).

BURGESS, C. R., 'Chantries in Fifteenth-Century Bristol', D.Phil. thesis (Oxford, 1982).

—— ' "For the Increase of Divine Service": Chantries in the Parish in Late Medieval Bristol', *JEH* 36 (1985), 46–65.

—— ' "By Quick and by Dead": Wills and Pious Provision in Late Medieval Bristol', *EHR* 102 (1987), 837–58.

—— 'A Service for the Dead: The Form and Function of the Anniversary in Late Medieval Bristol', *Transactions of the Bristol and Gloucestershire Archaeological Society*, 105 (1987), 167–91.

—— ' "A Fond Thing Vainly Invented": An Essay on Purgatory and Pious Motive in Late Medieval England', in S. J. Wright (ed.), *Parish, Church and People: Local Studies in Lay Religion, 1350–1750* (London, 1988), 56–84.

—— 'Late Medieval Wills and Pious Convention: Testamentary Evidence Reconsidered', in M. A. Hicks (ed.), *Profit, Piety and the Professions in Late Medieval England* (Gloucester, 1990), 14–33.

—— and KUMIN, B., 'Penitential Bequests and Parish Regimes in Late Medieval England', *JEH* 44 (1993), 610–30.

BYFORD, M. S., 'The Price of Protestantism: Assessing the Impact of Religious Change in Elizabethan Essex: The Case of Heydon and Colchester 1558–1594', D.Phil. thesis (Oxford, 1988).

CAMPBELL, J., 'The Church in the Anglo-Saxon Towns', in D. Baker (ed.), *The Church in Town and Countryside* (Studies in Church History, 16; Oxford, 1979), 119–35.

CARPENTER, C., 'The Religion of the Gentry in Fifteenth-Century England', in D. Williams (ed.), *England in the Fifteenth Century: Proceedings of the 1986 Harlaxton Symposium* (Bury St Edmunds, 1987), 53–74.

CARPENTER, D. A., 'Was There a Crisis of the Knightly Class in the Thirteenth Century? The Oxfordshire Evidence', *EHR* 95 (1980), 721–52.

CARR, D. H., 'The Problem of Urban Patriciates: Office Holders in Fifteenth-Century Salisbury', *WAM* 83 (1990), 118–35.

CARUS-WILSON, E. M., 'Evidence of Industrial Growth on Some Fifteenth-Century Manors', *Economic History Review*, second series, 12 (1959–60), 151–67.

—— and COLEMAN, O., *England's Export Trade 1275–1547* (Oxford, 1963).

CATTO, J. I., 'Religion and the English Nobility in the Later Fourteenth Century', in H. Lloyd Jones, V. Pearl, and B. Worden (eds.), *History and Imagination: Essays in Honour of H. R. Trevor-Roper* (London, 1981), 43–53.

—— 'John Wyclif and the Cult of the Eucharist', in K. Walsh and D. Wood (eds.), *The Bible in the Medieval World* (Studies in Church History, subsidia 4; Oxford, 1985), 269–86.

CATTO, J. I., 'Religious Change under Henry V', in G. L. Harriss (ed.), *Henry V: The Practice of Kingship* (Oxford, 1985), 97–115.

CHAMBERS, E. K., *The Medieval Stage* (Oxford, 1903).

CHENEY, C. R., *From Becket to Langton: English Church Government 1170–1223* (Manchester, 1956).

—— 'Rules for the Observance of Feast Days in Medieval England', *Bulletin of the Institute of Historical Research*, 34 (1961), 118–47.

—— *Hubert Walter* (London, 1967).

—— *Medieval Texts and Studies* (Oxford, 1973).

CHIBNALL, M., *Charters and Custumals of the Abbey of Holy Trinity of Caen* (London, 1982).

CHIFFOLEAU, J., *La Comptabilité de l'au-delà: les hommes, la mort et la religion dans la région d'Avignon à la fin du moyen âge (vers 1320–vers 1480)* (École Française de Rome, 1980).

CHRISTIAN, W. A., *Local Religion in Sixteenth-Century Spain* (Princeton, NJ, 1981).

CLARK, P., *The English Alehouse: A Social History 1200–1830* (London, 1983).

CLARK-MAXWELL, W. G., 'The Outfit for the Profession of an Austin Canoness at Lacock Wiltshire in the Year 1395', *Archaeological Journal*, 69 (1912), 117–24.

CLAY, R. M., *The Medieval Hospitals of England* (London, 1909).

—— *The Hermits and Anchorites of England* (London, 1914).

COATES, C., *The History and Antiquities of Reading* (London, 1820).

COLLINSON, P., *The Religion of Protestants: The Church in English Society 1559–1625* (Oxford, 1982).

—— *Godly People: Essays on English Protestantism and Puritanism* (London, 1983).

—— *The Birthpangs of Protestant England: Religious and Cultural Changes in the Sixteenth and Seventeenth Centuries* (Cambridge, 1988).

COLT-HOARE, R., *A Modern History of Wiltshire* (9 vols.; London, 1822–43).

CONSTABLE, G., 'Resistance to Tithes in Late Medieval London', *JEH* 13 (1962), 172–85.

COORNAERT, E., 'Les Ghildes médiévales (Vᵉ–XIVᵉ siècle)', *Revue historique*, 199 (1948), 22–55, 208–43.

CROSS, C., ' "Great Reasoners in Scripture": The Activities of Women Lollards 1380–1530', in D. Baker (ed.), *Medieval Women* (Studies in Church History, subsidia 1; Oxford, 1978), 359–80.

—— 'Monasticism and Society in the Diocese of York 1520–40', *TRHS*, fifth series, 38 (1988), 131–45.

CUNNINGTON, B. H., *Some Annals of the Borough of Devizes 1555–1791* (2 vols.; Devizes, 1925).

DAVIES, R. G., 'The Episcopate', in C. H. Clough (ed.), *Profession, Vocation and Culture in Later Medieval England* (Liverpool, 1982).

—— 'Lollardy and Locality', *TRHS*, sixth series, 1 (1991), 191–212.

DAVIS, G. R. C., *Medieval Cartularies of Great Britain* (London, 1958).

DAVIS, J. F., *Heresy and Reformation in the South-east of England 1520–1559* (London, 1983).

DAVIS, N. Z., 'Some Tasks and Themes in the Study of Popular Religion', in C. Trinkaus and H. Oberman (eds.), *The Pursuit of Holiness in Late Medieval and Renaissance Religion* (Leiden, 1974), 307–36.

DELARUELLE, E. F., CABANDE, E.-R., and OURILAC, P., *L'Église au temps du grand schisme et la crise conciliaire* (Histoire de l'église, xiv, ed. A. Fliche *et al.*) (Paris, 1962–4).

DE MAITRE, L., 'The Description and Diagnosis of Leprosy by Fourteenth-Century Physicians', *Bulletin of the History of Medicine*, 59 (1985), 327–44.

DICKENS, A. G., *Lollards and Protestants in the Diocese of York 1509–1558* (London, 1959).

—— *The English Reformation* (London, 1964).

—— 'The Early Experience of Protestantism in England 1520–1558', *Archiv für Reformationgeschichte*, 78 (1987), 187–222.

DICKINSON, J. C., *The Later Middle Ages* (London, 1979).

DOBSON, R. B., 'The Foundation of Perpetual Chantries by the Citizens of Medieval York', in G. J. Cuming (ed.), *The Province of York* (Studies in Church History, 4; Leiden, 1967), 22–38.

—— *Durham Priory 1400–1500* (Cambridge, 1973).

—— 'Urban Decline in Late Medieval England', *TRHS*, fifth series, 27 (1977), 1–22.

—— (ed.), *Church, Politics and Patronage in the Fifteenth Century* (Gloucester, 1984).

DODSWORTH, W., *An Historical Account of the Episcopal and Cathedral Church of Salisbury* (Salisbury, 1814).

DREW, C., 'Early Parochial Organisation in England: Origins of the Office of Churchwarden', *Borthwick Papers*, 7 (1954).

DUFFY, E., 'Holy Maydens, Holy Wyves: The Cult of Women Saints in Fifteenth- and Sixteenth-Century England', in W. J. Sheils and D. Wood (eds.), *Women in the Church* (Studies in Church History, 23; Oxford, 1990), 175–96.

—— *The Stripping of the Altars: Traditional Religion in England 1400–1580* (New Haven, Conn., 1992).

DUGDALE, W., *Monasticon Anglicanum* (6 vols.; London, 1817–30).

DUPARC, P., 'Confréries du Saint-Esprit et communautés d'habitants au moyen âge', *Revue historique du droit français et étranger*, fourth series, 37 (1958), 349–67.

DYER, A., *Decline and Growth: English Towns 1400–1640* (London, 1991).

DYER, C. C., *Standards of Living in the Later Middle Ages: Social Change in England c.1200–1520* (Cambridge, 1989).

—— 'Were There Any Capitalists in Fifteenth-Century England?', in J. Kermode (ed.), *Enterprise and Individuals in Fifteenth-Century England* (Stroud, 1991), 1–24.

EDWARDS, K. L., *The English Secular Cathedrals in the Middle Ages*, second edn. (Manchester, 1967).

ELTON, G. R., *Policy and Police: The Enforcement of the Reformation in the Age of Cromwell* (Cambridge, 1972).

ELTON, G. R., *Reform and Reformation, England, 1509–1558* (London, 1977).

FAITH, R., 'Berkshire: Fourteenth and Fifteenth Centuries', in P. D. A. Harvey (ed.), *The Peasant Land Market in Medieval England* (Oxford, 1984), 106–77.

FINUCANE, R. C., *Miracles and Pilgrims: Popular Beliefs in Medieval England* (London, 1977).

FLEMING, P. W., 'Charity, Faith and the Gentry of Kent 1422–1529', in A. J. Pollard (ed.), *Property and Politics: Essays in Late Medieval English History* (Gloucester, 1984), 36–53.

FLETCHER, J. M. J., *The Boy Bishop at Salisbury and Elsewhere* (Salisbury, 1924).

FOWLER, J., *Medieval Sherborne* (Dorchester, 1951).

GALPERN, A. N., 'The Legacy of Late Medieval Religion in Sixteenth-Century Champagne', in C. Trinkaus and H. Oberman (eds.), *The Pursuit of Holiness in Late Medieval and Renaissance Religion* (Leiden, 1974), 141–76.

GEERTZ, C., *The Interpretation of Cultures* (London, 1973).

GERBERT, M.-C., 'Les Confréries religieuses à Cacères de 1467 à 1523', *Mélanges de la casa de Velazquez*, 7 (1971), 75–113.

GEREMECK, B., *The Margins of Society in Late Medieval Paris* (Cambridge, 1987).

GITTINGS, C., *Death, Burial and the Individual in Early Modern England* (London, 1984).

GODFREY, C. J., 'The Chantries of Mere and their Priests', *WAM* 55 (1953), 153–60.

GRAHAM, R., 'An Appeal about 1175 for the Building Fund of St. Paul's Cathedral', *Journal of the British Archaeological Association*, third series, 10 (1945–7), 73–6.

GREYERZ, K. VAN (ed.), *Religion and Society in Early Modern Europe 1500–1800* (London, 1983).

GRIFFTHS, R. A., *The Reign of Henry VI* (London, 1981).

HAIGH, C. (ed.), *The English Reformation Revised* (Cambridge, 1987).

HAINES, R. M., *Ecclesia Anglicana: Studies in the English Church of the Later Middle Ages* (Toronto, 1989).

HARE, J. N., 'Lords and Tenants in Wiltshire *c.*1380–*c.*1520', Ph.D. thesis (London, 1975).

—— 'Durrington: A Chalkland Village in the Late Middle Ages', *WAM* 74 (1981), 137–47.

—— 'The Wiltshire Risings of 1450: Politics and Economic Discontent in Mid-Fifteenth-Century England', *Southern History*, 4 (1982), 13–31.

HARTRIDGE, R. A. R., *A History of Vicarages in the Middle Ages* (Cambridge, 1930).

HARVEY, B., *Westminster Abbey and its Estates in the Middle Ages* (Oxford, 1977).

—— *Living and Dying in England, 1100–1540: The Monastic Experience* (Oxford, 1993).

HARVEY, I. M. W., *Jack Cade's Rebellion of 1450* (Oxford, 1991).

HASKINS, C., 'The Church of St. Thomas of Canterbury, Salisbury', *WAM* 36 (1909), 1–12.

—— 'The Original Bederoll of the Salisbury Tailors' Guild', *WAM* 39 (1916), 375–9.

—— *The Ancient Trade Guilds and Companies of Salisbury* (Salisbury, 1917).

HEATH, P., 'Urban Piety in the Late Middle Ages: The Evidence of Hull Wills', in R. B. Dobson (ed.), *Church, Politics and Patronage in the Fifteenth Century* (Gloucester, 1984), 209–29.

HENDERSON, J., 'Confraternities and the Church in Late Medieval Florence', in W. J. Sheils and D. Wood (eds.), *Voluntary Religion* (Studies in Church History, 23; Worcester, 1986), 69–83.

HICKS, M. A., 'St. Katherine's Hospital Heytesbury: Prehistory, Foundations and the Refoundation 1408–1472', *WAM* 78 (1984), 62–9.

—— 'Chantries, Obits and Almshouses: The Hungerford Foundations 1325–1478', in C. M. Barron and C. Harper-Bill (eds.), *The Church in Pre-Reformation Society* (London, 1985), 123–42.

—— 'The Piety of Margaret Lady Hungerford', *JEH* 38 (1987), 19–38.

HILTON, R. H., *The English Peasantry in the Later Middle Ages* (Oxford, 1975).

—— *An Inventory of Historical Monuments: The County of Dorset* (5 vols.; Royal Commission on Historical Monuments; London, 1970–85).

HOLLAENDER, A., 'The Doom Painting of St. Thomas of Canterbury, Salisbury', *WAM* 50 (1944), 351–70.

HOSKINS, W. G., *The Age of Plunder: King Henry's England 1500–41* (London, 1976).

HOULBROOKE, R., *Church Courts and the People during the English Reformation 1520–70* (Oxford, 1979).

HUDSON, A., 'A Lollard Mass', *Journal of Theological Studies*, 23 (1972), 407–19.

—— 'The Examination of Lollards', *Bulletin of the Institute of Historical Research*, 46 (1973), 145–59.

—— *Lollards and their Books* (London, 1985).

—— *The Premature Reformation: Wyclifite Texts and Lollard History* (Oxford, 1988).

HUGHES, J., *Pastors and Visionaries: Religion and Secular Life in Late Medieval Yorkshire* (Woodbridge, 1988).

HUTCHINS, J., *The History and Antiquities of the County of Dorset* (4 vols.; Westminster, 1861–70; Trowbridge, 1973).

HUTTON, R., 'The Local Impact of the Tudor Reformations', in C. Haigh (ed.), *The English Reformation Revised* (Cambridge, 1987), 114–38.

INGRAM, M., *Church Courts, Sex and Marriage in England 1570–1640* (Cambridge, 1987).

JACKSON, J. E., 'Kington St. Michael', *WAM* 4 (1858), 36–124.

—— 'Ancient Statutes of Heytesbury Almshouse', *WAM* 11 (1868), 289–308.

JACOB, E. F., *Essays in the Conciliar Epoch* (Manchester, 1943).

JAMES, M., 'Ritual, Drama and Social Body in the Late Medieval English Town', *Past and Present*, 98 (1983), 3–29.

JONES, W. H., 'Terumer's Chantry at Trowbridge', *WAM* 10 (1867), 247–52.

JORDAN, W. K., *Philanthropy in England 1480–1660: A Study of the Changing Pattern of English Social Aspirations* (London, 1959).
—— *Edward VI: The Young King* (London, 1968).
—— *Edward VI: The Threshold of Power* (London, 1970).
KEEN, M. H., 'Wyclif, the Bible and Transubstantiation', in A. Kenny (ed.), *Wyclif in his Times* (Oxford, 1986), 1–16.
KEENE, D., *A Survey of Medieval Winchester* (2 vols.; Oxford, 1985).
KEISER, G. R., 'The Progress of Purgatory: Visions of the Afterlife in Late Medieval English Literature', *Analecta Cartusiana*, 117 (1987), 72–100.
KEMP, B., 'The Miracles of the Hand of St. James', *BAJ* 65 (1970), 1–19.
KEMPSON, E. G. H., 'A Shropshire Guild at Work in Wiltshire', *WAM* 57 (1958–60), 50–5.
KERRY, C., *A History of the Municipal Church of St. Laurence Reading* (Reading, 1893).
KIGHTLY, C., 'The Early Lollards: A Survey of Popular Lollard Activity in England, 1382–1428', Ph.D. thesis (York, 1975).
KINGSFORD, C. L., *English Historical Literature in the Fifteenth Century* (Oxford, 1913).
KITCHING, C. J., 'The Quest for Concealed Lands in the Reign of Elizabeth I', *TRHS* 24 (1974), 63–78.
KITE, E., 'Baynard Monuments in Lacock Church', *WAM* 4 (1858), 1–7.
—— *The Monumental Brasses of Wiltshire* (London, 1860).
KNOWLES, D., *The Religious Orders in England* (3 vols.; Cambridge, 1948–59).
—— *The Monastic Orders in England*, second edn. (Cambridge, 1963).
KREIDER, A., *English Chantries: The Road to Dissolution* (London, 1979).
LANDER, J. R., *Government and Community: England 1450–1509* (London, 1980).
LAWRENCE, C. H., *Medieval Monasticism: Forms of Religious Life in Western Europe in the Middle Ages* (London, 1984).
LE BRAS, G., 'Les Confréries chrétiennes: problèmes et propositions', *Revue historique du droit français et étranger*, fourth series, 19–21 (1940–2), 310–63.
LEFF, G., *Heresy in the Later Middle Ages* (Manchester, 1967).
LE GOFF, J., *La Naissance du purgatoire* (Paris, 1981).
LENNARD, R. L., 'Two Peasant Contributions to Church Endowment', *EHR* 67 (1952), 230–3.
—— *Rural England 1086–1135: A Study of Society and Agrarian Conditions* (Oxford, 1959).
LITTLE, F., *A Monument to Christian Munificence; or An Account of the Holy Cross and the Hospital of Christ Church in Abingdon* (Oxford, 1871).
LOGAN, F. D., *Excommunication and the Secular Arm in Medieval England* (Toronto, 1968).
MacCULLOCH, D., *Suffolk and the Tudors: Politics and Religion in an English County, 1500–1600* (Oxford, 1986).
McFARLANE, K. B., *John Wycliffe and the Beginnings of English Nonconformity* (London, 1952).

—— *Lancastrian Kings and Lollard Knights* (Oxford, 1972).

—— *The Nobility of Late Medieval England* (Oxford, 1973).

McHardy, A. K., 'The Dissemination of Wyclif's Ideas', in A. Hudson and M. Wilks (eds.), *From Ockham to Wyclif* (Studies in Church History, subsidia 5; Oxford, 1987), 361–8.

McIntosh, M. K., 'Local Responses to the Poor in Late Medieval and Tudor England', *Continuity and Change*, 3/2 (1988), 209–45.

McNeill, J. T., and Gamer, H. M., *Medieval Handbooks of Penance* (New York, 1938, repr. 1963).

McRee, B., 'Religious Guilds and Regulation of Behaviour in Late Medieval Towns', in J. Rosenthal and C. Richmond (eds.), *People, Politics and Community in the Later Middle Ages* (Gloucester, 1987), 108–22.

Malden, A. R., 'A Contemporary Poem on the Translation of the Cathedral from Old to New Sarum', *WAM* 30 (1899), 210–17.

Mann, J., *Chaucer and Medieval Estates Satire* (Cambridge, 1973).

Manning, B. L., *The People's Faith in the Time of Wyclif* (Oxford, 1929).

Margrett, E., 'St. Anne's Well and Chapel, Caversham', *BAJ* 12 (1906), 25–7.

Martin, J., 'The People of Reading and the Reformation 1520–1570', Ph.D. thesis (Reading, 1987).

Mason, E., 'The Role of the English Parishioner 1100–1500', *JEH* 27 (1976), 17–29.

Moffat, J. M., *The History of the Town and Abbey of Malmesbury* (Tetbury, 1805).

Mollat, M., *Les Pauvres au moyen âge* (Paris, 1978).

Moorman, J. R. H., *Church Life in England in the Thirteenth Century* (Cambridge, 1946).

Morrill, J., 'The Ecology of Allegiance', *Journal of British Studies*, 26 (1987), 456–67.

Morris, C., 'Equestrio Ordo: Chivalry as Vocation in the Twelfth Century', in D. Baker (ed.), *Religious Motivation: Biographical and Sociological Problems of the Church Historian* (Studies in Church History, 15; Oxford, 1978).

Morris, R. K., *The Church in British Archaeology* (Council for British Archaeology, Research Report 47; 1983).

—— 'The Church in the Countryside: Two Lines of Inquiry', in D. Hooke (ed.), *Medieval Villages* (Oxford Univ. Committee for Archaeology, Monograph 5; Oxford, 1985), 47–60.

—— *Churches in the Landscape* (London, 1989).

Munro-Cautley, H., *Suffolk Churches and their Treasures*, fifth edn. (Woodbridge, 1982).

Nash, A. E., 'Population Change in Late Medieval Wiltshire', Ph.D. thesis (Cambridge, 1984).

Nevill, E. R., 'Salisbury in 1455', *WAM* 37 (1911), 66–91.

Nocklen, C. von, 'Another Kind of Saint: A Lollard Perception of John Wyclif', in A. Hudson and M. Wilks (eds.), *From Ockham to Wyclif* (Studies in Church History, subsidia 5; Oxford, 1987), 429–43.

ORME, N., *Education in the West of England, 1066–1548* (Exeter, 1976).

OWEN, D. M., *Church and Society in Medieval Lincolnshire* (Lincoln, 1981).

OWST, G., *Literature and the Pulpit in Medieval England* (Oxford, 1961).

PALLISER, D. M., 'The Trade Guilds of Tudor York', in P. Clark and P. Slack (eds.), *Crisis and Order in English Towns 1500–1700: Essays in Urban History* (London, 1972), 86–116.

PENN, K. J., *Historic Towns in Dorset* (Dorset Natural History and Archaeological Society, Monograph series, 1; Dorchester, 1980).

PEVSNER, N., *The Buildings of England: Berkshire* (London, 1966).

—— and CHERRY, B., *The Buildings of England: Wiltshire*, second edn. (London, 1975).

—— and NEWMAN, J., *The Buildings of England: Dorset* (London, 1972).

PFAFF, R. W., *New Liturgical Feasts in Late Medieval England* (Oxford, 1970).

PHYTHIAN-ADAMS, C., 'Ceremony and the Citizen: The Communal Year at Coventry 1450–1550', in P. Clark and P. Slack (eds.), *Crisis and Order in English Towns 1500–1700: Essays in Urban History* (London, 1972), 52–85.

—— 'Urban Decay in Late Medieval England', in P. Abrams and E. A. Wrigley (eds.), *Towns and Societies: Essays in Economic History and Historical Sociology* (Cambridge, 1978), 159–85.

—— *Desolation of a City: Coventry and the Urban Crisis of the Late Middle Ages* (Cambridge, 1979).

PLATT, C., *The Parish Churches of Medieval England* (London, 1981).

—— *Abbeys and Priories of Medieval England* (London, 1984).

PLUMB, D. J., 'John Foxe and the Later Lollards of the Thames Valley', Ph.D. thesis (Cambridge, 1987).

PONTING, C. E., 'Notes on Churches', *WAM* 24 (1889), 154–6.

—— 'The Parish Church of S. Michael, Mere', *WAM* 29 (1896), 20–70.

POSTAN, M. M., *Essays on Medieval Agriculture and General Problems of the Medieval Economy* (Cambridge, 1973).

POWELL, J. W., 'A Sketch of the History of Hill Deverell', *WAM* 27 (1894), 245–60.

POWER, E., *Medieval English Nunneries* (Cambridge, 1922).

—— *The Wool Trade in English Medieval History* (London, 1941).

PRESTON, A. E., *The Church and Parish of St. Nicholas, Abingdon* (Oxford Historical Society, 99; 1935).

—— 'The Fourteenth-Century Painted Ceiling of St. Helen's Church at Abingdon', *BAJ* 40 (1936), 115–45.

RABAN, S., *Mortmain Legislation and the English Church 1279–1500* (Cambridge, 1982).

RABY, F. J. E., 'The Tomb of St. Osmund of Salisbury', *Archaeological Journal*, 104 (1947).

RAMSAY, G. D., *The Wiltshire Woollen Industry in the Sixteenth and Seventeenth Centuries* (London, 1965).

REDDWAY, T. F., 'The London Goldsmiths *c*.1500', *TRHS*, fifth series, 12 (1962), 49–62.

REYNOLDS, B., 'Late Medieval Dorset', MA thesis (London, 1958).

REYNOLDS, S., *An Introduction to the History of English Medieval Towns* (Oxford, 1977).

—— *Kingdoms and Communities in Western Europe 900–1300* (Oxford, 1984).

RICHMOND, C., 'Religion and the Fifteenth-Century English Gentleman', in R. B. Dobson (ed.), *The Church, Politics and Patronage in the Fifteenth Century* (Gloucester, 1984), 193–208.

—— 'The English Gentry and Religion *c*.1500', in C. Harper-Bill (ed.), *Religious Belief and Ecclesiastical Careers in Late Medieval England* (Woodbridge, 1991), 121–50.

ROCK, D., *The Church of our Fathers*, ed. G. W. Hart and W. H. Frere (4 vols.; London, 1903–4).

ROGERS, K. H., 'Salisbury', in M. D. Lobel (ed.), *Historic Towns*, i (London, 1969).

ROSSER, G., 'The Anglo-Saxon Guilds', in J. Blair (ed.), *Minsters and Parish Churches: The Local Church in Transition 950–1200* (Oxford Univ. Committee for Archaeology, Monograph 17; 1988), 31–5.

—— 'Communities of Parish and Guild in the Later Middle Ages', in S. J. Wright (ed.), *Parish, Church and People: Local Studies in Lay Religion 1350–1750* (London, 1988), 29–55.

—— *Medieval Westminster 1200–1540* (Oxford, 1989).

—— 'Parochial Conformity and Voluntary Religion in Late Medieval England', *TRHS*, sixth series, I (1991), 173–89.

Royal Commission on Historical Monuments, *Ancient and Historical Monuments in the City of Salisbury*, i (London, 1980).

Royal Commission on Historical Monuments, *The County of Dorset* (5 vols.; Edinburgh, 1970–2).

RUBIN, M., 'Corpus Christi Fraternities and Late Medieval Piety', in W. J. Sheils and D. Wood (eds.), *Voluntary Religion* (Studies in Church History, 23; Worcester, 1986), 97–109.

—— *Charity and Community in Medieval Cambridge* (Cambridge, 1987).

—— *Corpus Christi: The Eucharist in Late Medieval Culture* (Cambridge, 1991).

RUSHFORTH, G. McN., 'The Sacrament Window in Crudwell Church', *WAM* 45 (1930), 68–72.

SALZMAN, L. F., *Buildings in England: Down to 1540*, second edn. (Oxford, 1967).

SANCHEZ-HERRERO, J., *Las Diocesis del Reino de León, Siglos XIV y XV* (León, 1978).

SAUL, N., 'The Religious Sympathies of the Gentry in Gloucestershire 1200–1500', *Transactions of the Bristol and Gloucester Archaeological Society*, 98 (1980), 99–112.

—— *Scenes from Provincial Life: Knightly Families in Sussex 1280–1400* (Oxford, 1986).

SAVINE, A., *English Monasteries on the Eve of the Reformation* (Oxford Studies in Social and Legal History, 1; Oxford, 1909).

SCARISBRICK, J. J., *The Reformation and the English People* (Oxford, 1984).

SCRIBNER, R. W., *For the Sake of Simple Folk: Popular Propaganda for the German Reformations* (Cambridge, 1981).

SHEILD, I. T., 'The Reformation in the Diocese of Salisbury, 1547–62', B.Litt. thesis (Oxford, 1960).

SLACK, P., *Poverty and Politics in Tudor and Stuart England* (London, 1988).

—— 'Poverty and Politics in Salisbury, 1597–1666', in P. Clark and P. Slack (eds.), *Crisis and Order in English Towns 1500–1700: Essays in Urban History* (London, 1972), 164–203.

SLADE, C. F., 'Reading Records', *BAJ* 61 (1963–4), 48–59.

SOUTHERN, R. W., 'Aspects of the European Tradition of Historical Writing. IV: The Sense of the Past', *TRHS*, fifth series, 23 (1973), 243–63.

—— 'Between Heaven and Hell: Review of J. Le Goff La Naissance du Purgatoire', *Times Literary Supplement* (18 June 1982), 651–2.

—— *Robert Grosseteste: The Growth of an English Mind in Medieval Europe* (Oxford, 1986).

SPENCER, B., *Salisbury Museum Medieval Catalogue, ii. Pilgrim Souvenirs and Secular Badges* (Salisbury, 1990).

SPUFFORD, M., 'Puritanism and the Social Order?', in A. Fletcher and J. Stevenson (eds.), *Order and Disorder in Early Modern England* (Cambridge, 1989), 41–57.

STENTON, F. M., *Documents Illustrative of the Social and Economic History of Danelaw* (London, 1920).

STREET, F., 'The Relations of the Bishops and Citizens of Salisbury between 1225 and 1612', *WAM* 39 (1916), 185–256.

STROUD, D., 'The Cult and Tombs of St. Osmund at Salisbury', *WAM* 78 (1984), 49–54.

TANNER, N. P., *The Church in Late Medieval Norwich 1370–1532* (Toronto, 1984).

TAYLOR, C. C., *Dorset: The Making of the Landscape* (London, 1970).

THIRSK, J. (ed.), *The Agrarian History of England and Wales*, iv (Cambridge, 1987).

THOMPSON, A. H., *The English Clergy and their Organisation in the Later Middle Ages* (London, 1947).

THOMPSON, E. M., 'The Vision of Edmund Leversedge', *NQSD* 9 (1904–5), 19–25.

THOMSON, J. A. F., 'Tithe Disputes in Late Medieval London', *EHR* 78 (1963), 1–17.

—— 'Piety and Charity in Late Medieval London', *JEH* 16 (1965), 178–95.

—— *The Later Lollards 1414–1520* (London, 1965).

TIGHE, R. R., and DAVIS, J. E., *Annals of Windsor* (London, 1858).

TOUT, T. F., *Chapters in Medieval Administrative History* (6 vols.; Manchester, 1920–33).

UNDERDOWN, D., *Revel, Riot and Rebellion: Popular Politics and Culture in England*

1603–1660 (Oxford, 1987).

UNWIN, G., *The Gilds and Companies of London*, fourth edn. (London, 1963).

VALE, M. G., 'Piety, Charity and Literacy among the Yorkshire Gentry 1370–1480', *Borthwick Papers*, 50 (1976), 1–32.

VALLANCE, A., *English Church Screens* (London, 1936).

VAUCHEZ, A., *Religion et société dans l'occident médiéval* (Turin, 1980).

—— *The Victoria County History of the Counties of England: A History of Berkshire*, ed. W. Page and P. H. Ditchfield (4 vols.; London, 1906–24).

—— *The Victoria County History of the Counties of England: A History of Dorset*, ii, ed. W. Page (London, 1908).

—— *The Victoria History of the Counties of England: Gloucestershire*, ii, ed. W. Page (London, 1902).

—— *The Victoria History of the Counties of England: A History of Wiltshire*, iii–xiii, ed. E. Critall, R. B. Pugh, and D. A. Crowley (13 vols.; Oxford, 1956–91).

—— *The Victoria History of the Counties of England: Worcester*, ii, ed. J. W. Willis-Bund and W. Page (London, 1906).

WARDROP, J., *Fountains Abbey and its Benefactors 1132–1300* (Cistercian Studies Series, 91; Kalamazoo, Mich., 1987).

WEBB, E. D., 'Notes on Aldbourne Church', *WAM* 28 (1895), 156–60.

WEBB, S., and WEBB, B., *English Local Government in English Poor Law History*, i. *The Old Poor Law* (London, 1927).

WEBER, M., *The Sociology of Religion*, trans. M. Fischoff (London, 1965).

WESTLAKE, H. F., *The Parish Gilds of Medieval England* (London, 1919).

WHITING, R., 'Abominable Idols: Images and Image-Breaking under Henry VIII', *JEH* 33 (1982), 30–47.

—— *The Blind Devotion of the People: Popular Religion and the English Reformation* (Cambridge, 1989).

WICKHAM, A. K., *The Churches of Somerset* (London, 1952).

WICKHAM-LEGG, J. (ed.), *The Sarum Missal* (Oxford, 1916).

WILKINS, D., *Concilia Magna Britanniae et Hiberniae* (London, 1737).

WILLIAMS, G., *The Welsh Church from Conquest to Reformation* (Cardiff, 1962).

—— *Wiltshire Notes and Queries* (8 vols.; 1893–1916).

WOOD, S., *English Monasteries and their Patrons in the Thirteenth Century* (Oxford, 1955).

WOODGER, A., 'Post-Reformation Mixed Gothic in Huntingdonshire Church Towers and its Campanological Associations', *Archaeological Journal*, 141 (1984), 269–308.

WOOD-LEGH, K. L., *Perpetual Chantries in Britain* (Cambridge, 1965).

WOODRUFF, C. E., 'The Financial Aspect of the Cult of St. Thomas of Canterbury', *Archaeologia Cantiana*, 44 (1932), 13–22.

WORDSWORTH, C., 'Wiltshire Pardons or Indulgences', *WAM* 38 (1913), 15–33.

YOUINGS, J. A., *The Dissolution of the Monasteries* (London, 1971).

—— 'The South-western Rebellion of 1549', *Southern History* 1 (1979), 99–122.

Index

Abberbury, Richard de 210
Abbotsbury, abbey 32, 34; abbot Walter
 de Stokes 32; guild 132
Abingdon: abbey 26, 32 n. 27, 37, 38, 39,
 40, 41, 214, Abbot Athelm 68,
 relationship with town 37, 38, 39, 41,
 171; town 13, 20, 94 n. 8, 160, 193, 214,
 219, guilds 137, 144, 146, 171, 177,
 192, hospital 183, 187, 192, 193, 194,
 200, Lollardy 214, parish churches 37,
 41, 75, 93, 146, 251
Adlington 191
advowson 47, 116, 213
agriculture 8–9; *see also* settlement
Aiscough, William, Bishop 6, 37, 124,
 187, 217 n. 78; dispute with citizens 73
Aldbourne 129, 211
Aldworth 97 n. 16, 116, 126, 127
ales 55, 84, 87, 89, 91, 106, 119, 120, 207
Allington, hospital 185, 190, 191, 192
almshouses 15, 20, 181–201, 207, 244–5;
 see also charity, guilds, hospitals; altar
 lights: cathedral 52–4; monastic houses
 34, 36, 40, 47; parish 92–4, 96, 100,
 102, 105, 109; Reformation 226, 234,
 236; *see also* guilds
altars, portable 205
Alton Barnes 114
Amesbury 60; nunnery 30, 31, 35, 39
anchorites, *see* hermits
Andrew of Sancta Cruce 59
anniversaries: accumulation 109, 250;
 amalgamation 96, 110, 168, 173, 233;
 cathedral 52–4, 55, 56–7, 195; friaries
 44; monasteries 30, 34, 35, 36, 42, 47,
 213; parish 93, 94, 101–3, 105–6, 117,
 129, 222; and the poor 56–7, 101, 102,
 195, 196, 197, 198; problems with
 funding 96, 152, 167–8, 173, 233;
 Reformation 223, 235, 236, 246
antiphonaries 23, 145, 206 n. 23
Aport, John 164 n. 19, 173
appropriation 40, 41, 55, 58, 196
Arundell, Archbishop 208
Arundel, Sir Thomas 233

Ashford, John 151, 152
Ashleigh, William 162, 163, 166, 167,
 173 n. 51, 181
Athelstan, King (and 'wife' Maud) 7, 159
Aubrey, John 12, 41, 48, 88, 115, 127,
 197, 246, 259
Audley, Edmund, Bishop 217
Audley, Thomas 34, 39 n. 65
Augustinian order 27, 30
Ayleward bridge 149, 184

Baker, John 33, 163, 208
Baly, William 164
Bampton (Oxon.) 215
baptism: rights 68
barber-surgeons, *see* Salisbury, craft guilds
Barbour, John 22 n. 72, 114, 204 n. 11
Barnes, William 12
Basset, Sir Philip 187
Bath, abbey 35
Bath and Wells, diocese 62, 216
Baunfeld, Marion 31 n. 26
Bayly, Walter 64, 65
Baynard, family 47
Baynton 28, 212–13
Beauchamp, family 30; Sir William 64,
 209
Beauchamp, Richard, Bishop 6, 148, 184,
 216, 217; dispute with citizens 171–3
Beaulieu, abbey 195 n. 51
Beche, family 126, 127
bede roll, *see* guilds
beggars, *see* vagrancy
Bekot, John 163, 166, 167
bells 120, 129, 176
Benedictine order 8, 27, 28, 29, 30, 33, 37,
 43, 46, 206
Bere Regis 80, 210 n. 43
Berghe, John atte 60; Walter atte 53 n. 22
Berkeley, family 30
Berwick St James 114
Beryatt, Robert 227, 228
Betelcombe, Richard 235
Bettesthorne, John 127, 204
Bever, John 212

Beynton, Sir John 117
Bible 203, 228, 253, 254; Lollard 202, 211, 216, 217
Bikenore, Thomas 215, 216
Bindon, abbey 30, 32
Binfield 230 n. 34
Bingham, Bishop 185
Birton 86
Bisham: Lollardy 210, 219; well 6
Bishops Canning 5, 125
Bishopstone 211
Bitterleigh, John 163, 202
Black Death 9, 14; charity 185, 186, 196, 198, 200; church building 121; guilds 132, 138, 158; monasteries 33; parish 70–1, 90, 97, 110, 177–8, 203, 259
Blewbury 219
Bluet: Sir John 33, 42 n. 84, 47; Ralph 35 n. 44
Blythe, John, Bishop 217
Boket, William 16, 172
Bonham, Isabel de 206; Nicholas de 31 n. 26
Bonhommes, *see* Edington
Boniface IX, Pope 37, 146
books 33, 145, 203, 205–6, 208; Lollard 202, 203, 216, 225 n. 7; Lutheran 225; Reformation 228, 236; *see also* bible
Bottenham, Agnes 181
boy bishop 56
Boyton 116
Boyton, Thomas 114 n. 10, 205, 208
Bradenstoke, priory 18, 27, 30, 34, 35 n. 48, 36, 41, 46, 47
Bradford-on-Avon 17, 219, 236; chantry 36, 97, 106, 107, 118; St Lawrence's 114, 128
Bramshaw 55, 82 n. 48
Bray 74, 76, 77, 101, 107, 143, 170
Braybrooke, family 210; Joan 209
Bret, Walter le 185
breviary 92, 206 n. 23, 256
Brewer, John 211
Brickett, Thomas 164, 189, 245
bridges: bequests 198; building 38, 39; cults 40, 45, 69, 189; hermits 206; privileges 170; *see also* Ayleward, Caversham
Bridgewater 33
Bridport 13; burgess guilds 160–2, 170, 173, 174, 175, 176–7, 178, 179, 180, 261; friars 43; hospital 176, 192; parish 89, 95, 176; parish guilds 20,

134–7, 140, 145, 157; Reformation 245 n. 85; *see also* Munden
Bridport, Giles de, Bishop 5
Brinkworth 86 n. 62
Brinkworth, Roger 52 n. 19
Bristol 30 n. 37, 31, 216, 229; diocese 5
Brittany 170
Broad Chalke 103, 119
Broke, Sir Thomas (and son) 204, 208, 209
Bromham 230 n. 34
Broughton Giffard 210
Broughton, Thomas 214, 215, 216–17
Broune, Philip 214, 217
Browning, Alice 62
Brunanburh, battle 7 n. 27
Buckinghamshire 231
Buckland 93, 101, 109; priory 31 n. 26
Bulke, Robert 60
Bulkley, Charles 228
Bulkington 219
Burbage 205
burial: austerity in 204, 206, 208, 252; cathedral 54, 65; friaries 44; gentry 252, 253, 254; monasteries 30, 31, 33, 35, 36, 38, 47; mortuary fees 210; parish 35, 36, 47, 92, 100–1, 104–5, 126, 129, 253; preferences for 93, 253; Reformation 227, 246; rights 41, 68, 71, 181; *see also* cemeteries, charity, cloth industry, gentry, guilds, processions, tombs
Byconvil, Sir John 44
Byrde, William 236

Cade, Jack 6, 15, 49, 186
Calais 64
Calne: chantry 107, 191, 230; hospital 183; parish 83, 88, 89, 91, 95, 108, 244; town 248
Calne, William of 205 n. 17
Canford 94 n. 8
canonization 57–61
Canterbury 58 n. 47, 61
Caper, Sir Roger 129
Capgrave, John 202, 203, 222
capitalism 13–14
Cardmaker, John 107
Carpenter, William 215
Carrant, Sir William 230
Carthusian order 24, 28, 36, 206, 252
Carwood, Stephen 225
Castle Combe 13, 14, 15, 17, 81,

146 n. 49; Lollardy 216 n. 74, 219
Caversham 40, 45, 69, 93 n. 4
cemeteries 70–1, 74, 75, 219; *see also* burial
Cerne, abbey 43, 48
Cervington, Sir Walter 35
Chadenwhych chapel 107
Chaffyn, Thomas 239, 240, 242
Chafyne, John 207 n. 30
'chalk and cheese' 8, 9, 12, 17, 19, 62, 231, 259–60; *see also* agriculture; settlement
Chamber, John 63
chancel 250; *see also* church building
Chancery Court 230, 233
Chandler, John 18, 52, 53 n. 22
Chandler, John, dean: against citizens 43, 173; Bishop 16 n. 57, 78; visitations 79, 81, 82, 97, 119, 120 n. 37, 143, 145
chantries: burdens 241, 242; cathedral 52–4, 203–4; charity 97; commissioners 107, 110 n. 57, 143, 182, 195, 197, 255; concealment 233–4; failings 97, 230, 242; hospitals 191, 193; monasteries 33, 34, 36, 41, 46, 47; parish 1, 22, 23, 33, 47, 93–4, 95, 103–4, 106–7, 109, 110, 260; church building 111, 116, 118–9, 130, 131; separate chapels 36, 94, 103, 107; *see also* cloth industry, guilds
chapels: dependent 21, 41, 90; free 183, 191; and pastoral care 67–70, 71–4; private 46, 204–5, 207, 250, 252 *see also* chantries, church building, oratories
Chapleyn, Thomas 53 n. 22
Chardstock 82 n. 45
Charlton 41, 94 n. 8, 254
Charlyng, Alice 53 n. 20
charity 181–201, 251; cathedral 56–7, 195; children 196; clergy 195; discrimination 15, 20, 42, 182, 183, 185, 186, 190, 194–6, 197–9, 199–200; family 196; funeral doles 194, 196–9; monasteries 28 n. 13, 41–3, 47, 194–5; old 192, 196, 227; parish 197; Reformation 227–8, 235; *see also* almshouses, gentry, hospitals
Charminster 54, 128
Chaucer, Geoffrey 28
Chaucey, William 94 n. 8, 254
Cheney: Cecily 208; Hugh 202; John 209, 210; Katherine 51; Radulf de 205 n. 17

Cherton, Roger of 205 n. 17
Chichele, Henry, Archbishop 5
Chicklade 114
Chievely 82 n. 45, 103 n. 32
Chilterns 216
Chippenham 107, 143
Chipping Faringdon 216
Chirton 214
Chitterne All Saints 60
Cholsey 103 n. 32
Chubbe, William 31 n. 26
church building: parish 14, 20, 111–31, 192, 201, 222, 236; aisles 113, 114, 115, 121, 126, 130, 208, chancel 41, 111, 113, 114–15, 125, 126, 128, 129–30, 145, chancel and nave 67, 79, 125, chapels 113, 115, 116, 126, 130, clerestories 115, 127–8, help from monasteries 41, porches 115, 129 n. 69, roofs 115, 119; steeples 127, towers 14, 95, 113, 114, 115, 119, 125, 128–9, 176, *see also* chantries, cloth industry, gentry, guilds
churchwardens: accounts 19–20, 83–8, 94, 108; charity 189; Lollardy 218; Reformation 244; role 78–9, 250
Cirencester 31, 43
Cistercian order 27, 28, 30, 46, 195 n. 51
Clanvowe, Thomas 210
Clarence, duke of 51
Clarke, Robert 186
clay vales, *see* settlement
Cleche, Richard 193
Clement, Mararet 39 n. 65
clerestories, *see* church building
Clewar 236
Clifford, Sir Lewis 210
cloth industry 13, 14, 15, 16, 17, 19; anniversaries 95–6, 108; burial 101, 104–5, 108; chantries 95–6, 97, 110; church building 111, 117–9, 121, 127, 131; guilds 146, 178, 259; hospitals 186–7; Lollardy 16, 217, 218, 219, 222; monasteries 30 n. 17, 31 n. 26; parish 86–7, 87–8, 90, 95–6; Reformation 226, 248, 255; and religious life 14, 17, 259
Cluniac order 27
Clyffe Pypard 210
Cobham family 210; Joan 209
Codford St Mary 206 n. 26
Coke, Thomas 188, 189 n. 26
Coldstone, Henry 156, 164, 239, 242

Cole, Agnes 62
Colerne 86 n. 62
Collins, John 218; Robert 218
Colney, John 193; William 171
Colyns, John 225; Thomas 182
Combe 59
Compton Hawy 41
confessors 39, 44, 67, 203, 205; Lollardy 208
Cookham 43, 74, 77, 170, 219, 234
Coombe chapel 71, 75
Cornwall 236, 239
Cornwall, Edmund, Earl 40, 52
Corpus Christi 25, 85–6, 245, 253; fraternity 24, 233 n. 44
Corsely 76
Corsham 100, 107, 116
Corston 191
Corton, Elias, lord 34
Cotel, Ellis 41
Coterell, Margery 212
Cotswolds 9
Council of Constance 4–5, 59
Coventry 112
Coventry, family 117; Thomas 182, 189
Coverdale, Miles 236
Cox, Leonard 229
Cranbourne 129
Cricklade, hospital 183, 184
Cromwell, Thomas 63, 69, 228, 238
Crudwell 128
Cuddlestone 43 n. 86
Cuffe, William 152 n. 69, 155 nn. 82 & 83, 156, 165 n. 21
Culham 43 n. 86, 254

Dacy, Sir John 52
Damerham 212 n. 54
Danvers, Lady Anne 103 n. 32, 228, 252
Dauntsey 182, 204
Dauntsey, John 204, 208, 210; Thomas 253
D'Avranches, Hugh 50 n. 5
Davyson, dean 78
dead, the 3, 242; *see also* altar lights, anniversaries, burial, chantries, guilds, hospitals, monastic houses, Salisbury cathedral
decretals 206 n. 23
de la Mare, Sir Thomas 39
Delamere, Sir John 35 n. 44
Delawey, Matilda 31 n. 26
Deloney, Thomas 14

de Mere, John 127
de Montacute, John 32
Denchworth 92; breviary 92, 256
de Newburgh, Sir John 30; Richard 32; Robert 30
de Paveley, Walter 205 n. 17
Despenser family 30
Deverel chapel 107
Deverell Longbridge 137
Deverill, Hugh 45
Devizes 7, 50: almshouse 182, 187, 189; guilds 133, 173; Lollardy 216, 219, 222; parish 83 n. 54, 88, 89, 91, 95; chantry 107, church building 117, 119, Jesus light 86 n. 62; Reformation 225, 228, 234, 237, 244
Devon 236, 239
Diot, John 229
Dives and Pauper 111, 131
doles, *see* charity
Doom Paintings 128, 254
Dorchester 43, 44
Downton 9, 60, 62, 71
Draycot 41, 94 n. 8
Drayton, Sir John 254
Druweys, Sir Robert 41
Dunton 62
Durnford 212
Durrington 17 n. 61, 60, 109 n. 56

Early, John 68, 107
East Hendred 218, 230 n. 34, 247
East Lavington 182, 230 n. 34
Easter communion 102, 107, 127, 143
East Shefford 127
Easton, William 172
Easton priory 36, 41, 46, 190
eclipse 92
Edgar, King 39
Edington: hermit 206 n. 27; Lollardy 21, 212–13; priory 19, 28, 30, 35, 43 n. 85, 213; Reformation 225
education 31, 106–7, 229; gentry 253; *see also* schools
Edward IV 51; preaching against 82
Edward VI, Reformation 3, 223, 224, 237, 238, 239, 240, 243, 247
Eleanor of St Amand 51, 64
Elias de Durham 56
Elizabeth I, Queen 246
Elmeley, Richard 62
Enfeld, Edmund 54
Enford 71, 76, 77, 106

Englefield 230 n. 34, 233
Englefield, Sir Thomas 103 n. 32, 116; Sir
    Francis 233
Erasmus 229
Erghum, Ralph, Bishop 58
Erleigh 68, 69, 76, 107
Estbury family 116, 187; Sir John 116,
    191
Esturmey family 36, 46; Geoffrey 205;
    Sir Henry 101; Sir William 36, 42, 46
Ethelred, King 40
Eucharist 1, 3, 64, 105, 107; Lollardy
    202, 209, 210, 212, 214, 222, 225
excommunication 81, 203 n. 8, 210
executors 22, 23, 24, 65, 145, 152, 181
Exeter 258
Exeter, Thomas, Duke 51

Farleigh Hungerford 65, 196
Farman, Juliame 83, 212
Fastolf, Sir John 14
Fetiplace familu 187; Sir John 127; Sir
    William 103 n. 32, 253
Figheldean 121
Filliol, Sir William 254
Filmer, Henry 225, 230, 236, 248
Fishburn, Thomas 210
Fisherton Anger 44, 206, 207
Fisherton Delamere 196 n. 55
Fitz Waryn, Ivo 31 n. 26
font 37
Fordeham, Stephen 182
Fordington 80
Forest, John 155 n. 81
forests, and hermits 206
Forsett, John 225
Foxe, John 225, 229, 236
Foxley family 76
France: war 13, 64, 186
fraternity: cathedral 51, 59, 64; friaries
    44, 45; hospital 184, 192, 193–4;
    monastic house 26, 33, 39 n. 65 *see also*
    guilds
friars 19, 22, 26, 28 n. 13, 43–6, 202, 206,
    207; against bishop 45; *see also*
    fraternity, guilds
Frome 1, 24
funerals *see* burial
Fyfield 116, 126, 204; hospital 191

Gage, Richard 133 n. 7, 153 n. 70, 164,
    198
'gallants' 1, 203

Gamare, Michael 214, 258
Gandavo, Simon, Bishop 171
Garlyck, William 156
Gascoigne, Thomas 6
Gaunt, John, Duke 51
gentry: books 205–6, 252; burial 35 n. 48,
    126–7, 253, 255; cathedral 52;
    education 229; friars 44; hermits
    206–7; Lollardy 208–10, 252;
    monasteries 29, 30, 31, 32, 34, 35, 43,
    47, 48, 252; parish church building
    115–17, 121, 126–7, 131, chancels 125,
    253, chantries 126–7, chapels 179,
    seating 87, 179, 254–5, towers 128–9;
    piety 1, 2, 14, 46, 252–6; private
    devotion 203–7, 207–8; Reformation
    223, 254–6
Giffard family 116
Gilbertine Order 27, 28
Gillingham 43, 97
Gilpurne, Robert 31 n. 26
Glastonbury abbey 31 n. 26
Gloucester, Humphrey, Duke 51
Gobbet, Richard 234
Goddard, Richard 129; Thomas 31 n. 26
Godmanston, Margaret 163; Robert 53,
    54, 113–14
Golafre, Sir John 116, 126, 171, 187, 191,
    204
Goodall, John 238, 240
Goodhyne, John 35 n. 44
Gough, John 216
Gower, John: book 206 n. 23
Great Bedwyn 94 n. 8, 119–20, 132, 182
Great Chalfield 116
Great Faringdon 54–5, 94 n. 8
Great Marlow 6
Great Somerford 210
Great Wishford 60
Gregory IX, Pope 2, 58
Gresham 64
Grimstead 82 n. 45
Grosseteste, Robert, Bishop 78, 250,
    251 n. 2
Gryffyths, Robert 233
guilds: almshouses 164, 187–9, 192–4,
    altar lights 134–5, 138, 143, 149, 153,
    155; anniversaries 23, 132, 143, 149–52,
    163, 166–8, 169; bede roll 149, 156,
    157, 163–4, 245; burial 132, 134–5,
    136, 138, 142, 143, 165, 177; chantries
    143–4, 145, 151, 154, 158, 160, 161,
    165, 172; crafts 14, 45, 140, 146–57,

guilds (*cont.*):
185, 193, 245; foundation 132, 134,
137–8, 159; fund raising 135, 136, 141,
142; involvement with cathedral 53–6,
149, 153, 155, 165, 179, friars 153, with
monasteries 171; membership 135–7,
139–40, 142, 161, 162, 164, 177; outside
diocese 6–7, 133; records 20;
Reformation 226, 227, 234, 244–5;
relationship with parish 132–3, 142–6,
153–7, 160, 161, 175–7, 178–9,
179–80, church building 111, 145–6,
158, 179–80, visitations 144–5, 158;
town government 135–7, 146–8,
159–80; *see also* Jesus, Salisbury

Hailes, abbey 229 n. 31
Hakluyt, Giles 238
Hall, John 22, 63 n. 76, 169, 172
Hallum, Robert, Bishop 4–5, 58, 59
Halstede, John 173 n. 51; William 164,
167
Hancock, Thomas 237, 239
Harding, Nicholas 52 n. 20
Harreys, William 144
Harwell 81
Havilland, William 237
Haynes, Richard 154
Hell 2, 24
Hendy, Stephen 151 n. 66, 154, 156 n. 86,
157
Henry III, King 50
Henry IV, King 51
Henry V, King 51
Henry VI, King 6, 64; cult 84, 236
Henry VII, King 84
Henry VIII, King 69, 223, 242, 247
heresy, *see* Lollardy
hermits 203, 206–7
Herrying, Sir John 94–5, 117, 254
Heynes, William 13, 17
Heytesbury chantry 97 n. 16; hospital 18,
186, 189, 191, 196
Higden, *Polychronicon* 36, 206 n. 23
Highway 114
Highworth 230 n. 34
Hignell, Alice 215
Hill Deverill 107 n. 52, 111
Hilmarton 191
Hindon 76
Hinton charterhouse 24, 28, 36, 206
Hinton Waldrist 214
Hocktide 84, 88, 89, 120, 231, 241, 245,

246, 257
Holland family 100
Holme, William 63
Holnest 71, 82 n. 45
Holy Land 7, 32
Horton 254
Horton, Thomas 17, 36, 97, 118 n. 27
hospitals 20, 181–201; chantries 191;
foundation 14, 182–3, founders 187,
191, 200; monasteries 42; and the
parish 189, 190–1, 200; statutes 183,
184, 185; *see also* almshouse, charity
fraternity
host, *see* Eucharist
Huchyns, Simon 59, 66
Hull 112
humanism 31, 32, 229
Hungerford family 30, 39, 52, 100,
116 n. 18; almshouse 191; Edward 228;
Eleanor 100 n. 21; Margaret 52, 64,
184, 185, 186, 196, 203, 262; Robert,
Lord Moleyns 15, 64, 65; Thomas 196;
Walter 51, 52, 59, 64, 65, 196
Hungerford parish 69, 80, 83, 84 n. 55,
96; Lollardy 212, 214, 216, 219
Huntingdon, William 53 n. 21
Hurst 68, 77
Hyde, John 92; William 92, 256

images 39, 191; Lollardy 215, 216;
Reformation 235, 236; removal 230; *see
also* altar lights, saints
indulgences 5, 39, 40, 50, 124, 146, 161,
190, 227
Ingram, William 65
Ivychurch priory 35

Jerusalem 7
Jesus: Holy Name 1, 5, 86, 92, 248, 251;
guilds 55, 136–42, 154, 156–7, 178,
237
Jews 32
Johnson, Richard 225 n. 7

Kayleway, John 193
Keevil 118, 219, 225
Kellow, William 22
Kelsall, Henry 31 n. 26, 129, 139–40
Kemsing 39, 40 n. 70
Kingston chapel 76
Kingston Deverell 86 n. 62
Kington St Michael 30, 33, 34, 197

Kingswood abbey 223, 226
Knight, John 233
Knighton 55
Knook 114
Kyndeway, Lord Morgan 39
Kynsman, John 30

Lacock: parish 47; priory 18, 27, 30, 31, 33, 36, 46
Lacy, Margaret de 47; Emily de 94, 100, 103
Lamberd, Thomas 40 n. 70
Lambold, Jeronius 182
Lambourne 77, 107, 191
Langland, William 26
Langrysh, Richard 65
Langton, Thomas, Bishop 217
Lancaster, House of 47
Lateran Council, Fourth 4
Latimer, Hugh 229, 243
Latimer, Sir Thomas 209
Laurence of St Martin 209, 211
Laverstoke 60
Lee, Christine 164, 166, 167, 173
Leche, John 193
Legend, of Saints 205 n. 23
Leland, John 68, 118
leprosy 40, 183, 185–6
Letcombe Basset 210 n. 43, 216
Letcombe Regis 210, 215
Leversedge, Sir Edmund 1, 2, 16, 18, 24–5, 26, 203, 206, 250, 252, 253, 262
Levyng, Robert 60
Lewis, John 28
Lillyngston, Richard 16, 216 n. 74
Lincoln, diocese 6, 75
Little Horningsham 206
Littleton Drew 55
Little Okeborne 96
Locking 210 n. 43, 225
Lollardy 16, 20, 79, 82, 202–22; belief 211–7, 218; books 20, 217, 224; fear of discovery 214–15; knights 208–10, 250; in local society 218–19; Lollers Tower 216; network 216; occupation 217–8; preaching 202, 225; Reformation 224–5, 231, 236, 247
London 15, 61, 63, 133, 198, 213, 225, 230
London, Dr 69
Long Bourton 71
Long family 130; Robert 118, 128; Walter 229

Longspee family, Earls of Salisbury 30, 36, 46; Stephen 36, 94; William 46, 52
Loryng, Thomas 217
Loudres, Elizabeth de 204, 208
Lovel family 100, Lady Matilda 51
Lovell, Master 238
Low Countries 57
Lucas, Walter 31, 118, 128
Ludlow, Palmers' guild 133
Ludlow, Richard 207; William 111
Lutheranism 224, 225, 234
Lyme Regis 13, 43, 69, 81, 121, 256
Lyndewoode, William 4
Lytull, John 211

Macy, John 54
Maddington 227 n. 14
Madowell, John 238, 240
Maiden Bradley priory 34, 35; hospital 190
Maidenhead 74, 75, 170, 178, 207, 219
Makam, Robert 225
Malden, John 210
Malmesbury 7, 30, 41, 48, 106, 107, 191, 226; guilds 86 n. 62, 159, 160, 174; hospital 182
Malmesbury abbey 7, 8, 18, 27, 41; Abbot Loryng 7, 41; Abbot William Colerne 18
Manderville, William 213
Mandrel, John 225
Manselston, Thomas 223
Mapull, Thomas 62
Market Lavington 127 n. 55
Marky, Thomas 156
Malborough 20, 43, 75, 96, 101, 107, 121, 143, 175, 207; guilds 133, 139, 169; Jesus light 86; hospital 182, 183; Lollardy 216, 219, 222; Reformation 234
Marnhull 86
Marshill 182
Marston Bigot 216
Martival, Roger, Bishop 51, 52, 56
Martyn, Nicholas 30 n. 17; Robert 17 n. 61, 30, 109 n. 56; Thomas 30 n. 17, 189 n. 26, 194 n. 48, 207 n. 30, 227 n. 14
Mary, Queen 225, 231, 237, 238, 239, 240, 248
Mass of the Five Wounds 253
mass books 118, 128
Maudit, Thomas 205 n. 17

Mauger of Malcuvenant 26
Mautravers, Sir John 34
Maynard, William 144, 189 n. 26
Melancthon 225, 229
Melbury Sampford 62
Melcombe Horsey 76 n. 23
Melcombe Regis 9, 13, 45
Melksham 50, 93, 102
Mercer, William 114 n. 10
merchant tailors, London 133, 198
Mere 86 n. 62, 100, 127, 204
Meriot, Alice 24, 164, 258; Sir George
    173 n. 51, 255
Middleton, William 236
Miller, Agnes 215
Milton Abbas 124
Milton abbey 32 n. 27, 34, 43, 48
Minety 129
minster churches 8, 68–70, 71, 107, 219
miracles 6, 40, 125; *see also* St Osmund
missals 118, 206, 208
Mitford, Richard, Bishop 55, 196
Moleyns, Adam, Bishop 64
Mompesson, Sir John 35, 228; Edmund
    254
monastic houses 8; cartularies 18, 19, 40;
    chapels 40; disputes with townsmen
    37–9, 48, 171, 173; dissolution 48, 226,
    227, 243, 256; endowment 26, 27, 28,
    29, 30, 32–7, 39, 42, 46, 47; families
    30 n. 19, 31, 36, 46; and friars 45; and
    hermits 206; hospitals 187, 189–90;
    Reformation 23, 236; relationship with
    parish 36, 38, 40, 41, 47; shared
    churches 37; *see also* altar lights,
    charity, gentry, guilds, pilgrimage,
    saints.
Moner, John 163, 166, 167, 168, 188
Monkton Farleigh 35
Montagu, Earls of Salisbury: John 209,
    210; Thomas 51, 65
mortality 15, 79–80, 184, 185, 244, 248,
    250, 261–2; Reformation 224, 243–4
morbidity 1, 21, 203–4, 206, 252, 262
More, William 150, 155 n. 81
Mortimer family 30; Sir Hugh 35 n. 44
mortmain 33, 34, 130, 171, 174, 191, 193;
    Statutes 18, 28, 46, 130, 166, 200
Mulle, Emma atte 39
Munden, Michael (chantry) 177, 197, 275
murals 128, 203, 254
Myllys, John 227 n. 14
Myrc, John 256

mystics 203, 250

Netherbury 80, 81, 255
Neville, Robert, Bishop 251
Neville, Richard 51
new feasts 86, 92, 248, 253; *see also* Jesus
Newark 226
Newbury 13, 14; hospital 191, 257;
    Lollardy 209, 215, 219; parish 82 n. 45,
    86, 118; Reformation 224, 229, 233,
    236, 239 n. 64, 248
Newcastle 62
Newman, John 163
Nichol, Elias 52
Nicholas, Nicholas 86
Nicholas of Cusa 133
Norfolk 239
Norrys, Sir John 101
North Bradley 93 n. 4
Northmoor 214
North Standen 203 n. 34
Nothered, John 237
Notley priory 40
Nuttyng, Robert 101, 102

obits, *see* anniversaries
Oborne 71
Ogbourne St Andrew 70, 219
Okedon, William 205
Okeford, John 211
Old Sarum 4, 50, 68, 206 n. 26; hospital
    183
Oldcastle, Sir John 209, 211, 214
oratories 203, 205, 207, 208, 255; and
    pastoral care 76–7
Orcheston St George 83
ordinals 206 n. 23
organs 45, 118, 120
Orleans, duke of 64
Our Lady of Doncaster 62
Our Lady of Sorrows 86
Overcompton 71
Oxford University 1, 32 n. 27, 229, 253;
    Exeter College 210 n. 43; friars 45;
    Lollardy 210, 212

Page, William 228
pardoners 185; *see also* indulgences
parish 9–12, 67–131; church attendance
    74, 75, 81–3, 91, 129, 183, 191, 212;
    duties of parishioners 67, 77, 85, 90,
    179; endowment 92–6, 108; failings of
    priests 77, 170, 195; foundation 69–70;

fund raising 79, 83–8, 120, 214;
pastoral provision and failings 12, 40,
45–6, 219; 'frozen' structure 69–71,
74–7; reform 67, 250; Reformation and
continuity 245–7; seating 87, 89, 140,
250, 257; *see also* chapels, church
building, guilds, hospitals, monastic
houses, settlement, visitations
Parker, Roger 215
Parliament 64, 193, 209
Passelowe, John 49, 65
Passemar, John 218
Paston, John 64
Paraphrases 230, 231
Pater noster 18, 103, 119, 207, 216
Pecham, John, Archbishop 45
Peche, Sighert 234
Peerse, Joanne 23, 207 n. 30, 235
Peerson, Anthony 225, 229
penance 2, 32, 33, 124, 181, 209, 251
Pertwood 114
Petefyn, Richard 216
Petevyn, John 62
Phillips Norton 62
Picardy 40
pilgrimage: cathedral 54, 79; local cults
68, 69, 126, 183, 215; Lollard complaint
215; monastic houses 40, 42, 195 n. 51;
outside diocese 6–7, 32, 215, 229 n. 31,
236; Reformation 223, 229 n. 31, 236,
247; to Rome 7; St Osmund 57, 60–3
Pilgrimage of Grace 236
Pilgrimage of Souls 206 n. 23, 252
Pilton 247
Pinnok, John 150, 163; Richard 173 n. 51
plays 45, 88
Plush 258
Pokeswell, Agnes 80, 81
Polton, Thomas 119
Poole parish 83, 89, 95, 160, 189 n. 31;
hermit 206 n. 26; Reformation 229,
235, 237; town government 176
poor, *see* charity
Poore, Richard, bishop 4, 5, 187
Pope: petitions to 37, 58–60, 70–1, 76,
90, 146, 205; Schism 202
Popley, John 229
population 9, 13, 16; parish 74–5; *see also*
Black Death
porches *see* church building
portiforium 205
Portsmouth 242
Potterne 5, 125

Poughely 206 n. 27
Poulton priory 28, 36
Pownser, John 140
Poyntz, Nicholas 226; Thomas 223, 224,
247, 256
Prayer Book 247
preaching: anti-Yorkist 82; in cathedral
59; chantries 106–7; education 253;
friars 45; Lollard 210, 215, 216, 217,
219; in parishes 67, 205, 215; pulpit
140; Reformation 225, 228, 229, 230,
236, 237, 244, 248
Prentis: John 163, 165, 167; William 163
Preshute 75
pride 1, 2, 16, 131
primers 21
private devotion 128, 203–8
psalter 181, 190, 205, 206, 207
processions: cathedral 53; civic 140, 147,
165, 174–5, 179, 210, 250, 260–1;
funeral 39, 65, 100–1; guild (tailors)
149–50; Midsummer 149; parish 79,
251, 254; Reformation 242, 245
prostitution 15, 181, 192, 244, 260, 261
Protestantism 224, 225, 226, 233, 236–7,
246, 247
Pupilla Oculi 206 n. 23
Purgatory: origins 3; penance, cathedral
50, guilds 174, 177, hospitals 190,
monasteries 32, 33, 39, 47, parish 110,
124, 130–1; Reformation 223, 245;
vision 1, 2; *see also* indulgences,
penance
purification 191, 210, 256, 257
Purton 230
Purton, Thomas of 205 n. 17
Pymperne 86 n. 62
Pynnok, William 53 n. 20

Quidhampton 60

Radipole 45
Ramsbury 106, 197, 206 n. 26, 230 n. 34
Ramsbury, William 16, 210, 211, 213, 219
Reade, Morgan 237
Reading 13, 14, 20, 21, 43, 160, 193;
almshouse 185, 194; burgesses 171,
173, 176; friars 45; guilds and parish
145; Jesus guilds 138, 139, 140,
146 n. 49, 157; Lollardy 211, 218, 219;
parishes 83, 85, 91, 107, 108, 121, 143,
260; Reformation 231, 237; St Giles
87, 96, 108, 110; St Laurence's 38, 45,

Reading (*cont.*):
  82 n. 48, 86, 87, 96, 105, 108, 110, 120,
    125, 176, 185, 225, 257
Reading abbey: Caversham chapel 40;
  endowment 27, 32; hand of St James
  26, 39; hospital 31, 38, 42, 184, 185,
  187, 200; relationship with town 37, 38,
  44, 171, 173, 193; school 31, 229
Reformation 8, 17, 223–49: attitudes
  towards: acceptance 240–7, 249,
  ambivalence 241, caution 234–5,
  conservatism 231–40, 237, 238–9,
  desire for change 225–31, opposition
  239; continuity 244–7, 251, 261–2; *see
  also* altar lights, anniversaries, chantries,
  charity, monastic house, settlement
relics 39, 58, 66; Lollardy 214, 215; *see
  also* pilgrimage
Restwoode, Thomas 45
Reve, William 146
Riborgh, Richard 163, 198
Ringbourne family 46
roads 193, 198
Robin Hood play 85, 88
Rochett, Richard 193
Rockley 70
Rogation 245
Roger of Cherlton 205 n. 17
Rogers, John 45
Rolle, Thomas 85
Rome, *see* Popes, pilgrimage
Romsey 31 n. 26
rood cross 128, 176; Reformation 237,
  247
Rous, Sir John 28, 35 n. 44, 212–13;
  Walter 60
Ruscombe 68
Rutland, Edward, Earl 51
Ryckeman, Thomas 81
Ryme 81, 82 n. 45

Saints, cults and relics: Aldhelm of
  Malmesbury 8, 39 n. 67, 48; Bearnwold
  of Bampton 215; Benedict 194;
  Bernard 230; Blaise at Lyme Regis 69;
  Catherine 12; Christopher 33; Cirius at
  Sonning 68, 69, 126; Cuthberga of
  Wimborne Minster 8, 85, 86, 88;
  Cuthbert of Durham 40 n. 69; Edward
  of Westminster 63, 92; Edith of Wilton
  39–40, Erasmus 215; Giles at
  Wimborne St Giles 215; Godric of
  Finchdale 60 n. 58; Frideswide of

Oxford 60 n. 58; James of Compostela
  7, 32, 61; James at Reading 26, 39;
  Laurence at Hungerford 69; Osmund
  4, 19, 22, 50, 57–63, 92, 153, 227, 235,
  245, 251, 259: miracles 60, 61–2;
  Oswald 12; Osyth 12; Petroc at Lyme
  Regis 69; Thomas of Canterbury
  58 n. 47; Whyte of whitchurch
  Canonicorum 8, 126; Wulfstan of
  Worcester 57 n. 43, 60 n. 58

Salisbury: burial 101, 197; cloth trade 13,
  effect on civic life 101, 115, 121, 260–1,
  effect on guilds 14, 146, 158, 177–9;
  craft guilds 56, 153; economy 4, 17, 61,
  66, 187; foundation 4, 5; friary 22, 43,
  44–5; hospitals, bede row 182, 188,
  189, 194, charity 198, 199, and
  reformation 244, 245, St Nicholas 183,
  184, 185, 187, 188, 189, 190, 201,
  Trinity 18, 22, 23, 181, 182, 183, 184,
  188, 189, 190, 191, 192, 193, 201;
  Lollardy 15, 202, 214, 216; monasteries
  28, 31, 44, 47; parishes, foundation 70,
  parish guilds 20, 137, 138, 142, 157,
  population 74, visitations 82; private
  devotion 204, 205, hermits 207;
  Reformation, acceptance of change
  242–8, ambivalence 239–41,
  susceptability to reform; bequests
  226, 227–8, 230, 235, conservatism
  235–6, 238–9, decrees 223–4,
  Protestantism 225, reaction to
  reforming bishop 238, 240, relationship
  with bishop 5–6, 49, 64, 166, 171–3,
  250, 238, 239, 248, 258–9; risings
  (1431) 15, (1450) 49, 63–4; St
  Edmund's church 5, and altar
  lights 105, building 113–14, 120, 124,
  125, 128 n. 63, and cathedral 55, 56, 63,
  and chantries 94 n. 8, 97, 100, 153,
  college 104, 105, 175, fund raising 87,
  88, 89, 96, 108, 257, and guilds 137,
  152–7, and Jesus guild 86, 138, 139,
  140–2, 143, 144, 145, 153, 154, 156,
  174, 175, 227, indulgence 69, liturgical
  goods 85, and town government 166,
  167; St Martin's 5, 54, 113–14, 153,
  167, 238; St Thomas's 5, 19, 22, 89, 96,
  104, 108, and cathedral 54, 55, 58, 63,
  65, 196, and chantries 22, 23, church
  building 111, 113–14, 125, 126, 128,
  131, 208, 255, and guilds 137, 139, 154,

155, and Reformation 230, 238, 239,
240, 241, and tailors 149, 150, 151, 153,
154, 156–7, and town government 167;
tailors' guild 60, 146–58, and cathedral
149, 150, 153, chantry 151–2, obits
149–52, parish 111, 152–7, procession
147–8, 149, 150, 153, and Reformation
227, 233, 235–6, 241, 245, rules
146–52; town government: 5, 160, civic
processions 165, 174–5, endowment
and obits 23, 162–4, 166–8, guild
chantry 165, and guild (St George) 20,
56, 162–70, 178, 192, 208, 227, 235,
241, 242, 244, 250, quarrels 16, 22,
168–9, 172, 179–80, *see also* Trinity
hospital, Reformation; Vaux college
5, 57, 195; weavers' guild 142 n.30, 152,
153, 154, guilds outside city 133
Salisbury cathedral 4, 9, 15, 19, 24, 44,
49–66, 78, 202; attacks on canons 49,
63–5, 214; building 58; foundation and
endowment 5, 50–4, 65; and parishes
53–5, 56, 58, 63, 65, 111; prebends 5,
19, 49, 50, 54–5, 61; *see also*
anniversaries, burial, chantries, charity,
fraternity, guilds, St. Osmund,
visitations
Salisbury, Ela, Countess 42
Salle, William 163
Sambourne, Nicholas 31, 35 n. 44
Sandehus, John 97
Sandhurst 68
Sarum Use 4, 5, 59, 66
Savage, Sir John 31 n. 26
Say, Thomas 252
Says, Joan 85
Schotte, John 45
Scochyn, Thomas 218
Scrop, William 152, 155 n. 81
Scrope, Lord 65
Seend 17, 102, 127
settlement, effect on: parish structure 9,
74, 80, 91, 259; endowment 95–6, 108,
110, 260; church building 115, 121,
123, 131; Reformation 231, 241; *see also*
chalk and cheese
Seyman, William 234
Seymour family 46; Alice 36; Thomas 28
Seyntloo, John 230
sermons, *see* preaching
Sextayn, Thomas 21–2 n. 72, 204 n. 11
schools 32, 44, 57, 195, 198; *see also*
education

Shaftesbury 31 n. 26, 35, 86, 235 n. 49
Shaw 210
Shaw, Ralph 236
Shaxton, Nicholas, Bishop 223, 228, 238,
239, 240
Sherborne 13: abbey 32 n. 27, 37, 38, 41,
48; almshouse 183, 184, 186, 187, 193,
200; castle 212; friars 43; guilds 143,
Jesus 86; hermit 206 n. 27; parish 62,
70, 71, 83 n. 54, 85, 89, 95, 257;
Reformation 230, 239 n. 64
Shinfield 76 n. 23
Shirley, Walter 52 n. 20, 164, 173 n. 51
Shrivenham 107
Sindlesham 68
Smith, Richard 140
Smyth, Thomas 214; William 117
Southbroom 182
Southe, Thomas 235 n. 52
Somerset 28, 64, 247
Somerset, John, Earl 51
Sonning 68–9, 71, 74, 75, 76, 77, 79, 107,
126
sorcery 18
Southampton 64
Southend, Katherine 105
South Newton 7, 41, 88, 196 n. 55, 197
Sparsholt 247
Speen 82 n. 45, 216
Stamford, John 62
Stanley abbey 41
Stanton St Quintin 206 n. 26
Stapleton, Miles 97 n. 17
Star Chamber 224, 230, 238, 240
Staunton 105 n. 41
Staveley, John 156 n. 86, 157
Steeple Ashton 31, 88, 118, 128
Stephen of Tisbury 36
Stere, Augustine 215 n. 67, 216
Stilman, Robert 211, 225 n. 7
Stoke family 17, 127, 130; John 127
Stone, Anne 35, 207 n. 30; John 31 n. 26,
207 n. 30
Stourbridge 86 n. 62
Stourpayne 55, 86
Stourton, Edward, Lord 248; Sir John
51, 64, 100 n. 21, 182; William 204,
206, 209
Stratfield Mortimer 76 n. 23
Studley, Sir Alexander 35 n. 44
Stumpe, William 226
Sudden, Richard 156
Suffolk, Duke 15, 64

Surrey 26
Sutton Courteney 196 n. 55
Swanage 137
Swayne: Henry 63, 111; John 82, 214;
    Margery 214; William, chantry 53,
    54 n. 25, 100, 104, 111, 131, 227, church
    building 111, 130, city benefactor 164,
    dispute with citizens 63 n. 76, 169, 172,
    involvement with cathedral 52 n. 20,
    53, 51, 63 n. 76, and tailors' guilds 152,
    will 22, 24
Symonds, William 236
Syon abbey 228

Tailor: Alice 215; Thomas 211, 216
Talbot, John 163
Tanner, William 63
Tarrant Kaines 39
Tavener, William 16
taverns 15, 16, 64, 169 n. 41, 184, 207,
    216 n. 74, 219, 244
Taylor, Nicholas 163, 208
temporale 205
Tenterelles, John 173 n. 51
Terumber, James 17, 97, 103, 104, 106,
    118–19, 183, 186, 191
Testwood, Robert 225, 236
Teynterer, William 24, 53, 163, 166, 167,
    168
Thames 6, 68, 108
Thatcham 86, 186, 189, 206 n. 26, 210,
    219
Thatcham, William 102
Thomas of Purton 205 n. 17
Thornford 80, 143
Thornham 62
Tilehurt 16 n. 57
Tinhead 212
tithes 2, 19, 27, 45, 105, 195, 196;
    Lollardy 202, 210, 212, 213, 222;
    refusals to pay 77, 81, 91, 230
tombs 59, 111, 116, 119, 126–7, 130, 204;
    see also burial
Touker, Nicholas 205
Transfiguration, new feast 86, 92
transubstantiation 202, 215
Tregonwell, Sir John 233
Trenchard, Sir Thomas 128
trentals 34, 44
Treve, Richard 49
Trinitarian order 27
Tropenell family 130, 213; Anne 100;
    Christopher 35 n. 50, 100, 103 n. 32;

Thomas 35 n. 50, 116, 125, 131
Trowbridge 17, 35, 121, 186, 233 n. 44;
    almshouse 183, 189, 191; chantry 97,
    103, 104, 107; guilds 143; Jesus guild
    86; Reformation 229
Tubervyle, Richard 234
Tudworth, Reginald 100, 143–4
Turleigh 219
Twynhoo, Margaret 39 n. 65
Twynyng, Christopher 54
Tyndale, William 225

Ullerston, Richard 59
Upton 219
Upton, John 163, 208, 212; Nicholas 49,
    58, 64, 65
Upton Scudmore 191
Urchfont 219

vagrancy 15, 186, 195
Valor Ecclesiasticus 42, 43, 195
Vaughan, John 106
vestments 32, 35, 55, 85, 118, 156, 157,
    212
Viresden, John 45
visions, *see* Edmund Leversedge
Visitation, feast 86
visitations: parish failings 19, 55, 68, 69,
    70, 79–82, 96–7, 100, 120; Reformation
    230–1, role 4, 77–9, 90, 250

Wagyn, John 155 n. 82, 156
Wakeham, William 211, 216, 222
Wales 50
Wallingford 20, 70, 74, 143, 173,
    206 n. 26, 216, 219, 241; hospital 190;
    priory 32 n. 27
Wallop, John 163, 167
Walsingham, Thomas 209
Waltham, John, Bishop 19, 69, 79, 81, 82,
    97, 210
Walter, William 23, 163, 166, 167, 168,
    173
Wanborough 95, 119, 125, 129, 191
Wantage 86, 97 n. 16, 182
Wareham 86 n. 62
Warminster 76, 77, 82 n. 45, 94, 102, 107,
    240; chantry 100, 103; chapel 205 n. 17
Warmwell, William 24, 163, 197, 199
Warve, Thomas 216
Warwick, Countess 69
Warwick, William 53, 54 n. 25, 100, 164,
    182, 189

Watkyns, Humphrey 230
Wattes, Dr 238
West, Alice 204
West Kington 229
Westbury 15, 24, 76 n. 23, 86, 92, 93, 106,
    107, 208, 214
Westbury William 107
Westminster 63, 245 n. 86
Westmorland, Joanna, Countess 51
Weymouth 7, 170, 178
Wherwell 62; abbey 31
Whistley 68, 75
White, John 54; Thomas 237; William
    52, 216, 218
Whitchurch Canonicorum 8, 126; *see also*
    St Whyte
Whithorn, John 216
Wichford, William 163, 167
Wigmorland 213
Wilcot 41
Willensford 82
William of Pagula, Oculus Sacerdotis 4
Williams, William 155, 227, 228
Wilsford 210, 214
Wilton 44, 54, 70, 105, 239 n. 64; abbey
    31 n. 26, 35, 39, 40; burgesses' guild
    169, 174; church building 115, 121;
    hospital 190, 192, 193
will: burial 93, 253, 254; cathedral 54;
    charity 196–9; church building 114;
    clergy 251; evidence 21–5, 28; friaries
    44; guilds 139, 142 n. 31, 155–6;
    hospitals 183, 188, 200; monasteries 29,
    40; private devotion 204, 208;
    protestantism 22; Reformation 226,
    227, 228, 234, 235, 236; St Osmund
    62–3
Wimborne Minster: charity 197; college
    8, 195; guild 146 n. 49; hospital 189;
    parish funding 83, 84–5, 86, 88, 89,
    church building 117, 119, 120, 129,
    254, endowments 94–5, 96, 104, 105,
    107, 108, 241; Reformation 234, 241
Wimbourne St Giles 214, 258
Winchecombe, John 14, 118

Winchester 62, 120 n. 36
Winchester, Agnes 22
Winchester, bishop 9, 28, 57 n. 41, 81
Windsor 13, 20; almshouse 182; chantry
    103 n. 32; Lollardy 216; Reformation
    224, 225, 229, 230, 236, 245 n. 86; town
    government 160, 173, 176; watch 63
Winkfield 77
Winsley 219
Winterbourne Whitchurch 117
Winterslow 19, 83, 85, 88, 91, 95, 104,
    108, 231, 241
Witham 230 n. 34
Witham charterhouse 24, 28, 31 n. 26,
    206, 230 n. 34
Winton, William 100
Witherington 9
Wodeford, Robert 53, 54, 105
Wodewell, Richard 61
Wokingham: parish 68, 69; Jesus guild
    86; hospital 182, 187; Lollardy 219
women 256–8: altar lights 56; heresy 215,
    258; guilds 135, 140, 152; parish fund
    raising 120, 257; seating 87; *see also*
    purification
Woodhill, Richard 212
wool 9, 13, 17; *see also* cloth industry
Wootton Basset 182, 185, 187
Wrastely, Henry 235 n. 52
Wrottesly 69
Wyclif, John 6, 202, 210, 211, 215, 217,
    222, 224, 225 n. 7
Wycombe 6
Wyke Regis 170, 178
Wykes, John 35

Yatminster 86
Yatton Keynell 62
York 49 n. 4, 112; diocese 66, 75; minster
    61
York, Richard, Duke 64 n. 77
Yorke, William 106, 197
Yorkshire 62, 206

Zeals 107